Hitler's
Air Bridges

Hitler's Air Bridges

The Luftwaffe's Supply Operations of the Second World War

DMITRY DEGTEV AND DMITRY ZUBOV

AIR WORLD

AIR WORLD

HITLER'S AIR BRIDGES
The Luftwaffe's Supply Operations of the Second World War

First published in Great Britain in 2022 by
Air World
An imprint of
Pen & Sword Books Ltd
Yorkshire – Philadelphia

ISBN 978 1 39901 562 2

Typeset by SJmagic DESIGN SERVICES, India.
Printed and bound in the UK by CPI Group (UK) Ltd.

Pen & Sword Books Ltd incorporates the imprints of Pen & Sword Archaeology,
Air World Books, Atlas, Aviation, Battleground, Discovery, Family History, History,
Maritime, Military, Naval, Politics, Social History, Transport, True Crime, Claymore
Press, Frontline Books, Praetorian Press, Seaforth Publishing and White Owl

For a complete list of Pen & Sword titles please contact:

PEN & SWORD BOOKS LTD
47 Church Street, Barnsley, South Yorkshire, S70 2AS, UK.
E-mail: enquiries@pen-and-sword.co.uk
Website: www.pen-and-sword.co.uk

Or

PEN AND SWORD BOOKS,
1950 Lawrence Roadd, Havertown, PA 19083, USA
E-mail: Uspen-and-sword@casematepublishers.com
Website: www.penandswordbooks.com

MIX
Paper | Supporting
responsible forestry
FSC
www.fsc.org
FSC® C013604

Contents

Introduction

Ukraine. February 1944. German tanks, sinking in the mud, rush to help the 50,000 German troops, surrounded by the Russians in the area of the city of Korsun. Due to the thaw and Rasputitsa (season of bad roads), heavy armored vehicles consume three times more fuel than usual. But the fuel trucks are hopelessly stuck. The crews have no choice but to resort to delivering fuel on foot in buckets. However, the 'carriers' do not cope well with the task, soldiers' boots constantly get stuck in the clinging mud, then in the soft snow. Shells are also sorely lacking. It seems that the Germans will not be able to break through to their surrounded comrades in such conditions...

But soon, out of the fog at a low level, splattered with mud and covered with soot, appear outwardly-clumsy Ju 52 transport planes! To get away from anti-aircraft fire, desperate pilots descend almost to the ground, literally hiding behind trees or low hills. Containers of ammunition, gasoline, and food rations fall to the sides of muddy roads. Mud and snow so soften the impact of the container on the ground that even packed in heavy boxes, shells for tank guns do not suffer any damage. With the delivery of gasoline things are more difficult. Every fifth barrel of fuel explodes on impact. But the rest reach the 'addressees'! When night falls and the frost hardens the mud, the most experienced pilots land in the open area along the roads by the beam of their headlights. And the German soldiers understand that nothing is impossible for the aircraft affectionately nicknamed 'Aunt Ju'...

Such is a typical episode from the combat work of Luftwaffe transport aircraft during the Second World War. This book is dedicated to these dangerous and dramatic missions and their bitter results.

Initially, this type of aviation was created in the Third Reich to serve the airborne forces. In October 1937, during another Luftwaffe reorganization, the 4th group of the 152nd bombardment squadron 'Hindenburg' (IV./KG 152) was converted to KGr.zbV (special purpose combat air group). In the summer of 1939, it was reformed as a special purpose combat squadron (Geschwader) KGzbV 1. However, the transport Geschwader was rather an exception, mainly the Luftwaffe command followed the path of creating separate air groups (Gruppen). Until the end of 1939 were additionally formed KGr.zbV 101, KGr.zbV 102, KGr.zbV 103, KGr.zbV 104, KGr.zbV 105, KGr.zbV 106, KGr.zbV 107 and KGzbV 172. By September 1939, the Luftwaffe had a total of 400 Ju 52/3m, and transport aircraft was thus already a fairly impressive force.

These units were first used during the Polish campaign in 1939. Then they were applied during the occupation of Denmark, Norway, Holland, Belgium, and Greece. Airborne forces captured airfields, fortresses, and strategic bridges. Parachutists suddenly descended from the sky directly on the heads of the enemy, preparing a beachhead for the main landing. But even if some airfields could not be captured on the move, the Ju 52s still landed directly under fire, ensuring success.

Already in early May 1940, transport planes was first assigned the task of supplying German troops cut off behind enemy lines by air. During this period, a critical situation developed in the north of Norway. General Eduard Dietl's 3rd mountain division was blocked by the Allies in the Narvik area. Air groups KGr.zbV 107 and KGr.zbV 108 received an order to supply this division by air. In fact, this was the first Luftwaffe air bridge in history between the rear and the blocked German troops. In addition to ammunition, food and medicine, cargo aircraft delivered a large number of soldiers' boots to German sailors who ended up on the beach after a battle with the British fleet. And later, KGr.zbV 102, which joined the operation, delivered a battery of 75 mm mountain guns and shells to them.

Some of the aircraft in these missions were, in essence, used only once. The fact is that canisters of fuel, unlike conventional cargo containers, could not be dropped by parachute. Therefore the Ju 52 pilots had to land on the ice of lakes in the area of Bardufoss. The length of these lakes was too short for the plane to take off again, however. Used in this way transport planes had to be simply abandoned, and the crews had to join the ground forces. Then, during the spring ice melt, the planes sank.

On 12 May, the Allies occupied the northern part of Narvik after prolonged fighting, and on 28 May, they liberated the entire city and forced the Germans to withdraw to Vestfjorden. But the difficult situation in France forced them to evacuate all their troops from Norway on 3–8 June. On 10 June, the Norwegian army capitulated, and by 16 June, the Wehrmacht had captured the whole of the country. In the overall success of this adventurous operation, the share of transport planes was very significant. In fact, it was here that the real combat capabilities of airborne forces and transport aircraft were shown for the first time. In total, during the Norwegian campaign, German transport aircraft performed 3,018 sorties, transported almost 30,000 people, and delivered 2,376 tons of cargo (including 1,180 tons of gasoline).

The last major operation of this kind was the capture of the island of Crete in May 1941. In the future, airborne forces were rarely used, and the main mission of transport aircraft was to supply the ground forces. In June, Germany attacked the Soviet Union, and Hitler's Panzer divisions rushed deep into the vast country. There, the Germans faced a lack of normal roads, an almost complete lack of civilization in entire regions, severe weather, and other difficulties. Military communications stretched for many hundreds and thousands of kilometers, and it was impossible to organize supplies by traditional methods. Therefore, such missions were increasingly performed by transport planes. At first, only four air groups were used to supply the troops: IV./KGzbV 1, KGr.zbV 50, KGr.zbV 102 and KGr.zbV 106. They were later joined by I./LLG 1, I. и II./KGzbV 1, KGr.zbV 101, KGr.zbV 104 and KGr.zbV 105. In addition, DFS 230, Go 242 gliders and even the Me 323 'Giant' had to be used for cargo delivery. All of them were created for airborne operations, but eventually went to Russia to carry food and ammunition.

In the autumn of 1941, already entire divisions, and even armies, cut off from communications by impassable mud, were supplied by air. As the supply situation continued to deteriorate by winter, and the railways could not cope with transportation, on 17 December Hitler personally ordered the formation of five new transport air groups. These units, KGr.zbV 700, KGr.zbV 800, KGr.zbV 900 and KGr.zbV 999 were immediately transferred to Fligerkorps VIII (VIII.Fl.Korp.), which operated in the 'Mitte' Army Group band. There they were engaged in delivering reinforcements and supplies to the front line. Then the Luftwaffe command had to form five more transport air groups from training units: KGr.zbV 4, KGr.zbV 5, KGr.zbV 6, KGr.zbV 7 and KGr.zbV 8. However, there were not enough Ju 52s for all of them, so some units had to be equipped with old Ju 86 and He 111 E/P aircraft.

As it turned out, the increase in transport aviation was very timely. The Red Army launched a counteroffensive, but Hitler forbade his troops to retreat. He demanded that numerous strong points and cities be held, even if they were in the deep rear of the enemy. Hitler, a former Gefreiter of the German Empire, because of the peculiarities of his pathological psyche, learned only one lesson from his military past. He was a staunch supporter of fanatical defense to the last soldier. As a result, in January–February 1942, the Russians completely surrounded several divisions of the 16th Army in the area of the settlement of Demyansk, as well as a small garrison in the town of Holm. The Luftwaffe received orders to supply this fortress by air…

In the era of tanks and cars, it seemed to many that the era of fortresses as such was forever in the past. Moreover, during the First World War, a great many resources were spent on huge fortresses surrounded by rows of impregnable forts, which completely failed to justify the hopes placed on them. 'The war was a battle test for the fortresses, which, according to the majority, they did not pass.' Russian professor V.V. Yakovlev wrote in his 1931 book *History of the fortresses*:

> Even those who had criticised the fortresses before the war were struck by the rapid fall of the Belgian and French fortresses and outposts in 1914 and the Russians in 1915. Liege held for 12 days, Namur – 6 days, Maubeuge – 10 days, Antwerp – 12 days, the outpost fort Manovillier surrendered after 54 hours of heavy artillery fire, Kovna held for 10 days, Novogeorgievsk – only 9 days, after the process of completely blocking the fortress was completed.

The only exception was the Austrian fortress of Przemysl. The advanced Russian units approached this citadel in September 1914, after which they began to prepare for an assault. The Przemysl fortress consisted of eight defense sectors. The first two were represented by an inner contour with a length of 15 km and a radius of 6 km. In total, eighteen forts and four batteries were built as part of the inner contour of the fortress. The outer perimeter of the fortress, with a total length of 45 km, was divided into six defense sectors consisting of fifteen main and twenty-nine auxiliary forts. Twenty-five artillery batteries were placed between the forts. Due to the talentless command of incompetent, and frankly stupid, tsarist military leaders, the siege Przemysl lasted for six months and became one of the largest battles of its kind during the First World War.

The capture of Przemysl was celebrated in Russia with great fanfare and even led to a sharp, though short-term increase in the popularity of the incompetent Russian Tsar Nicholas II, as well as the belief in victory in a senseless and bloody war. However, people who were closely familiar with the events understood that the 'great victory' was a strong exaggeration. 'On March 9, Przemysl fell', Mikhail Rodzianko, Chairman of the State Duma (Russian Parliament) in 1911–17, recalled.

> Without an assault, almost without a fight. General Selivanov, desperate to take Przemysl, was about to lift the siege, but

suddenly, almost on the same day when they were going to leave, Przemysl surrendered... It turned out that there was not enough food in the fortress and that the Slavs were at war with the Hungarians. Kumanek, the commandant of the fortress, was threatened with death by soldiers locked up in Przemysl... Przemysl – the last word of military science, where the natural conditions were supplemented by the miracle of fortification: it seemed that it was impossible to take it, and only the betrayal of Kusmanek helped to surrender the fortress.

The First World War completely debunked the theory of so-called 'fortresses of unlimited resistance', that is, bastions that can independently to hold and defend themselves until the end of the war, distracting significant enemy forces. 'Novogeorgievsk was, perhaps, the last surrounded fortress, taken after taxation [complete encirclement],' recalled the German Generalfeldmarschall Ludendorf. French engineer Benoit, in an article entitled 'Long-term Fortifications during the War', wrote:

Fortresses with a belt of forts have outlived their time. They cannot resist modern artillery and its huge expenditure of shells. One of the conclusions of the last war is that an isolated fortress, as it was understood until now, can no longer withstand the range of guns and the monstrous number of projectiles fired.

Well, the German Blitzkrieg of 1939–1941, with its rapid advances into enemy territory, quick encirclement and crumbling defenses of a demoralized enemy, seemed to have finally put an end to the fortresses as medieval remnants.

However, Yakovlev, Benoit and Ludendorf, like many of their contemporaries, were wrong. The fortress, as a system of some long-term and impregnable shelters, walls and towers, had really gone into the past and lost its tactical significance. But the idea of a fortress, including an isolated one, not only did not die, it received a new life during the the Second World War. Moreover, this period has become the 'triumph' of isolated fortresses.

Starting in 1942, one of the characteristic methods of warfare of the Wehrmacht was to hold cities and strongholds that were in the rear of the advancing enemy forces; the role of forts and bastions passed to the ruins of houses and factories. To replace the underground passages of old came the city streets, staircases and basements. And the development of aviation solved the seemingly unsolvable problem of fortresses of the past: external supply.

And all this was made possible by a psychopath who, with the connivance and sometimes criminal assistance of numerous political forces in Germany, climbed to the top of power and declared himself the Führer of the German people. The 'strategy' of holding fortresses was a direct consequence of the pathological features of Hitler's psyche. His official point of view was based on the statement that the long-term defense of such Festung (fortresses) is, from a military and political point of view, an effective means of struggle, especially against the Soviets. He believed that it 'diverted significant enemy forces', and at the same time provided a great propaganda effect. However, the true motive for such a commitment to Hitler, to the disastrous 'strategy' for the Wehrmacht, was his panic and fear of admitting the obvious fact of complete incompetence in the management of troops. And the Führer's fanatical desire to hold on to any piece of land that came under his control, created endless crises for the Wehrmacht and the Luftwaffe, and in the end, inevitably led to the collapse of the Nazi empire.

In this book, based on numerous German and Russian archival documents, most of the air bridges organized by the Luftwaffe in 1942–45 are described in detail. This is the first complete encyclopedia of such operations, in which the authors tell not only about the actions of German aircraft and give detailed lists of losses, but also reconstruct unknown details of the battles themselves in 'Pockets' and Festung. The book uses a huge number of documents that are not available to Western researchers, and which demonstrate this component of the Second World War in a completely new way.

The creation of this book would not have been possible without the great help of our colleagues, aviation enthusiasts and experts on the history of the Luftwaffe. The authors express special gratitude to Sergey Bogatyrev (Ukraine) for his invaluable assistance in compiling lists of lost aircraft and aerial victories.

In addition, the authors thank:

- archivist of Kampgeschwader 27 'Boelcke' Walter Waiss (Germany) for the materials and photos provided;
- Luftwaffe historian Mikhail Zefirov (Russia) for the materials provided;
- Theodor Mach (Germany) for additional information on transport aircraft losses;
- historian Yuri Borisov (Russia) for technical advices.

Chapter 1

Air bridge in the 'Arse of the World'

'Don't allow a single German out of Demyansk'

Operation Barbarossa did not achieve its goal; Moscow and Leningrad were not taken and it was not possible to reach the Volga River line, the oil-bearing areas of Baku were also not captured. In December 1941 the Red Army itself launched a counteroffensive. On 7 January, the Soviets struck in the area of the Valdai Hills. This vast forest region, located midway between Moscow and the Baltic Sea, was one of the largest wastelands in the European part of Russia. In this area, the size of the whole of Hungary, there was not a single large city or highway. There were only villages and hamlets scattered among the forest thickets, connected by narrow and winding dirt roads. In these forests, bears and other dangerous predators could easily be found, wolves howled all over the area at night, and people were afraid to leave their homes. German soldiers who came to Valdai in the autumn of 1941 immediately called this region 'the arse of the world'. There was none of the usual European water supply and drainage, and even electricity was perceived by the population as exotic.

In early 1942, Valdai Hills again became the scene of violent fighting. The Soviets intended to make a deep break here into the rear of the Army Groups 'Nord' and 'Mitte'. Through these thickets and wastelands opened a direct road to Smolensk, Vitebsk, and Pskov. The 16th German army was too weak to defend this region, so after the first Russian attacks, its units quickly withdrew to the west across the Lovat river, and southwest to the towns of Velizh and Demidov. At the end of January, the Russian north-western front, which consisted of five armies, broke through 120–150 km, forming a huge Andreapolsky arc. On the map, this ledge looked threatening, but the Soviets failed to achieve strategic success. The Russian troops collided with a chain of German strongholds: Staraya Russa, Holm, Velikiye Luki, Velizh, Demidov, and Beliy. In the area of Demyansk, the Germans were able to hold a large area measuring 60 by 70 km. At the same time, the 9th German army also repulsed desperate Russian attacks near the village of Olenino and the town of Rzhev.

Meanwhile, the Führer forbade any further retreat, including breakouts from the encirclement, ordering troops everywhere to 'stand to the death'. As a result, on 22 January, the German garrison in the town of Holm (on the Lovat river) was completely blocked by the Soviets; 3,500 soldiers were surrounded.

The Russians, overcome with optimism, continued their advance, moving in several directions at once in this wild and almost uninhabited wilderness. They blocked the German garrison at the little town of Velizh and continued to advance along the western Dvina river towards Vitebsk and Rudni. There was a real threat of Soviet troops entering the deep rear of the Army Group 'Mitte' to the west of Smolensk. On 2 February, the Russian 4th Shock Army reached the small town of Demidov and surrounded another German garrison there. Around the same time, the garrison at the little town of Surazh was surrounded.

On the morning of 3 February, the 249th rifle division's advanced units reached the Vitebsk–Nevel highway and railway. The Russian infantry reached an area 450 km west of Moscow and 135 km northwest of Smolensk. It was a fantastic success for the Red Army. Its advanced regiments were already in the territory of Belarus, while the German 4th Panzer army held the front 300 km to the east in the area of town Gzhatsk. The front line was taking on more and more impossible curves and outlines – the Russians were in the west and the Germans were in the east. At the same time, there was no solid front line, huge gaps yawned between Army Groups 'Nord' and 'Mitte', the Germans were defending in several blocked cities.

However, this moment was the culmination of the Russian breakthrough. Having dispersed its infantry divisions along the huge front from Lake Ilmen to the city of Rzhev, the Kalinin front could no longer conduct large-scale attacks. The Germans managed to transfer reserves to the Vitebsk region and drive the Russians away from the city. In the area of Velikiye Luki, the 3rd Shock Army was unable to encircle the German garrison, stopping at the approaches to the city. On 7–8 February, fierce battles for Velizh and Demidov took place. Russian infantry broke through several times to the central part of these small towns, but were repulsed in desperate counterattacks.

On 17 February, the garrison of the little town of Surazh was unblocked. A few days later the blockade of Velizh was lifted, and in early March, the

Germans also released Demidov. From now on, the defense in the southern part of the Andreapol arc was built along the network of strongholds Beliy, Demidov, Velizh, Velikiye Luki.

On 8 February, the Russians were able to close the encirclement around the city of Demyansk. Immediately, 96,000 soldiers from six German divisions were in a complete blockade. General der Infanterie Walter Graf von Brockdorff-Ahlefeldt, 53-year-old commander of II. Armeekorps, took overall command of these units. Von Brockdorff-Ahlefeldt was a typical First World War veteran who had participated in the famous battle of Verdun. This battle, which cost huge sacrifices but did not bring any success to either side, has forever become a symbol of senseless carnage. The experience gained in Verdun was very useful to von Brockdorff-Ahlefeldt on the Eastern front of the Second World War.

Despite the emerging crisis, the general situation in this sector of the front did not seem critical to the command of Army Group 'Nord'. There was no solid front line, and the blocked divisions were separated from the main forces by a distance of only 30 to 40 km. The encirclement of Demyansk seemed only a temporary problem – and this assessment was not entirely wrong. Demyansk was located on a hill and was a crossroads, a logistics center in this remote area. The German divisions that had taken up a circular defense were located in convenient positions and strongpoints around a chain of small towns and villages. There were huts with stoves and firewood in unlimited quantities, without which life in this area in the winter season is impossible. The Russians were in the role of hungry 'wolves', who watched with envy the 'sheep' hiding in warm houses and not letting them in the door.

Already on 11-12 February, the German 16th Army made its first attempt to break through the blockade ring south of the little town of Staraya Russa. But the attack made by the 18th motorized infantry division did not achieve its goal. At the same time, the Russian 11th Army and 1st Shock Army, despite the lack of troops, food, and ammunition, launched a new offensive south of Lake Ilmen. The goal was to surround the little town of Staraya Russa. In this regard, there was a risk of creating another 'Pocket'. But at the crucial moment, the Soviets lacked air support. On 17 February clear and frosty weather set in and Stukas and twin-engine bombers appeared in the sky. The Russians recorded 400 flights of German aircraft that day, and the next day there were about the same number again. German Bf 109 fighters also provided great support to the ground forces. They were flying at a low level over snow-covered fields where all the targets

3

were clearly visible. From a height of 30–50 meters, Bf 109s fired at the Russian infantry, inflicting heavy damage. These flights, when planes roared overhead, also had a strong psychological effect on young Soviet soldiers. Already, on 18 February, some divisions of the 1st Shock Army were unable to move due to continuous air attacks. Two days later, the headquarters of the 11th Russian army reported: 'All the attacking units were pinned to the ground by bombing and air assault attacks, and were unable to advance.'

Using the strong support of the Luftwaffe, the Germans managed to tighten their reserves and organize a reliable defense. It was based on a network of well-fortified strongpoints, provided with all types of artillery and infantry weapons. These 'forts' were supplied by the Pskov–Dno–Staraya Russa railway line, and then by automobile convoys moving under the protection of tanks and armored personnel carriers. Control of railway communications in this region was vital. The Russians were unable to take control of the Bologoe–Staraya Russa railway line. As a result, they had to unload supplies and troops far in the rear, and then take them along poorly equipped roads to the front line.

The last major Soviet success was the capture of the Pola railway station and the bridge over the Pola river (30 km east of Staraya Russa). After that, the front line in this area stabilized. On 25 February, the headquarters of the north-western front received a directive from Stalin. In it, the dictator expressed outrage at the slow pace of the offensive and ordered the front commander, General Kurochkin, to capture or destroy a group of German troops in the Demyansk area as soon as possible – and do it so that no German escaped. The order said:

> Continuously and persistently compress the ring of encirclement of the Demyan group. Take all measures to ensure that in no case will even a part of the encircled enemy troops break through to the west and south to the rear of the 3rd and 4th Shock Armies of the Kalinin front.

In addition, Stalin ordered the air force to systematically scatter leaflets in German over the Pocket. The text of the leaflets called on German soldiers to 'stop further futile struggle and surrender'. Three or four days were allowed for the implementation of this directive. The Soviet command continued to underestimate the determination and ability of the Wehrmacht. It seemed to the Russian generals that all they needed to do was increase the pressure a little and the German troops, not adapted to the cold and snowy weather, would panic and run west. At the same time, the ruthless Stalin and his generals overestimated the capabilities of their own soldiers. They believed that Russians were used to winter and frost from childhood, so it was easier for them to adapt to heavy physical loads and extreme conditions of fighting. But Demyansk showed that German soldiers can fight in winter conditions no worse than their enemies.

Stalin's categorical directive did not mention anything about the actions of Russian aviation (except for the delivery of propaganda leaflets) or about countering the German air bridge. The Soviets did not even assume that the completely blockaded II and X army corps wouldn't try to break through the Pocket, and that the Luftwaffe could supply 100,000 soldiers by air for a long period.

The decision to supply Demyansk on a large scale by air was made on 12 February, when the first weak attempt to break through the encirclement ring failed. This mission was extremely difficult, given the winter weather, terrain features, and volume. The daily needs of the group locked in the wilderness, were about 300 tons of cargo. One transport airplane Ju 52 could deliver 2 tons of cargo per flight, and it turned out that it was necessary to make at least 150 flights to the Pocket every day, and in any weather! The Luftwaffe had never had the experience of such operations.

To provide an air bridge to Demyansk in February-March 1942, the following aviation groups and Staffel were allocated:

- KGr.zbV 9 Oberstleutnant Jansen, 1./KGzbV 172, KGr.zbV 105 Oberstleutnant Deffner and the training unit KGr.zbV 'Oels' were based at Plescau-Sud airfield (Pskov-south, near the city of Pskov);
- IV./KGzbV 1 Hauptmann Fridolin Vath, 11./KGzbV 1 and II./KGzbV 1 Oberstleutnant Neundlinger and the training unit KGr.zbV 'Posen' at the airfield Ostrov-Sud (Ostrov-south, near the city of Ostrov);
- KGr.zbV 500 Major Theodor Beckmann, KGr.zbV 700 Major Muggenthaller, KGr.zbV 900 Hauptmann Stioschultz, KGr.zbV 999, at Plescau-west airfield (Pskov-west);
- KGr.zbV 600 and KGr.zbV 800 Major Lalepke at Korovye Selo airfield;
- KGr.zbV 4 Major Rudolf Kraus and KGr.zbV 5 Hauptmann Zan at Riga airfield;
- KGr.zbV 211 at Warsaw airfield.

In addition, various auxiliary units were used to supply the Pocket, such as the transport squadron headquarters Fliegercorps XI (Tr.St./XI.Fl.Korps), equipped with Ju 52s and some other types of aircraft.

Management of all these units was entrusted to the commander of transport aircraft under General-Quartiermeister Luftwaffe, former KGzbV 1 commander Oberst Fridrich-Wilhelm Morzik. The Air transport command 'Ost' at the 1st air fleet (Lufttransportführer Ost Luftflotte 1) was created specifically for it.

To supply Demyansk and additional support for the troops of the 16th Army, bomber units were also involved. This was the first time that the Kampfgeschwader was used en masse for cargo delivery. At the beginning of February, II./KG 27 'Boecke' fully completed their rest and activities to replenish the personnel of the combat unit up to full-time strength at Langenhagen airfield (Germany). But instead of joining their comrades who were fighting in the Crimea and southern Russia, this air group was suddenly sent on a 'business trip' to the north. II./KG 27 arrived at the Korovye Selo air base (south of Leningrad).

Its first mission in this sector of the front was a bombing attack against a railway station on the western shore of Lake Ladoga (the Russians used it to supply Leningrad). Then German bombers carried out the first supply missions to the blockaded garrison at Holm, dropping cargo containers on parachutes. After that, He 111s regularly flew cargo to Demyansk and Holm, and bombed Soviet positions on the Volkhov river and around Lake Ilmen. Periodically, the bombers carried out passenger transport on German territory, and even courier flights from Pskov to Helsinki (Finland).

Among the flight personnel involved in this complex operation were crews who had experience of transport flights over Norway, Belgium, the Balkans and the Mediterranean, and newcomers who had just finished training in flight schools. In addition, instructors from various Luftwaffe educational institutions participated in the flights. But here, on the front line, thanks to the close interaction of veterans and young people, novices quickly gained experience and did not lag behind their elders.

The main base for servicing the air bridge was the large air base Pleskau-Süd (city of Pskov). The bulk of the cargo for the encircled troops was delivered there by rail. Wounded German soldiers taken out of the Pocket were also unloaded there. In Pskov, there were capital barracks for personnel, fuel supplies and everything necessary. The nearby Pleskau-west airfield was often used as a backup. The other alternate airfield in Daugavpils was a minor take-off area with limited services, while Korovye

Selo airfield did not have enough hangars or runways, and there were only temporary barracks for pilots.

Things were much worse with the necessary infrastructure for receiving transport planes in the Pocket itself. The so-called Demyansk airfield was located near the north-eastern edge of this locality (near the village of Glebovschina). It did not have any airfield structures and hangars, and consisted of only one runway with small areas for taxiing and unloading. In order for 100 to 150 planes a day to land here, it was necessary to develop a strict schedule of landings and take-offs so that the serving staff could unload the car and load the injured into it, so that too many planes were not concentrated on the site. Often, the frozen lake Mosylinskoe, located near the northern outskirts of Demyansk, was used as an alternative for landings and take-offs.

Many difficulties arose with the maintenance of transport planes. In such difficult weather conditions as deep snow, frosts, snowstorms, thaws and ice, even the undemanding Ju 52 presented unpleasant surprises to technicians. Pilots from KGr.zbV 500, Major Theodor Beckmann's unit which was transferred to Pskov from far Africa, felt the contrast especially vividly. Here they had to get acquainted with such amazing things as freezing of oil pipes and fuel tanks, hydraulic failures and radio equipment. During frosts, the engines on the Ju 52 had to be warmed up for four or five hours, and sometimes they did not shut down at all, only filling the tanks with more fuel.

The Germans had to organize several field points for aircraft maintenance under the command of experienced technicians and engineers. All this, together with regular deliveries of spare parts from factories, allowed increasing the interval between engine overhauls from 450 to 500 hours and constantly maintaining 50 to 80 per cent of the aircraft in good condition.[1]

Great difficulties arose during the thaw, when airfields were literally sinking in the mud. This led to delays in loading, unloading and taxiing. It was impossible to maintain the established schedule. Instead, the planes began to take off in pairs or groups of six planes as soon as they were ready. During the return flights from Demyansk, all transport planes, regardless of their unit affiliation, gathered in groups and flew together until they crossed the front line. Only after they were over German territory were transport planes separated and returned to specific bases depending on their deployment.

---

1 Pegg M. Transporter Volume One: Luftwaffe Transport Units 1937-1943. Luftwaffe Colours. – Classic Publications, 2007. p. 35.

In March, the Peski airfield, located 12 km south-west of Demyansk, began operating as a reserve. However, due to its small size and narrow runway (about 30 meters), only experienced pilots could land there, and then no more than six aircraft at a time. At the final stage of the operation in April–May, the condition of the airfields significantly improved, and the weather conditions became more favorable. This made it possible to restore and maintain the flight schedule. Transport planes were escorted by specially designated Bf 109s from I./JG 51 and 9./JG 54.

The greatest danger to transport planes was fire from the ground. The distance from Pskov to Demyansk was 250 km, so the Ju 52 simply did not have time to climb to a high altitude and usually flew at the level of 1,500–2,000 meters or lower. According to the pilots' recollections, almost all Soviet soldiers fired at them, often even with pistols. One Ju 52/3m even crashed after its pilot, who was flying at a low altitude, was severely injured by submachine gun fire from the ground.

The Red Army air force did not pose a serious threat to the air bridge for a number of reasons.

First, after heavy losses in 1941, the Soviets had not yet been able to restore the number of their aircraft. They still had a lot of aviation regiments and squadrons, but none of them was even half-staffed. In many fighter aviation regiments there were four or five aircraft, and sometimes less.

Secondly, these weak units were evenly distributed over the entire huge front and could not operate in a concentrated area. The Russians did not use their scant aircraft centrally. Most aviation regiments were distributed among the air forces of the armies. For example, the air force of the 34th Army (VVS 34th Army), which carried out the blockade of Demyansk, in mid-February included three aviation regiments: 661 LBAP (light bomber aviation regiment), 677 LBAP and 402 IAP. There were forty-six aircraft (fifteen R-5, 20 U-2B and eleven MiG-3), of which only twenty-four were serviceable (combat-ready). Russian aviation at that time was aimed at 'exhausting actions' (harming the Germans and not letting them sleep), but was not capable of performing serious tactical and even more strategic missions.

The northwestern front air force (VVS SZF) had about 200 aircraft in mid-February, but most of them were R-5, U-2B, and UT-2 light night bombers. These were low-speed, two-seat training aircraft, converted to drop small incendiary, fragmentation and high-explosive bombs. German soldiers called them 'flying sewing machines' for their unsightly appearance and the characteristic click of the engines. At night, these Russian bombers flew low over German territory and dropped bombs on villages and homes. They had no sights, and the bombs were often dropped manually by a second crew member. These bombs rarely reached their targets, but they exhausted the nervous system, not only of the Germans, but also of Russian civilians. During daylight hours, light biplanes were used for reconnaissance of German positions and meteorological reconnaissance. In addition to converted training aircraft, the Russians actively used TB-3 and SB night bombers in this sector of the front.

The few Russian twin-engine bombers were less intense, but equally ineffective. They never flew further than 70–100 km from the front line, so the German air base at Plescau was completely safe. In mid-February, the main target of Russian bombers was the Dno-Griwotschki air base, located 150 km west of Demyansk. German fighters and tactical reconnaissance aircraft were usually based there.

Dangerous flights 'Aunt Ju'

In the early days of the German air bridge, the air force of the north-western front (VVS SZF) practically had no opposition with its work. But transport planes still suffered losses. On 19 February, west of the village of Zvyagino, Ju 52 W.Nr. 7382 'VK+PB' from KGr.zbV 999 went missing. The fate of the five crew members and two passengers of the plane remains unknown. During the flight to Demyansk, Ju 52 W.Nr. 5006 'CO+TJ' from KGr.zbV 700, with three pilots, disappeared without a trace and 4./KG 27 also suffered the first loss on this day. During take-off from the Korovye Selo air base (mission-supply of Demyansk), He 111 H-6 W.Nr. 4901 '1G+GP' collided with a Ju 52 W.Nr. 6130 from Transportstaffel I. Fl.Korps. The 'Aunt Ju' was damaged during the return from the Pocket and made an emergency landing. As a result of the accident, both aircraft caught fire, and the pilot of the He 111 Feldwebel, Adam Albert, was killed. The other four members of the bomber's crew were injured. Only one person was killed in the transport aircraft crew. In the Pocket area at the time there was favorable weather – calm and light frost (-10°C).

On 20 February in the area of Demyansk, Ju 52 W.Nr. 2841 'DS+AE' from KGr.zbV 700 and Ju 52 W.Nr. 5167 '1Z+FF' from KGr.zbV 900 disappeared, together with their crews. One of them, near the village of Kuzemkino (north-west of Demyansk), was shot down by 2 LaGG-3 from the 163rd IAP. At the Pleskau-west airfield, one Ju 52 from KGr.zbV 9 made an emergency landing (with 25 per cent damage) due to engine failure. Also with engine failure, Ju 52 W.Nr. 7185 from KGr.zbV 105 crash landed in the village of Manshino and suffered 90 per cent damage. In the area of the city of Krasnogvardeysk, Ju 52 W.Nr. 7127 from Tr.St./XI.Fl.Korps crashed due to icing. All five crew members were injured.

On 21 February, two aircraft from 1./KGr.zbV 105 were lost. One Ju 52 (W.Nr. 5703) crashed on take-off, another (W.Nr. 6829) during landing.

The next day, the Ju 52 W.Nr. 5546 'TA+DA' from KGr.zbV 9 went missing with the entire crew of four people. Another transport airplane, Ju 52 W.Nr. 7082 from the same group, was broken up in an accident during take-off from the airfield in Demyansk.

On 23 February, two Ju 52s W.Nr. 7415 '4V+ED' and W.Nr. 6118 '4V+CU' from I./KGzbV 172 were shot down by fire from the ground near Demyansk. Nine members of their crews added to the list of missing persons. And in the area of Zaluchye two Ju 52 (W.Nr. 2962 and W.Nr. 7359) from KGr.zbV 600 were shot down. One crew of five people went missing, in the other, two pilots were killed and the rest were able to reach the German positions.

Heavy snowfall in the area of Demyansk meant 24 February was a difficult day for transport planes. There were numerous accidents; nine transport planes were put out of action at once, including four from II./KGzbV 1. Ju 52 W.Nr. 2961 crashed during an emergency landing after firing from the ground (100 per cent damage). Ju 52 W.Nr. 7262 crashed (80 per cent damage) at the airfield of Demyansk. Two more (W.Nr. 5431 and W.Nr. 7174) failed (50 per cent and 40 per cent damage) for non-combat reasons as a result of accidents. Two losses were recorded in I./KGzbV 172: Ju 52 W.Nr. 6992 'V4+DT' went missing with a crew of four, and Ju 52 W.Nr. 5616 crashed in an accident at the Demyansk airfield. Ju 52 W.Nr. 2913 from KGr.zbV 105 was shot down by a Russian fighter; one member of its crew was killed and another was injured. Ju 52 W.Nr. 6088 from KGr.zbV 600 in the area of Lake Velikoe was shot down by anti-aircraft fire, but the full crew escaped. Ju 52 W.Nr. 7029 from KGr.zbV 900 crashed (75 per cent damage) during take-off at the airfield of Demyansk. But in general, the losses in personnel were small: four missing, one killed and two wounded.

On 25 February, the weather in the area of Demyansk improved again. A clear sky and a slight frost provided favorable flying conditions. For the first time, the Soviet air force launched air attacks against the airfield at Demyansk. The day before, the 253rd IAP was relocated to Kresttsy airfield (north of Demyansk) as part of 11 LaGG-3. Their first mission was to escort Il-2 group aircraft to attack an airfield near the hamlet of Glebovshchina. In parallel, the pilots were assigned the task of controlling the actions of attack aircraft. This practice was common among Russians. The commanders did not trust their pilots; they saw treason and cowardice everywhere. They believed that the pilots of bombers and attack aircraft would evade the task; afraid they would be shot down, that they would deliberately drop bombs past the target. Therefore, the pilots of the escort fighters had to monitor their charges and inform on them to their commanders.

In the area of the airfield, a group of Soviet aircraft was shelled by anti-aircraft fire, but returned safely to the base. As a result of the attack, the Russians counted ten aircraft destroyed, including eight Ju 52 and two Ju 88. According to German data, as a result of Russian air raids at the Demyansk airfield, three Ju 52/3m were destroyed (W.Nr. 3178, 6062 and 6955) from KGr.zbV 9, two pilots were killed. In addition, on the route Korovye Selo–Demyansk on this day, three more Ju 52/3m disappeared along with the crews (W.Nr. 5344 'CN+BL' from KGr.zbV 600, W.Nr. 5095 'DB+QC' from KGr.zbV 700 and W.Nr. 6596 'CI+HA' from KGr.zbV 900). Another transport from the 900th aviation group received combat damage, but was able to return to the air base. When landing in Daugavpils, one Ju 52 from KGr.zbV 800 crashed. The crew was not injured.

Then, on the night of 25–26 February, forty-five Russian TB-3, SB and R-5 bombers made a second raid on the airfields of Demyansk and Dno-Griwotschki. In parallel, U-2B biplanes carried out 239 sorties to bomb villages inside the Pocket. The north-western front air force (VVS SZF) losses during these raids were two aircraft (U-2B and R-5).

At 14.00 on 26 February, nine LaGG-3s from the 253rd IAP again accompanied Il-2 aircraft to an air attack on the Demyansk airfield. This time, the strike group reported the destruction of five Ju 52s and one Ju 88 on the ground. However, this time the losses are not confirmed by German data. Only one Ju 52/3m W.Nr. 5438 from KGr.zbV 900 crashed during take-off. At night, Russian biplanes appeared over the Pocket again. Five U-2B from the 661st LBAP attacked the airfield, and thirteen R-5 dropped bombs on the Molvotitsa stronghold.

On 27 February, transport planes again suffered heavy losses. At night, the air base inside the Pocket was bombed by Russian TB-3 and SB night bombers. In parallel, raids were carried out on the Dno railway station, the Soltsy and Dno-Griwotschki airfields. At 14.45, five LaGG-3 from the 253rd IAP independently launched an air attack against the Demyansk airfield. They fired twenty-eight unguided RS-82 rockets, 730 20-mm ShVAK shells and 695 12.7 BS cartridges. The pilots reported five Ju 52s destroyed on the ground and two more Ju 88s shot down in the air. Then at 15.50, nine LaGG-3 again accompanied attack aircraft Il-2s to the same target. Again, according to reports from Russian pilots, the raid was a complete success: eight to ten planes were destroyed on the ground and two Ju 52s were shot down in the air (one was recorded as a personal victory for Senior Lieutenant Peter Petrov). Another Ju 52 shot down in this sector of the front was reported by the pilots of three Yak-1 from the 744th IAP.

In fact, only one Ju 52 W.Nr. 6231 from KGr.zbV 'Posen' was seriously damaged at Demyansk airfield as a result of an air attack by the Soviet air force. Also badly damaged (40 per cent) at the airport was Bf 109 F-4 W.Nr. 7534 from 8./JG 3. A Ju 52/3m was shot down over the Demyansk airfield W.Nr. 2925 from KGr.zbV 999. One pilot from its crew was killed and two were injured. On flights between Soltsy and Demyansk / Demyansk and Ostrov, Ju 52s W.Nr. 5073 'RJ+NK' from KGr.zbV 600 and W.Nr. 7116 'DE+TI' from III./KGzbV 1 went missing. One He 111 P-2 W.Nr. 2730 'SA+DF' from KGr.zbV 5, making a long-distance flight from Warsaw to Demyansk, went missing along with a crew of five people. Two more transport planes were damaged during emergency landings. Thus, the Luftwaffe transport units that supplied the encircled German troops lost five aircraft in one day..

On this day, aircraft from II./KG 27 also suffered losses. But their mission took place 200 km north of Demyansk, in the area of the little town of Chudovo. At the end of February, there was another crisis situation. General Andrey Vlasov's 2nd Shock Army crossed the Volkhov river and broke through to the rear of the German 18th Army. The supply routes of the German troops on the West Bank of the Volkhov were partially cut, and they had to be supplied by air. On 27 February, during such a mission, He 111 H-6 W.Nr. 4873 '1G+KN' of 5./KG 27 went missing. The Germans considered the alleged cause of the bomber's demise to be an attack from the ground 3 km west of small village Olkhovka.

On 28 February, the first major air battle between Russian and German fighters took place south of Lake Ilmen. Patrolling over the south Bank, four LaGG-3s from the 253rd IAP were suddenly attacked by a group of Bf 109s. Junior Lieutenant E.S. Markov was the first to be shot down. His plane crashed into a thicket on the coast and exploded. The LaGG-3 of Senior Lieutenant Sorochan was also shot down, while the pilot himself was injured in the shoulder and arm and with great difficulty sat on the fuselage right in the middle of the village of Vdal. The fighter of Senior Lieutenant Agapov was also literally riddled with bullets and made an emergency landing on the edge of the forest. The pilot was injured in the head and leg. The least damage was received by the fighter under the control of Junior Lieutenant Smirnov. He was also wounded in the shoulder, a shell pierced through the dashboard, and gasoline hoses were interrupted. However, the pilot managed to reach the air base and land on the landing gear. Returning from a mission at 16.15, LaGG-3 under the control of Junior Lieutenant Zalivchiy not far from the airfield, was attacked by a pair of Bf 109 F-4. With great difficulty, he was able to break away from his pursuers and land the damaged fighter. After landing, it turned out that the tail was almost completely broken by bullets and shells. In just one day, the 253rd aviation fighter regiment lost almost half of its aircraft, one pilot was killed, and three were sent to hospitals. According to German data, the Soviet fighters shot down in this sector of the front were recorded in the combat accounts of Hauptmann Hans Fhillip (09.35 – 09.36 – 2 'I-18'), Unteroffizier Gerhard Proske from St.I./JG 54, Oberleutnant Frahz Beyer from 8./JG 3 (10.30 – 'I-301'); Hauptmann Heinrch Jung from III./JG 54 (16.36 – 16.40 – 2 'I-26'). But the Germans also suffered losses. Bf 109 F-4 W.Nr. 8089 of 9./JG 54, severely damaged in battle, crash landed at Demyansk air base. The plane was not repaired and just sent to the dump.

On this day, KGr.zbV 5 suffered serious losses. Ju 52 W.Nr. 3189 'BJ+EY' went missing on a flight from Warsaw to Demyansk, and He 111 P-2 W.Nr. 2636 'TU+NG' also disappeared during the flight to Demyansk from Riga. Ju 52 W.Nr. 3082 'BR+AQ' from KGr.zbV 600 was shot down by Soviet fighters (these were 2 I-16s from the 728th IAP, piloted by young pilots Sergeants M.S. Baranov and A.E. Borovykh) near the village of Lyakhovichi. Two members of the transport airplane crew jumped out with parachutes, and two more were missing. In addition, the I-16 pilots also shot down a Ju 88 A-4 bomber in this flight W.Nr. 4618 'V4+UM' from 4./KG 1 'Hindenburg'. All four pilots from its crew were killed.

In early March, weather conditions in the area of the Valdai hills changed dramatically. A southerly wind blew, the temperature rose to -5°C, and heavy snowfalls began, typical for the European part of Russia at this time of year. Unable to capture Staraya Russa and break through to the little town of Dno, the Soviets nevertheless continued their brutal attacks in this direction. The 11th Army was fighting near the village of Bolshoe Orekhovo in order to reach the Staraya Russa–Dno railway line from the north, while the 1st Shock Army was advancing from the south. But the German troops staunchly held the defense. At the same time, the 34th Soviet army was fighting around the Pocket.

During this period, the most powerful Russian attacks were directed against the bridgehead on the west bank of the Pola river. Thus the Soviets sought to compress the blockade ring and move it away from the main forces of the German 16th Army. Fierce fighting unfolded for Zaluchye – a strongpoint in the area of the Pola and Lovat rivers. The 1st Guards rifle corps, which Stalin had pinned special hopes on, operated there. It was in the Western part of the blockaded end that the fiercest fighting unfolded. But the Stalinist guard in this sector had a worthy opponent – the motorized infantry division of the SS-Infanterie-Division 'Totenkopf' (Death's Head) under the command of the ardent Nazi Theodor Eicke. This unit was characterized by incredible cruelty to enemies and civilians and boundless fanaticism and loyalty to Hitler. Here, in the Western sector of the blockade ring, this fanaticism was prevalent. At the same time, the Russians led attacks from the north (near the small village of Lychkovo) and south (near the large village of Molvotitsy).

The airbridge continued to function smoothly. On 1 March, a Ju 52 went missing while flying from Dno-Griwotschki airfield to Demyansk, W.Nr. 7146 'KD+IM' from KGr.zbV 600. Another He 111 P-1 W.Nr. 1484 from KGr.zbV 211 crashed during an emergency landing due to engine failure in the area near the small town of Holm. In addition, in the area south of the village of Pogarino, I-16 (pilot Lieutenant V.S. Komarov) shot down a He 111 H-2 W.Nr. 2715 'GB+MS' from KGr.zbV 5. Another transport airplane – Ju 52 W.Nr. 3192 'PD+KB' from KGr.zbV 700 went missing with the crew in an unspecified area. On this day, experienced pilots of 3 LaGG-3 fighters from the 5th Guards IAP (Captains N.P. Gorodnichev, P.E. Bundelev and A.V. Petrov) were recorded on the combat account of three downed Ju 52s in the area of the settlements of Arteminka–Butskino–Dubrovka.

On 2 March, at 10.15, a pair of LaGG-3s of Major Pankov and senior political officer Mandura from the 33rd IAP Air Defense took off for reconnaissance in the Pocket area. In the area of Kamennaya Gora (in the north-eastern part of the Pocket), they saw an airfield with 150 Ju 52s! The pilots decided to attack the target. Dropping to a height of 250 meters, the LaGG-3s fired at the transport planes. Senior Political Officer Mandura after returning to the air base reported the destruction of eight Ju 52s. But his partner, Major Pankov, was missing. At 13.25, three LaGG-3s (Senior Political Officer Mandur, Senior Lieutenant Kostin and Junior Lieutenant

Gankevich) took off in the direction of Demyansk. At 13.39, they saw a single Ju 52 flying at an altitude of 300 meters and shot it down. Then 'Stalin's falcons' appeared over the air base of Demyansk at an altitude of 300 meters, where they saw a lot of German aircraft. They attacked them twice from a low level and reported six destroyed Ju 52s and five Ju 88s. Only two LaGG-3s returned to their airfield. Senior Political Officer Mandura went missing, just as his partner had gone missing a few hours earlier…

Already at 14.20, six LaGG-3s from the 253rd IAP appeared over the Demyansk air base. The fighters completed three passes, firing twenty-two unguided rocket projectiles, 614 20-mm shells and 493 BS cartridges at the target. The pilots immediately reported twenty destroyed Ju 52s, and along the way 150–200 killed German soldiers and officers. In addition to the pilots of the 33rd IAP, three Yak-1s from the 744th IAP claimed to have shot down the Ju 52. In reality, all these Russian reports were a big fantasy. German transport planes at the airfield were not affected. But there were losses due to technical reasons. During take-off they encountered two Ju 52 (W.Nr. 2971 and W.Nr. 5097) from KGr.zbV 9. Due to difficult weather conditions two aircraft from KGr.zbV 999 and KGr.zbV 'Posen' (W.Nr. 5487 and W.Nr. 3067) crashed. In the area of Demyansk anti-aircraft artillery was shot down Ju 52 from KGr.zbV 4. On the flight from the Dno-Griwotschki airfield was shot down a Ju 52 W.Nr. 6132 '4V+AM' from KGr.zbV 9. Luftwaffe's total losses for the day were six transport planes.

On 3 March, transport aircraft lost four more Ju 52s, including two (W.Nr. 6594 and W.Nr 6924) from I./KGzbV 172, which were destroyed by Soviet field artillery fire at Staraya Russa airfield. Ju 52 W.Nr. 7430 'SN+FX' was shot down by a link of three I-16s from the 728th IAP directly over Demyansk (all four pilots were killed). Ju 52 W.Nr. 7138 'KD+J' from KGr.zbV 'Posen', which took off for Demyansk from the Dno-Griwotschki airfield, went missing along with the crew.

At 13.21 on 4 March, three LaGG-3 from the 253rd IAP took off to reconnaissance the airfield in Demyansk. 'At Glebovschina airfield up to twenty-five Ju 52, observed the take-off of three Ju 52 aircraft, two Bf 109 are in the air, did not join the battle', the report read. On this day, the weather improved (the snowfall ended, and the frost hit again). For the Luftwaffe, the day passed without loss.

On the night of 5 March, the air force of the north-western front (VS SZF) carried out another air attack against the airfield in Demyansk. Russian pilots reported several fires in the target area.

On 6 March, at 16.05, a pair of junior lieutenants, Fyodor Semyanenkov and Kuzma Garkusha, flew a reconnaissance flight to the Pocket in LaGG-3 fighters. At the airfield, they saw seven or eight Ju 52s standing, loading and unloading, a couple more maneuvering on the airfield to prepare for take-off and one coming in for landing. Taking advantage of good visibility, Semyanenkov and Garkusha calculated that there were about fifteen heavily damaged transport planes in the area of the airfield. In addition, in the area of the large village of Molvotitsy (south of Demyansk), a levelled area was discovered that could be used for landing transport planes. On this day, over the ring of the blockade, Soviet fighters shot down a Ju 52 W.Nr. 6892 from II./KGzbV 1 (all four pilots were killed). Two more transport planes (He 111 P-2 W.Nr. 1522 from KGr.zbV 211 and Ju 86 W.Nr. 0249 from KGr.zbV 7) made emergency landings on the fuselage on German territory after being damaged by fire from the ground.

On 6 March, a frost of -30°C set in the area of Demyansk. German transport aircraft suffered heavy losses on this day. In the Pocket were lost Ju 52s W.Nr. 3187 'BJ+EW' from KGr.zbV 4 and W.Nr. 6486 'PF+FT' from KGr.zbV 'Oels' and also W.Nr. 7245 from KGr.zbV 'Posen'. A Ju 52 W.Nr. 7191 'KO+RO' from KGr.zbV 800 was shot down by Soviet anti-aircraft artillery. All four members of its crew were missing. This was not a day without accidents, either. During take-off from the Pleskau-Süd airfield, weather reconnaissance plane Ju 88 A-5 W.Nr. 2190 from Wekusta 1 collided with two transport planes that were standing on the tarmac. Transport planes (W.Nr. 7105 and W.Nr. 7371) from KGr.zbV 9 received 70 per cent of the damage. The cause of the crash was poor visibility. Two He 111 H-2s from KGr.zbV 211 also failed due to damage. Their number includes transport airplane W.Nr. 6886, which was later decommissioned on the airfield of Demyansk. In total, eight German transport planes were out of service for the day. The Soviets lost four planes near Demyansk.

At 15.10 on 7 March, junior lieutenants Garkusha and Rodionov from the 253rd IAP again appeared over Demyansk. There they saw two Ju 52s preparing to land and immediately attacked them. According to the report of the pilots, after three attacks, both 'Aunt Ju's' fell in the area of the airfield. According to German data, the Soviet fighters shot down Ju 52/3m W.Nr. 6326 of II./KGzbV 1 in the area of the airfield Demyansk. In the evening, the same pair of LaGG-3s again flew to the Pocket along with attack aircraft Il-2. They carried out an air strike on the airfield, and fighters attacked anti-aircraft batteries. Since it was already getting dark, the pilots did not observe the exact results of the attack, reporting only that 'a large fire broke out at the airfield in several places'.

On this day, in the area of Demyansk, the Germans lost two Ju 52/3ms from KGr.zbV 4 (W.Nr. 6569) and KGr.zbV 'Posen' (W.Nr. 7303). Two Ju 52s W.Nr. 5778 'NA+HK' and W.Nr. 7421 'KA+VZ' from KGr.zbV 600 were shot down by Soviet anti-aircraft artillery over the blockade ring near the village of Zaluchye. Six members of their crews were killed. Two more crew members of these transport planes managed to jump out with parachutes over German territory, but were injured. In addition, four more Ju 52s were damaged in accidents (from 15 to 30 per cent).

On 8 March, the Russians continued their attempts to interfere with the air bridge. At 08.35, six LaGG-3s from the 253rd IAP and 38th IAP flew to intercept German transport planes in the Demyansk area. The operation was unsuccessful, and no German planes were found in the air. Later, a pair of LaGG-3 piloted by Lieutenant V.I. Stanovov and Senior sergeant F.S. Petuhov from the 33rd IAP air defense covered the troops in the western part of the blockade ring. At 10.55 am, they saw a group of five Ju 52s flying from the west at an altitude of 1,500 meters. Anti-aircraft artillery shells were exploding around the transport planes, but they were flying steadily towards Demyansk. Stanovov and Petuhov decided to attack them and gave the signal: 'I'm a friendly aircraft', after which the Russian anti-aircraft guns stopped firing. Soviet fighters attacked a medium Ju 52 and shot it down near the village of Vzglyady. The remaining transport planes persisted in heading for Demyansk. Lieutenant Stanovov attacked the second plane at close range and shot it down over German territory in the area of the small village of Korchevka. At the same time, Petuhov's LaGG-3 came under fire from German anti-aircraft artillery and was shot down.

At 16.06 another group of Russian fighters made a second flight to Demyansk. This time, the 'Stalin's Falcons' saw five Ju 52/3m in the sky, which had recently taken-off from the airfield. One of them was attacked and shot down by Junior Lieutenant Vasily Kiselenko from the 253rd IAP. The transport airplane fell near the village of Kolomna. Another Ju 52 was shot down by a pair of I-16 fighters operated by young pilots M.S. Baranov and A.E. Borovykh from the 728th IAP.

The Soviets once again exaggerated their achievements in the fight against the German-organized air bridge. According to German information, on the Soltsy-Demyansk route, Ju 52 W.Nr. 2867 '1Z+DQ' from KGr.zbV 'Oels' went missing along with the crew of a transport airplane. Two more aircraft from this air group were damaged at the airfields of Pskov and

Demyansk. A Ju 52 W.Nr. 7419 from 1./KGzbV 172, Ju 52 W.Nr. 6312 from KGr.zbV 9 and Ju 52 W.Nr. 6324 from KGr.zbV 999 also received varying degrees of damage.

On 9 March, the weather in the area of the Valdai hills changed again abruptly and unexpectedly. The icy north wind was replaced by a south-easterly wind, the air temperature increased, visibility deteriorated, and snow began to fall. The weather hid vulnerable transport planes from Russian fighters and anti-aircraft artillery. The number of accidents was also minimal. During a landing in Demyansk, transport airplane He 111 H-2 W.Nr. 2779 from KGr.zbV 211 was attacked by two I-16s from the 728th IAP and crashed, with one of its crew members injured. Despite poor visibility, the Russians again tried to interfere with the operation of the air bridge, but this time they completely failed. The journal of combat operations of the 253rd IAP reported:

> At 09.30–10.27, Junior Lieutenants Garkusha, Rodionov and Kiselenko took off to intercept bombers in the Demyansk area. In the area of the Vysoky Bor settlement at an altitude of 1,500 meters, they were suddenly attacked by 4 Bf 109s. As a result, the plane of Junior Lieutenant Rodionov was severely damaged, and fell 3 to 4 km south of the village of Lutovka in the forest. The plane crashed, the pilot was bruised and slightly injured. Junior Lieutenant Kisilenko was repeatedly attacked and when trying to land the damaged plane, during the last attack at an altitude of 10-20 meters was killed, after that the plane began to fall apart randomly. Junior Lieutenant Garkusha, repelling the enemy's attacks, fired 2 bursts at the enemy from a gun and a BS machine gun. After Junior Lieutenant Kisilenko was killed and Rodionov was shot down, Junior Lieutenant Garkusha dived out of the battle and on a low-level flight was forced to leave for the Kresttsy airfield.

According to German sources, Oberleutnant Karl-Henz Langer and Leutnant Erkhardt Hübner of 7./JG 3 (which was based at Soltsy airfield during this period) recorded two aerial victories (09.30 – 10.27 – 2 'I-61'). At 10.30, Oberfeldwebel Karl Fuchs from 2./JG 54 near the village of Dolgie Nivy shot down I-16 Starshina A.E. Novikov from the 728th IAP. After this battle, only two serviceable aircraft remained in the 253rd IAP. Such a deplorable situation was typical for Soviet fighter aviation regiments.

On 10 March, the snowfall increased, so that the air force of the north-western front (VS SSJ) did not take to the air at all. Only some of the most experienced Luftwaffe crews operated from the German side.

The next day, the sky was also free of Russian aircraft, while the Germans continued to fly and deliver cargo to Demyansk. At the same time, one Ju 52 (W.Nr. 6234 from KGr.zbV 900) went missing and two other aircraft were slightly damaged.

On 12 March, in the small village of Dekhino, LaGG-3 Lieutenant N.F. Leonov of the 38th IAP shot down a Ju 52 W.Nr. 3182 from KGr.zbV 999. The crew escaped by parachutes and returned to the air base. Another Ju 52 from II./KGzbV 1 south of Demyansk came under fire from the ground and received minor damage (15 per cent). At the same time, one of the crew members was killed on board.

Snowfall, snowstorms and thaws in this environment became allies of the Wehrmacht. The Soviet troops, whose positions were mostly in the open, among fields and forests, completely lost their mobility. The soldiers were stuck in snow and mud, which precluded any rapid attacks. Supplies, which were carried out along muddy and broken forest roads, were chronically disrupted. As a result, many Soviet infantry regiments received less food and ammunition than the Germans who were under siege! The 370th rifle division of the 34th Army reported in the combat log:

> In the period from 9 to 13 March, the division did not receive any supplies. Taking into account the fact that even before this cargo was delivered with interruptions, a critical situation has developed that threatens to massively undermine the morale of the soldiers. In some companies, the soldiers were given only a few frozen potatoes for two days. There are very few shells for divisional artillery, and none for regimental artillery at all. There are no shells for mortars, no cartridges for machine guns.

The division several times unsuccessfully tried to capture the village of Turginovo. The main incentive for the soldiers was the possibility of finding some food there or taking it from the Germans!

As supply problems became more and more difficult, the Russian air force had to deal with a new task – providing air support supply to its units. At first, these missions were performed by R-5 biplanes from the 677th LBAP. During the day and night, they reached the positions of their troops and dropped containers of food and ammunition to them from a low level. In the future, as the snow cover increased, the supply of Russian divisions became more and more difficult, and the Red Army air force had to deal more and more with cargo delivery. From now on, two air bridges operated in the Demyansk area – German and Russian!

On 10 March, the 23rd rifle division managed to capture the large village of Molvotitsy, located south of Demyansk, after a long battle. The Germans retreated north to their other stronghold, 'Bel'-1', having previously created a new impregnable center of defense there. On all other sections of the blockade ring, all Soviet attacks were repulsed.

On 13 March, the weather conditions changed dramatically again. Already at night, a freezing north wind blew, and the air temperature fell to -25°C. In the next two days the cold intensified even more. Although March is considered a spring month in Europe, in Russia it is often just a continuation of winter. The Red Army air force immediately stepped up its activities. At night, the Russians carried out almost 500 sorties on this sector of the front, setting a kind of record. The main targets were German strongholds inside and outside the blockade ring. While the huge TB-3 planes dropped incendiary and high-explosive bombs from a great height, the small U-2s flew one after another directly over the roofs of houses and the tops of trees. Numerous silhouettes of these biplanes, resembling the aircraft of the First World War, were clearly visible in the light of the moon and complemented the fantastic picture of fighting in this wild and frozen wilderness.

During the day, the air force of the north-western front (VS SZF) was much less active. They completed a total of seventy-nine flights and claimed two downed aircraft. At 11.20 two LaGG-3, flown by Lieutenant V.I. Stanovov and Sergeant N.F. Denchik from the 33rd IAP, attacked a pair of Ju 52s flying at an altitude of 30–59 meters above Lake Zavaly. First, they launched unguided rocket projectiles at them from a distance of 600 meters, then they started firing machine guns at them from a distance of 100–200 meters. According to the pilots, after a while one transport airplane crashed into a forest 3 km north of the village of Latkino. The second plane, despite a prolonged attack, was able to escape. According to German data, a Ju 52 W.Nr. 5199 'CU+SX' from KGr.zbV 800 went missing that day along with a crew of four. At the Demyansk airfield, a plane crashed due to engine failure (W.Nr. 6918) from KGr.zbV 'Posen', but the pilots in this case were not injured. Another aircraft from that aircraft group (W.Nr. 6669) crashed during taxiing.

Russian losses were four aircraft. Among them was the LaGG-3 of Senior Lieutenant I.F. Kononenko from the 38th LAP, which according to Soviet documents 'did not return from a combat mission'. According to German data, it was shot down by Hauptmann Dietrich Hrabak from St.II./JG 54, in the documents of which was confirmed destruction of a Soviet fighter 'I-18' at 16.47. The next night, the Soviets suffered their first loss when supplying their troops from the air. In the area of the village of Knevitsy, anti-aircraft artillery fire shot down plane R-5 with a crew consisting of Sergeants Roller and Vesnin from the 677th LBAP. During the emergency landing, the plane was completely destroyed, and the pilot Sergeant Roller was seriously injured. From now on, the Russians also began to regularly lose planes on their air bridge.

On 14 March, the northwestern front air force (VS SF) flew eighty-nine sorties during daylight hours. There were several air battles, as a result of which the Russians claimed eight downed aircraft. 2./KGr.zbV 600 lost two Ju 52s at once, of which at least one was shot down by LaGG-3 fighters from the 38th IAP. It was a Ju 52/3m W.Nr. 4029 'NG+VO' from 2./KGr.zbV 600 (mobilized from the airline 'Deutshe Lufthansa' Ju 52 'D-AKEP' 'Fritz Rumey'). The plane crashed 10 km south-southwest of Demyansk. It was recorded as a personal aerial victory for Senior Lieutenant N.A. Gruzdev. A second Ju 52, W.Nr. 7351 'NG+VR', was destroyed during the crash. Three members of their crews were killed and four were injured. Also, during the attack of Russian fighters, the Ju 52 W.Nr. 7351 from KGr.zbV 9 was damaged. He 111 P-2 from KGr.zbV 211 on the way back from the Pocket was damaged by anti-aircraft fire, resulting in an emergency landing on the fuselage near the airfield Ostrov.

On the same day, an air battle in the spirit of the First World War took place near Demyansk. In the air, Russian R-5 and German Hs 126 accidentally met. There was a short air battle between the biplanes, which according to Soviet information ended in their favour. The Russians own losses on 14 March amounted to eight aircraft. The next day, 15 March, was more propitious for transport planes. In the area of Demyansk, a Ju 52 W.Nr. 3128 from KGr.zbV 900 suffered 95 per cent damage from anti-aircraft artillery fire and crashed during an emergency landing. One crew member was killed and three were injured. All the rest of the flights passed without incident. However, Senior Lieutenant M.N. Zhukov of the 38th IAP on this day recorded in the account of the combat two aerial victories over Ju 52s (one south of the small village of Anino, the second, 4 km north-east of the small village of Ohrino). The next day, there were no losses at all among the German transport aircraft.

Interestingly, in the first half of March, Russian combat reports record almost no Luftwaffe air attacks against ground troops. In the middle of the month, during clear and frosty weather, the Russians recorded eighty to a hundred German aircraft overflights daily, but they did not drop bombs nor fire from the air. These were mostly reconnaissance flights. This indicated that the situation in the Demyansk area had finally stabilized, and the ground forces no longer needed strong air support. The Luftwaffe's main efforts were concentrated in other sectors, such as the Chudovo area. In many of the crises that arose endlessly on the Eastern front that winter, the German air force invariably saved its troops by performing the role of 'flying artillery'. However, the effectiveness of such support for the Luftwaffe ground forces in reality was not so high and did not always correspond to the optimistic reports of the bomber pilots. Such conclusions can be drawn from the report of the commander of Luftflotte 1 Generaloberst Alfred Keller on 15 March 1942. It read as follows:

> The evaluation of the target images makes it clear that the hit of the bombs is partially very bad. Comparison with reports of success received from units' shows that the actual effect achieved has no relation to the reported effect. This poor use of precious resources is unacceptable and, in addition, can shake the confidence of the troops in the skill of the bomber crews and in the reliability of their reports of success. I require all crews to increase the effectiveness of their weapons to the maximum level, that is, not only to fly well, but also to attack targets well.
> The following three points should be made by the commanders:
>
> 1) Bombing, depending on the task or weather conditions, should be carried out mainly from the height most favorable for targeting and accuracy;
> 2) The difficulty in recognizing targets requires particularly careful aiming and bombing. Constant training and guidance is required;
> 3) Success reports should be given in accordance with the facts. Embellishment or justification of error leads to an incorrect assessment of the actions and misconceptions. You should report what you actually saw, not what you would like to see.[2]

---

2 Boelcke Archiv

'The number of enemy aircraft in the air is literally huge'

On 16-17 March, extremely cold weather continued in the area of Demyansk, with a north-easterly wind blowing, and frost reaching -30°C. On the afternoon of 16 March, the Russian air force carried out eighty-five sorties and reported two downed aircraft and four more destroyed at air bases. In fact, this day passed successfully for transport planes. The Luftwaffe lost only two Ju 87 D-1s (W.Nr. 2031 and W.Nr. 2035) from 2./StG 2, which were shot down in the Podberezye–Dvorec sector.

However, on 17 March, the transport planes again suffered significant damage, mostly from anti-aircraft fire. In the area of Demyansk a Ju 52 W.Nr. 6681 'KB+NB' from KGr.zbV 9 was shot down. Ju 52 W.Nr. 7113 '1Z+IQ' from KGr.zbV 'Posen' also 'disappeared in the white haze', the fate of the crew remaining unknown. The pilots of the Ju 52 from I./KGzbV 172 were much more fortunate. After being damaged, the plane was able to make an emergency landing near the village of Porkhov. Two of its crew members managed to jump out with parachutes and reach their troops, while two others were killed.

II./KGzbV 1 lost two Ju 52s: W.Nr. 3064 'KF+UN' and W.Nr. 6068 'DA+CF'. But they went missing along with their crews far enough from Demyansk – namely, north of the city of Smolensk, in the area of the city of Demidov – in the village of Volbovichi.

On 18 March, the weather was still clear and frosty. Russian aviation was very active. At night, it carried out almost 500 flights, and 151 during the day. A mid-air collision in this desert region still was a rarity. There were only two recorded air battles in which the Russians claimed one downed aircraft with two lost. Most likely, we are talking about the Bf 109 F-4 W.Nr. 7519 from 7./JG 3, which was shot down over Demyansk, but its pilot escaped by parachuting out. This victory was claimed by LaGG-3 pilots from the 160th IAP and Yak-1 pilots from the 744th IAP.

Meanwhile, the air bridge continued to collect its victims and recorded as missing was the crew of the Ju 52 W.Nr. 6861 'G6+AX' from 1./KGr.zbV105. On the way back from Demyansk to Ostrov, Ju 52 W.Nr. 2929 'NL+ON' from KGr.zbV 'Posen' disappeared without a trace. After the night bombing of the Russian air force at the Demyansk airfield, Ju 52 W.Nr. 5777 from KGr.zbV 'Oels'was written off.

On 19 March, Soviet anti-aircraft artillery shot down a Ju 52 W.Nr. 3207 '4V+BV' from I./KGzbV 172 near the village of Telyatino, and near Demyansk a Ju 52 W.Nr. 6890 'CF+JD' from KGr.zbV 4 went missing.

By 20 March, the total strength of the Soviet northwestern front (SZF) was 161,000 soldiers. They were armed with 1,500 guns and 2,500 mortars, fifty tanks, 244 aerosleds, and eighty-three multiple rocket launchers (the Germans called them 'Stalin's Organs'). The outer ring of the blockade and the front on the Lovat river were occupied by the 11th and 1st Guards, which numbered 74,500 soldiers. The inner ring of the blockade around Demyansk was occupied by the 34th Army and a separate 1st Guards rifle corps (86,500 soldiers). This almost corresponded to the number of German troops surrounded (about 100,000 people, including auxiliary personnel). The Soviets had almost no tanks in this direction, no armored vehicles at all, and almost no anti-aircraft guns. In the 11th Army there were only fifteen anti-aircraft guns, in the 1st Shock Army there were five, in the 34th Army, twenty-six, in the 1st guards rifle corps – zero! Thus, the air defense of the troops was practically absent. The main means of transportation in deep snow and off-road was aerosled, armed with a single 12.7 mm machine gun.

On the morning of 20 March, after a heavy artillery barrage and air attacks, the German 16th Army suddenly launched an offensive south of Staraya Russa. The Germans managed to concentrate a strong shock group in the 8th Jager, 122nd, 127th and 329th infantry divisions under the command of General der Artillerie Walther Kurt von Seydlitz-Kurzbach without the Russians noticing. At the same time, the Soviets did not suspect anything about the enemy's plans, and they explained the unusual and mysterious lull in the night from 19 to 20 March by saying that 'the Germans are listening and watching'. Only when the Ju 87 armada appeared in the sky at 08.00 did they realize that something serious was afoot!

The next day, units of the 1st Shock Army were forced to evacuate in disarray the bridgehead on the Western bank of the Porus'ya river. On 22 March, despite Stalin's categorical order from Moscow to 'stand to the death', the Russians continued to retreat to the East. The Germans, with strong support from the Luftwaffe, captured the settlements of Maryino, Nagatkino, and Vasilyevschina and reached the Staraya Russa–Holm highway. 'The enemy aircraft conducted continuous bomb attacks on the army troops,' reported a panicked report from the headquarters of the 1st Shock Army. 'It has caused huge losses to the units of the army, killing many people and vehicles... The number of enemy aircraft in the air is literally huge and it decides the success of the battle.' And this emotional statement was not an exaggeration. Several rifle brigades of the Red Army were almost destroyed as a result of air attacks, and the surviving soldiers were demoralized and frightened. The commander of the north-western front, Lieutenant General Kurochkin, begged the command to give him more aircraft, but in response received another very original order from the cruel Stalin: 'Don't cringe, but be cheeky and behave as impudently as possible with the enemy.'

With massive support from the Luftwaffe, the Germans crossed the Redya river and captured the localities of Onufrievo, Malyie Gorbi, Kozlovka and Borisovo. By 25 March, the strike group had managed to drive a deep wedge 15 km deep and about 13 km wide into the Russian defense. Only 16 km remained before the blockade ring was broken. At the same time, the Soviets had no reserves to close the gap.

The success of the ground forces raised the morale of Luftwaffe pilots, and they, despite heavy losses, continued to fly in the Pocket. On 20 March Ju 52 W.Nr. 7376 'AU+KP' from IV./KGzbV 1 and Ju 52 W.Nr. 4052 'DD+MF' from KGr.zbV 900 went missing along with their crews. During take-off at Riga airfield, He 111 H-5 W.Nr. 5547 from KGr.zbV 211 collided with a Ju 52 W.Nr. 7263 from KGr.zbV 4, resulting in both aircraft receiving 80–85 per cent damage and being written off.

On 22 March, a pair of Yak-1 fighters from the 744th shot down two Ju 52s near Soltsy W.Nr. 6953 and W.Nr. 7058 from KGr.zbV 105. One crew remained intact and in the second, four pilots was injured.

On 24 March, during an emergency landing at Pleskau air base, a Ju 86 W.Nr. 0456 from KGr.zbV 7 crashed (90 per cent damage). One crew member was killed.

On 25 March, a Ju 52 W.Nr. 2829 'KI+AA' from KGr.zbV 600 went missing along with the crew.

On 26 March, heavy snowstorms and snow falls started again in the Demyansk region. Low clouds hung over the area of operations at an altitude of 200–300 meters, visibility was from 300 to 1,000 meters. All this was accompanied by a squally wind. The weather ruled out the planned actions of the Luftwaffe. In addition, Hitler during this period insisted on an urgent operation 'Eisstoss' ('Breaking the ice') – an air attack against the ships of the Soviet Baltic fleet, which were on winter berths in Leningrad. In this regard, in early April the 16th Army suspended the offensive. Heavy fighting broke out in the western part of the blockade ring.

Despite the bad weather, German transport aircraft continued its work. Every day, the air bridge reaped its bountiful harvest of victims.

On 26 March, in the sector east of Demyansk, a group of Yak-1 of the 163 IAP shot down three Ju 52s: W.Nr. 5737 'DB+QL' and W.Nr. 7386

'VK+PF' from KGr.zbV 700 and W.Nr. 7144 'X8+GH' from KGr.zbV 900. All three crews were missing. The battle account of Lieutenant Blokhin recorded that he personally had shot down a Ju 52, the rest were 'victories in the group' to all pilots who participated in this battle.

On 27 March, four Ju 52s went missing along with their crew: W.Nr. 7361 'NJ+KJ' from KGr.zbV 4, W.Nr. 7306 'DG+ST' from KGr.zbV 8, W.Nr. 6687 from 1./KGr.zbV 105 (this aircraft was shot down in the area near the small village of Lipovka, by I-16 Lieutenant Baranov from 728 IAP – the highest scoring Soviet pilot in this sector of the Eastern front) and W.Nr. 3151 'BC+RM' from KGr.zbV 700.

On 28 March, a Ju 52 W.Nr .2989 'G9+DV' from II./KGr.zbV 1, which flew from Dno airfield to Demyansk to supply German troops went missing.

On 30 March, the same cruel military fate befell the Ju 52 W.Nr. 7341 'VV+OP' from KGr. zbV 800, which took off from Korovye Selo airfield in the direction of Demyansk.

The operation to supply the Pocket and its unblocking was not without losses for other German air groups. For example, II./KG 27 lost five aircraft in one week. On 22 March, a He 111 H-6 W.Nr. 4927 '1G+KP' from 6./KG 27 was shot down by ground fire while flying out to bomb the 11th Army troops in the village of Bolshie Gorki. The plane made an emergency landing on German territory in the hamlet area of Glushitsa; the Navigator Feldwebel Helmut Dietrich was injured. On 23 March, two He 111 H-6s (W.Nr. 4840 and W.Nr. 4846) crashed while landing at Korovye Selo airfield and were virtually destroyed (70 per cent damage). On 25 March, a He 111 H-6 W.Nr. 4854 '1G+GM' from 4./KG 27 went missing along with a five-man crew while flying to support ground forces in the area south-east of Staraya Russa. On 29 March, a He 111 H-6 W.Nr. 4863 of 5./KG 27 was hit by small arms fire from the ground during an air attack at low altitude of Soviet supply lines east of Lake Ilmen. The plane made an emergency landing on Russian territory. His crew set fire to their bomber, crossed Lake Ilmen on ice, and reached the German positions. By the end of the month, the II./KG 27 'Boelcke' had twenty-five aircraft, of which only eleven were in combat readiness.

The unexpected success of the Wehrmacht south of Staraya Russa made a significant difference. The encircled troops were given a new incentive to resist further, and the Russians were forced to ease the pressure on them in an attempt to strengthen the ring of blockade. The few Russian aviation forces were also diverted from the air bridge. For example, the new 568th assault aviation regiment (568th SHAP), recently transferred to the Valdai Hills, was ordered to attack the Demyansk airfield on 21 March. The raid involved eight Il-2s, which were accompanied by nine LaGG-3 fighters from the 24th IAP. Forty FAB-50 high-explosive bombs and fifty-two RS-82 unguided rocket projectiles were dropped on the airfield. The pilots reported ten Ju 52 and Fw 200 aircraft destroyed. According to German data, the aircraft destroyed at the airfield were Ju 52 W.Nr. 6513 'V4+GW' from I./KGzbV 172 (100 per cent), and reconnaissance aircraft Hs 126 B-1 W.Nr. 2347 from 4.(H)/23. The Russians did not note any German anti-aircraft artillery opposition. But the next day, the 568th SHAP received orders to attack German troops advancing from the west, and did not re-appear over Demyansk until 30 April.

'X-X' is 'Hurricane'!

At the end of March, clear weather was established in the area of Demyansk, which favored the actions of aviation. At this point, several additional aviation regiments were transferred to the Valdai Hills, which were merged into the reserve Group of the Main Command No. 6 and the reserve Group of the Main Command No. 2 (RGC No. 6 and RGC No. 2). This allowed the Soviets to launch the first large-scale operation against the air bridge, which included transport plane attacks on the flight route and massive air attacks against Luftwaffe air bases.

On 1 April the first major air battle took place in this region. The Russian air force carried out 287 sorties and claimed twenty-nine downed Ju 52s, while another eight Bf 109s and two Ju 88s were destroyed at airfields. Own losses amounted to twenty-two aircraft, comprising fifteen Soviet fighters and six Il-2 attack aircraft which all went missing, and a Pe-2 dive bomber which was shot down by anti-aircraft fire. At night, Russian night bombers carried out 428 sorties, most of which was carried out using U-2B and R-5 biplanes. While they attacked German positions inside the blockade ring and on the 1st Shock Army front, DB-3 and SB twin-engine bombers raided airfields at Kresti, Dno-Griwotschki, Soltsy and railway stations. On German air bases, He 111 H-6 W.Nr. 4420 from 6./KG 4 (45 per cent), and Ju 88 A-4 W.Nr. 4636 from 3./KG 3 (50 per cent) were damaged.

The next major air battle took place on 4 April. The Russian air force carried out 186 sorties, claimed nineteen downed aircraft and forty-four destroyed at air bases (including thirty-five Ju 52s). Their own losses amounted to eighteen aircraft (10 per cent of the number of sorties), of which fourteen were missing (ten LaGG-3 and four Il-2), the rest were severely damaged and made emergency landings on Soviet territory. At night, the Russian air bridge had already started working. R-5 biplanes and even TB-3 heavy bombers not only dropped food containers for Soviet troops cut off from supplies, but also made landings and transported wounded soldiers to the rear. These huge planes were equipped with ski landing gear, so they could land and take off on any flat ground. On the afternoon of 5 April, the Soviets carried out 214 sorties and claimed thirty downed and forty-seven destroyed aircraft at air bases (including forty Ju 52s).

Here, it is necessary to explain to the reader the degree of reliability of the Russian documents recording the declared victories: the real German losses were nine to ten times less than indicated in the Soviet archival sources. Russian losses amounted to twenty-two aircraft, of which seventeen were missing.

On 6 April, the Russian air force carried out 112 sorties, claimed fourteen downed in the air and forty-one destroyed at German air bases German plane. Own losses amounted to thirteen aircraft. One LaGG-3 fighter was shot down in air combat, one crashed during landing, and eleven more (seven LaGG-3, two Il-2, one Yak-1 and one Pe-2) 'did not return from the mission'. At night, the Russians carried out 437 sorties, including thirty-four for the supply of troops and the removal of the wounded. But in the following days, due to the sharp deterioration of weather conditions and the losses incurred (from 1 to 6 April, ninety aircraft were shot down and missing), the Soviet aviation could no longer maintain the same intensity. And from 9 to 11 April, the air force of the north-western front (VS SZF) did not operate at all.

Interestingly, in the flight book on 8 April, Captain A.N. Dekhtyarenko recorded four Ju 52s personally shot down in the area of the settlement of Istoshino. And on that day, the Germans did really lose three of these aircraft (from KGr.zbV 800 and KGr.zbV 900).

By this time, the Demyansk area had warmed dramatically. Recent severe frosts have been replaced by a positive temperature, and the sky was shrouded in low clouds. Sleet turned to rain. This weather led to a terrible Rasputitsa, all roads turned into a mess of mud and deep puddles, air bases that did not have a hard surface, also failed. Off-road movement of troops became almost impossible.

On the afternoon of 14 April, active Russian aviation operations resumed. The Red Army air force carried out 112 sorties and reported nine downed aircraft. Own losses amounted to six aircraft. Two LaGG-3s were shot down in air battles and made emergency landings on their territory, another Pe-2 and three aircraft of non-specified types were destroyed at the air base as a result of German bombing.

The next day, the Russians flew ninety-five sorties and claimed three downed planes. Their own losses were four aircraft missing (two LaGG-3 and two Yak-1). At night, the Russians flew 111 sorties, seventy-eight of them to supply their troops (four U-2B were lost).

On 16 April, the Russian air force flew 166 sorties. The pilots reported sixteen downed aircraft (ten Bf 109, three Ju 88, one Ju 87, one 'He 113' and one 'Fw 187').[3] The authors do not have complete data on Luftwaffe losses for April 1942, but it can be expected that this information would have been greatly exaggerated by the Russians. On this day, during a flight to Demyansk, a Ju 86 W.Nr. 0286 'PF+QU' from KGzbV 7 (pilot Feldwebel O. Rudolph) went missing. The Soviets' own losses were seven aircraft (three Yak-1, two Pe-2 and two LaGG-3). Another twenty Soviet aircraft were destroyed or damaged as a result of German air attacks against Soviet airfields. At the same time, forty-seven pilots and technical personnel of the airfields were killed and injured. At night, the Soviets carried out 152 sorties, 124 of them to supply their troops. TB-3 bombers and PS-84 passenger planes dropped cargo near the village of Ramushevo and in other sectors. In total, Russian transport airplanes delivered 70 tons of cargo to its troops.

On 17 April, the northwestern front air force (VS SF) reported seven enemy aircraft shot down. At the same time, their own losses amounted to four aircraft (three fighters crashed in accidents at airfields). At night, ninety-three sorties were carried out to supply troops, while one TB-3 was missing.

On 18 April, the 'Stalin's Falcons' flew 175 sorties and claimed seven downed aircraft. Their losses were nine aircraft (three LaGG-3, three Yak-1, two X-X and one Il-2). At night, 111 sorties were carried out to supply Soviet troops, with one TB-3 being (presumably) shot down by a German night fighter.

On 19 and 20 April, the Russians claimed to have shot down ten German planes daily. Their own losses were also heavy: twenty-seven aircraft in two days (including again three X-X). The 'X-X' symbol in Soviet military documents of that period denoted the British and American 'Hurricane' and

---

3 These types of German experimental aircraft were specified in Soviet manuals. Although they were never used on the Eastern front, for various reasons, Russian pilots and ground observers during the war persistently alleged to have 'noticed' and even shot them down.

'Kittihawk' fighters that were received from the lend-lease allies. Planes were re-equipped with the 157th, 191st, 438th, 485th and other fighter aviation regiments that fought in this sector of the front. Although imported aircraft were used in Russian aviation for a long time (since November 1941), they continued to be considered secret. Therefore, they were encrypted in reports with a mysterious code. From whom the Soviet military authorities hid the presence of British and American aircraft is not clear. Perhaps this is due to the stupid total secrecy that flourished in the conditions of Stalin's bloody regime, when they tried to hide absolutely everything that had at least some relation to military equipment and military production.

Meanwhile, the Germans continued their offensive. The 16th Army concentrated its main efforts on the section of the Borisovo-Ramushevo highway. This road ran along an embankment, around which were extensive marshes. The Germans systematically drove a wedge into the Russian defense, and on 20 April, with the powerful support of Ju 87s, they managed to push back the units of the 397th rifle division, 41st and 44th rifle brigades. By the end of the day, they had captured the village of Ramushevo – a key point on the way to Demyansk – and reached the frozen river Lovat. This was the last water barrier in the ring of the blockade. The positions of the II and X army corps were only a few kilometers away. At the same time, a specially assembled strike group from the SS-Infanterie-Division 'Totenkopf' (mot.) under the command of an ardent Nazi, Theodor Eicke, launched a breakthrough from inside the Pocket on 17 April. Two days later, the SS made their way to the river Lovat in the area of Muccino. On 20 April (the Führer's birthday), Theodor Eicke received the title SS-Obergruppenführer und General der Waffen-SS and was awarded the Knight's Cross of the Iron Cross. This spurred the SS on, and the next day they made a final decisive push. On the evening of 21 April, soldiers of the Totenkopf division broke through to the village of Ramushevo and met with soldiers of the 8th Jaeger division. The blockade ring was broken!

Interestingly, the Soviet command had no information about what was happening in the area between the rivers Lovat and Pola. Russians did not know that German troops had established contact with the encircled Demyansk. Due to warming, the water level in reservoirs began to rise rapidly, flooding began and numerous swamps also melted and became impassable. Communication between Soviet units was disrupted, and the roads were full of Rasputitsa. The Germans also had many difficulties. Despite the break of the blockade ring, it was impossible to organize supplies along the narrow corridor that had formed. Everywhere there was impassable mud and swamps, it was necessary to build a crossing over the Lovat. Therefore, the air bridge continued to operate in the same mode. Meanwhile, the Russians conducted continuous attacks in the Ramushevo area, simultaneously attacking this locality from the north and from the south.

On 28 April, the Russian air force launched massive attacks against German air bases in Demyansk, Khani, and Ilyina Gorka. The pilots reported the destruction of forty-eight aircraft on the ground at once, including about thirty-five Ju 52s. Another six aircraft were shot down in air battles. Own losses amounted to four aircraft (two Il-2 and two Yak-1). According to German documents, only one Ju 52 W.Nr. 6753 from KGr.zbV 700 was destroyed (100 per cent) at the Demyansk air base.

On 29 April, the Russians flew 175 sorties, shot down five aircraft (three Bf 109 and two Hs 126), and destroyed another ten at the Khani airfield. This time, the losses of the air forces of the north-western front (VS SF) and groups of the reserve of the main command amounted to twelve aircraft, of which ten were missing.

On 30 April, the Soviets carried out ninety-four sorties, shot down one plane and destroyed twelve at air bases (not confirmed by German documents). Russian losses were again very large: eleven downed and missing aircraft, including six Il-2. For example, a composite four Il-2 from the 568th SHAP and 299th SHAP, accompanied by four LaGG-3, carried out an air attack on the Demyansk air base. In the target area, the group was hit by heavy anti-aircraft fire, resulting in all four attack aircraft missing.

In early may, the 1st Shock and 11th Soviet Armies launched an offensive, trying to converge attacks from the north and south to cut the resulting 'Ramushevsky corridor'. In addition, the Russians launched new attacks against the German II army corps from different directions. But they all ended unsuccessfully. The German defenses proved impregnable along the entire front.

The Russian air force mainly focused on supporting the offensive. Bombers attacked German troops in the area of Ramushevo, bombed crossings over the rivers Lovat and Pola, and roads in the rear of the enemy.

On 2 May, the northwestern front air force (VS SZF) flew ninety-eight sorties and lost four aircraft. On this day, during a mission east of the little town Staraya Russa, designated in German documents as 'monitoring roads east of Lake Ilmen', came under fire from a He 111 H-6 '1G+LN' of 5./KG 27. The plane took off from the Korovye Selo air base at 12.15 (Berlin time), and at 14.15 returned on one engine.

But not all such flights ended so well. The next day, during a similar reconnaissance flight east of Lake Ilmen, a He 111 H-6 W.Nr. 4830 '1G+LM' of 4./KG 27 went missing. None of the five crew members returned… This was the last loss of the II./KG 27 'Boelcke' during a combat mission to the northern sector of the Eastern front.

On 5 May, the Russians first decided to use armored Il-2s attack aircraft to intercept transport planes. Sergeant I.P. Vovkogon in a single-seat Il-2 from the 299th SHAP in the area of Demyansk shot down an Ju 52 from KGr.zbV 500. The Russians decided to use attack aircraft intended for attacking ground targets against transport planes because of the high survivability of the Ju 52. Very often, Soviet fighters went on the attack, fired all the ammunition, but did not cause visible damage to the transport airplane. Il-2 was equipped with two 20mm guns and three machine guns, making the power of its salvo much higher than that of the fighter.

On 7 May, aviation operations intensified. The Luftwaffe actively supported their troops in the area of the 'Ramushevsky corridor' and village Naluchi. The Soviet air force carried out 201 sorties, and the pilots reported seven downed planes. One of them was again on the account of Il-2 Sergeant I.P. Vovkogon from the 299th SHAP. According to German data, a Ju 52 from KGr.zbV 500 was shot down as a result of the 'Zementbomber'[4] attack near the Hani airfield. Another twenty transport planes, according to Soviet data, were destroyed at the Demyansk air base. According to German reports, two planes were destroyed at the Demyansk air base: Ju 52 W.Nr. 3172 and Ju 52 W.Nr. 5131 from KGr.zbV 500. The Russians own losses were eleven aircraft.

At 10.40 on 15 May, a pair of Il-2 piloted by Junior Lieutenant Feoktistov from the 568th SHAP and Il-2 Junior Lieutenant Okunev from the 299th SHAP flew to intercept Ju 52s in the area of the settlements of Shumilov Bor and Vysokii Bor. No transport planes were found, but a short-range reconnaissance aircraft Hs 126 was intercepted, which was attacked and shot down by Feoktistov. At 14.30, the same pair of Il-2s went on a second flight to intercept the Ju 52s. At 14.50, a group of German transport planes was discovered in the area of Vysokii Bor. The Russians went on the attack and shot down four Ju 52s at once. The Okunev plane was hit by German anti-aircraft artillery and made an emergency landing on Soviet territory. Interestingly, in both flights, the armored Il-2 was accompanied

---

4 'Zementbomber' is a common nickname of the Russian attack aircraft Il-2, which is apparently associated with the unreliability and clumsiness of this poorly designed and poorly built aircraft, which Stalin liked very much.

by a group of LaGG-3 fighters, which did not participate in the attack. Up to 1 June, the 299th and 568th SHAP carried out eighteen joint sorties to intercept transport planes. Soviet pilots reportedly shot down five Ju 52s.

By 16 May, the German 16th Army had managed to expand the Ramushevsky corridor to 12 km long and 4 km wide, creating a network of wire fences, minefields, and strongpoints on both sides. On either side of the corridor stretched impassable forests and swamps, into which the Germans had pushed the Russians. On 17 May, warm weather was established in the area of Demyansk. A pleasant south wind blew, and the air temperature rose to +24°C. On this day, the first large automobile caravan, which delivered a large cargo to the II army corps, proceeded towards Demyansk.

Stalin's order at the end of February demanding 'not to release a single German from Demyansk' ironically turned out to be prophetic. The battles in this 'Arse of the World' were just beginning. The Germans were not going to leave and were ready to defend the remote forest area for as long as necessary. But that's another story…

On 20 May, most of the aviation groups serving the air bridge were withdrawn. Only three of them still continued to fly to Demyansk in the following months. From mid-February to 17 May, 265 aircraft (mostly Ju 52/3m) were lost as a result of enemy action, accidents and forced landings, but many of them were only 10 to 40 per cent damaged and were subsequently restored.[5] Losses in Luftwaffe personnel amounted to 383 people killed, injured and missing. There was also indirect damage. Over a period of four months, flight schools lost 300 aircraft, which could only affect the speed and quality of training.

In total, from January 1942 until the final evacuation of the Demyansk salient at the beginning of the following year, transport planes made 33,086 flights to this fortress. During this period, 64,844 tons of supplies and 30,500 troops were delivered, and 35,400 wounded or sick were evacuated back to the German rear.

---

5 Pegg M. Transporter Volume One: Luftwaffe Transport Units 1937-1943. Luftwaffe Colours. – Classic Publications, 2007. p.36.

Chapter 2

'Osgiliath' on the Lovat river

'We had pistols in our equipment to kill ourselves'

In Holm – a little old Russian small town located on two banks of the river Lovat – the German garrison of 3,500 people was surrounded by Russians. But this situation was not a disaster for them. The Germans were located in a compact settlement, they had stoves and firewood, and they had food and ammunition supplies. The Russian divisions, on the contrary, found themselves in an open and desolate area, without a roof over their heads and without fuel to save them from the cold. Not only did they have no hot food, but no food at all! To warm themselves up, Russian soldiers had to chop down wet and frozen trees with axes, pour gasoline on them and set fire to them. In addition, the Russian soldiers were exhausted by long marches on snow-covered roads and forests and chronic malnutrition. They were short of ammunition and shells. Therefore, they could not attack the Germans defending the town of Holm. It was a siege in which the besieged Germans felt much more comfortable than the besieging Russians.

These circumstances allowed the commander of the 281st security division (Sicherungs-Division) Generalmajor Theodor Scherer to prepare well for defense. All the big brick buildings of the small town were turned into forts, and pillboxes and bunkers were built between them from improvised materials. The small central city square was turned into a citadel, which was surrounded by trenches and barriers. At the same time, the German garrison had almost no heavy weapons, they had to rely mainly on heavy machine guns, mortars and personal weapons. Only the Tellermines 43 was available to fight against Russian heavy tanks.[1] Having

---

1 Tellermine 43 is a push-action anti-tank mine, developed in Germany and adopted in 1943. It is a flat rounded metal box, inside which an explosive charge is placed and a fuse is installed. The explosion occurs when a tank track or a car wheel presses on the cap of a mine.

dug-in and evenly distributed his modest forces, Scherer prepared for the arrival of 'Aliens'. This improvised German fortress went down in history as Holm Pocket.

The first major Soviet attack on Holm Pocket began on the morning of 13 February. The infantry was supported by thirteen British 'Matilda' tanks from the 146th tank battalion. These vehicles crawled very slowly through the snow, but the German shells bounced off their armor like peas. On 16 February, the soldiers of the Russian 33rd rifle division managed to break through to the city center from the east. At the same time, the 391st rifle division, attacking from the south, could only advance as far as the outskirts. On 19 February, this division launched a new attack and occupied three blocks of the city.

On 20 February, the newly arrived 37th rifle brigade joined the assault. By 06.00 the next day, they managed to capture several houses on the northern edge of the city. The Russians thought that victory was not far away. But then the Germans launched a desperate counterattack and drove Red Army men into the woods north of Holm Pocket. The Matilda tanks that reached the central streets were destroyed in close combat with grenades and Tellermines. The first assault on the fortress failed, although from this moment on, 'Aliens' were constantly located directly in the city.

Supplying the Scherer garrison was a very difficult mission. The territory defended by the Germans was only 2 km in diameter and had a curved shape. The ring of blockade gradually shrank. A small airfield was located in the northern part of town and was constantly under fire. Transport planes were forced to descend and come in low-level for landing, coming under fire from Russian infantry.

Therefore, it was impossible to organize a standard air bridge here. But the Germans found a way out. It was decided to use cargo gliders to supply Scherrer's group, as well as drop cargo containers on parachutes. For this purpose, for the first time it was decided to attract bomber aircraft. He 111 from KG 4 'General Wever' were engaged in towing Go 242 'Gotha' gliders, while Ju 52/3m dragged lighter DFS 230 gliders. A special landing squadron of the 1st air fleet (LS LFl 1)[2] was created for Go 242 gliders. Bombers from KG 4, for the first time, but not the last, had to perform the role of transport planes. The flights took place in conditions of severe frosts and snowstorms, the engines started poorly, and consumed an extremely large amount of fuel (which shortened the range). Frequently, aircraft iced

---

2 Gundelach K. Kampfgeschwader 'General Wever' 4. – Motorbuch Verlag Stuttgart, 1978. p. 165.

up in the air. Because of bad weather and fog, flights often took place at a low altitude, so that the bombers were constantly at risk of being hit by fire from the ground.

The Go 242 glider, nicknamed the 'flying container' by the Germans, was first used in 1941 on the Eastern front. It was designed on a double-girder system, which made it possible to make the rear part of the fuselage recline on hinges, so that it could be used for loading and unloading. The rear position of the loading hatch was also convenient in case the glider collided with an obstacle during landing, which was common. In this case, usually only the nose of the fuselage suffered, the tail hatch remained intact, and there were no problems with rapid unloading in a combat situation. The main material in the Go 242's construction was wood. Three sprung skis were used for landing, and for take-off, a two-wheeled cart that was dropped when lifting off from the ground. The tow rope was attached to a special lock in the nose of the glider and could withstand a load of 6 tons. The crew consisted of two pilots who sat side by side in the front cockpit, which had an excellent view.

The Go 242 A-1 modification was intended specifically for cargo transportation, while the Go 242 A-2 variant was intended for delivering paratroopers or necessary equipment on restricted landing sites. The glider had a braking parachute that was ejected before landing and significantly reduced mileage. In addition, an extra door appeared on the hinged rear part of the fuselage. Go 242 gliders could transport up to 3,500 kg of food, fuel or medicine, as well as ammunition of all calibers, up to shells for heavy field howitzers. The glider's braking distance was only 183 meters, so it could land even on a small meadow or street.

To minimize losses from artillery fire, sorties were usually carried out early at dawn or at dusk. A straight street in the center of the city (Staraya Russa – Holm highway) was used as the 'airfield'. At the same time, cargo gliders were only able to be used once, since it was not possible to take them back. After unloading, they were simply dragged to the side of the road and abandoned. However, the discarded gliders were not wasted! Soon the fuselages were simply sawn up for firewood, which was also in short supply in the fortress. Glider pilots did not stay long as guests of the surrounded garrison, they were operatively evacuated on light-engine aircraft Fi 156 'Storch'.

This legendary aircraft was developed in 1935. Initially, it was intended for correcting artillery fire, communication, rapid evacuation of the wounded, and as a personal aircraft for high-ranking military and officials.

The Fi 156 was characterized by amazing maneuverability and the ability to stay in the air at an extremely low speed, only 53 km/h. A very short runway was required for the 'Storch' to take off and land; in fact, it could take to the sky from any meadow or football field. The Fi 156 was chosen from various competing models because of its very simple and reliable design, based on a light and strong steel tube frame. One of the advantages of the aircraft was also the simple and unpretentious Argus As 10 engine. The unique design allowed the aircraft to take off after a run of only 65 meters, and stop 20 meters after contact with the ground. With a strong wind, turning in its direction, 'Storch' could almost hover in the air, like a helicopter.

The Fi 156 was built in various versions, which differed mainly in the glazing of the cab. The most popular modification was the Fi 156 C. If necessary, skis could be attached to the aircraft instead of a wheeled chassis, and even a tracked chassis was experimentally installed on the Fi 156 E. For defense, the Storch had a single 7.9 mm MG15 machine gun in the rear of the cockpit, but their pilots when facing the enemy still preferred to rely on the excellent handling and maneuverability of this aircraft.

On 14 February, the Luftwaffe suffered their first losses while supplying the Holm garrison. Two Ju 52s (W.Nr. 6118 and 6513) from I./KGzbV 172 were hit by machine gun fire from the ground when approaching the city. In one of the planes, two pilots were injured. The next day, the Russians first documented the fact that the garrison was being supplied by air. The 3rd Shock Army's combat log records: 'The enemy tried to support the Holm garrison by parachuting people and supplies.'

Not all gliders landed safely in Holm Pocket. On the approach to the target, Soviet soldiers and anti-aircraft guns opened up on them with a barrage of fire from all barrels. Russian fighters sometimes also circled the approaches to the city and managed to intercept German gliders. Some of them were damaged, but still reached the street where they could land, others fell near the fortress. For example, on 16 February, two Go 242s with the side numbers 'K5+2-10' and 'K5+2-11'were shot down near Holm.

According to Soviet data, these gliders shot down three I-16s from the 728th IAP (pilots Junior Lieutenant N.P. Ignatiev, Sergeants M.S. Baranov and A.E. Borovykh). On 20 February, a He 111 H-6 W.Nr. 4001 '5J+AL' from 3./KG 4 (crew: Leutnant Gunther Brox, Unteroffizieres Ernst Fahring, Gefreiter Heinz Langenstein and Obergefreiter Friedrich Bachmann) went missing while flying to Holm. The Go 242 'SF+HM' being towed fell in the Holm area, and its pilot was killed. He 111 P-2 W.Nr. 547 from

KGr.zbV 211 in the Holm Pocket area was damaged by machine-gun fire from the ground, one crew member was killed, and another was injured.

On 23 February, two more gliders, 'Gotha' 'SF+HR' and 'SF+CH' from LS LFl 1, fell in the Holm area. The next two gliders (onboard codes 'SF+HV' and 'SCH+2-4') did not reach their goal on 4 March. At the same time 'Gotha' 'SCH+2-4' crashed, three members of its crew were killed. On 5 March, 2 Go 242 ('VC+FR' and 'VC+FP') were lost. One of their pilots was killed. On 7 March, another 'Gotha' with the tail number '5K+2-15' was lost at Holm.

In addition to ammunition and food, reinforcements were also delivered to Holm Pocket, as the garrison suffered constant losses and its numbers gradually decreased. Support from the strike aircraft was weak, because all units were involved in the sectors of Staraya Russa, Demyansk, Chudovo and others during this period. But in the most critical moments, Luftwaffe still helped the Scherer group. For example, on the morning of 22 February, Ju 87s conducted a series of air attacks against the 33rd rifle division in the eastern part of Holm Pocket. As a result, the Russians suffered heavy losses and were temporarily demoralized. The planned attack was thwarted. At the same time, a Ju 87 B-1, W.Nr. 0292 'NG+ID', from 9./StG 2 was shot down. Its crew was killed.

On 25 February, several transport planes landed at the airfield in the northern part of Holm Pocket. But soon Russian planes suddenly appeared from behind the forest and dropped bombs on the parking lot. As a result, three Ju 52s (W.Nr. 3178, 6062 and 6955) from KGr.zbV 9 were damaged, two pilots were killed. On the same day, Soviet fighters shot down the He 111 H-6 W.Nr. 4216 '5J+AK' from 2./KG 4. Of its crew, commander 2./KG 4 Hauptmann Erich Frhr von Wernherr was killed, and Leutnant Helmut Heisig was wounded. The other pilots were able to escape.

In late February, the makeshift landing pad for transport planes in the northern part of Holm Pocket was completely deactivated as a result of constant artillery attacks and attacks by Russian infantry. From now on, the garrison could only receive cargo using gliders and cargo containers dropped from transport planes.

On the way to Holm on 1 March, He 111 P-1 W.Nr. 1484 from KGr.zbV 211 was attacked by Russian fighters. The plane made an emergency landing on German territory and was completely destroyed. On 2 March, a He 111 H-6 W.Nr. 4876 '1G+BM' from 4./KG 27 was shot down during a Holm Pocket supply mission. The crew of five (pilot

Leutnant Otto Hartmann, navigator Unteroffizier Franz Metzner, radio operator Obergefreiter Julius Bohrmann, flight mechanic Unteroffizier Bruno Rogge and side gunner Obergefreiter Adolf-Karl Pamperin) were missing.

Such losses strongly affected the morale of German pilots. The idea of suddenly being in the territory occupied by a cruel and merciless enemy, literally terrified them. This was especially true for young pilots who were not yet used to the constant threat of death. And Soviet captivity in a war of mutual destruction on the Eastern front did not allow hope for the Geneva Convention. The Germans came up with different ways to deal with this stress. H. Schlue from KG 27 recalled:

> We sang in the airfield barracks the German version of the song 'Sowjetstern', the song of the Red air force! At the same time, instead of the words 'Heil Hitler', we sang 'Heil Moscow', but no one scolded us for it. Such 'parties' with a large amount of vodka always occurred when the crews did not return from missions. It was more of a howl than a chant, but we had to deal with the frequent desperation. After we found the crew killed by the Russians, we were very scared. We had pistols in our equipment to shoot ourselves if we landed behind Russian lines. The dead crew, of course, motivated us to 'close combat with knives', the fear of capture – this was the worst in the Russian war.[3]

Many German aircraft crews disappeared without a trace, and nothing is known about their fate until now. Many years later, it turned out that of the crew of the He 111 '1G+BM' that disappeared in the Holm Pocket sector, only Leutnant Otto Hartmann survived (he was 21 in 1942). He was captured by the Russians, then sent to the Stalin's Lager No.74 (Oranki, a large village in the Gorky region). From there, Hartmann was moved around a lot in the Soviet Union. He was in camp No.99 (Yelabuga, Central Russia), camp No.27 (Krasnogorsk, near Moscow), then in Karaganda (Kazakhstan). Yet Hartmann was among the lucky ones. He survived and returned to Germany in June 1953, eleven years after the fatal mission to Holm. Then he was already 32 years old. Otto Hartmann had spent a third of his life as a prisoner of Stalin's Gulag.

---

3 Boelcke Archiv.

'Transport planes of the enemy dropped 120 cargo-packages'

Meanwhile, the Soviets continued to try to destroy the garrison under Scherer's command. The battle order for the 3rd Shock Army dated 3 March stated: 'The enemy Garrison in the city of Holm has suffered more losses, but is not surrendering. We must destroy it.' The Russians sent twelve tanks to help the infantry, including 4 T-34s, 2 KV-1s, and 6 T-60s. Heavy and medium tanks were sent to the eastern part of the city to help the 33rd rifle division, while light T-60 tanks were sent to the southern and northern parts of the city. By the morning of 5 March, the Russian 33rd division occupied ten blocks in the eastern part of Holm Pocket, the 391st rifle division occupied three blocks in the southern sector, and the 37th rifle brigade occupied positions in the area of the airfield.

On 21 March, near Holm, Soviet fighters shot down two Ju 52s from KGr.zbV 9 (W.Nr. 6115 'V4+HL' and W.Nr. 6355 'V4+FL'). One of them fell on German territory (five pilots were killed), the second on Soviet territory (four crew members were missing). On 25 March, a He 111 H-6 W.Nr. 4331 '5J+CH' from 1./KG 4 (crew: Leutnant Werner Hochgraber and three Obergefreiters Karl Siebrecht, Otto Krautscheider, Robert Fritsch) went missing during a Holm supply mission. The next day, a similar, sad military fate befell the Ju 52 W.Nr. 7144 'X8+GH' from KGr.zbV 'Posen'.

For a month, in the city there was continuous fighting for every destroyed house, but the Russians failed to achieve serious success. 'Enemy aircraft during 27 March showed great activity, bombed and shelled the battle lines of our troops in the Holm sector,' the journal of combat operations of the 3rd Shock Army reported. 'Transport aircraft of the enemy dropped 120 cargo packages with ammunition and food during the day.' On 29 March, the Russians recorded the dumping of sixty cargo containers.

On the night of 1 April, Soviet aircraft carried out a massive raid on Holm Pocket. When the smoke from the explosions and the resulting fires dissipated, at 05.00 the 33rd rifle division launched another offensive. At the cost of heavy losses, Red Army men managed to capture block No.8 and break into block No.7 of the city. However, by the next morning, the Germans had knocked them out and forced them to withdraw to their original positions. On this day, the Russians recorded the dumping of 120 cargo containers for the besieged garrison.

Despite the strong defense, the situation of the German garrison gradually deteriorated. In the fortress, a typhoid epidemic raged, disabling more soldiers than the enemy's attacks. All the horses were eaten, and the daily ration of bread was reduced to 300 grams per day per person. All food supplies from the surviving local population were mercilessly requisitioned, which doomed most of the city's residents to starvation.

On 5 April, soldiers of the 33rd rifle division managed to capture two gliders on the northern edge of Holm. One of them had not yet been unloaded; it contained ammunition and food. Suffering from hunger, Red Army men were able to have a hearty lunch and dinner for the first time in many weeks.

During 6 April, units of the 3rd Shock Army claimed that three transport planes and three He 111s were shot down by rifle and machine gun fire in the Holm Pocket area. Two of the lost German aircraft were accounted for by soldiers of the 391st rifle division. And this information was close to reality.

During the mission to supply Holm Pocket, II./KG 27 lost three aircraft at once on this very unfortunate day. In the target area He 111 H-6 W.Nr. 4902 '1G+HP' from 6./KG 27 was missing; 9 km southwest of Holm, He 111 H-6 W.Nr. 4850 '1G+BP' of 6./KG 27 fell into a swamp on Soviet territory. He 111 H-6 W.Nr. 4870 '1G+GN' from 5./KG 27 also went missing. At first, all fifteen crew members of these bombers were reported missing. This mass loss was a real disaster for their comrades. But the capricious 'military fate' still showed some German pilots a little favor. Soon the II./KG 27 headquarters at Korovye Selo air base received a radio message from Feldwebel Gerhard Reppe, radio operator He 111 H-6 '1G+GN'. He said that during the dumping of cargo containers, the plane came under fire from the ground and received a lot of damage. Pilot Oberleutnant Gottfried Kappes was able to make an emergency landing on the territory of the city of Holm in no man's land. At the same time, the crew removed the radio from the plane, and then – with the help of a bicycle – the German pilots were able to generate electricity to send a radio message.

The next day, at 15.00 (Berlin time), bombers from II./KG 27 flew back to Holm. In addition to cargo containers, they dropped off a supply of warm clothing and food for Gottfried Kappes' crew. But this mission also brought new victims. In the western part of Holm, He 111 H-6 W.Nr. 4929 '1G+GP' from 6./KG 27 fell for an unknown reason. Its entire experienced crew of pilot Oberleutnant Hans-Theo Ewerhardt (25 years old), navigator Feldwebel Kurt Ehlig (30 years old), radio operator Unteroffizier Hans

Lehle (22 years old), flight mechanic Unteroffizier Hans Gehlen (22 years old) and flight gunner Unteroffizier Fritz Langenbach (29 years old) added to the sad list of missing (the short lifespan of a transport airplane pilot allowed us to consider this crew very 'old'). The further fate of the crew of Gottfried Kappes, for which their comrades did not spare their lives, is not known. We can only assume that they joined the German garrison of Holm Pocket.

On 10 April, the Soviets launched a new offensive. After heavy fighting, by the evening of the next day, the 33rd rifle division managed to occupy several blocks located on the Lovat bank. On 13 April, the Russians managed to reach the destroyed bridge over the river. The eastern part of the city was completely captured.

After a brief respite, another attack began at 16.00 on 16 April. As a result, the Russians managed to occupy another four blocks of the city. It already seemed to them that a few more attacks must be made and the German garrison would fall. In reality, however, these events were the culmination of the battle for the Holm. The headquarters of the 3rd Shock Army received reconnaissance data that the Germans were soon going to launch a deblocking attack from the area west of the hamlet of Khvoroshino. Divisions occupying the outer ring of the blockade received urgent orders to prepare for defense and build two lines with long-term nodes of resistance. At the same time, it was planned to complete the work in two stages: the main line of defense by 20 April and the rear line (in the area of the hamlet of Kuzemkino) by 5 May. These actions forced the Soviets to suspend the assault on Holm Pocket and throw all available units and reserves to strengthen the blockade ring.

At 04.00 (Moscow time) on 28 April, a powerful artillery barrage began, then a large group of Ju 87s appeared in the sky, and struck the positions of Soviet infantry and artillery. At 05.00, a German shock group from the 39th (XXXIX) army corps launched an offensive from the hamlets area of Mazurovo and Khvoroshino in the direction of Holm. Already at 09.30, the Germans captured the settlements of Varavinka and Lisichkino. During the day, the Russians recorded the dumping of 120 cargo containers for the Holm garrison. The Russian air force conducted air attacks against the defending Germans, with one plane being shot down by anti-aircraft artillery and falling on the 44th quarter of the city in the location of the Soviet troops.

The order of the Luftwaffe General Command described the tactics of aviation actions during the deblocking attack:

Luftflotte 1 supports the XXXIX army corps attack with all its strength and in the following way:

a) before the start of the attack, the strike deployment of aircraft: 'Stukas' against resistance nests and positions close to their own front, Kampfverbände against the deployment and nests of resistance in the depth of the battlefield. The attack begins after the last plane takes off.
b) during the mobile operation 'Stukas', in accordance with the preparation of the attack, must destroy the resistance nests directly in front of the advancing infantry and artillery positions. Kampfverbände attack positions located in the depth, as well as suppress the flank impact of the enemy with heavy bombs.[4]

On 29 April, the strike group continued its offensive, capturing the settlements of Zamoshye, Maksovo, and Chashchevka. 'Three enemy planes landed in the city of Holm,' the 3rd Shock Army's combat log reported. 'Presumably the landing is made within the city limits on the Holm – Staraya Russa highway. Enemy transport aircraft dropped up to 100 parachutes with cargo into the city of Holm.' Within two days, Soviet infantrymen reported two aircraft shot down by infantry weapons fire, including one glider tug.

On 30 April, the Luftwaffe was active again. Ju 87 and He 111 bombed the Snopovo–Toropets and Holm–Kamenka roads, along which reinforcements for the Soviet troops were moving. The supply of the garrison Holm Pocket by air also continued. There were several air battles in the area of the city, and Russian pilots reported downed Ju 87 and Ju 88 aircraft.

At dawn on 1 May, fearing that the city would be unblocked, the Soviets launched a desperate offensive against the German garrison. By 10.00, soldiers of the 33rd rifle division and the 'fresh' 26th rifle brigade managed to capture several blocks in the north-western part of the city. But at a critical moment, Ju 87s appeared in the sky, which struck the Soviet troops and inflicted heavy losses on them. Three tanks were destroyed by direct hits of bombs.

On 2–3 May, heavy fighting took place in the Holm area, but although the garrison was weakened (by that time there were over 1,000 wounded

---

4 Boelcke Archiv

soldiers in the infirmaries located in the basements of brick houses) they managed to repel all attacks.

On the morning of 4 May, the Germans concentrated a strike group with ten assault guns in the area of the small village of Pronino. At 16.30, after heavy artillery and mortar fire and an accompanying Ju 87 air attack, the Germans launched a final offensive along the road to Holm. At 20.30, the defenses of the Russian 3rd Guards rifle brigade located there were breached, and the strike group captured the small village of Kuzemkino. The blockade ring was broken. During the night, the first supply trucks arrived at Holm.

On 5 May, the soldiers of the German 121st infantry division arrived in the city and completely drove the Russians out of the Central and northern part of the city, creating a new perimeter of defense. The supply of the garrison by air continued for several more days. During 7 May, thirty cargo gliders landed in the western part of the city. Now they were no longer cut for firewood, but were taken back. The parachuting of cargo containers continued until 9 May. In total, the Luftwaffe delivered 24,303 tons of cargo and 15,445 soldiers to a beleaguered garrison during the blockade. Within a month, the Germans completely cleared Holm Pocket of the Russians, and the city itself was gradually turned into a powerful stronghold. Despite regular attacks, Holm remained under Wehrmacht control for two more years...

Back on 16 April, Chief Lufttransportführer Ost Luftflotte 1 Oberst Friedrich-Wilhelm Morzik had been awarded the Knight's Cross for the successful organization of air bridges to Demyansk and Holm, as well as for his previous great achievements.

The battle for Holm was somewhat reminiscent of the fairy tale battle for the city of Osgiliath from the movie *Lord of the Rings*, in which hordes of orcs from the east attacked this ruined old city, located on two banks of the river Anduin and connected by a single bridge. Holm was also an ancient city, a monument of the old Russian Novgorod Republic, which in the fifteenth century was mercilessly destroyed by bloodthirsty Moscow princes. It was also located on two banks of the river, along which the ancient 'trade route from the Varangians to the Greeks' passed, the western and eastern parts of the city were connected by a single bridge... At the same time, the brutal battle for this small town was only a rehearsal for subsequent similar battles for numerous cities on the Eastern front...

On 30 June, Hitler dined with his entourage at the Wolfschanze. The commander of the Army Group 'Nord', Georg von Kuchler, was present and was awarded the title Generalfeldmarschall on that day. The Führer listened with unusual delight to his account of the fierce defensive battles on the rivers Volkhov and Lovat. Kuchler told the impressionable dictator that 'the Russians fought like animals to the last breath', and that 'they had to be killed one by one'. In addition, the Führer was pleased to learn that the Red Army soldiers who were captured in this swampy area also died, as they could not be helped.

Hitler saw these battles as analogous to the Roman Empire of the later period, when the Romans had to constantly hold off barbarian attacks on their northern border. The basis of defense then was a network of strong points – fortresses, which often found themselves isolated in the environment, but continued to defend themselves. The troops came from the depths of the empire, unblocked these 'Festing' and restored the situation. The Führer decided that Staraya Russa, Demyansk, Holm, Velizh, Demidov, Rzhev and other cities under his leadership were the chain of strongholds that successfully held off the 'Bolshevik hordes' attacking from the depths of the dense forests. Imagining himself a new Roman emperor, Hitler decided that such a strategy (first capturing a vast territory, and then holding it with the help of a line of fortresses) in the future would lead him to victory.

Chapter 3

The fire hill

'Migratory birds' III./KG 4

After successful missions to supply Demyansk and Holm, the experience of using bombers in the role of transport planes was actively continued. First of all, this concerned KG 4 'General Wever', which had a lot of experience in performing such missions. By the beginning of Operation Barbarossa, this combat unit was a specialized unit and was mainly engaged in strategic air attacks and mining of enemy water areas by dropping Luftmine. But by the middle of 1942, the I. and II./KG 4 had actually turned from specialized to conventional bomber aviation groups, no different from the others.

Only III./KG 4, which has been headed by Major Wolfgang Queisner[1] since 31 July, still retained its special status. In early 1942, at Fassberg air base, it received additional training in towing Go 242 cargo gliders. It was assumed that during the upcoming offensive in the Caucasus, III./KG 4 would be involved in amphibious operations. In fact, this group was mainly involved in transport operations, throwing groups of agents and saboteurs behind the front line and pinpointing air attacks on important strategic objects. From 8 July, this unit was based at the Nikolaev-Ost airfield (a city in the southern part of Ukraine), then in Kharkov and Makeyevka (a city in the south-east of Ukraine).[2]

One of the group's most successful operations was a daylight raid by fourteen He 111s on the city of Astrakhan on 9 September. The main attack was on oil storage facility No.5; in addition, the oil storage facility in the village of Ilinka and the ship repair yard 'Lenin' was bombed. As a result

---

1 On September 6, he was replaced by Major Werner Klosinski, who commanded III./KG 4 until May 1943.

2 Gundelach K. Kampfgeschwader 'General Wever' 4. – Motorbuch Verlag Stuttgart, 1978. p. 178 – 179.

of numerous direct hits of heavy incendiary bombs, Brand C50A and Brand C250A on two oil storage facilities containing about 400,000 tons of petroleum products were set on fire, the resulting fire took on a colossal, apocalyptic scale. The flames rose hundreds of meters, merging into huge fire tornadoes. Then a huge column of black smoke rose over the steppe, which could be seen for tens of kilometers. After that, III./KG 4 carried out several more raids on Astrakhan, and on 27 September participated in a massive air attack on industrial buildings in the northern part of Stalingrad.[3]

On 5 October, the air group returned to Germany, and soon the 7th and 8th Staffel were transferred to southern Italy to participate in the supply of the Panzer army 'Africa'. The troops under the command of Generalfeldmarschall Erwin Rommel were severely short of fuel, and any available aviation units were used to transport it.

On 26 October, the bombers arrived at Kalamaki airfield near Athens. From here, they towed Go 242 cargo gliders loaded with gasoline and ammunition to Tobruk. The flights were conducted at low altitude to avoid attacks by Allied fighters.

However, on the 30th, III./KG 4 received orders to fly to San Pancrazio air base in the Lecce region in southern Italy. From here, the flight of the He 111 to the target with the 'Gotha' in tow took six hours. And all this time, both crews were in constant tension, as the pilots had to simultaneously monitor the sky and at the same time not to hit objects that rose above the ground. During this period, a strong wind raised high waves on the sea, and storms often occurred. Therefore, the control of both aircraft at low altitude presented great difficulties. As a result, after landing in Tobruk the crews had to rest for almost a day and only then go on the return flight.

In this regard, the commander of the group, Major Werner Klosinski, suggested that cargo gliders should be abandoned altogether, and that the He 111 bombers themselves should be loaded to capacity. Thus, in his opinion, cargo turnover increased, and pilots were less exposed to dangers. This suggestion was adopted and from mid-November, the bombers began flying without gliders. In addition to Tobruk, the port of Benghazi and other air bases on the North African coast were often the landing point. Combat losses were insignificant and were close in numbers to standard operating losses. On 15 November, He 111 from 9./KG 4 was lost (two pilots were missing), and on 16 November, He 111 from 8./KG 4 was crushed (four wounded).

---

3 Gundelach K. Kampfgeschwader 'General Wever' 4. – Motorbuch Verlag Stutgart, 1978. p. 211 – 212.

Sometimes German bombers carrying cargo to Africa were attacked by British fighters; 17 November was the most difficult for III./KG 4. On that day, thirteen He 111, carrying a total of seventy-five barrels of gasoline, went on another flight from Lecce to Benghazi. Landing in Benghazi was very difficult because of the soft soil, eroded by the autumn rains. The difficulties did not end there however.

When the last bombers were still landing, and the first planes were already being unloaded on the ground, twenty British fighters suddenly appeared in the sky at once, catching the Germans at the most inopportune moment. As a result of the rapid attack, two He 111s coming into land were immediately shot down. However, one of them still managed to make an emergency landing, although the crew members were injured. The pilots from the second plane jumped out with parachutes. Meanwhile, Supermarine Spitfire fighters tried to attack another plane coming in to land; its pilot noticed the danger in time, picked up speed abruptly and went into the clouds. In addition, British aircraft simultaneously bombarded the airfield, destroying four Italian Savoia-Marchetti SM. 82 and the already unloaded He 111 '5J+KR'. Another eight aircraft from III./KG 4 were damaged in various ways. Surprisingly, with such a powerful and unexpected attack, the Germans had very small losses in terms of personnel. Obergefreiter Erich Jurczyk, Gefreiter Reinhard Engmann, Feldwebel Siegfried were killed, and six other pilots (all from 9./KG 4) were wounded or injured.

It was not possible to repair damaged planes in Benghazi. And the failure of eleven vehicles at once seriously undermined the group's combat capability. However, the pilots made the bold decision to take off. As a result, the damaged He 111s went on a long flight over the sea. Many had their fuel and oil tanks shot through, some with a deactivated hydraulic system, and others with faulty radios and navigation equipment. The most affected aircraft were operated by Hauptmann Gopel, Feldwebel Schutze, Gefreiteres Matz and Orisch. All the He 111s were eventually able to land safely in Lecce.[4]

The trip to the Mediterranean lasted a month and a half. The aviation group essentially traveled from cold regions to warm ones and back again, like migrating birds. In early December, III./KG 4 returned to Russia, this time to the Smolensk-Nord airfield. The next target area of this special group was the town of Velikiye Luki …

On 24 November, the Soviets launched an offensive in the upper reaches of the Lovat river. The purpose of the operation of the 3rd Shock Army

---

4 Gundelach K. pp. 214–217.

was to capture the important stronghold of Velikiye Luki, as well as the railway junctions at Novosokolniki and Nevel. The Russians wanted to cut the rocade railway[5] Vitebsk–Staraya Russa, which was important for supplying the German 16th Army and its strongholds along the Lovat river. In addition, the Soviets sought to prevent the transfer of German divisions to the Rzhev salient and Stalingrad. On 25 November, operation Mars was launched – another attempt to break through the front of the German 9th Army near the city of Rzhev.

After several days of heavy fighting, by the evening of 28 November, the 381st and 9th Guards rifle divisions met in the area of Ostrianj station. 7,000 German soldiers from the 83rd infantry division were blocked in the town of Velikiye Luki. After that, the troops of the 3rd Shock Army launched an attack on the small town of Novosokolniki. But by this time the Germans had pulled the 291st infantry division and the 20th motorized infantry division into the breakout area. They managed to localize the break and close the gaps in the front line, and in early December, the fighting took a positional character.

When the situation in the area of Velikiye Luki was reported to Hitler, he, as usually happened in such situations, gave orders to defend this fortress to the last opportunity, as well as prepare a deblocking strike and organize the supply of the garrison by air. To all the objections of the command of the Army Groups 'Mitte' and 'Nord' (the breakthrough occurred at the junction of their positions), the Führer refused. He used the 'heroic defense of Holm Pocket' the previous winter as an example.

On 11 December, German troops made their first attempt to unblock the Velikiye Luki Pocket. The main attack was carried out from the south-western direction from the Chernozem station area. Three days later, the Wehrmacht managed to push back the Russians and capture the village of Gromovo. But the Soviets had the experience of fighting for Holm. Now they had many reserves at their disposal, and they did not spare the soldiers, gradually throwing them into battle to the southwest of Velikiye Luki. As a result, the Russians suffered heavy losses, but were able to hold the front on the outer ring of the blockade. Fierce fighting continued until 25 December.

Meanwhile, the blockaded garrison of Velikiye Luki Pocket was preparing to defend itself. The main line passed through suburban settlements, each of which was adapted to a circular defense. All the stone buildings of this

---

5 Rocade railway – a railway that runs parallel to the front line and is intended for rapid transfer of troops and supplies from one section of the front to another.

ancient Russian city were turned into forts. The most fortified defense hub was the complex of railway station buildings. Lofts of tall buildings were equipped for observation posts and machine-gun emplacements. The Bastion-type fortress located in the center of the city became the citadel of defense. This structure was built during the Great Northern War of the early XVIII century by order of the Russian Tsar Peter I.[6] An irregular hexagon consisting of six bastions at the corners and ravelins between them, it towered menacingly above the terrain. The height of the earthen rampart from the outside was 50 meters, the circumference of the ramparts reached 2 km.

Initially, the commander of the garrison was General Theodor Scherer – the hero of the defense of the Holm Pocket. But Hitler did not want to risk this 'man-legend', and ordered him to evacuate from Velikiye Luki. Scherer was flown out of the fortress in a Fi 156, and was replaced by the commander of the 277th infantry regiment, Oberstleutnant von Sass.

'The enemy uses Ju 87 aircraft to deliver food and ammunition'

Given the catastrophic situation at the front, the organization for the air bridge was undertaken mainly by bombers from III./KG 4. There were simply no other transport aviation groups at the disposal of the Army Group 'Nord' – all the planes had been sent to Stalingrad! Weather conditions, like a year ago in the Demyansk Pocket sector, left much to be desired: snowfall, frost, constant icing. Flights had to be performed at low altitude, exposed to the risk of firing from the ground. He 111 aircraft towed cargo gliders, and also dropped containers of food and ammunition in the location of the German troops. At the same time, cargo gliders in such situations, as it was previously in Holm Pocket, became disposable, because after landing, the pilots could not take to the air again. The pilots themselves were evacuated by special units flying the Fi 156. In addition

6 Great northern War (1700–1721) war with Sweden, unleashed by the Russian Tsar Peter I in alliance with a number of European States. After a series of embarrassing defeats, the Russians were able to turn the tide of the war, and eventually Sweden was defeated. As a result of the war, Russia gained access to the Baltic sea and the former Swedish colonies in the Baltic States. Russian Tsar Peter I was Stalin's idol and had much the same pathological qualities, except that the Tsar, unlike Stalin, had a high intelligence. The victory over Sweden resulted in the complete ruin of Russia and the extinction of 30 per cent of the population from hunger, disease and backbreaking slave labour.

to supplies, He 111 aircraft periodically bombed the positions of Soviet troops besieging the city.

The Russians planned to launch an assault on the city on the morning of 12 December, but a heavy fog forced them to postpone the attack for one day. At noon on 13 December, after a long artillery barrage and massive air attacks, the 257th and 357th rifle divisions began their assault. By evening they managed to reach the Lovat river and capture the bridge. On the morning of 14 December, the Russian air force launched a massive air attack on the eastern part of the city. It involved forty-one Il-2 attack aircraft from the 292nd assault aviation division (292nd SHAD). It included three assault regiments (667th, 800th, 820th) and one fighter regiment (427th). Due to the lack of air bases in the area of operation, the Russian air force operated mainly from the large Andreapol air base (110 km from the town of Velikiye Luki). By evening, the Russians had occupied almost the entire western part of the city, except for the citadel built in the time of Tsar Peter I.

The first losses in KG 4 occurred on 16 December. Gefreiter Kurt Schirrmacher from 7./KG 4 and Unteroffizier Theodor Mietzner from 14.(Eis)/KG 4 (Staffel was formed in late October 1942, but was disbanded in early January 1943) were killed (apparently as a result of infantry fire from the ground). On 17 December, the Luftwaffe launched powerful attacks on Soviet positions in the area of Velikiye Luki. At the same time, the Russians recorded for the first time the dropping by parachute of 150 cargo containers.

German air attacks slowed the advance of Soviet infantry and tanks, but could not stop them. On the Eastern bank, the Soviets captured the German stronghold of Sovkhoz Nikulino.[7] However, the losses of the attacking Russians were huge. From 10 to 20 December alone, the 3rd Shock Army lost 15,000 men, including 5,000 killed.

The Shock Army resumed the assault after transferring the 249th rifle division and the 47th mechanized brigade to the city. On the morning of 25 December, Soviet aircraft made a massive raid on the eastern part of the Pocket, which involved thirty-eight Il-2 attack aircraft from the 292nd SHAD. At the same time, several air battles took place in the area of the city, and the Il-2 crew of Barzilov and Shitov claimed to have shot down a Ju 52.

---

7 Sovkhoz (sovetskoye khozyaistvo) is a state-owned farm, a perverse and pathologically ineffective form of organization of agricultural workers in the USSR.

After three days of fierce fighting, the soldiers of the 257th rifle division and the 47th mechanized brigade reached the central part of the city. The garrison desperately asked for the Luftwaffe's help. Soon, Ju 87s appeared in the sky and launched a series of attacks on Soviet tanks and infantry. This slowed the attack, but the commanders and commissars continued to drive their soldiers into the attack, despite the huge losses. 'A heavy twin-engine enemy plane was attempting to parachute ammunition to the garrison surrounded by our troops,' the 357th rifle division's combat log for 28 December reported. It circled for a long time, descending and then climbing again.

> 'I will treat him to armor-piercing incendiary bullets', decided the platoon commander of anti-tank guns Starshina I.P. Semikov. He chose a convenient position and gave a well-aimed burst from a light machine gun at the enemy aircraft. The plane caught fire and crashed down like a rock. It burned up in the air before it reached the ground. The crew burned down with it.

It was probably He 111 of 14.(Eis)/KG 4. In its crew, one person (Unteroffizier Peter Luger) was killed, and the rest were injured, but escaped.

On 30 December, Soviet attack aircraft again bombed neighborhoods in the central part of the city. While accompanying them, Yak-1 and Yak-7 fighters from the 427th IAP conducted several air battles and shot down three aircraft (Hs 126, Bf 110 and Ju 88). In reality, the Luftwaffe lost two Ju 87 D-1s (W.Nr. 2312 and 2420) from 9./StG 1 in the area of the Velikiye Luki Pocket. Pilots Leutnant Martens, Unteroffiziere Borghoff and Steinbohmer were missing. Of the entire crew, only one flight gunner managed to get to his troops. By 31 December, only the railway junction and the citadel remained in German hands.

At the beginning of January, in the area of Velikiye Luki, there was solid cloud cover which hindered aviation plans. From 1 to 4 January, soldiers of the 12th Separate Anti-aircraft Division (12th OZAD), whose positions were located south-west of the city, recorded the passage of only twelve German aircraft (including six He 111 and two Ju 88). They were mainly engaged in supplying the garrison. On 2 January, one plane dropped bombs on Soviet troops in the area of Velikiye Luki Pocket. Russians saw a He 111 drop five cargo containers from a height of 1,000 meters at 16.00, but the wind carried them to the territory occupied by the Russians. On 4 January, a pair of Ju 88s bombed the northern edge of the city.

On 5 January, the Russians again recorded only one He 111, which dropped cargo containers on the Velikiye Luki Pocket. But again, the starving Germans did not get them. When the bomber went on a reverse course at an altitude of 1,000 meters, near the village of Tokolovo, it came under fire from two batteries of the 12th OZAD (12th Separate Anti-aircraft Division). After the fourth salvo, the left engine of the bomber flared up, and the flames quickly spread throughout the plane. According to the Soviet anti-aircraft gunners, the pilot of the He 111 did not attempt to make an emergency landing. Instead, he flew the burning aircraft on the concentration of Soviet troops near Tokolovo! The plane crashed on the northern edge of the village and exploded. As a result, twenty-eight people were killed, along with seventeen horses, and the destruction of two field kitchens, four trucks and three Katyusha multiple rocket launchers (the Germans called them 'Stalin's Organs'). This 'German kamikaze' was probably Leutnant Josef Haga from 9./KG 4. Crew of the He 111 H-6 W.Nr. 7483 '5J+KT' consisting of Unteroffiziere Herbert Olle and Karl Huppemann, Feldwebel Hans Geiger is reported missing on this day.

Meanwhile, on 4 January, after heavy artillery training, a German strike force consisting of the 20th motorized infantry division, 205th infantry division, and 6th air field division launched a new offensive against Velikiye Luki from the southwest. By the evening of the next day, the Germans managed to break through the front and capture the village of Borschanka. This unpleasant event forced the Soviet command to withdraw part of the troops from the inner ring of the blockade to the outer ring and throw the last reserves into battle.

On 6 January, the main forces of the Soviet air force switched to attacks on the deblocking group. For example, thirty-three Il-2 attack aircraft from the 292nd SHAD (Ground-attack Aviation Division), accompanied by thirteen Yak-1 fighters, struck a sector southwest of Velikiye Luki. At the same time, according to Soviet data, two Yak-1s from the 427th IAP were shot down by several German Zerstorer Bf 110. One of the fighters was piloted by the navigator of the regiment, Senior Lieutenant A.G. Shukhov. He was seriously injured, but jumped out with a parachute and died on the ground. According to German data, only a few reconnaissance aircraft Bf 110 from 8.(H)/23 were operating in this sector of the front, so exactly which German planes shot down a couple of Soviet fighters is not clear.

The next day, the Luftwaffe attacked twenty-three Il-2 attack aircraft from the 292nd SHAD. In the area of Velikiye Luki, the group was suddenly attacked by Bf 109s (of 8./JG 54 and 9./JG 54), which shot down six Russian aircraft at once. Aerial victories were recorded by Oberleutnant

Gunter Fink (at 07.55 – Il-2, at 08.00 – Il-2 and 08.07 – Il-2), Feldwebel Siegfried Müller (at 07.51 – Il-2 and at 08.08 – Il-2), and Unteroffizier Heinrich Sterr (at 07.56 – Il-2).

In the following days, the Russian air force was inactive due to bad weather. In the area of Velikiye Luki there was cloud cover at an altitude of 200–300 meters and heavy fog.

On 6 January, the Luftwaffe became more active. Diving Ju 87 bombers in groups of six to fifteen bombed Soviet positions around the Velikiye Luki Pocket, He 111 from III./KG 4 operated singly and in groups of three or four aircraft. On this day, the Soviets recorded several flights into Velikiye Luki by cargo gliders, which were towed by Hs 126 and Fw 189. For example, over the positions of the 2nd battery of the 12th OZAD at an altitude of 1,200 meters, a Hs 126 appeared, pulling a DFS 230 glider. Anti-aircraft guns began firing. With the second salvo they managed to knock out the cargo glider, which went into a tailspin and fell near the village of Gorushka. After that, the Hs 126 dropped to an altitude of 100 meters and went on a reverse course. In the small village area of Ivantsevo, it came under fire from a quadruple Maxim anti-aircraft machine gun and was shot down. When the Russians reached the wreckage of the glider, they found the dead crew and a cargo of rifles and machine guns. On the same day, the 12th anti-aircraft division reported a downed Fw 189, which was also towing a glider towards the Velikiye Luki Pocket. According to them, the plane crashed near the railway station of the city. For these successes, eleven Russian soldiers of this division were awarded the Order of the Red Banner.

But according to German data, the loss of Fw 189s in this sector of the front were noted only on 8 January, when two aircraft (Fw 189 A-2 W.Nr. 2150 '5D+FM' and Fw 189 A-2 W.Nr. 2236 '5D+HM' from NAGr. 3) went missing, along with six pilots in the area of the settlements of Dno, Novosokol'niki and Tolubeevo.

Despite snowfalls, poor visibility and fanatical Russian resistance, the German shock group, going to the aid of their surrounded comrades, slowly moved towards the goal. By 9 January, the fighting unfolded 4–5 km from the city of Velikiye Luki, in the area of the villages of Dones'evo and Belodedovo. From the old fortress, which towered over the city on a high hill, skirmishes and the approaching German tanks could clearly be seen.

The von Sass headquarters constantly broadcast panic messages on the radio, complaining that almost all the cargo containers dropped from the He 111 were going to the Russians. The area of the fortress was only 550 x 300 meters, so the cargo, dropped from a height of 1,000 meters, was carried away by the wind beyond its limits. As a result, starting on 4 January, the surviving soldiers of the garrison began to experience a chronic shortage of food.

In this regard, the Luftwaffe decided to use Ju 87 diving bombers for supply! On 11 January at 16.12 (Moscow time), twelve 'Stukas' from StG 1 appeared over the Velikiye Luki Pocket. After circling the fortress, they dropped the containers from the dive. After ten minutes, another group of Ju 87s appeared, which also dropped cargo containers from a height of 300 meters. In total, the Russians recorded the dumping of thirty containers from diving bombers, and this time most of the cargo hit its intended destination. At the same time, Russian anti-aircraft gunners claimed four downed 'Stukas'. 'To deliver food and ammunition to the besieged garrison of the fortress of the city of Velikiye Luki, the enemy uses Ju 87 aircraft, which dropped containers on parachutes into the fortress from a dive,' says the journal of combat operations of the 12th OZAD. Interestingly, despite the fact that the Ju 87 dropped 'safe' cargo, there were still victims: in the 257th rifle division, two Soviet soldiers were killed by a direct hit from a cargo container!

By 12 January, the German strike group managed to break through the Russian defense in the direction of Velikiye Luki on a section 10 km long and 3 km wide. The Germans captured the village of Litvineko, located 3.5 km from the city. This was the culmination of a fierce battle that took place in the snow-covered forests. The rescue mission was coming to an end, but there was almost no one left to save. By this time, most of the garrison at Velikiye Luki Pocket had already been killed or captured. Under these conditions, there was no point in continuing the risky offensive. German intelligence received information that the Russians were drawing up troops to the flanks of the shock breakthrough. The commander of the garrison received an unofficial authorization from the headquarters of the Army Group 'Mitte' to break out of the Pocket, but the committed Nazi von Sass refused to violate the order of his Führer.

The supplies dropped from the Ju 87 were not enough for the defenders of the fortress. By 15 January, the soldiers had eaten all their supplies and were completely without food. But they still had seven serviceable assault guns, which were safely hidden and disguised. The citadel was on a high hill, so the Russians could not see what was happening inside it. The defenders of the fortress prepared the last surprise for the Soviets when they made a decisive assault on the fortress. The final fight was held in the spirit of the 'Battle of Helm's Deep' in Middle-earth!

At 11.25 on 15 January, after an artillery barrage and aerial bombardment, the 357th rifle division's assault detachments launched an attack. By evening, at great cost to the Russians, they managed to overcome the steep and slippery rampart and capture the north-eastern Bastion. But soon, out of the darkness, appeared a German squad with seven assault guns, which threw the enemy back with a desperate attack. But throughout the night, the Russian mobs fanatically continued to climb the rampart of the fortress, which was covered in ice and littered with the dead. The main siege technique was Ampulomets,[8] which threw ampoules containing flammable liquid at the defenders. The fiercest battle was fought in the flickering glare of fires and explosions. By morning, after losing several hundred soldiers killed, the 357th rifle division had managed to capture almost all the bastions.

When it became clear to the Germans that their fate was sealed, they, in the spirit of King of Rohan Théoden, did the impossible. At the moment when the Soviets were already celebrating their victory, a group of about 100 soldiers ran out of the last bastion and rushed to break through with wild shouts. The Germans had prepared a plan of departure in advance; in the western part of the rampart, they prepared a narrow ice path leading to the ruins of the old warehouse. Here, the soldiers used a makeshift sledge, on which they descended the rampart on the ice path at high speed and ended up outside the citadel. These daredevils, hidden in the smoke and fog, managed to overcome the Russian barriers and leave in the direction of the village of Rybiki (south-west of Velikiye Luki). The next day, the 'hundred Spartans', having overcome incredible difficulties and adventures, went out to meet the German troops.

By midday on 16 January, the citadel had only one remaining point of resistance – the headquarters led by Oberstleutnant von Sass, hidden in one of the deep casemates. At 15.30, a special Russian detachment under the command of Major E. Lemming managed to break into this last shelter. Fifty-two soldiers and officers were captured there, including von Sass himself.

Thus, the failure of the defense of the Velikiye Luki Pocket was an alarming harbinger of the terrible catastrophe of the German 6th Army in Stalingrad, which occurred just two weeks after the events described in this chapter.

Meanwhile, the Russians attacked the base of the deblocking wedge, forcing the Germans to withdraw to their original positions. By 21 January, the front line had stabilized. The pilots of the III./KG 4 after the fall of the Velikiye Luki Pocket did not have to rest for long. They were waiting for the way to the south-east – to Stalingrad…

---

8 Ampulomet (ampulla mortar) – a type of capsule flamethrower, in which a capsule (ampoule) with a fire mixture that does not have its own accelerant is delivered to the target using a propellant charge.

Chapter 4

The air bridge into the Darkness

'Hold on, Führer will help you out!'

On 19 November 1942, Soviet troops launched an offensive north and south of Stalingrad. On 23 November, they pushed back the Romanian units and surrounded the 6th Army Wehrmacht. In the resulting Pocket were twelve infantry divisions, three tank divisions, three Wehrmacht motorized infantry divisions, one Jäger Division (light infantry division), and one Romanian infantry division (twenty divisions in total). The total number of encircled troops was 265,000 people! Interestingly, the Russians themselves estimated the number of blocked troops at twenty divisions and 90,000 soldiers. According to their information, there were 1,400 guns, 10,000 vehicles and 400 tanks in the area of Stalingrad. The length of the huge Pocket at the beginning of the blockade was 65 km from west to east and 35 km from north to south.

On 21 November, Hitler ordered the 6th Army to take up a circular defense, adding that its supply would be carried out by air 'for some time'. On the night of 23-24 November, the commander of the army, Generaloberst Friedrich Paulus, sent a radio message to Hitler, in which he asked for permission to break out of the Pocket. His position was supported by the head of Generalstabes des Heeres Generaloberst Kurt Zeitzler. He insisted that the current situation would not allow the 6th Army to be unblocked by an offensive from outside. Zeitzler also soberly estimated that the Luftwaffe (especially given the simultaneous crisis in Africa) would not be able to supply the Pocket by air. The arguments of the head of the Generalstabes des Heeres originally made an impression on the Führer. However, the chief of the Oberkommando der Luftwaffe, Generaloberst der Flieger Hans Jeschonnek, assured the Führer that the Luftwaffe was able to supply the encircled troops in sufficient numbers. It should be noted that Reichsmarschall Göring was not aware of the situation at the time, he was presiding over the Carinhall Oil Conference. Only after it ended was Göring informed of the decision. He did not deeply analyze the opportunities and the Luftwaffe to deal with the testing of complex statistical data. Instead, the Luftwaffe commander-in-chief, like almost everyone else involved in crafting the solution, suggested that the encirclement would be 'temporary' and supported Jeshonnek, assuring the Führer that the Luftwaffe would do everything possible to meet the needs of the 6th Army. The Führer himself from the very beginning was inclined to declare Stalingrad a fortress ('Festung'). He was sorry to give the Soviets these ruins, for which so much German blood had been spilled. In addition, with sadness he had already announced to the whole world the seizure of the city named after Stalin.

Thus, when Hitler met Göring at the Berghof, the Reichsmarschall was presented only with figures and calculations previously prepared by the chief of the Oberkommando der Luftwaffe. As Göring himself, who was not very intelligent, later slyly pointed out, the calculations were presented to him in such a way that he could only agree with them. Jeshonnek himself quickly realized that his initial calculations were incorrect. However, he did not have the courage to report this directly to the Führer, and Generaloberst der Flieger only notified his immediate superior of the error. Jeschonnek asked Göring to report the real situation to Hitler. Göring, however, was reluctant to risk spoiling his cordial relationship with Hitler and therefore spoil his own comfortable position. Instead, he simply went to auctions in Paris to buy more works of art for his collections.

As a result, the stupidity, incompetence, indecision, adventurism and vanity of all the main actors of the military elite of the Nazi state became the main arguments for the decision to organize the infamous air bridge to the encircled Stalingrad and doomed the 6th Army to total destruction.

Initial optimistic calculations estimated the needs of the encircled group at 750 tons per day. However, this figure was soon reduced to more than 500 tons. Later calculations carried out first at the Führerhauptquartier Hitler and the 6th Army headquarters showed that an absolute minimum of 300 tons per day would be required. However, all these calculations were obviously wrong. Later, at the end of December, Soviet intelligence managed to intercept information from the headquarters of Army Group 'B', which reported that the real daily demand of the 6th Army was at least 1,000 tons of cargo per day! Moreover, most of the needs were not food at all, but ammunition and fuel for vehicles and tanks. German experts calculated that if such a volume of supplies was not provided, the

6th Army would quickly lose its combat capability and maneuverability. With a shortage of shells and fuel by the beginning of January, it would not be able to hold a stretched defensive perimeter. Thus, for the normal supply of the Pocket, according to the headquarters of Army Group 'B', it required at least 600–800 flights of transport planes per day! Such intensity could only be maintained if the entire transport aircraft of the Luftwaffe was concentrated in the Stalingrad area. But this was not possible, since the air bridge to Tunis started operating during the same period.

From the very beginning, the military functionaries who were entrusted with the operation to supply Stalingrad expressed doubts and reservations about this. In particular, the commander of Luftflotte 4 Generaloberst der Flieger Wolfram von Richthofen immediately said that during the summer offensive, transport aircraft is severely depleted and at that moment it had only eighty aircraft at its disposal. And they were not able to supply the Pocket, especially in winter weather conditions. The commander of Fligerkorps VIII (VIII.Fl.Korp.) Generalleutnant Martin Fibig exclaimed: 'A whole army?! This is absolutely impossible!' It was the weather that bothered him most. In southern Russia, according to Fibig, there was an extremely unpredictable climate. Clear weather could very abruptly become overcast, not to mention fog and sleet. It must be admitted that by the end of 1942 there were still signs of intelligence at the middle level of the military leadership, but it was no longer possible to counteract directly Hitler's murderous desires in the conditions of Nazi totalitarianism.

Despite uneasy forebodings about the madness of the order, it was carried out, and on 24 November the air bridge to Stalingrad began to operate. The direct responsibility for its provision was initially assigned to Generalleutnant Martin Fibig and the VIII. Fl. Korp. On the same day, German transport aircraft suffered its first losses. At Pitomnik airfield, two Ju 52s from KGr.zbV 9 and KGr.zbV 50 were lost for reasons not specified in the documents. One pilot was killed and one injured. The next day Ju 52 W.Nr. 2981 from Tr.St.VIII.Fl.Korp went missing with the entire crew. On 26 November, over the Pitomnik airfield, another Ju 52 W.Nr. 0328 from the same Staffel was shot down. On 27 November, Generaloberst Paulus issued an order for the 6th Army:

> Our army is surrounded, and it's not the soldiers' fault. The enemy will not be able to achieve their goal – to destroy us. The Führer promised help, you must hold out until reinforcements arrive. Hold on, the Führer will help you out!

On this day, 27 Ju 52s delivered 28 tons of cargo to the Pocket and took out 210 wounded. Over the Pitomnik airfield Soviet fighters shot down Ju 52 W.Nr. 3235 of KGr.zbV 500.

Immediately, measures were taken to increase the number of transport aircraft in this direction. In fact, all available Ju 52/3m were requested for the 6th Army. First of all, KGr.zbV 500 and KGr.zbV 700 were replenished, which were the first to fly into the Pocket. By 1 December, ten more aviation groups were expected to arrive at the Morozovskaya and Tatsinskaya airfields. Most of them received Ju 52s from Luftwaffe aviation schools. In addition, temporary aviation groups were formed from pilots-instructors of these schools: KGr.zbV 20, KGr.zbV 21 and KGr.zbV 22. The first was armed with the old He 111 Ps, and the other two were also equipped with far from new Ju 86 aircraft.

In good weather, transporters flew to the Pocket whole Staffel or groups of 5–6 aircraft accompanied by fighters. During bad weather, only experienced crews took off in groups, while others reached their destination singly. In the most difficult conditions were pilots from educational institutions, with no experience of flying in such difficult combat conditions. Winter cold, a long and dangerous flight to Stalingrad Pocket and back over enemy territory under fire from anti-aircraft guns and fighter attacks, frequent icing of aircraft and technical problems, all this presented difficulties even for experienced Ju 52 pilots.

However, the measures taken were not enough. During the five days from 26 to 30 November, they managed to deliver an average of only 75 tons per day. On 28 November, the Russians recorded a flight of eighty transport planes. In the early days, German planes landed not only at Pitomnik airfield and other air bases inside Stalingrad Pocket, but also near infantry positions along the perimeter, using landing sites in Basargino, Voroponovo and Sovkhoz 'Gornaya Polyana'. The headquarters of the Stalingrad front reported: 'The exceptional activity of enemy transport aircraft on the routes Tatsinskaya – Gumrak, Rostov – Gumrak deserves attention.'

On 28 November transport planes suffered their first major losses: Ju 52 W.Nr. 5087 and W.Nr. 6227 of KGr.zbV 105, of the Ju 52 W.Nr. 3186 of KGr.zbV 900 and Ju 52 W.Nr. 5009 from KGr.zbV 50 went missing along with their crews. Also missing were six members of the crew from He 111 H-5 W.Nr. 5593 from KGr.zbV 5. Another Ju 52 W.Nr. 6189 from KGr.zbV 9 was shot down south of the Karlovka airfield, three pilots from its crew were killed. On this day, 'personally shot down' Ju 52s were recorded on the combat accounts of Captain I.L. Bendeliani, Senior Lieutenant T.G. Bugaev (both from the 237th IAP) and Sergeant A.A. Mikelich from the 13th IAP. Senior Lieutenant A.P. Savchenko said that he shot down a transport airplane of the Savoia type (Savoia-Marchetti SM.79 Sparviero) in the area of settlement Berezniki, and his partner V.S. Sukhin said that he had shot down a He 111.

All these days in the area of Stalingrad were warm and cloudy, the air temperature was kept around 0°C. Periodically it snowed, and visibility was from 4 to 10 km. Sometimes clouds and mists covered the entire sky, reducing visibility to 150–300 meters. For example, on 29 November, it was cloudy and snowing in the Stalingrad area. The air temperature was +3 – +5°C. Transporters completed fifty-nine flights in the Pocket during the day, of which thirty-eight were on the Ju 52 and twenty-one on the He 111. At the same time, the Luftwaffe again suffered serious losses. Ju 52 W.Nr. 5473 'DB+OJ' from KGr.zbV 700 was missing, and the Ju 52 transporting the wounded from VIII.Fl.Korp crashed near the village of Makeyevka (100 per cent damage). KG 55 lost five aircraft at once: He 111 H-6 W.Nr. 4234 'G1+BK' of 2./KG 55, He 111 W.Nr. 4660 and He 111 W.Nr. 7678 of 5./KG 55, He 111 W.Nr. 4158 and He 111 W.Nr. 7829 of 6./KG 55.

It soon became clear that transport aircraft alone were still not enough to support the 6th Army, so it was decided to additionally use He 111 bombers for this purpose. On 29 November, the 1st air transport command (LufttransportFührer 1) was created to coordinate the actions of all Kampfgruppen based at the Morozovskaya air base (the Germans called it 'Moro' for short), located 150 km from the 6th Army positions. It was headed by the commander of KG 55 'Greif' 53-year-old Oberst Ernst Kuhl. In operational terms, KG 27, KG 55, part of KG 53, and I./KG 100 were subordinate to him.

The payload capacity of the He 111 bomber (depending on the series) was no more than 1.5 tons in the fuselage, four to eight cargo containers (Abwurfbehälter) Mun C250 or Tank C250 (with fuel), or one to three cargo containers Mun C1000. Large loads could not be loaded, as the He 111 entrance hatch was too small. When transporting light but space-consuming cargo, the load capacity was significantly reduced, since the cargo space was too small. The Mun C250 container contained 50–80 kilograms of food and 100–150 kilograms of ammunition. The Tank C250 container contained 110 liters of fuel. The Mun C1000 container contained 150–250 kg of food and 300–400 kg of ammunition.

However, the containers contained not only the necessities of life and war. The German command also made sure that the starving soldiers in Stalingrad were not bored. H. Nowak of 8./KG 27 recalled:

> Out of pure curiosity, I once, before starting a supply operation, carefully examined the contents of one of the supply containers that were stored in the hall. It was filled with completely insignificant things, such as card games, games 'Man-do not irritate-do not irritate' ('Mensch-ingere-Dich-nicht') – stupid marketing products! I don't know how it was possible! Of course, we dropped and food and ammunition, and clothing, but the thing just described still gave me a shock.

In cloudy weather, He 111 bombers flew singly into Stalingrad Pocket, each crew individually choosing the route, altitude and approach path. The main landmark in the Pocket was the characteristic bend in the western part of the city of Stalingrad. In clear weather, to protect against Russian fighters, they had to fly in formation. But the experienced crews of He 111 from KGr.zbV 5 of the previous winter flying in the Demyansk Pocket, offered the simplest formation for the flight – the 'chain'. The planes flew in links (triangles and rhombuses) one after the other at a short distance and at the same height. Any Russian fighter that came into the attack, regardless of whether he attacked from above, from the side or from below, was caught in the crossfire of several He 111s at once. The 'chain' became the usual formation of bombers in such operations.

In cases when landing in the Pocket was impossible (due to weather, accidents at the air base or attacks by Russian aviation), the aircraft had to drop the cargo from the air to a site marked with special warning lights. Sometimes the reset was performed by a radio beacon. In cases where these signals were not available, containers (often referred to by the Germans as 'Food bombs' – Verpflegungsbomben) should be dropped over the eastern half of the ring of the blockade – closer to the city of Stalingrad. There, the probability that they would be found was higher than on the western parts of the Pocket. But dumping cargo from the air was considered a last resort, because there was not enough fuel to collect and transport the containers by car. In addition, they were poorly visible in the snow due to the white color of the parachutes.

Often there were cases when one German plane did three or four missions to the Pitomnik airfield and back in a day. The specialized Kampfgruppe I./KG 100 Major Paul Claas, which had recently been engaged in air attacks on tankers and the dropping of Luftminen in the Caspian sea, also participated in the supply of Stalingrad, including the commander of the 1st Staffel Hauptmann Hans-Georg Bätcher. By 28 November 1942, he had already made 422 combat sorties and became one of the best pilots of the bomber aviation. The first transport flight Bätcher made to Stalingrad Pocket took place on the morning of 30 November. According to records in his Fligerbuch, the bomber took out eight wounded, and on the way was attacked by four Soviet fighters. After that, between 11.58–14.45, He 111 Bätcher once again flew with cargo to Pitomnik, taking out eight people on the return flight. Thus, just on 30 November, the bomber piloted by Bätcher saved sixteen wounded soldiers from imminent death.[1]

After some time, Russian intelligence established the obvious relocation of German aircraft and the work starting on the air bridge. The journal of combat operations of the Stalingrad front for 25 November stated:

> Intelligence has established that in Millerovo there is a concentration of the 1st, 2nd and 3rd groups of the 27th bombardment squadron [KG 27] previously noted on distant air bases. In Gumrak recorded the work of the airfield, which is intensively flown to by transport aircraft from Tatsinskaya and Kamensk... at 16.00, 10 transport planes landed in the area of Central'nyi[2] airfield.

Frontline intelligence gathered information with the help of agents located in the German rear, actively using the local population. In addition, to conduct reconnaissance, the Russians constantly secretly sent groups of their soldiers across the front line to the German rear. The practice of regularly capturing prisoners from advanced positions (the Russians called them 'tongues'[3]) was established.

However, this flurry of activity brought rather modest results. Scouts even collected gossip and rumors that were spread on German territory, processed them and tried to understand the plans of the Germans based on their analysis. Sometimes Russian frontline intelligence was able to get fairly accurate data. For example, on 27 November, the Soviets received

---

1 Fligerbuch Hans Georg Bätcher. p. 136 – 137.

2 The Germans called this airfield 'Stalingradskii'.

3 A prisoner of war captured for the special purpose of obtaining important information about the enemy.

information that 'fresh' German units and tanks were concentrating in the small town area of Kotelnikovo. Soon the Russians realized that it was from there that the deblocking strike would be launched in the direction of Stalingrad. On 4 December, Russian intelligence determined that the '100th bombardment group' (I./KG 100) had been transferred from air bases in the cities of Armavir and Maikop to the Morozovskaya air base and operated flights to Pitomnik airfield.

Russian intelligence knew much more about the difficulties in relations between the Germans and their Romanian allies. The garrulous German prisoners did not conceal the shameful details of the quarrels between the allies. The Germans blamed the Romanians for the crisis and treated them like cattle. In particular, most of the Romanian soldiers were stripped of their weapons ('as soldiers, you're no good anyway', the Germans told them) and sent to heavy construction work. However, despite the fact that all this 'information' collected by a 'thorough' analysis of rumors and gossip was interesting to the Russian commanders, no practical use was made of it.

As a result, Russian intelligence, busy with small details, knew almost nothing about its opponent. The Soviets were confident that the 6th Army would break out of the blockade ring to the west. So instead of throwing all their forces into narrowing the blockade ring, the Russians used a lot of manpower building defenses in the western and southwestern sectors. The Soviets also did not know for a long time that German He 111 bombers were used for cargo delivery.

When organizing the blockade of the German 6th Army, Russian soldiers also experienced unbearable difficulties. By the end of 1942, the incompetent and ruthless style of command had not changed. The Russian command did not take into account the huge loss of life and did not care about the regular supply of soldiers. At the end of November, the Volga became covered with ice and crossing on river vessels became impossible. The troops of the 62nd and 64th armies stationed in Stalingrad had to be supplied by air every night. At the same time, Russian aviation did not have fully fledged cargo containers, products were dropped from a low altitude in bags. Most of them were damaged when they hit the ground, and the contents were a mash. The Russian soldiers were constantly starving and having to eat garbage; many died of starvation, stomach diseases, and poisoning. On some nights, Russian transport planes carried out up to 300 sorties to supply troops. From 20 to 30 November alone, the 8th Air Army dropped 868 bales to its soldiers. In fact, as with other Pockets, two air bridges simultaneously worked together in the area of Stalingrad.

On the night of 30 November, the Soviets intercepted a rather mysterious radio message transmitted by the 6th Army's main radio station near the Basargino railway station. The Russians deciphered it as follows: 'At the moment I take command, waiting for support from all units. The situation that is unfavorable for defense must be eliminated at all costs. In any case, I will act decisively with all the units entrusted to me and the means at my disposal.' Under the radiogram was the mysterious signature 'Gubner'. Now the Russians could ponder the question, who was Gubner and what did it mean? They also noted that after this proclamation was uttered, the resistance of German troops sharply increased in almost all sectors on the inner and outer ring of the blockade (in all probability 'Gubner' is Generalfeldmarschall von Manstein).

On 30 November, the Russians recorded 100 transport planes landings in various areas in the Pocket. This was the first time a landing was recorded at the Pitomnik air base. On this day, the air force of the Stalingrad front (8th Air Army) conducted the first large-scale operation against the air bridge. In the morning, the first air attack on German air bases, including Pitomnik, was made by Il-2 aircraft from the 622nd SHAP. However, it ended in complete collapse. Six Il-2s did not return, and five more aircraft were severely damaged and made forced landings. Among the dead was the deputy commander of the regiment, Captain Dobrokhotov. No German aircraft were damaged...

Russian pilots reported thirty-three downed transport planes. The most reliable applications for aerial victories over the Ju 52 are from the commander of the 283rd IAD Colonel V.A. Kitev, Lieutenants N.F. Kirillov from the 181st IAP, I.G. Vikhlyaev from the 517th IAP and A.A. Mikelich from the 13th IAP.[4] Another four German transport planes were shot down by Russian anti-aircraft artillery.

German documents confirm the loss of four transport planes. Missing along with the crews: Ju 52 W.Nr. 3188 from KGr.zbV 900, Ju 52 W.Nr. 3235 from Tr.St.Lw.Kdo 'Ost', Ju 52 W.Nr. 3117 from Feldwerft(mot) 'Rostow' and Ju 52 W.Nr. 5490 from Verb.Kdo.(S)V. One heavily damaged transport aircraft made an emergency landing near the village of Gavrilovka. The crew was captured. During the interrogation, one of the pilots said that there are about 100 transport planes at the Tatsinskaya airfield. Each of them could deliver 1.8 tons of fuel to Stalingrad.

---

4 The total losses of the 8th Air Force (8th VA) for 30 November were ten aircraft.

Russian long-range artillery also strenuously bombarded German air bases inside the Stalingrad Pocket. At night, the operation to counter the supply of German troops continued. U-2 biplanes flew over the Pitomnik, Gumrak and Basargino air bases at low altitude, which, as indicated in the report, 'prohibited the landing of transport planes'.

December 1 was warm and cloudy, the 8th Air Army flew 117 sorties and reported four downed transport planes. Major A.M. Zhuravlev from the 15th IAP, Captain Ya.D. Varlov, Senior Lieutenant L.I. Borisov from the 581st IAP and Sergeant L.F. Kravchuk from the 239th IAP claimed the downed Ju 52s. According to German data, forty-two flights were made, of which seventeen were on the account of the Ju 52 crews (fifteen successful) and twenty-five on the account of the He 111 crews (all ended safely); 85 tons of cargo were delivered to the encircled army. Losses amounted to three aircraft. Ju 52 W.Nr. 7596 from KGr.zbV 50 went missing along with the crew. Ju 52 W.Nr. 2954 from KGr. zbV 900 and Ju 52 W.Nr. 6126 of Kurierstaffel crashed (both 60 per cent damaged) during emergency landings on German territory.

On 2 December, Russian observers recorded a flight of 179 transport planes over the blockade ring. At the same time, groups of Ju 52s landed in different places, delivering supplies directly to the divisions' positions. Thirty-nine Ju 52s landed in the area of Bolshaya Rossoshka farm, thirty in the area of Sovkhoz 'Opytnoye Polye', forty in the area of Kuzmichi village, and nineteen in the area of Voroponovo railway station. Observers of the 57th Army recorded the landing of thirty-five transport planes near the village of Rokotino (in the southern sector of the Pocket). According to German data, seventy-eight sorties were completed, including thirty-seven Ju 52 (thirty-one successful) and forty-one He 111 (thirty-nine successful); 120 tons of cargo were transported. Only one Ju 52 W.Nr. 3335 from Tr.St.IV.Fl.Korps was lost during the day.

On 3-6 December, the Soviet air force did not operate due to bad weather, although the Germans continued to fly. On 3 December in the area of Pitomnik airfield Ju 52 W.Nr. 5457 from KGr.zbV 500 and Ju 52 W.Nr. 7566 '7V+CA' from KGr.zbV 700 went missing. Another Ju 52 W.Nr .7561 'DG+KG' from the 700th air group was shot down by anti-aircraft fire.

On 4 December, the Russians recorded a flight of eighty transport planes in Stalingrad Pocket. According to German data, eighty-eight flights were made, of which sixty-four were on the account of Ju 52 crews (fifty-two successful) and twenty-four on the account of He 111 crews (twenty-two successful). On this day, Hans Bätcher made his next flight to Pitomnik.

The bomber took off from 'Moro' at 10.23 and an hour later it landed in the Pocket. Unloading and loading took only 23 minutes, at 11.45 Bätcher took off again. At 12.27 pm the He 111 returned to Morozovskaya air base. In total, 143.8 tons of cargo were delivered to Stalingrad, including 55 tons of shells (including 3 tons of cumulative for 75-mm anti-tank guns), 46 tons of fuel, 12.6 tons of bread, 4 tons of spikes for tank tracks, 300 kg of liquid chocolate, mail, radio equipment, etc. However, the Luftwaffe suffered only one loss: the Ju 52 W.Nr. 5423 of KGzbV 172 was shot down in the area of Kotluban farm, all five members of its crew were killed.

On 5 December, a flight of forty-two transport planes was recorded. Planes still landed in various sectors of the Stalingrad Pocket, delivering cargo directly to the front line. According to German data, only Ju 52s flew on this day to supply the 6th Army. They completed thirty-seven sorties (twenty-nine successfully). In the area of Pitomnik two Ju 52 (W.Nr. 5485 and W.Nr. 7335) from KGr.zbV 500 were lost.

On 6 December, in the area of Stalingrad, there was a continuous low cloud with fog at an altitude of 200–300 meters, drizzling rain. The Luftwaffe carried out ninety-six flights to Festung, of which twenty-four were on the account of Ju 52 crews (sixteen successful) and seventy-two on the account of He 111 crews (twenty-eight successful). A total of 72.9 tons of cargo were delivered to the 6th Army. Losses were six aircraft, KGr.zbV 500 lost two Ju 52s (W.Nr. 7491 'CK+QQ' and W.Nr. 10021 'NI+MT'). One of them made an emergency landing in no-man's land at 16.30 and by 22.00 was destroyed by artillery fire (and both sides were firing at the aircraft). Ju 52 W.Nr. 5566 of the KGr. zbV 700 was shot down over Pitomnik air base, the entire crew was killed. Anti-aircraft artillery shot down two He 111 P-2 (W.Nr. 1297 and W.Nr. 1736) from KGr.zbV 20. In addition, He 111 F W.Nr. 2386 '6N+AA' from St./KG 100 crashed during an emergency landing at Tatsinskaya airfield. Two pilots were killed.

On the evening of 6 December, He 111 '1G+NN' Oberfeldwebel Ludwig Havighorst from 5./KG 27 landed at Pitomnik. After unloading, the plane was ready for the return flight, but the crew was ordered to stay there until morning. At 06.00, the wounded were loaded into the plane, and 40 minutes later, the chief of staff of the Army Group 'Don' Generalmajor Schultz arrived. Five minutes later, the bomber took off. 'A Soviet fighter plane appeared behind us and the crew opened fire on it,' Havighorst recalled. 'The General turned to me and asked: "Oberfeldwebel, what is it?" "Attacking enemy fighters, herr General." He nodded and silently stared straight ahead. At 07.39 we landed in Morozovskaya…'.

On 7 December, it warmed up to +5°C, and it was still raining. Despite the adverse weather conditions, the Russians recorded a flight of 145 transport planes at once to Pitomnik and back. According to German data, 190 flights were made, of which eighty-eight were on the account of Ju 52 crews (fifty-nine successful) and 102 on the account of He 111 crews (seventy-six successful). Given that the flight was considered 'successful' when the crew was able to reach the target area and complete the mission, it turns out that 135 aircraft arrived in Festung. The amount of cargo delivered was a record 362.6 tons, including 160 tons of shells, 72 tons of fuel, 2 tons of antifreeze, 50 tons of food (mainly bread); 704 wounded were taken out on return flights.

But the losses were also impressive – nine Ju 52 and four He 111. Overloaded Ju 52 W.Nr. 2892 from KGr.zbV 5 crashed during take-off from Basargino airfield, killing the entire crew. The KGr.zbV 50 had two losses: the Ju 52 W.Nr. 3019 'BI+YU' went missing with the crew, and of the Ju 52 crew W.Nr. 6859 only one person escaped. Ju 52 '6G+BX' and Ju 52 W.Nr. 7355 'NJ+KD' from KGr.zbV 500 were also missing. Two Ju 52s (W.Nr. 3175 and 7488) of the KGr.zbV 500 were lost in Pitomnik. One crew escaped, and the second had three dead. One Ju 52 from KGr. zbV 600 (W.Nr. 5279) was lost and one Ju 52 (W.Nr. 6667) from KGr. zbV 700 went missing with the crew.

The losses of the He 111 were significantly less. He 111 H-5 'TK+NH' from KGr.zbV 20 was missing. He 111 H-5 W.Nr. 4090 'L5+HL' from KGr.zbV 5 was shot down by anti-aircraft fire east of Morozovskaya. In addition, He 111 H-5 of 4./KG 55 was lost. But it was not possible to establish what mission it carried out, transport, or bombing. The first loss during the transport mission was suffered by KG 27 'Boecke'. He 111 H-6 W.Nr. 7844 '1G+HM' from the 4th Staffel on the way to the Pocket was hit by an anti-aircraft shell in the starboard engine, and then fell on Soviet territory. The entire crew of Feldwebel Paul Mnich, Unteroffizier Johann Hass, Obergefreiter Karl Zähringer, Josef Bieniek and Rudolf Fricke were missing. In fact, the He 111 '1G+HM' fell in the zone of operations of the Don front, and at least one of the pilots was captured. During the interrogation, on the same day, he admitted that he had served in KG 27, that his Kampfgeschwader was based at Millerovo air base and operated transport flights to Stalingrad.

According to Soviet data on this day, the pilots of the 181st IAP shot down ten Ju 52 and one He 111. The 3rd Guards IAP had five Ju 52s on its combat account, and the 13th IAP and 239th IAP had two Ju 52s each. One Ju 52 was shot down at 12.00 in the 57th Army lane and fell 5 km north-east of the village of Verkhne-Tsaritsynsky. Along with the plane, twenty-three officers from the 384th infantry division headquarters were killed.

By 1 December, on the order of the commander of the 8th Air Army, Major General Khryukin, the 214th attack aircraft aviation division (214th SHAD) Colonel S.U. Rubanov, which at that time numbered seventy-seven Il-2s, was relocated to Abganerovo airfield. A group of nineteen Il-2s from the 206th SHAD also arrived there. Several fighter aviation regiments arrived in Abganerovo for tactical interaction with attack aircraft. The command of the entire combined air group was assigned to the commander of the 206th SHAD Colonel V.A. Sravkin. At the same time, the command of the 16th Air Army allocated 228th SHAD Lieutenant colonel G. I. Komarov for attacks on German air bases.

Air attacks on airfields have never been an advantage of the Red Army air force. Most often, during such raids, the Soviets did not achieve any results, but suffered huge losses. The reasons for this were poor training of pilots, primitive tactics, imperfect planes, lack of normal sights and poor weapons. In this case, the attacks were planned 'traditionally', that is, based on false reports about the alleged high effectiveness of previous attacks. The commanders of Russian aviation regiments put the emphasis on hidden approach routes, the suddenness of appearance over the target and low-level flight strikes. However, it was never possible to observe all this in practice. The German surveillance service always detected the approach of the Il-2 in advance, referred to by the Luftwaffe as 'Zementbomber' for their clumsiness. Above the target, they did not appear in strict order of battle, but in a long, extended formation. Bombs were dropped from the first approach, and the pilots were guided not by the sight, which was actually not on the Il-2, but by the leading aircraft; when he dropped – everything was dropped. Having turned around after the attack, the planes flew in a straight line towards their airfield.

The fighter escort also left much to be desired. Bf 109s from JG 3 'Udet' usually patrolled far beyond their air bases, ready to engage at any moment. As a result, long before the approach to the target Soviet fighters were tied up in battle and left the Il-2 to its fate. In turn, the departure of Russian fighters greatly unnerved the pilots of 'Zementbombers'. Many of them were panicked and, before reaching the goal, dropped bombs anywhere.

For these reasons, the raids on German air bases in Stalingrad Pocket and beyond proved completely ineffective and involved heavy losses. During the week of fighting, the combined aviation group of the 8th Air Army lost 14 Il-2s, and dozens of others were damaged. On 8 December, only five serviceable 'Gorbatyj',[5] as the Soviet pilots called their Il-2, remained in its composition. The fighters also suffered heavy losses. At the same time, only two Ju 52s from KGr.zbV 500 were destroyed in Pitomnik during this period, but whether this was the result of air attacks is unknown. Nevertheless, the Soviet attack aircraft raids continued.

On 8 December, the Russians observed the landing of twenty transport planes on the western outskirts of Stalingrad (in the area of Mamayev Kurgan hill[6]). In addition, some aircraft dropped cargo containers directly on the positions of the German troops – in the sector Plant No.221 'Barrikady'.[7] In total, the flight of 150 transport planes over the blockade ring was recorded. According to German data, 126 sorties were carried out, of which fifty-seven were on the account of Ju 52 crews (forty successful) and sixty-nine on the account of He 111 crews (sixty-seven successful).

The Russians reported twenty-four planes shot down. Soviet fighters announced seven shot down by a Ju 52. The greatest success was achieved by Captain V.S. Galkin and Lieutenant Kozyrev from the 34th IAP, who shot down three transport planes in the Gumrak area. Senior Lieutenant S.Ya. Zhukovsky from the 13th IAP in the Basargino area shot down a Ju 52. Senior Lieutenant M.A. Zuev from the 11th IAP, Senior sergeant V.V. Lukoshkov from the 181st IAP and Senior Lieutenant L.D. Goryachkov from the 239th IAP also claimed the downed 'Aunt Ju'. According to German reports, the Russian fighters shot down Ju 52 W.Nr. 2953 from KGr.zbV 9 (the crew died) and Ju 52 W.Nr. 5377 from KGr.zbV 700. Ju 52 W.Nr. 5964 from San.Flugber.3, which was being used in a medical role, was shot down by a Soviet fighter over Pitomnik air base, and its entire crew was killed.

In the area of the gully, Korovatka made a forced landing of He 111 P-2 W.Nr. 1383 'L5+JM' from KGr.zbV 5. His crew of five people were taken prisoner. During the interrogation, the pilots said that they served in the 5th aviation group, which had forty He 111 aircraft. Their mission was to deliver chocolate, bread and vodka to Pitomnik. In the area of the settlement Buzinovka made a forced landing another one He 111 H-6 W.Nr. 7467

---

5 Russian nickname of the Il-2 attack aircraft

6 Mamayev Kurgan – a hill on the right Bank of the Volga on the western outskirts of Stalingrad

7 The Tsaritsyn gun factory was laid down on 27 June 1914 and began to be built under a concession agreement by the British company Vickers Limited, but construction was halted following the start of the First World War and the Russian revolution. The plant was completed by the Bolsheviks and was named Plant No. 221 'Barrikady'. In the 1930s, the plant produced B-4, Br-2, Br-5, Br-17, Br-18 artillery guns.

'VH+IA' of St./KG 55. The crew of four men and eight passengers (wounded soldiers from the 4th, 376th and 384th infantry divisions and the 14th Panzer division) were also captured. The plane's radio operator told his interrogators that they flew from Berlin to Taganrog on 2 December. After that, He 111s made several missions to the Pocket to deliver upplies. Wounded soldiers were taken out on return flights. Also, a captured German radio operator said that at the Pitomnik air base, he saw thirty aircraft standing on the unloading area. The wounded themselves, who were prematurely sent to the cruel Russian captivity by 'military fate' instead of their homeland, also turned out to be talkative. They gave the Soviets a lot of information about the situation in Stalingrad Pocket, hospitals and the lives of soldiers. German prisoners said that they were in the infirmary from 21 to 22 November and waited two weeks for their turn to be evacuated.

On December 8, another He 111 P-2 W.Nr. 1497 'KB+BW' from KGr. zbV 20 went missing along with the crew. According to Soviet data, it was shot down by anti-aircraft guns of the 2nd battery of the 1080th anti-aircraft artillery regiment near the village of Peschanka. Ju 52 W.Nr. 5390 from Tr.St.IV.Fl.Korps which was flying to Pitomnik, was shot down by fire from the ground, all four pilots were missing. According to Soviet data, it was shot down by the 1st battery of the 1080th anti-aircraft artillery regiment (1./1080 ZenAP) near the Voroponovo railway station.

As the result of an air attack against the airfield of Pitomnik, Ju 52 W.Nr. 3087 from KGr.zbV 9, Ju 52 W.Nr. 7512 'DP+EK' of KGr.zbV 700, Ju 52 W.Nr. 3239 of I./KGzbV 172 were damaged. Ju 52 W.Nr. 5186 from Fl.Komp./Ln.Rgt.38 was destroyed at Tatsinskaya airfield during a raid by Soviet aircraft. Ju 52 W.Nr. 0512 from KGr.zbV 50, Ju 52 W.Nr. 3331 and Ju 52 W.Nr. 6098 from KGr.zbV 700 were damaged in accidents due to icing in the air.

Until 8 December, the Soviets tried to compress the blockade ring around the 6th Army by continuous attacks from various directions. But the Germans managed to maintain a solid defense along the entire stretched perimeter. The headquarters of the Stalingrad front had to admit that the Germans were able to quickly create reliable lines consisting of strong points, barriers, and minefields. Due to good interaction with artillery and mortars, the infantry was able to effectively repel all attacks. And to eliminate breakthroughs, mobile assault detachments were formed with tanks and armored vehicles, which acted as 'fire brigade'.

But despite these temporary successes, the 6th Army has already begun to have serious problems. The artillery began to run out of ammunition supplies, so it was necessary to set standards for their consumption. Howitzers and mortars began to fire less intensively. Russian pilots noted that starting in the second decade of December, anti-aircraft fire from the Pocket became weaker. A captured German soldier from the 295th infantry division confirmed the deterioration of the situation of the encircled German troops in Stalingrad. He said that in the first days of the month, the food situation deteriorated significantly. Since the beginning of December, the soldiers received an average of 300 grams of bread per day.

On 9 December, the situation changed dramatically. Russian intelligence had received numerous reports that in the area around the small town of Kotelnikovo and the settlements of Nizhne-Chirskaya and Tormosin are concentrated strong German shock groups that are soon to go on the offensive. Reconnaissance planes photographed many tanks, armored vehicles, and trucks in these sectors. Intelligence reported that the operation to unblock the 6th Army should begin on December 14-16, and would be commanded by General Monstein.

On this day, small groups of the Soviet air force made several successful raids on German airfields. As a result, four Ju 52s were destroyed at the Tatsinskaya air base ('Tazi') (W.Nr. 2881, 3275, 7528, 7533) from KGr. zbV 9 and KGr.zbV 900, and also fuel and ammunition depots. At the Basargino airfield (inside the Stalingrad Pocket), a Ju 52 was destroyed W.Nr. 3244 from KGr.zbV 500. In addition, He 111 W.Nr. 2594 'L5+AL' from KGr.zbV 5 went missing along with a crew of five people.

From 1 to 9 December, thanks to the arrival of new Luftwaffe units, 6th Army deliveries were increased to an average of 117 tons per day, but even this was far from the required minimum amount of cargo. Meanwhile, the Luftwaffe command continued to collect all available transport planes. Three additional groups of Ju 52/3m were transferred from the Mediterranean, the operation involved the company 'Deutsche Lufthansa', liaison and courier units, and even industrial and technical squadrons. Planes and crews were assembled on the principle of 'every little bit helps', and sent to Luftflotte 4.

On 10 December the weather in the area of Stalingrad turned sharply cold, to -13°C, but it was still snowing heavily. The Russians recorded 120 transport planes flying over the blockade ring. For example, at 13.20, twenty transport planes landed at the central airport of Stalingrad. Russian observers recorded this activity from the upper floors of tall buildings and Mamayev Kurgan hill (height 102 meters). Commander 1./KG 100 Hauptmann Bätcher went on a supply mission for the 6th Army at 05.45. An hour later, his bomber landed in Pitomnik. Taking on board seven wounded, He 111 Bätcher flew back in 'Moro'.

The Russians again tried to counteract the work of the air bridge. On the morning of 10 December, seven Il-2s from the 622nd SHAP Captain I.A. Yemelyanov, under the cover of four La-5s from the 13th IAP, took off to attack the Pitomnik airfield. This airfield actually became a major air base and played a key role in supplying Paulus's 6th Army. Right in the middle of the steppe were the parking lots of transport planes, bombers and fighters, repair shops, warehouses with food and fuel, barracks and earth-houses for the wounded, a road junction, and so on. The object was heavily protected by anti-aircraft artillery, and several Bf 109 G fighters constantly covered it from air attacks. A composite Staffel from I. and II./JG 3 was permanently based at Pitomnik airfield. It is clear that sending seven attack aircraft with an escort of just four fighters to this 'hornet's nest' was suicide.

Already on the approach, the La-5 fighters were scattered by anti-aircraft fire and attacks by Bf 109 patrollers. As a result, 'Zementbombers' approached Pitomnik alone. The first link, led by Junior Lieutenant Opalev, was completely destroyed by German fighters. Sergeant Dol'beridze managed to drop the bombs and turn back, but soon his flight gunner reported that two pairs of Bf 109s appeared from behind. The pilot gave full throttle and began to throw the aircraft from side to side. The Il-2 was shot down over the front line and made an emergency landing on Russian territory. Two more burning Il-2s landed on the fuselage in no man's land near the German trenches. Only three attack aircraft riddled with bullets and shrapnel returned to the Abganerovo air base. The very same combat mission was once again unfulfilled. According to German data, on 10 December, one Ju 52 W.Nr. 7066 from KGr.zbV 50 was severely damaged (80 per cent) in Pitomnik.

The Russian 8th Air Army carried out 150 sorties and claimed forty-two downed aircraft, including twenty-four transport planes. This day marked the first losses of Ju 86 from KGr. zbV 21 and KGr.zbV 22. Ju 86 W.Nr. 0424 was destroyed (100 per cent) after the attack by Soviet aircraft at Basargino airfield. Ju 86 W.Nr. 5111 was damaged after an emergency landing at the Soldatskoe airfield; 2 km east of Sovkhoz Krep' Soviet fighters shot down a transport airplane (a Ju 86 W.Nr. 5104 'RD+RS'), which fell on Russian territory. The bodies of three pilots and nine wounded soldiers were found in the wreckage. Military air forces of the Don front (16th Air Army) had carried out 116 missions. They bombed Gumrak and Bolshaya Rossoshka airfields, claiming thirty-one aircraft destroyed on the ground. In fact, only one Ju 52 W.Nr. 7348 from KGr.zbV 700 was destroyed. Another Ju 52 W.Nr. 7293 from KGr.zbV 9 was shot down by anti-aircraft fire while approaching Gumrak, but fell on German territory.

The He 111 planes suffered heavy losses that day. KGr.zbV 20 lost four planes at once from attacks of fighters (W.Nr. 1287, 1289, 1729, and 5342). But the loss of personnel was relatively small – four missing, one killed and two wounded. Fighters shot down and He 111 P-4 2988 'CC+KC' from 3./KGr.zbV 5. The Soviet pilots' claims for the downed He 111s are close to reality: one aircraft was shot down by Captain V.N. Makarov from the 512 IAP (near the village of Peskovatka), Senior Lieutenant V.D. Lavrinenkov from the 9th IAP (near Pitomnik) and Senior Lieutenant A.A. Murashev from the 3rd IAP (near farm No.3). The losses of Russian aviation for the day amounted to eighteen aircraft.

On 11 December, the Russians recorded eighty-seven transport planes flying over the blockade ring. At 15.00, ten transport planes landed at the central airfield (Stalingrad). According to German data, 141 flights were made, of which fifty-one were on the account of Ju 52 (twenty-five successful-cargo delivered), and ninety on the account of He 111 (eighty-two successful) and eleven on the account of Ju 86 (ten successful).

Taking advantage of the improved weather conditions, the Russian 8th and 16th Air Armies flew 527 sorties. The pilots claimed forty-three downed aircraft, including seventeen transport planes. Also, Russian aircraft carried out an air attack on the Bolshaya Rossoshka airfield. The pilots reported ten Ju 52s destroyed on the ground. The losses of German transport aircraft began to take catastrophic proportions. On this day twelve aircraft were lost:

- Ju 52 W.Nr. 2936 '9P+FN' from KGr.zbV 50 (the crew was killed);
- Ju 52 W.Nr. 5230 from KGr.zbV 105;
- Ju 52 W.Nr. 7043 '4V+FW' from KGzbV 172 (the crew was missing);
- Ju 52 W.Nr. 2870 'KM+BX' and Ju 52 W.Nr. 3095 'KJ+MS' from KGr.zbV 500 (both crews are missing);
- Ju 52 W.Nr. 3051 '7V+BP', Ju 52 W.Nr. 3059 '7V+BG', Ju 52 W.Nr. 3332 '7V+AE', Ju 52 W.Nr. 10024 from KGr.zbV 700 (three crew missing, in the fourth 1 killed and 2 injured);
- Ju 52 W.Nr. 6956 'G5+PH' from Tr.St.Lw.Kdo 'Ost' (crew missing);
- Ju 52 'KM+MS' from KGr.zbV 500 was forcibly landed at Bolshoy Chapurnik airfield by a Senior Lieutenant E. D. Basurin fighter from the 239th IAP;

- He 111 H-5 W.Nr. 5476 from KGr.zbV 20 was shot down by fighters over the Pitomnik air base (this aerial victory was claimed by Senior Lieutenant I.G. Korolev from the 9th IAP and Senior Lieutenant G.S. Dubenok from the 512 IAP).

According to Soviet data, the bodies of German officers with documents from the headquarters of the 234th tank regiment were found on a Ju 52 shot down near the farm Tsybenko.

'The encircled enemy offers fierce resistance, still shows great tenacity and fights for every meter, for every trench, conducts counterattacks with tanks,' said the report of commander of the Stalingrad Front General Alexey Yeryomenko and Chief Commissar of the Stalingrad Front Nikita Khrushchev sent to Headquarters of the Supreme Command.

The brutality of the fighting is evidenced by the fact that the 38th rifle division of the 64th Soviet army lost 1,700 men in three days. The unit lost its combat capability and was withdrawn to the rear.

On 12 December, at 06.30 (Moscow time), the German 4th Panzer army launched an offensive from the small town area of Kotelnikovo. The attack was preceded by powerful air attacks by Ju 87, Hs 123 and Bf 109. The Russian 302nd rifle division, which was in the direction of the main attack, suffered heavy losses and was forced to retreat hastily.

The Soviets recorded a flight of 80 transport planes over the blockade ring and claimed to have shot down 35 of them. In addition, a second bombing of the Bolshaya Rossoshka airfield was carried out. The pilots reported eleven Ju 52s destroyed on the ground.

According to German documents, only He 111 P-2 W.Nr. 2362 from KGr.zbV 20 and He 111 H-5 W.Nr. 4035 from KGr.zbV 5 were lost that day as a result of a raid on the Pitomnik air base. In the same sector He 111 E W.Nr. 0035 'ND+DZ' from St.I./KG 55 (crew missing) and He 111 'L5+CB' from KGr.zbV 5 were shot down by Russian fighters. In the area of Tatsinskaya, He 111 W.Nr. 3566 and He 111 W.Nr. 4035 from KGr.zbV 5, He 111 H-2 W.Nr. 5358 'LO+RG' (crew missing) and He 111 W.Nr. 5557 (three dead and one injured in the crew) from KGr.zbV 20 were shot down. According to Soviet data, pilots from three fighter aviation regiment reported on the German He 111 planes shot down that day, namely: Captain E.P. Melnikov from the 237th IAP (near the farm Perelazovsky), Lieutenant M.I. Mudrov from the 3rd IAP (near Pitomnik) and Junior Lieutenant V.V. Lukoshkov from the 181st IAP (west of the Trudboy railway station).

Ju 52 W.Nr. 6308 'G5+BH' from Tr.St.Lw.Kdo 'Ost' was missing along with the crew. Ju 52 W.Nr. 5426 from KGr.zbV 900 was lost in the area of

Tatsinskaya (two pilots were injured). Ju 52 W.Nr. 7631 of KGr.zbV 500 was shot down in the Pitomnik area (three killed and one injured). Ju 52 W.Nr. 3258 from KGr.zbV 50 was shot down by anti-aircraft fire (the crew remained intact). Commander of the 9th Guards IAP Major Lev Shestakov in the area of Zeta airfield shot down a twin-engine German aircraft, which he identified as 'Do 215'. It was actually a Ju 86 W.Nr. 0129 'RD+NI', which went missing with the crew in this sector.

On 13 December, the area of Stalingrad again warmed to 0°C. At 10.00, the Luftwaffe carried out a very successful air attack on the Abganerovo railway station. As a result of bomb hits, twenty-two ammunition wagons exploded there.

The Soviets recorded a flight of forty-one transport planes in the Pocket, including thirteen 'Hamburg 142' (Ha 142/Bv 142). Most likely, the Ju 86 was mistaken for the Ha 142. According to German data, ninety-five flights were made, of which forty-two were on the account of Ju 52 crews (thirty-one successful), thirty-four on the account of He 111 (twenty-nine successful) and nineteen on the account of Ju 86 (thirten successful); 133.7 tons of cargo were delivered to the Pocket.

The losses were small compared to the previous days. Ju 52 W.Nr. 3228 'TR+CR' from KGr.zbV 500 missing with crew, Ju 52 W.Nr. 5338 from the same air group crashed during an emergency landing southeast of Pitomnik. At the Basargino airfield soviet aircraft destroyed Ju 52 W.Nr. 3294 from KGr.zbV 700.[8]

The next day there was heavy cloud cover in the area of Stalingrad. The Soviet air force did not operate. Ludwig Havighorst of 5./KG 27 recalled:

> On December 14, due to a thick fog, we once again stayed in Pitomnik, spending the night in a bunker on the outskirts of the airfield. The air temperature was minus 24°C,[9] and the next morning we had great difficulty starting the engines. The plane was packed to the limit with wounded. We have already exceeded the maximum allowable take-off weight by taking two additional people on board. The remaining ones begged to

---

8 The next day, the Ju 52 W.Nr. 7553 from KGr.zbV 500 was officially decommissioned at this landing site. The plane was slightly damaged during one of the air attacks, but its repair in the Pocket was impossible.

9 In fact, the air temperature was about 0°C. Years later, the memory of the 'terrible Russian winter' was so embedded in the memory of the Germans that they remembered it only in the form of constant frosts.

be taken but we were forced to refuse them. It was a terrible
picture that will remain in my memory forever.

Despite the bad weather, the Luftwaffe made ninety-eight transport flights
to Festung, of which fifty-nine were on the account of Ju 52 (fifty-two
successful) and thirty-nine on the account of He 111 (thirty-three successful).
A total of 135 tons of cargo were delivered. The only loss of the day was the
Ju 52 W.Nr. 3831 'H6+PD' from KGr.zbV 700, who went missing. In fact,
it made an emergency landing in the strip of the Russian 64th Army (in the
southern part of Stalingrad Pocket). The plane was loaded with 2,800 liters
of gasoline in barrels, and three pilots were captured.

On 15 December there was a solid cloud cover, which hindered flight
plans. However, the Russians recorded the passage of several transport
planes over the blockade ring. According to German data, fifty-seven
flights were made, of which eleven were on the account of Ju 52 crews
(ten successfully) and forty-six on the account of He 111 crews (forty
successfully). The 6th Army received 91.5 tons of cargo.

The Luftwaffe lost only one aircraft – He 111 W.Nr. 1380 'L5+DK' from
KGr.zbV 5 was missing. In fact, when approaching the target area, it was hit
by anti-aircraft artillery of the 1st battery of the 1080th ZenAP and made an
emergency landing on Russian territory in the area of altitude 123.3 (west
of the village of Beketovka). The crew of four was captured; 800 liters of
gasoline and twenty-eight trays with anti-tank shells were found in the plane.
During the interrogation, the German pilots said that 200 Ju 52s from the
50th, 300th, 500th, 700th and 900th transport aviation groups (KGr.zbV) and
fifty Ju 88 bombers were based at the Tatsinskaya air base ('Tazi').

On 16 December, in the area of Stalingrad, there was still bad weather
with heavy clouds. Soviet aircraft were inactive, but at least fifty transport
planes flew over the blockade ring. According to German data, 129 sorties
were carried out, of which thirty-eight were on the account of Ju 52 crews
(twenty-eight successfully), seventy-nine on the account of He 111 crews
(sixty-five successfully) and twelve on the account of Ju 86 crews (four
successfully). On this day, Hauptmann Bätcher flew three supply missions
for the 6th Army (07.30 – 12.35; 429th–431st combat sorties). On return
flights, he took twenty-three wounded soldiers out of the Pocket. Almost
all flights took place during daylight hours without any opposition from the
Soviet air defense.

Losses amounted to eleven aircraft. Ju 52 W.Nr. 7590 'HB+GH'
from KGr.zbV 900 missing along with the crew, Ju 52 W.Nr. 7181 of
KGzbV 172 was shot down near Tatsinskaya (all 5 pilots were killed).

During the flight to Pitomnik, a He 111 H-6 W.Nr. 7023 '6H+BL' from 3./KG 100 went missing. According to Soviet data, anti-aircraft gunners from 2./1080 ZenAP and 12./1082 ZenAP shot down a He 111, which fell in the area of the Maslozavod and burned with a cargo of ammunition and bread. In addition, eight Ju 86s were also lost. Ju 86 W.Nr. 0048 crashed (100 per cent damage) at Tatsinskaya air base due to icing of the fuselage, Ju 86 W.Nr. 0002 due to icing crashed south of Tatsinskaya, and Ju 86 W.Nr. 4067 crashed northeast of Tatsinskaya. Another three Ju 86s were lost in the same sector for unknown reasons (W.Nr. 0047, 0311, 5084).

Several transport planes apparently went off course and flew over the positions of the 64th Army near the village of Beketovka. Soviet anti-aircraft artillery opened fire on low-flying planes and shot down three of them. One transport airplane crashed and burned, the second made an emergency landing. These were the Ju 86 crews W.Nr. 0167 'S17+M20' and Ju 86 W.Nr. 0225 'S17+M22', which according to German data were missing along with the crews. One crew of four people was captured.

On the same day, German tanks from the deblocking group came to the Aksai river and began to ford it. They had about 60 km to go to the southern part of Stalingrad Pocket. But the Soviets were not idle. The 2nd Guards Army, consisting of six guards rifle divisions and three guards mechanized brigades, was concentrated in the area of the breakthrough.

On 17 December, weather conditions in the area of Stalingrad changed dramatically. A northerly wind blew, driving away the clouds, and the temperature dropped to minus 15°C. Russian aviation has become more active. The 8th Air Army carried out 576 sorties in the village of Aksay – small town Kotelnikovo sector. Only the Don front air force operated over Pocket, which completed 164 sorties. Russian reconnaissance planes found thirty-four Ju 52s at Bolshaya Rossoshka airfield, and about 300 trucks were also noticed. Forty transport planes and bombers were found at Gumrak airfield and there was a truck shelter in gullies southeast of the air base.

It was a successful day for the Germans. There were seventy-one flights to Festung, of which forty-six were on the account of Ju 52 crews (twenty-eight successful), thirteen on the account of He 111 crews (eight successful) and twelve on the account of Ju 86 crews (eleven successful). In total, 129.9 tons of cargo were delivered to the Pocket.

Losses amounted to two aircraft. Ju 52 W.Nr. 7655 'GG+FG' from KGr.zbV 500, which took off from Tatsinskaya to Pitomnik went missing; according to Soviet data, it was shot down by Captain A.A. Gubanov from the 13th IAP. He 111 E W.Nr. 1214 'VB+MD' from KGr.zbV 20 also went missing with the entire crew. According to Soviet data, Senior Lieutenant

I.G. Korolev from the 9th GIAP in the area of Zeta airfield shot down a He 111.

On 17 December, the pilot of a Zerstorer Bf 110 was captured by the Soviets near the Zeta airfield. During interrogation, he admitted that he had fought as part of ZG 1. He spoke about the locations of his Geschwader, as well as the fact that III./ZG 1 was currently located in Africa. It was probably Unteroffizier K. Laasser from the crew Bf 110 E W.Nr. 4368 'S9+KL', which was shot down by a Soviet fighter in the square Qu4958. The next day, another Zerstorer pilot was captured in the same sector and confessed that he had served in ZG 1. It was probably a member of the crew Bf 110 C W.Nr. 2122 'S9+RK' from 1./ZG 1, which went missing in the same square. ZG 1, which supported the 4th Panzer army's attack on Stalingrad, suffered heavy losses during this period. On 16 December, three planes were shot down and another one sustained 80 per cent damage. The next day, three Bf 110s were lost, and four on 18 December. Eleven crew members were killed and missing.

On 18 December, the Luftwaffe made forty-six flights to Stalingrad, of which thirty-two were on the account of Ju 52 crews (twenty-three successfully), four on the account of He 111 crews (three successfully) and ten on the account of Ju 86 crews (five successfully). In total, 85 tons of cargo were delivered to Festung during the day. One aircraft dropped cargo containers directly on German infantry positions at hill 102 (Mamayev Kurgan). Probably it was a Ju 52 W.Nr. 7644 '7V+DD' from KGr.zbV 700, which later went missing, along with the crew. According to Soviet data, shortly after the cargo was dropped, the plane was attacked by a fighter from the 866th IAP, which was piloted by Starshina G.T. Turuev.

Russian reconnaissance planes found twenty Ju 52 and 7 Bf 109s at Bolshaya Rossoshka airfield. The 16th Air Army carried out air attacks against the Bolshaya Rossoshka and Gumrak air bases, flying 459 sorties. The pilots reported the destruction of sixteen aircraft, including fourteen transport planes. German documents do not confirm such figures. Only one Ju 52 W.Nr. 3229 from I./KGzbV 172 was lost at Pitomnik airfield due to an air attack by Soviet aircraft. Russian losses for the day amounted to ten aircraft.

On 19 December the weather in the area of Stalingrad was good for aviation. A north-easterly wind was blowing, and the temperature was minus 6°C. The Luftwaffe threw all their forces in support of their troops. About 1,000 sorties of bombers and direct support aircraft were carried out. The positions of the 2nd Shock Army were subjected to heavy bombardment and shelling. At the same time, the work of the air bridge had also increased. Russian observers recorded a flight of 171 transport planes over the blockade ring. Most often, the transport planes route went along the Morozovskaya-Stalingrad railway, over the Logovsky-Marinovka railway crossing. The landing approach to the Pocket was made from the south-western direction. The same route used by transport planes on the return flights. Landing was carried out not only in Pitomnik and Gumrak, but also directly at the front line. At 08.00 (Moscow time), nine Ju 52s landed in the area of the Sovkhoz 'Opytnoe pole' (in the north-eastern sector of Stalingrad Pocket). At 10.30, fourteen Ju 52s landed near the Sovkhoz No.1 stronghold (in the northwest sector Pocket). These planes were clearly seen by Russian soldiers sitting in snow-covered trenches. At 12.00, another nine Ju 52s landed near the village of Baburkin in the same sector. Soviet artillery fired on unloading planes, but with no visible results. After loading the wounded on board, the Ju 52s took off one by one and disappeared into the darkness...

According to German data, 179 flights were made, of which eighty-one were on the account of Ju 52 crews (fifty-three successful), ninety-four on the account of He 111 crews (ninety successful) and four on the account of Ju 86 crews (three successful). In total, 273.3 tons of cargo were delivered (16.4 tons of kerosene, 85.4 tons of bread, including 56.5 tons of canned food, 10 tons of oil, 14 tons of sausage, and 6.8 tons of ammunition). On return flights, 632 wounded soldiers and thirty-two bags of mail were taken out.

The Russian 8th and 16th Air Armies flew 697 sorties and claimed forty-eight downed aircraft, including twenty-three transport planes. This was a very strong exaggeration. A group of Ju 86s during a flight from Tatsinskaya to Pitomnik was attacked by a group of Yak-1 fighters from the 9th Guards IAP. As a result a Ju 86 was shot down W.Nr. 0177 (the crew managed to return to German territory), two more Ju 86s (W.Nr. 0120 and W.Nr. 5162) were severely damaged and made emergency landings on German territory north of the small town of Kotelnikovo. Senior Lieutenant Arkady Kovachevich, a participant in this air battle, was recorded on the battle account as having personally shot down 'Do 215' and another group victory, also over 'Do 215'. Ju 52 W.Nr. 10027 '4V+CK' from KGr.zbV 9 south-east of the village of Vasilyevka was shot down by Major Lev Shestakov. He 111 H-6 W.Nr. 7780 of 3./KG 55 also went missing. It was probably shot down by Lieutenant A.V. Chilikin near the Zeta airfield. The Russian air force's own losses on this day amounted to nineteen aircraft.

Meanwhile, the German deblocking group defeated the Soviet 3rd Guards mechanized corps, destroying almost all of its soldiers, then broke through the front and by evening reached the Myshkova river in the village of

Nizhnekumsky. It was a real winter blitzkrieg, in one day the German tanks overcame 15 km of snow and mud. But the south-western part of the Pocket was still 55 km away. At the same time, inside Stalingrad, 6th Army soldiers began preparing to strike towards breakthroughs. It was supposed to start when the tanks of the deblocking group approached 15 km.

Despite the desperate efforts of the Luftwaffe, the food situation in the 6th Army continued to deteriorate. For example, German and Romanian soldiers of the 297th infantry division in mid-December received only horsemeat soup and 125 grams of crackers per day. By 20 December, this very modest food ration was reduced to 100 grams of crackers.

On 20 December the weather in the area of Stalingrad was quite warm (minus 3°C). The Luftwaffe held the advantage in the air in the Pocket area, making about 1,000 sorties. The Soviet air force carried out 600 sorties during the day. At the same time, the Russians recorded 300 flights of transport planes over the ring of the blockade. Seventy-six Ju 52s again landed directly in the area of German positions along the northern front of Stalingrad Pocket. Many crews were working to the limit of their capabilities. According to German data, the Luftwaffe carried out 128 transport flights, of which seventy were on the account of Ju 52 crews (sixty successfully), fifty-six on the account of He 111 crews (fifty-two successfully) and two on the account of Ju 86 crews (one successfully); 215 tons of cargo were transported. Commander 1./KG 100 Hauptmann Bätcher made three flights to Pitomnik during the day. The first time the Bätcher plane took off at 05.20, and at 06.10 landed in the Pocket. This speed was possible due to the proximity of the Morozovskaya airfield and the clear organization of unloading and loading of aircraft in Pitomnik. After resting for one hour, the Bätcher takes to the sky again at 07.05 and returned to Morozovskaya at 08.00. The next flights[10] took place at 10.15 and 13.25 Berlin time. Each time eight wounded soldiers were loaded on board the bomber, so Hauptmann Bätcher saved the lives of twenty-four people during the day.[11] The next day, during his 443rd and 444th combat sorties, he took eight more soldiers out of Stalingrad. Each flight lasted exactly 55 minutes.

On 20 December, the Soviets claimed forty downed planes, including twenty-seven transport planes. The claims of 'Stalin's falcons' as usual exceeded all imaginable limits. In fact, the German transport planes marked with only one loss: a He 111 D W.Nr. 2491 of KGr.zbV 5 was shot down

---

10 Combat flight in this case was considered a flight in one way flight

11 Fligerbuch Hans Georg Bätcher. p. 140 – 143.

by the Russian fighter. Probably, this aerial victory was on the account of Lieutenant L.I. Borisov of the 581st IAP, who shot down the He 111 near the village of Alekseevskaya.

On 21 December, the 4th Panzer army continued its attacks and, with massive support from the Luftwaffe, managed to capture a bridgehead on the north Bank of the Myshkova river. The next day, the Soviets expected another full-scale offensive by the Generaloberst Hoth group to the northeast. However, the attack did not happen. On the contrary, the Germans began to strengthen their positions. In fact, this and the next two days were the culmination of the battle to save the 6th Army, and the last chance for its soldiers to save their lives. Paulus headquarters received an unofficial offer from Generalfeldmarschall Manstein to break through to meet the Hoth battle group (Armeeabteilung Hoth). But he gave no answer...

This day was one of the most successful in the work of the air bridge. The Luftwaffe carried out 180 transport flights to Festung, of which seventy-two were on the account of Ju 52 crews (fifty-two successful), ninety on the account of He 111 crews (eighty successful) and eighteen on the account of Ju 86 crews (twelve successful). In total, 362.3 tons of cargo were delivered to Pocket, including 128 tons of food. Losses amounted to only two Ju 52 (W.Nr. 2097 and 7563) of KGr.zbV 700 which were damaged at the aerodromes of Pitomnik and Tatsinskaya during a Russian air attack.

But on 22 December, the volume of cargo deliveries decreased. Only 142 tons were delivered to Stalingrad Pocket. The Luftwaffe lost three transport planes. Ju 52 W.Nr. 2897 and Ju 52 W.Nr. 7569 from KGr.zbV 700 were damaged at Pitomnik air base, and Ju 52 W.Nr. 7302 'DG+SP' from KGzbV 172 crashed during an emergency landing on German territory.

'A ring of dead metal'

According to the plan of Manstein, immediately after the Hoth group reached the Myshkova river line, the second deblocking group, the Hollidt combat group (Armeeabteilung Hollidt), was to go on the offensive from the Chir river area (Nijne-Chirskaya village). But this phase had to be canceled due to a new crisis.

On 16 December, the troops of the Russian south-western front launched an offensive from the bridgeheads near small town Boguchar and the village of Vishenskaya on the Middle Don. The goal of the new operation called 'Saturn' was the city of Rostov-on-Don. With this offensive, Stalin intended to cut off all German troops in the Caucasus and the southern Don. But at the last moment, the Soviet command changed the plan, directing the axis of attack to the southeast – to the rear of the battle groups Hoth and Hollidt. With much superior forces, the Russians attacked the positions of the 8th Italian army. Two days later, the defense in this area began to rapidly collapse, and hundreds of T-34 tanks rushed to the south and south-east. Soon the German air bases from which the 6th Army was supplied were under threat.

This unexpected disaster adversely affected the supply of the 6th Army. Luftflotte 4 had to drastically reduce supplies, switching some bombers to air attacks against Soviet tank and infantry columns south of the Don river. For example, the He 111 Hauptmann Bätcher took off four times on 18 December to drop high-explosive and fragmentation bombs on the advancing Russians. On the same day, bombers from I./KG 27 (based at Urasow air base) also bombed enemy tank and cavalry columns. While shooting from the ground damaged He 111 '1G+BL' Oberfeldwebel Wiethaup. However, the pilot still managed to reach the Urasow airfield. The bomber was destroyed during an emergency landing (70 per cent damage), but the crew survived. In addition, I./KG 27 periodically bombed the Povorino–Stalingrad railway line, along which more Soviet troops were arriving in the region. During a similar mission, anti-aircraft fire shot down a He 111 H-6 '1G+CL', led by the same Oberfeldwebel Wiethaup. The plane crashed on Soviet territory, but the pilot Wiethaup and navigator Unteroffizier Walter Holzapfel were able to reach their troops four days later.

KG 27 in these days had to deal with the supply of German troops, cut off east of the village of Chertkovo (50 km north of Millerovo). On 24 December, during a similar mission, He 111 H-6 W.Nr. 4883 '1G+ML' of 3./KG 27 went missing with the entire crew of five people.

Meanwhile, Soviet tanks were rapidly approaching the Tatsinskaya and Morozovskaya air bases. On the morning of 20 December, navigator Karl Licher of 2.(F)/Ob.d.L. once again flew his Ju 88 D-1 north of Tazi to locate the Russians. Part of the 2nd Staffel of the Rowehl group, engaged in strategic air reconnaissance, was based at Tatsinskaya air base from October. In mid-December, the crews were assigned to monitor Soviet tanks moving from the north on a daily basis.

The reconnaissance plane took to the sky at 10.55 (Berlin time). Due to the dense clouds, the flight took place at a low level – 300 meters from the ground. Just 40–50 km from the airfield, Licher noticed some vehicles moving in a southerly direction. Making a circle over the column, the pilots realized that they were T-34 tanks. Painted in white camouflage, they waded through snowdrifts and rolled across the steppe. Radio operator of the reconnaissance plane immediately reported what he saw to headquarters, and Licher took a picture of the column with a pocket camera. At the same time, the second Ju 88 D of 2.(F)/Ob.d.L. found another unit of Soviet tanks north of the railway stretch Tatsinskaya-Morozovskaya.

Despite the alarming situation, the Luftflotte 4 command did not rush to evacuate. This was done at the direct command of Hitler, who ordered the evacuation of air bases only in the event of a threat of their direct capture. At this time, the tanks of the Hoth battle group were still rushing to Stalingrad Pocket from the southwest. In these circumstances, the uninterrupted supply of the 6th Army was of the utmost importance. Dozens of loaded Ju 52s continued to take off every hour into the frosty haze.

At 07.00 on 23 December, during the next departure of the Ju 88 D-1, Unteroffizier Rudolf Kiesch from 2. (F)/Ob.d.L. found Russian tanks already 5–6 km from their own air base; when the reconnaissance plane returned there, the first shells were already exploding on the outskirts of Tatsinskaya. At that time, for the defense of the airfield, the Germans could only use one 88-mm anti-aircraft gun, six Oerlikon 20 mm cannon and 120 men of the airfield guard company.

Only after that, all four crews of 2.(F)/Ob.d.L. were ordered to relocate in Rostov-on-Don, where was the other part of their unit. 'It is impossible even to describe the chaos that was going on there,' recalled navigator Max Lagoda. 'Snow, minus 35°C[12] and rings of burnt-out aircraft around the square.' Shortly before take-off, Max Lagoda observed the crash of transport planes, which hit the landing gear in the shell crater. But the pilots of the Rowehl group were lucky, all four reconnaissance aircraft managed to take off safely and landed at the new air base two hours later.[13]

As soon as the emergency evacuation order was issued, with visibility less than 600 meters, dozens of Ju 52s simultaneously roared their engines and prepared to take off. In the post-war years, German pilots often described this evacuation from Tatsinskaya as 'indescribable confusion and chaos', accompanied by numerous accidents. Allegedly, Ju 52s rushed to the

---

12 Max Lagoda's memory failed a little. Actually, on 23 December, there was warm weather in the area of Stalingrad, the air temperature was about 0°C.

13 Lagoda M. Ein Blick in die Vergangenheit. Kriegsernnerungen eines Fernaufklarers aus Russland und dem Orient. Helios, 2011. p.108.

runways from all corners of the huge airfield at the same time, overtaking and crossing each other's paths, while ground personnel also in a hurry loaded on cars and fled in a south-westerly direction. In fact, all 124 aircraft left the base safely, and no Ju 52 losses were recorded that morning. This fact proves that it is not always possible to believe the emotional memories of former soldiers, even if it is only about the weather!

The aviation group KGr.zbV 22 based in Tatsinskaya fared worse, and the 'chaos' referred to has partial confirmation. As a result of the untimely evacuation and subsequent attack by Soviet tanks, the group lost fifteen of its Ju 86s at the airfield at once (W.Nr. 0047, 0068, 0098, 0238, 0311, 0434, 0435, 0465, 0786, 3017, 3322, 4015. 4045. 5043, 5084). KGr.zbV 21 had better luck; the bulk of its old aircraft managed to escape, and the Soviets got only three Ju 86s as trophies (W.Nr. 0123, 0163, 0231). From the number of aircraft that managed to take off from air base Tatsinskaya, Ju 86 W.Nr. 0274 'HG+PF' and Ju 86 W.Nr. 0314 went missing along with their crews and aircraft technicians. Ju 86 W.Nr. 5071 crashed near the city of Shahty, Ju 86 W.Nr. 0139 crashed during an emergency landing at Pitomnik airfield. At the Verbovka airfield two more Ju 86s were destroyed by their crews (W.Nr. 0438 and W.Nr. 5149).

But this moment was the culmination of the raid of the Russian 1st Guards army into the German rear. Soon, troops from the Hollidt battle group, previously intended to deblock the 6th Army, were moved to the area. They managed to recapture Tatsinskaya, pushing the Russians 30 km to the north and delaying the collapse in this sector of the front. Despite the crisis, the air bridge continued to operate.

Russian observers recorded a flight of 130 transport planes over the blockade ring on 23 December. According to German data, only thirty-seven Ju 52s flew that day, which delivered 83.8 tons of cargo to Stalingrad Pocket. In the area of small town of Salsk (probably as a result of weather conditions), three Ju 52s were lost (W.Nr. 7642 'DM+WP' and W.Nr. 7650) from KGr.zbV 500 and W.Nr. 6535 from KGr.zbV 900. There was also a raid of Soviet aircraft which destroyed Ju 52 W.Nr. 2897 and Ju 52 W.Nr. 7568 from KGr.zbV 700.

On 25 December, the Hoth battle group, under the onslaught of the Red Army, evacuated the bridgehead on the north bank of the Myshkova river, retreating to the south bank. On this day, the temperature dropped to minus 15°C. At the same time, the Russians noted a sharp decrease in traffic for transport aircraft flights. Despite the clear weather, only fifteen transport planes flew over the blockade ring. According to German data, only nine He 111 were flying in Festung.

On 26 December, the deblocking group began its retreat to the small town of Kotelnikovo. From now on, the fate of the 6th Army was sealed. At the same time, there were the first serious interruptions in the operation of the air bridge. On this day, Russian observers recorded a flight of forty-three transport planes over the blockade ring. According to German data, forty-nine transport flights were made, of which forty were on the account of Ju 52 crews (thirty-four successful), six on the account of He 111 crews (two successful) and three on the account of Ju 86 crews (one successful). A total of 78 tons of cargo were delivered. The loss of transport aircraft amounted to four aircraft. Ju 86 W.Nr. 5016 'DD+JV' went missing along with the crew during a flight from the small town of Kotelnikovo to Salsk. Ju 86 W.Nr. 3093 crashed (80 per cent damage) during an emergency landing near the village of Novomikhailovsky. One Ju 86 W.Nr. 4016 was abandoned in Kotelnikovo, apparently due to a technical malfunction. Over Stalingrad, anti-aircraft gunners of the 242nd ZenAP shot down a Ju 52 W.Nr. 7515 from KGr.zbV 9.

Due to the changed situation, Eremenko and Khrushchev issued an order to the troops to immediately begin destroying the 6th Army. In addition, they demanded the supply of Stalingrad Pocket by air to be stopped. The commander of the Stalingrad corps air defense area was ordered to create two rows of anti-aircraft gun positions on the approaches to the inner ring of the blockade. The 8th and 16th Air Armies were ordered to strengthen the air blockade, using 50 per cent of the fighters to intercept transport planes.

On 27 December, the weather was frosty and clear. The Russians recorded a flight of ninety transport planes over the blockade ring. According to German data, ninety-five flights were made, of which forty-three were on the account of Ju 52 crews (thirty-three successfully) and fifty-two on the account of He 111 crews (forty-six successfully); 127 tons of cargo were delivered in Festung. Among the transport planes again was the He 111 commander 1./KG 100 Hauptmann Bätcher. He completed two missions between 'Moro' and Pitomnik, delivering food and ammunition to the encircled troops, and on the way back took out sixtteen wounded soldiers. During the first flight at 07.10–08.05, Soviet fighters were seen in the air.

On 28 December, traffic again decreased significantly. In Stalingrad Pocket, only thirteen flights were completed (ten successful) and only 35.4 tons of cargo were delivered.

At 09.25 on 29 December, Hauptmann Bätcher delivered 600 liters of gasoline and other cargo to Stalingrad. At 11.15 am, his bomber was on its way back again. After taking off from Pitomnik, the plane was attacked immediately by eight to ten Soviet fighters. As a result, the wounded soldiers on board received many new injuries. However, Bätcher still managed to cope with the situation and at 12.05, flew safely to the Morozovskaya air base.

On this day, the Russians recorded a flight of 150 transport planes over the blockade ring. At the same time, for the first time, the supply of the Pocket was carried out at night. In fact, 106 transport flights were completed, of which sixty-one were on the account of the Ju 52 crews (fifty-seven successful) and forty-five on the account of the He 111 crews (thirty-nine successful); 124.2 tons of cargo were delivered, including 10 tons of candy for Christmas.

The Soviets claimed to have shot down twenty transport planes. In fact, the Luftwaffe lost only five. Ju 52 W.Nr. 7153 from I./KGzbV 172 was deactivated in Pitomnik. Ju 52 W.Nr. 3323 from KGr.zbV 102, Ju 52 W.Nr. 5651 and Ju 52 W.Nr. 6740 from KGzbV 172 were lost at Basargino airfield (in the southern part of Stalingrad Pocket). Ju 52 W.Nr. 3006 from San.Flugber.17 was shot down by Russian fighters.

But the most painful loss on this day was suffered by Italian aviation. SM.81T 'M.M.20257' from the 246th transport squadron, following take-off from Pitomnik airfield at 14.18, was shot down by a Soviet fighter 4 km north-east of the village of Yuganovka. At the controls of this aircraft was the commander of the Italian Air Force on the Eastern front (ARMIR) Generale di brigata aerea Enrico Pezzi. The entire crew and all passengers aboard were killed, including the chief medical officer of the Italian 8th Army, Colonello Franchesko Boccetti and staff officer of an infantry division 'Torino' Maggiore Romano. With a high probability, we can say that SM.81T was shot down by the commander of the 9th Guards IAP Lieutenant Colonel Lev Shestakov. It was in this area and at this time that he reported a downed Ju 52.

Helmut Weltz, who fought in the 6th Army as part of one of the sapper battalions, described what was happening in Pitomnik:

> On the edges of the airfield are fighters, several Ju 87 diving bombers, and in one of the corners – a lone dilapidated and stripped cargo glider. Heaven only knows how this soldier from the Western front came to us. To the left is the radar tower, a pointed structure twenty-five meters high. In front of it are the dugouts of the supply headquarters, which, according to the instructions of the army, distributes incoming cargo between corps, divisions, and battle groups. On the right – the premises of the airfield command. Behind you can see two

large hospital tents. At the entrance to them – ambulances, stretchers, hobbling figures of the wounded and businesslike scurrying staff...

A Ju 52 is just approaching the airfield. It is still rolling on the ground, and everything is already in motion. Soldiers are running from dugouts, tents and snow pits to the plane. A car is racing on the right, two cars on the left. Officers in thick fur coats jump out of them and hurriedly set a course for the plane, followed by batmen with suitcases. Everyone wants to fly away, and a semicircle forms around the cabin door.

But there is room on the plane, perhaps, only for a quarter of those who want to. And there are more and more of them. They storm the plane, pushing their way forward, elbows and fists pushing others away, fighting, pulling each other away. Hats and caps fly to the ground, canes flash, those who are weaker fall. The first soldiers are already clambering up the ladder, clinging to the rungs, to the door, to the bottom of the cabin. Officers are squeezed in among them, you can hear them cursing and yelling at the top of their voices, threatening, but it doesn't have any effect. There is no rank, no insignia, has decided strong fists and a healthy grip of the hand. Meanwhile the plane is intended for the evacuation of the seriously injured and sick...

And even further back, the seriously injured are lying on stretchers. The medical orderlies dragged them across the airfield, but they can't get them into the plane. Only then the crowd is pushed back by the soldiers of the airfield service; this is probably not the first time for them, since they do their job well. Now, finally, we can start loading the plane.[14]

The report of von F. Weltner from KG 27, 'Versorgungsansätze nach Stalingrad' stated:

The number of wounded taken with them was determined according to the condition of the walkers or actually lying down. On average, we invited 12 to 18 wounded people to our plane, depending on their condition. During the return flight, they were in a euphoric mood. They believed that

---

14 Welz G. Soldiers who were betrayed: notes of a former Wehrmacht officer. – Smolensk: Rusich, 1999. pp.190-192.

nothing else could happen, and they were saved. The soldiers seemed surprisingly calm in this situation. Severe weather conditions, insufficient food, and constant fighting caused indifference mixed with physical infirmity. Therefore, most of the soldiers were not able to think clearly. It was different with the wounded, with whom we make personal contact during loading and who had a return ticket. Their will to live was clearly greatly activated by the possession of tickets for the return flight. Despite their more or less serious injuries, and despite their fatigue, they were in many cases alert and took every opportunity to take a seat on the plane. If this hope was not fulfilled due to the overload of the plane, their mood changed to aggressive. They tried with force and recklessness to get to the plane. To prevent such events, we provided bread and part of our onboard food to the commandos, who were supposed to organize the loading of the wounded, as well as to monitor the wounded. It happened that some of the wounded clung to the entrance hatch (under the fuselage of the plane) and crouched there, so that take-off was impossible.[15]

Meanwhile, the situation of the 6th Army itself was getting worse. In the huge Stalingrad Pocket, there was not enough food, but also firewood. A third of the troops lived in bunkers and basements, and many slept in earth-houses in the middle of the barren steppe. In December, there were countless cases of frostbite and thousands of soldiers froze to death. The situation of the huge number of wounded was particularly alarming. Hundreds of them were taken to the Pitomnik airfield, where they waited in the snow for evacuation, often also dying of cold. Even experienced crews returning from the Pocket experienced a real shock from what they saw there. Nothing like this was observed in Demyansk, which had been surrounded ten months earlier.

One transport staff member claimed to have seen a truck completely filled with frozen corpses. Another pilot was struck by a huge number of lice in bandages and on the clothes of the injured. According to him, all their bodies were literally infested with parasites. Commander 2./KGzbV 172 Hauptmann Werner Muller saw soldiers piled on top of each other in houses in order to save themselves from frostbite. According to him, it was the worst thing he had ever seen in his life. Loading into planes often took place under the supervision of an employee with a gun in his

---

15 Boelcke Archiv.

hand. However, at the beginning of each take-off, many soldiers still tried to cling to the plane traveling on the runway.[16]

Until the end of December, some of the German bombers were still used in a direct profile – for air attacks against the advancing Soviet troops and their supply routes. But the gradual deterioration of the situation forced them to divert all available He 111 to aid in the supply of Stalingrad. From 29 December, the transport operations were joined by I./KG 27. At this point, the entire Kampfgeschwader 27 was forced to leave the Millerovo air base and relocate to Novocherkassk.

Navigator bomber Hans Reif of 3./KG 27 wrote:

> The disastrous situation in Stalingrad, we have experienced it ourselves. In the early morning of 30.12 we were woken up and ordered to immediately relocate to Novocherkassk. We landed there around 9.40, and the next evening we had our first supply flight to Pitomnik, where we boarded at 14.20.
>
> For a whole month, we had to be like fighter pilots, not drop bombs, but only fly with cargo. We took food, fuel, ammunition, blankets, medicine, soldiers returning to their units after a rest period to Pocket and took out the wounded. We were warned before our first flight of extremely strong and fairly accurate anti-aircraft fire.[17] However, we flew in very bad weather, which we would never have flown in other circumstances, we did not notice any air defense.
>
> Wide, located on the plain below Stalingrad, Pitomnik, which, like the surrounding area, is covered with a monotonous blanket of snow, is still clearly visible, now surrounded by a ring of their damaged, wrecked aircraft and debris. Will we ever fill this ring? We had these thoughts constantly at this extraordinary moment... We recalled this picture from the countless wreckage of shattered hopes, this ring of dead metal that exactly corresponds to the word 'ring', a deadly ring around the besieged... After unloading at Pitomnik, we invited

---

16 Pegg M. Transporter Volume One: Luftwaffe Transport Units 1937-1943. Luftwaffe Colours. – Classic Publications, 2007. p. 56.

17 By December 20, there were 235 medium-and small-caliber anti-aircraft guns and 241 anti-aircraft machine guns in the western part of the blockade ring. During this period, the Soviets still had a shortage of anti-aircraft guns, which allowed the Germans to fly relatively safely in Stalingrad.

the injured to the car. Night unloading – at 16.30 it was already a dark night… We were glad when we were lucky enough to be back on the ground with our wounded.

The conditions in which the German pilots lived in Novocherkassk were also far from comfortable. 'Our housing was terrible, – Reif wrote. – Two Staffels were located in a large hall on the first floor of a building where Romanians used to live. Beds on this base appeared only over time. The windows were mostly broken and boarded up with plywood. But so far it was a Paradise compared to Stalingrad!'[18]

On 30 December, the Russians recorded a flight of 153 transport planes over the blockade ring and claimed seven downed transport planes. At the same time, some of the planes again landed directly at the infantry positions. At 10.00 in the area of the settlement of Podsobnoe hozyaistvo (in the northern sector of the Pocket) ten Ju 52 landed. At 13.40–15.40, thirteen transport planes landed near the Drevnii Val railway station (in the north-eastern part of Stalingrad Pocket).

According to German data, the Luftwaffe made ninety-one transport flights in Festung, of which sixty-two were on the account of the Ju 52 crews (fifty-nine successful) and twenty-nine on the account of the He 111 crews (twenty-six successful). For the 6th Army they delivered 224.9 tons of cargo, including sixty-two tons of food (twenty-seven tons of bread).

Before Christmas, the personal aircraft of the leaders of the Nazi party, Göring and Ribbentrop, as well as that of the leader of the German Workers' Front (DAF) and the founder of Volkswagen, Robert Ley, were sent to participate in the work of the Stalingrad air bridge. Two planes from the courier staffel at the Führer's headquarters also went to Stalingrad. A total of six additional Ju 52s.

The Russian 16th Air Army flew 134 sorties over the northern sector of the blockade ring. The pilots claimed five downed aircraft, including two transport planes. Among them was the Ju 52 W.Nr. 7429 of KGr.zbV 102. Staffel Hauptmann commander Karl Harhisch was also killed, along with the crew. Immediately after taking off from Pitomnik, Ju 52 W.Nr. 6668 from the Courier Staffel at the Führer headquarters (Kuriersstaffel des Führers) was also shot down. The entire crew of Major Alfred Noack and fifteen passengers were killed. Interestingly, this Ju 52 was shot down not

---

18 Waiss, W. Chronic Kampfgeschwader Nr. 27 Boelcke. Teil 3. 01.01.1942 – 31.12.1942. Helios Verlag, Aachen, 2005. p. 173.

by a fighter, but a Il-2 ground-attack aircraft from the 285th SHAP, which was piloted by a young Sergeant N.P. Myasnikov. Damaged Ju 52 '7V+CJ' from KGr.zbV 700, was luckier, it crashed on German territory. Two pilots were killed and two others were injured.

On 31 December, the Russians recorded a flight of 152 transport planes over the blockade ring. In fact, 177 flights were completed, of which eighty-nine were on the account of Ju 52 crews (seventy-two successful) and eighty-eight on the account of He 111 crews (eighty-six successful). Hauptmann Bätcher delivered a total of 3.8 tons of gasoline to the encircled troops during three sorties to Pitomnik and took out twenty-four wounded soldiers. In total during the month, commander 1./KG 100 'Viking' made twenty-three sorties to supply the encircled 6th Army. The last one, at 13.15–13.55, a few hours before the New Year, became the 458th combat flight for Bätcher. After that, the pilot, who took about 100 people out of the 'Stalingrad hell', received a well-deserved long vacation.[19]

Losses during the implementation of the air bridge amounted to five aircraft. Missing Ju 52 W.Nr. 2928 and Ju 52 W.Nr. 7129 'DE+TR' from KGr.zbV 102, Ju 52 W.Nr. 2876 from St.I./KG 100. The authors managed to discover the fate of one of the missing planes. At 22.00, soldiers of the Soviet 15th guards rifle division saw the Germans signalling with colored missiles for transport planes coming in to land near the Prudboy railway station (in the western part of the Pocket). The Russians decided to cheat and fired several signal missiles of a similar color. A few minutes later, a Ju 52 appeared out of the darkness and landed on Soviet territory. The plane was seized. Four pilots surrendered, and a cargo of 1.5 tons of bread was found in the fuselage.

Also missing was a Ju 52 that took off from Berlin (the information was recovered based on the testimony of the captured pilot Oberfeldwebel Oskar Paust) to Stalingrad W.Nr. 6477 'BB+MQ' from a separate transport squadron at the Kriegsmarine headquarters (Kurier St. OKM). At the beginning of September, a group of naval officers and specialists was sent to the army of Paulus. It was assumed that the Germans would seize Russian ships during the offensive, and the intention was for the Kriegsmarine officers who arrived to create a German military flotilla on the Lower Volga and the Caspian sea from captured Soviet vessels. In all likelihood, these

---

19 On 2 January, I./KG 100 moved to Novocherkassk, where it continued to fly to Stalingrad until 27 January. After that, for a month, the unit was transferred to the Crimea at the Saki airfield, and then brought to the rear for rest and reformation. As a result, the next 459th combat flight of Hans Bätcher was not undertaken until 29 April 1943, dropping two Luftmine BM1000 into the Volga.

sailors were forgotten for a long time, and perhaps the missing plane was flying to pick them up from the Pocket.

On the night of 31 December to 1 January, He 111 H-6 of 1./KG 100 went missing during a flight to Pitomnik.

Meanwhile, the condition of the Geschwader bombers that provided the air bridge had deteriorated significantly by the end of the year. Due to constant breakdowns and a lot of wear and tear, fewer and fewer aircraft remained in combat condition. For example, in KG 27 'Boelcke' as of 30 November, there were sixty-four He 111, including twenty-seven serviceable ones. A month later, the Kampfgeschwader had fifty-six aircraft, of which only fifteen remained in airworthy condition.[20] More information is shown in the tables below.

Table 1. Availability of aircraft in KG 27 on 30 November 1942[21]

Gruppe	Staff number	Total He 111	Combat-ready planes
Stab/KG 27	4	1	1
I./KG 27	37	16	11
II./KG 27	37	21	9
III./KG 27	37	26	6
In total	115	64	27

Table 2. Availability of aircraft in KG 27 on 30 December 1942

Gruppe	Staff number	Total He 111	Combat-ready planes
Stab/KG 27	4	1	0
I./KG 27	37	23	6
II./KG 27	37	23	9
III./KG 27	37	9	0
In total	115	56	15

20 Waiss, W. Chronic Kampfgeschwader Nr. 27 Boelcke. Teil 3. 01.01.1942 – 31.12.1942. Helios Verlag, Aachen, 2005. pp. 159, 173.

21 Excluding IV./KG 27, which was a training unit based at an airfield in the city of Poltava.

However, losses of bombers during transport missions during this period were still rare, especially from the impact of the enemy. For the entire month of December, KG 27 lost only the mentioned He 111 H-6 W.Nr. 7844 '1G+HM' from the 4th Staffel.

'We hope, by praying to the Lord God, that he will bless us'

On 1 January, 6th Army soldiers received a 'New Year's greeting' from Hitler from Wolfschanze. It spoke of the 'tremendous military successes of Germany', the current situation, and the need to hold the defense on all fronts until complete victory. Then the atheist Hitler suddenly remembered God... 'God spare Europe, if the Jewish plot succeeds, then Europe will definitely perish,' said the Führer. 'If the Lord gave us the strength to overcome the winter of 1941–1942, then we will survive this winter and the coming year.' In his appeal, he did not mention national socialism, and in conclusion called on everyone to pray for victory: 'We hope, by praying to the Lord God, that he will bless us this year, as he did last year.' But the soldiers themselves, addressed by their commander-in-chief, no longer believed in God, but in 'Aunt Ju'! 'Not a miracle can help us here in this steppe, but only the good old 'Aunt Ju', if it will often fly to us,' wrote one of the soldiers of the 6th Army in a letter.

Meanwhile, the situation in the area of Stalingrad was becoming worse for the encircled troops. By 1 January, the nearest German units were already 115 km from the Pocket. At the same time, the Soviets continued to throw new divisions into battle and pressed the Germans everywhere. Already on 2 January, the Morozovskaya air base had to be evacuated. From this point on, the closest air base to Stalingrad was Salsk airfield, and the He 111 bombers moved to Novocherkassk. The distance to Pitomnik from there was 300–330 km, and this was almost at the limit of the range of the Ju 52/3m. Naturally, this led to a reduction in the number of payloads in each aircraft. Overspending of fuel and excessive engine wear led to more and more aircraft being repaired and unable to participate in the operation. The old He 111 E, He 111 F and He 111 P aircraft had to be removed from the air bridge system altogether. Their range did not allow them to fly to the Pocket and back, and if the crew was not able to land at Pitomnik, these old planes might not have enough fuel for the return flight.

In Salsk, the Ju 52 crews faced a new problem, namely a strong steppe wind blowing at a speed of 80 km/h, as well as constant snowstorms. It was especially difficult for transport units arriving from the warm Mediterranean sea with no experience of working in such cold weather. The problem was solved by adding gasoline to the engine oil. This made it possible to change the viscosity of the oil so that it flowed more freely, and the engine was easier to start. After a long warm-up, the gasoline evaporates, and the oil viscosity is restored to normal levels; this had to be done before each flight to Stalingrad Pocket.

In the first days of January, the weather around Stalingrad was warm and overcast. The Soviet air force did not fly at all, and the Luftwaffe, on the contrary, did everything possible to supply the 6th Army. On 1 January, Russian observers recorded a flight of 112 transport planes over the blockade ring. And this figure was close to the real one. According to German data, the Luftwaffe carried out 130 transport flights to Festung. Seventy-three were on the account of Ju 52 crews (thirty-nine successful) and fifty-seven on the account of He 111 crews (thirty-nine successful). The 6th Army received 205 tons of cargo. J. Wolfersberger of 5./KG 27 wrote:

On January 1, 1943, the 'old dance' continued, with only the word 'Stalingrad' being heard everywhere. When we were before bedtime, each of us thought with horror about the fate of these soldiers. In order to do something and not to watch idly, we were always ready. In silence we entered the cabin to receive the command to start, and in the same silence we left it again. The plane is loaded so that we could not even get through the lower hatch, the crew climbed into their seats in the cabin passing across the wings. It was a grey sky, grey everywhere, as if the whole world was conspiring against us. We climbed about 2,000 meters and set a course for the target. Complete silence in the cabin, until suddenly anti-aircraft guns roared around us in the Kalach-na-Donu area. But the shells missed. Given the cruel fate of so many comrades, we did not feel this danger. I put a little pressure on the throttle, and we were out of danger again. However, now the navigation values and calculations no longer coincided, and it was possible to get out of the clouds not over the Pitomnik airfield, but already beyond the Volga. So it was this time, the Volga was still frozen and therefore not immediately distinguishable. So, until we were 'warned' by the Russian anti-aircraft gunners, we were over the Kotluban station, from which Pitomnik could be reached in two minutes at a course of about 220 degrees. The landing was quick. Everything went like clockwork, then we again took on board eight wounded and set a course for Morozovskaya.[22]

Losses amounted to three aircraft. Missing with their crews: Ju 52 W.Nr. 5924 '4V+FL' from KGr.zbV 9, He 111 H-5 W.Nr. 3667 'CM+KE' from KGr.zbV 20 and He 111 H-6 W.Nr. 7968 'G1+DF' from St.IV./KG 55.

On 2 January, the Russians recorded a flight of only twenty-one transport planes in Stalingrad. This was due to the relocation of transport planes to other air bases and bad weather.

On 3 January, the Russians recorded a flight of forty-four Ju 52 and forty-five He 111. According to German data, 123 flights were made, of which thirty-one were on the account of Ju 52 crews (eighteen successful) and ninety-two on the account of He 111 crews (seventy-nine successful). They transported 168.4 tons of cargo. Among them were He 111 bombers from KG 27. One of the reports by 2./KG 27 stated:

On January 3, we flew numerous times from Novocherkassk to supply Stalingrad Pocket and to transport the wounded day and night. We mostly landed at Pitomnik airfield, regardless of the weather conditions. Sometimes the lower border of clouds was at an altitude of 50–100 meters. In the immediate vicinity of the landing strip were lighthouses, to which we descended in a spiral. At the same time, other planes took off. So this arrival and departure was always a touchy business. The airfield itself could hardly be overlooked when looking at the ground, as there were countless damaged and crashed aircraft around it and its surroundings. Night landings were particularly nerve-wracking. All we saw was a simple, glowing landing path.

Once I circled over the airfield for more than an hour, because the airfield post was constantly turning this luminous path on and off. Russian bombers formed a circle and dropped bombs on the runway! In the end, I just landed in the dark with the landing lights on. Fortunately, I didn't fall into a bomb crater... We mostly delivered food. In the bomb bays hung containers with supplies, and in the aisles were stacked in pile of bread and boxes of canned food. Hungry soldiers unloaded the planes, and they often scraped broken bread crumbs on

---

22 Boelcke Archiv.

the ground. Hardly anyone dared to steal anything for fear of being shot. We gave our poor comrades what we had in our rations. On the return flight, we usually took with us 10 or more wounded who were freezing in the fuselage.[23]

During one of the return flights He 111 H-6 W.Nr. 7896 '1G+AK' went missing, along with the commander of that Staffel. The plane (pilot Feldwebel Willi Wunderlich, navigator Hauptmann Bernhard von Hasselbach, radio operator Feldwebel Siegfried Ost, flight engineer oberefreiter Hans Alles and air gunner Oberfeldwebel Gerhard Althuis) took off from Novocherkassk at 08.30 (Berlin time). After unloading, seven wounded soldiers were taken on board. After take-off, Staffel gathered in the usual order of battle ('chain') and headed west. Almost the entire flight route was obscured by cloud cover. In such ideal flight weather, the He 111 usually kept directly above the clouds to be able to quickly hide from Russian fighters. But in this case, the lead He 111 for some reason flew 1,000 meters above the clouds. This allowed two Russian fighters to sneak up behind them and shoot down one plane before the group had time to disappear into the clouds; 10 km north of the village of Kalach He 111 H-6 W.Nr. 7896 '1G+AK' disappeared from view. The comrades of the experienced Hauptmann von Hasselbach were sure that the crew had died. In fact, the bomber made an emergency landing near the city of Kalach-na-Donu. The Russian summary reported: 'The crew consisting of Hauptmann, Feldwebel and three Gefreiter captured.'

In addition two Ju 52s were lost in the Pitomnik area (W.Nr. 3325 and W.Nr. 7587 'NB+GK') from KGr.zbV 102, He 111 P-2 W.Nr. 2882 '9K+UA' from KGr.zbV 5 and He 111 'L5+FH' from KGr.zbV 5. Aerial victories over the Ju 52 on this day were credited to account Captain V. Ichensky from the 563rd IAP (in the area of the settlement Peskovatka) and Senior Sergeant G.S. Kravtsov (in the area of the settlement Baburkino). He 111 W.Nr. 7049 from 2./KG 100 was damaged by anti-aircraft fire in the area of Stalingrad, but managed to return to base. An air gunner in its crew was injured. Faulty Ju 86 W.Nr. 5061 was destroyed on the Morozovskaya airfield by its crew.

On 4 January, in the area of Stalingrad, the temperature dropped sharply (to minus 11°C). The Russians recorded 300 transport planes flying over the blockade ring at once. According to German data, 170 transport flights were made, of which 103 were on the account of Ju 52 crews (eghty-four successful) and sixty-seven on the account of He 111 crews (sixty-one

---

23 Boelcke Archiv.

successful). 270.9 tons of cargo was delivered to Festung, including 107 tons of food and 67 tons of bread.

In the evening, while returning from the Pocket, a large group of He 111 from KG 27 was suddenly attacked by Russian fighters while crossing the front line. As a result, He 111 H-6 W.Nr. 7702 was damaged (25 per cent), but flew safely to the Novocherkassk air base. The crew of the He 111 H-6 W.Nr. 4551 '1G+IL' from 3./KG 27 were much less fortunate. An air gunner and a flight engineer were killed in the attack. The pilot of the Feldwebel Dieter was barely able to make an emergency landing near the village of Papchino (150 km north of Novocherkassk). The bomber was completely destroyed, and the injured navigator and radio operator were blocked in the cockpit. The only pilot remaining on his feet, Dieter went to get help, but got lost. At the same time, a Fi 156 plane with a doctor, I./KG 27 J. Fähndrich, took off in search of the plane and made an emergency landing itself due to icing. As a result, the two injured pilots spent the entire night in the cockpit of the bomber and were very cold. Dieter arrived in the morning with a peasant sledge team on which the wounded were taken to the village of Papchino. For some time, the pilots were holed up in a peasant hut, until the Fi 156 ambulance plane with doctor Fähndrich came for them on the second attempt. As a result, when the frostbitten Obergefreiter Ernst Gröning was finally taken to a hospital in Rostov-on-Don on 7 January, doctors had to amputate the young man's right leg, but this was not the cruellest manifestation of a capricious 'military fate'; 21-year-old Gröning at least survived and returned to his homeland after severe hardships. The war ended for him at that moment. The further 'military fate' of his other comrades was still unknown.

There were other losses. Ju 52 W.Nr. 7211 'G6+GX' from 1./KGr. zbV 105 and Ju 52 W.Nr. 7610 'DI+KJ' from II./KGzbV 1 were missing. Ju 52 W.Nr. 5700 from Tr.St.Lw.Kdo 'Don' was destroyed at Kantemirovka airfield during an Il-2 air attack. He 111 P-2 W.Nr. 3762 'L5+D5' from KGr.zbV 5 was damaged by anti-aircraft fire and crashed during an emergency landing at Novocherkassk airfield. Two crew members were killed and five injured.

At the Morozovskaya railway station, during the retreat, echelons (several hundred wagons) with cargo prepared for the 6th Army were destroyed. 3,000 tons of ammunition, 1,500 tons of grain, 540 tons of flour, 200 tons of canned meat and 12 tons of marmalade were lost.

On 5 January, the Russians recorded a flight of 270 aircraft (mostly He 111 and Ju 52) over the blockade ring. According to German data, ninety-five transport flights were made to Festung, of which sixty-eight were on the account of Ju 52 crews (thirty-one successfully) and twenty-seven on the account of He 111 crews (twenty-two successfully); 161.3 tons of cargo were delivered. At the same time, transport planes suffered heavy losses. On the night of 4 to 5 January and the day of 5 January, the following aircraft were lost:

- Ju 52 W.Nr. 6560 '1Z+KR' from 5./KGzbV 1 missing with crew;
- Ju 52 '1Z+AC' from St.II./KGzbV 1 crashed at night near the city of Salsk, killing the entire crew and seventeen wounded soldiers who were on board the plane;
- Ju 52 W.Nr. 10034 'NM+EG' of I./KGzbV 1 lost for an unknown reason;
- Ju 52 W.Nr. 7677 'G6+FY' from KGzbV 172 crashed at the airport Basargino (three killed, one wounded);
- Ju 52 W.Nr. 3302 'KI+LU' from II./KGzbV 1 lost for an unknown reason;
- Ju 52 W.Nr. 6787 from KGr.zbV 50 missing;
- He 111 H-6 'G1+DR' from 7./KG 55 crashed during an emergency landing at Novocherkassk airfield (five crew members were killed and seven injured).

On 6 January, the Russians recorded a flight of 170 transport planes. According to German data, fifty-six flights were made, of which twenty were on the account of Ju 52 crews (one successful) and thirty-six on the account of He 111 crews (twenty-eight successful). Most of the crews were unable to complete the mission due to bad weather, and only 49.5 tons of cargo was delivered to Stalingrad. Three aircraft from KGr.zbV 9 were severely damaged during emergency landings: Ju 52 W.Nr. 7454 – at Pitomnik airfield, Ju 52 W.Nr. 2838 and Ju 52 W.Nr. 6696 '4V+CB' (crew missing) – southwest and west of Salsk.

On 7 January, the Russians recorded 270 flights of German aircraft over the blockade ring. However, the accuracy of these observations was very low due to poor visibility. The Russians often identified and counted German aircraft by sound. According to German data, 102 flights were made, of which forty-five were on the account of Ju 52 crews (thirty successfully) and fifty-seven on the account of He 111 crews (thirty-three successfully); 125.5 tons of cargo was delivered.

Losses amounted to four aircraft. A He 111 H-6 W.Nr. 4426 '1G+FK' from 2./KG 27 crashed at Novocherkassk airfield during the take-off.

The plane was completely destroyed, two crew members were killed and three were injured. He 111 H-6 W.Nr. 4736 of 3./KG 100 was shot down by anti-aircraft fire in the area of Stalingrad. As a result of a direct shell hit in the cockpit, the pilot and radio operator were killed, but the navigator and flight engineer managed to leave the plane by parachute and landed on German territory. Later, both were taken out of the Pocket on another plane. Ju 52 from Fl.Komp./Ln.Pgt.4 was lost for an unknown reason. Ju 52 W.Nr. 10033 'NM+EE' from Tr.St.Lw.Kdo 'Don' was missing. Russian aviation in these days mostly did not fly because of the heavy haze and clouds.

During the first days of 1943, on average, only 123 tons of cargo per day were delivered to Stalingrad Pocket. The needs of the encircled group also changed in comparison with December. The 6th Army needed less food due to losses and the evacuation of some people by air. But at the same time, the need for ammunition and fuel increased, the reserves of which were greatly reduced due to the fighting.

On 8 January, the Soviet command issued an ultimatum for Paulus, which suggested that the 6th Army surrender. The text also mentioned the work of the air bridge. The ultimatum said:

> The German transport aviation, which is carrying you starvation rations of food, ammunition and fuel, because of the rapid advance of the Red Army is forced to frequently leave their bases and fly to Stalingrad from afar. In addition, the German transport aircraft is suffering huge losses in aircraft from attacks by Russian aviation. Its assistance to the encircled troops becomes unrealistic. The situation of your surrounded troops is difficult. They experience hunger, disease, and cold. The harsh Russian winter is just beginning. Severe snowstorms, frosts and cold winds are still ahead….

The Soviets promised to provide soldiers and officers of the 6th Army with comfortable conditions, food and medical care in the event of surrender. For Paulus, this was the last chance to save the lives of many soldiers. But the loyal Hitler general, of course, did not use it and thus doomed his army to a terrible death.

On that day, in the area of Stalingrad, it warmed to 0°C, there was a heavy snowfall. But the air bridge continued to function. During the day, the Russians recorded the passage of 216 aircraft over the blockade ring, including seventy-nine He 111 and sixty-eight Ju 52. According to German data, 101 flights were made to Festung, of which thirty were on the account of Ju 52 crews (thirteen successfully) and seventy-one on the account of He 111 crews (sixty-three successfully). They delivered 117.6 tons of cargo. German transport aircraft suffered heavy losses on this day – seven aircraft. Missing: Ju 52 W.Nr. 7591 'NB+GO' from KGr.zbV 102, Ju 52 W.Nr. 6339 'CH+HR' from KGr.zbV 500, Ju 52 W.Nr. 5244 'RF+AN' of KGr.zbV 700, Ju 52 W.Nr. 3052 'KF+UB' of KGr.zbV 900. Ju 52 W.Nr. 6363 from KGzbV 172 was found wrecked with the dead crew inside. In the crew of the Ju 52 W.Nr. 3046 from KGr.zbV 500, two pilots were killed and two injured.

In the south-western sector of the Pocket, Junior Lieutenant P.M. Boikov of the 897th IAP shot down a transport airplane in an air battle, which fell on the positions of the Soviet 57th Army. It was a Ju 52 W.Nr. 6729 '4V+CB' from KGr.zbV 9, which according to German data was missing. One crew member managed to jump out with a parachute. During the interrogation, the pilot said that he flew from the air base of Shahty with a cargo of bread. Another Ju 52 was shot down at 22.00 by infantry fire in the northern sector Pocket. According to German data it was a Ju 52 W.Nr. 1307 from Tr.St. IX.Fl.Korp (with double side code 'RK+AR' and 'D2+HH'). Its crew was also missing. Shot down by the 303rd separate anti-aircraft battery of the 346th rifle division, the Ju 52 fell on the Vlasov farm. Fifteen bodies were found in the wrecked plane, and two wounded survivors were captured. In 13.46 1./1082 ZenAP shot down another Ju 52, which fell 7 km north of the settlement of Trudposelok No.3. One pilot managed to jump out with a parachute and was captured, the rest were killed.

On 9 January, the Russians marked the passage of 167 transport planes over the blockade ring. According to German data, 124 transport flights were made, of which fifty-six were for Ju 52 crews (forty-six successful), fifity-two for He 111 crews (forty-six successful), nine for Ju 86 crews (seven successful) and seven for Fw 200 crews (seven successful); 385.7 tons of cargo were delivered to Stalingrad (a record figure) and 156 wounded were taken out on return flights. Losses were minimal – four aircraft. Lost for unknown reasons were: Ju 52 W.Nr. 2891 from I./KGzbV 1 (two killed, two wounded), Ju 52 W.Nr. 4066 '6C+AE' from 2./KGr.zbV 50 (two injured), Ju 52 W.Nr. 7507 'DP+EG' from KGr.zbV 102 (three killed, one injured). Ju 86 W.Nr. 4031 was intercepted and shot down by Soviet fighters in the square Pl.Qu.25613/44, but its crew escaped by jumping out with parachutes.

Periodically, the Soviet air force launched air attacks against transport aircraft bases outside of the Pocket. On 9 January, seven Il-2s from the 622nd SHAP, accompanied by eight Yak-1s from the 236th IAP, raided Salsk airfield, where a large number of He 111 and Ju 52 aircraft were based. This time, low clouds helped the Soviet pilots to approach the target unnoticed, which was very rare. At 11.08 'Zementbombers' suddenly fell out of the clouds and began to dive into the parking lot of aircraft. From a height of about 400 meters, they dropped twenty-six high-explosive bombs, after which they made several more passes under the fire of anti-aircraft artillery, firing guns and rockets. The rockets and shells exploded in various places, sending up columns of fire, snow, and earth. However, the German planes themselves were not affected. The attackers own losses were three Il-2s and five Yak-1 fighters, almost half of the attacking group.

'The supply of Stalingrad continues day and night'

Until 10 January, despite the difficulties, the overall situation in the fortress remained relatively stable. The 6th Army firmly held a huge defensive perimeter. Inside the Stalingrad Pocket carried out intensive road transport. The air bridge functioned relatively steadily. In addition, until this moment, the weather was relatively comfortable, without severe frosts. Hitler was confident that the 6th Army would hold out for another couple of months and promised to unblock it nearer spring.

Combat losses were surprisingly small. According to the chief of supply of the 6th Army Oberstleutnant von Kulowsky, on 23 November 1942, the total number of the encircled group numbered 220,000 people. During the period from 23 November to 10 January, the losses of the 6th Army amounted to only 5,000 people killed, during the same time, about 20,000 wounded were evacuated by aircraft. As a result, by 10 January, there were about 195,000 people in the fortress.

But after this date, the situation changed dramatically. On the morning of 10 January, the Russians launched an offensive simultaneously in the northwestern and southern sectors of the German defense perimeter. Their plan was to capture Pitomnik air base with converging strikes and divide the 6th Army into two isolated units.

The Russians recorded a flight of 213 transport planes over the blockade ring. On this day, for the first time since the New Year, the Russian air force was also active. The 16th air force flew 513 sorties, and many air battles took place over Stalingrad Pocket. Russian pilots reported twelve downed aircraft (ten Bf 109, one He 111 and 1 Fw 200). Own losses amounted to eleven aircraft.

According to German data, 137 transport flights were made, of which sixty-four were on the account of Ju 52 crews (forty-three successful), sixty-six on the account of He 111 crews (fifty-three successful) and seven on the account of Fw 200 crews (six successful); 162.2 tons of cargo were delivered to Festung. Hans Reif of 3./KG 27 wrote:

> Our supply of Stalingrad continues day and night. Now we have to fly to our comrades for 250 km, i.e. there and back about 500 km over enemy territory. What a blessing that we had at least some cloud cover. However, the weather was often too bad. Over the airfield there are always a lot of planes that constantly interfere with each other. Sometimes, when you see the shadows pass by at a ramming distance, the last hair on your head stands up under your hood. Such a mission costs more nerves than a real combat operation.[24]

In the area of the village of Vertyachii, anti-aircraft artillery shot down two Ju 52. According to Soviet information, both crews were killed. In fact, it was two Ju 86 (W.Nr. 0073 and W.Nr. 5143) missing along with the crew and passengers on board. In the list of passengers missing were two pilots – Oberleutnant O. Genrich of 2.(F)/11 and Oberleutnant O. Grotzmann of St./ KG 77. In the morning (at 08.08) anti-aircraft gunners 1./1080 ZenAP shot down He 111 W.Nr. 1266 from KGr.zbV 23.

This day marked the first flight to Stalingrad of a four-engine Ju 290, which delivered 10 tons of cargo at once and took out seventy-eight wounded.

German historians still argue about the feasibility of transferring four - engine Ju 290 and Fw 200 aircraft from France, Italy and Germany to the Eastern front, from which a new transport aviation group was formed – KGr.zbV 200. The lack of suitable airfields for them, spare parts and qualified aircraft technicians led to the fact that the efforts of this air group were ineffective and ended in heavy losses. The first missions on 9 January were successful, but the next day the 'Condors' were intercepted

---

24 Boelcke Archiv.

by Russian fighters. Fw 200 C-2 W.Nr. 0018 'GF+GF' was shot down while landing at Pitomnik. The plane crashed on German territory, and all six crew members of the Oberfeldwebel Werner Brune were killed. This aerial victory belonged to Junior Lieutenant N.V. Kharitonov and Senior Sergeant V.F. Makarov from the 520th IAP.

Fw 200 C-4 W.Nr. 0151 'F8+HW' landed safely and unloaded, then took on board the seriously injured and took-off again. But on the way back, south-east of the village of Kletskaya, 'Condor' was intercepted and shot down three Yak-1 from the 910th IAP air defense. According to German data, all six crew members of the Oberfeldwebel Eugen Reck and twenty-one wounded soldiers were killed. According to Soviet information, the plane crashed 4 km east of the village of Ventsy. Four German pilots managed to jump out with parachutes and were captured. The Russians claimed that thirty-two corpses of high-ranking German officers and banners of German divisions were found in the wrecked plane.

The aerial victory (this was the first Fw 200 shot down by the Soviets) was divided between Captain E.A. Kozlov, Senior Lieutenant S.G. Ivanov and Junior Lieutenant B.S. Ivlev, who each recorded one-third of the Fw 200 shot down in their flight books.

On 10 January, the Lufttransportführer II (LTF II) was formed in the city of Voroshilovgrad (now Lugansk) in order to improve the supply of Festung Stalingrad, led by KG 27 commander von Beust. It consisted of Stab./KG 27, III./KG 4, II./KG 53, 15./KG 6,[25] KGr.zbV 20 и KGr.zbV 23. The LTF I (Oberst Kühl) consisted of: Stab KG 55, I./KG 55, III./KG 55, I./KG 27, II./KG 27, III./KG 27 and I./KG 100.

III./KG 4 arrived in Voroshilovgrad from the northern sector of the front, where it had just been supplying the garrison of Velikiye Luki Pocket. The group was supplemented with new He 111 H-16 aircraft, which had more powerful defensive weapons. Every day, three or four bombers with experienced crews covered a distance of 300 km. The He 111 usually carried eight passengers in its fuselage, but some crews managed to take up to fifteen people out of Stalingrad![26]

---

25 15./KG 6 were an experimental Staffel of pathfinders. It was equipped with He 111 and Do 217 aircraft.

26 Gundelach K. Kampfgeschwader 'General Wever' 4. – Motorbuch Verlag Stutgart, 1978. p. 220 – 221.

Table 3. Availability of aircraft in KG 27 on 10 January, 1942

Gruppe	Staff number	Total He 111	Combat-ready planes
Stab/KG 27	4	1	0
I./KG 27	37	19	7
II./KG 27	37	19	5
III./KG 27	37	19	19
In total	115	58	31

On 11 January, despite fog and snowfall, the Russians recorded a flight of 213 transport planes over the blockade ring. According to German data, 134 flights were made, ninety-six of which were successful (the cargo was delivered to Pitomnik). The 6th Army received 189.6 tons of ammunition and food.

At 10.10–10.30, a group of He 111s from 4./KG 27 took off from Novocherkassk air base and headed for Stalingrad. The flight took place in conditions of poor visibility (500 meters) and solid clouds. When approaching Pitomnik He 111 H-6 W.Nr. 4553 '1G+FP' was attacked (according to flight gunner Unteroffizier Ludwig Decker) by a fighter. As a result, the elevators were damaged and the bomber crashed during landing. In this case the pilot, Oberleutnant Albert Gropp, navigator Unteroffizier Josef Dischl, and Flight Engineer Ernst Lenniger were killed, while Decker and radio operator Unteroffizier Herbert Klein were injured. Around the same time, a He 111 H-6 crashed in Pitomnik W.Nr. 4291 '1G+EN' (pilot Feldwebel Wilhelm Ebbinghaus). The plane was 60 per cent damaged, and all the pilots were injured. After unloading planes, all six injured pilots were evacuated to Novocherkassk on other bombers. In addition, nine Ju 52s were lost for non-combat reasons (three from KGr.zbV 700, two from KGr.zbV 50 and KGr.zbV 102, and one from KGzbV 172 and KGr.zbV 500). The Russian 16th Air Army was again inactive that day due to bad weather.

Despite starvation and lack of ammunition, the 6th Army put up a desperate resistance along the entire perimeter, and in places the Germans even launched fierce counterattacks. As a result, in the first two days of the offensive alone, the Soviet Don front lost 8,000 men killed and wounded!

On 12 January, the period of relatively warm weather finally ended, and severe frosts began. On this day, the Russians recorded a flight of 111 transport planes in Stalingrad. According to German data, sixty-four transport flights were carried out. Fifty-one aircraft delivered cargo, the rest either failed to reach the target area, or dropped cargo with parachutes. Festung received 61.7 tons of cargo, including 34.5 tons of food.

On 13 January, according to Russian data, 268 transport planes flew over the blockade ring. According to German data, ninety-two flights were made (sixty-nine successful), and 224.5 tons of cargo were delivered.

German bombers continued to suffer losses due to weather conditions that were more dangerous than enemy interceptors. During take-off from Novocherkassk air base, a He 111 H-6 crashed W.Nr. 4948 '1G+GP' (pilot Oberfeldwebel Herbert Thiele) from 6./KG 27. The entire crew of five people died. Two more bombers were lost by 2./KG 100, they were shot down over the Don river during a flight in Stalingrad Pocket. One crew was able to escape and reach German territory. But the crew of the He 111 H-6 W.Nr. 7941 '6H+AK' commander of this Staffel Hauptmann Lars Garms[27] was missing.

But the most painful was the loss of the Ju 290 A-0 W.Nr. 290-11-0150, which delivered 10 tons of cargo to the Pocket. Due to incorrect loading of stretchers with the wounded at Pitomnik airfield, the plane crashed during take-off. Five pilots of the six Valter Hënig crew and seventy-one wounded out of eighty-six taken on board were killed. A second Ju 290 A-1 W.Nr. 0151, which took off from Pitomnik with ten wounded soldiers, made an emergency landing before reaching its air base in Zaporizhia. Later, this aircraft was dismantled and sent by rail to Tempelhof for repair, but no information was found that it was able to re-enter service.

On this day, the Soviets finally managed to break through the front in the western part of Stalingrad Pocket and capture the village of Karpovka. There, surprised Russian soldiers were convinced that the 6th Army still had a lot of supplies! In Karpovka, they captured two warehouses full of ammunition. There were 3,000 shells, 53,000 rounds of ammunition, 3,700 rounds for mortars, and a large number of various weapons. In the south-western sector, the Russian 57th Army captured the village of Rokotino.

On 14 January, the Russians recorded a flight of 239 transport planes over the blockade ring. The 6th Army unsuccessfully tried to hold the new line of defense along the banks of the Rossoshka and Chervlennaya rivers. But it was no longer possible to hold back the men of the Red Army who were advancing with wild shouts of 'Hooray'.

---

27 Garms was a very experienced pilot and had previously commanded 4./KG 26.

On 15 January, in the area of Stalingrad, the temperature dropped to minus 28°C. The 'real Russian frosts' came, which were more deadly for the 6th Army than the attacking Red Army men. On this day, the advanced units of the Soviet 21st Army broke through to the village of Dubinin and the settlement of Molochno-tovarnaya ferma, from which Pitomnik was only 4 km away. To the south, the 57th Army captured the Basargino railway station and also moved east. Russian observers recorded a flight of 199 transport planes in the Pocket.

The 16th Air Army was again activated and flew 545 sorties. The pilots reported eight transport planes shot down and eight transport planes destroyed on the ground. Among the attackers was a large group of twin-engine Li-2VV bombers from the 62nd long-range aviation division. Their target was Pitomnik air base. As a result of the bombing, no aircraft were damaged, but five Li-2VV were shot down and Several experienced crew embers were missing. In the area of the settlement boundary, Soviet fighters shot down a He 111 H-6 W.Nr. 4869 '1G+MN' from 5./KG 27. The entire crew of five people was missing.

Trying to improve the situation in the doomed Stalingrad Pocket, Hitler took new administrative measures. He ordered Generalfeldmarschall der Flieger Erhard Milch to leave immediately for the city of Taganrog and personally head the air bridge command to Stalingrad. The Führer gave him extraordinary powers. Arriving at Luftflotte 4 headquarters on 16 January, Milch hastily formed the Sonderstab Gen.Feldm. Milch. The energetic (but absolutely stupid) Generalfeldmarschall, inspired by the trust of the Führer, immediately tried to increase the number of flights to the Pocket by various 'administrative' methods. In particular, Milch threatened to personally shoot officers who disrupted the supply of the 6th Army. Field court Fliegerkorps VIII (Das Feldgericht des VIII. Fliegerkorps) immediately received an order to interrogate 'judicially' all the crews who, instead of landing in Stalingrad, dropped the cargo on parachutes. The court had to find out whether it was really impossible to land in Stalingrad for objective reasons, or whether there was 'cowardice in the face of the enemy'. In addition, it was necessary to interrogate the pilots who made the landing, in order to obtain reliable information about the state of the airfields in Stalingrad.

However, all these idiotic measures were clearly too late, and there was absolutely no reason to suspect Luftwaffe pilots who risked their lives every day to save their comrades. However, Milch had no desire to interrogate 'judicially' the real traitors and cowards responsible for the disastrous situation of the 6th Army, which undoubtedly were Hitler and Göring.

On 16 January, the temperature dropped to minus 32°C. On this terrible morning for the 6th Army, an event occurred that finally buried it. Shortly after dawn, the soldiers of the Russian 298th rifle division of the 21st Army launched an attack. This time they met with no resistance. In the misty morning haze, the soldiers saw only frozen trucks, guns, and tanks. Moving quickly forward, at 09.00 the Russians saw an apocalyptic spectacle. There were dozens of wrecked and damaged aircraft of various types in the vast space. Many of them were already covered with snow and looked like frozen prehistoric monsters. This cemetery of aircraft technology stretched for several kilometers in the distance. Anti-aircraft guns also stood motionless there, their barrels pointed at the frosty sky. Even more soldiers were astonished by a huge cluster of trucks – there were thousands of them! This was the 'ring of dead metal' – Pitomnik air base.

In total, in the Pitomnik area, the Soviets captured 13,000 vehicles, 1,632 motorcycles, 270 tanks and self-propelled guns, seventy anti-aircraft guns, 350 bicycles and about 300 aircraft (almost all of them were faulty). Among those abandoned at the airfield was a four-engine Fw 200 C-3 W.Nr. 0046 'SG+KV'[28] from KGr.zbV 200. Moreover, all six pilots from its crew could not fly and were missing. The retreating Germans abandoned several ammunition and food depots, as well as two hospitals full of wounded. These poor devils were definitely not destined to return to Germany…

On the external (relative to Stalingrad Pocket) front, the situation was also disastrous. On 14 January, the Russians launched an offensive against the 2nd Hungarian army south of the city of Voronezh and immediately broke through the front. Already under the threat of complete encirclement was the 2nd German army. At first, Hitler planned to ban the retreat in this sector and declare Voronezh the next Festung, but he no longer had any available aircraft to use for the next air bridge. This fact made Hitler more compliant and soon (though dangerously late) he sanctioned the withdrawal from Voronezh. In the sector of the Army Group 'Don', the Red Army also continued to advance, and on 16 January the Germans had to evacuate the Salsk air base. The Ju 52 transport aviation groups were once again forced to change their location. They flew to Zverevo airfield (north of Shahty). Now the 6th Army was 275 km away from the nearest Wehrmacht positions.

But despite the crisis caused by the loss of Pitomnik and Salsk, the air bridge was still active. The Russians recorded a flight of 200 transport

---

28 Later, this aircraft was tested at the research Institute of the Red Army Air forces at Chkalovsky airfield, and was subsequently on display for a long time at the exhibition of captured equipment in Moscow in the Gorky Park.

planes over the blockade ring. But almost all of them dropped their cargo on parachutes. Most of the crews referred to the 'impossibility of landing' in Gumrak. And in the evening, as part of the 'investigation', Feldwebel Ospel from II./KG 27, who had just returned from Stalingrad Pocket, was questioned. He said:

> Landing at Gumrak 11.45, starting at Gumrak 13.10. The runway at Gumrak consisted of rolled strips about 400 meters long, 5-10 meters wide. The tractor with the roller was still working in the snow. Outside the rolling track, the snow was about knee-deep. To the south of the runway lay the wreckage of a Bf 109 and a Ju 87. There were craters and some aircraft in the vast expanses around them. The bomb craters at the airfield were filled in. There was no landing cross. A cross made of canvas signs lay off the runway at the northern end of the airfield. There was no starting post or direction indicator for the unloading point. Landing was difficult due to the short length of the runway, not very strong snow and surrounding pits. The place was unsuitable for night landings. The unloading teams were not in place. The crew unloaded the plane. There was a fuel tanker for refueling. The organization of unloading, allocation of wounded for the return flight could not be found. During unloading, 4 Il-2s attacked the airfield and 2 standing He 111 for 15 minutes. The anti-aircraft defense consisted of 3 light guns that fired moderately. About 300 injured people were stationed in the aircraft parking lot, trying to take shelter in one truck. The crews of Ju 87 and 6-8 pilots from Jagdgeschwader 'Udet', who arrived from Pitomnik, were also here and tried to fly out of the fortress. They reported that their planes in the early morning hours of 16.01.1943 were damaged by enemy tank fire at Pitomnik airfield, and they were unable to fly away.[29]

On this day, new He 177 'Greif' bombers from I./FKG 50 took part in the supply of Stalingrad for the first time. These unusual planes, which had been expected for several years, had just arrived at the Zaporizhia air base for long-range bombing raids. But instead, He 177 bombers were also sent to assist with air bridge. Five planes led by Major Schede took to the air

---

29 Boelcke Archiv.

in order to drop containers with cargo to the encircled troops. But the first combat mission of the newest 'Greifs' ended in failure. Two aircraft were forced to return prematurely due to technical problems and engine failures, and another crew was unable to find the target. As a result, only one bomber reached Stalingrad. But the worst part was that the He 177 A-1 W.Nr. 15233 'E8+FH' commander I./FKG 50 Major Karl Schede did not return to the base. What happened to the plane remains unclear and the entire crew were added to the list of missing persons.[30] Hauptmann Heinrich Schlosser was appointed acting commander of the I./FKG 50.

On 17 January, the 6th Army occupied the former inner circle of the Stalingrad fortified area. This perimeter defense was hastily built by the Soviets in the summer of 1942, 15–20 km west of Stalingrad to contain the advancing German troops. Now it was the other way around, the Red Army was attacking from the west, and the Germans were defending in the east! On this day, 114 transport planes flew over the blockade ring. The operation again involved I./FKG 50. Five He 177s were loaded with cargo containers and flew to the Pocket, but the 'Greif' mission was again unsuccessful. One of the He 177, 100 km west of the city of Stalino (now Donetsk), caught fire, which forced the crew to jump out with parachutes. Another He 177 A-1 W.Nr. 15242 'VD+UQ' was lost 'as a result of enemy action'. As a result, only two aircraft reached the target area and dropped the containers. One of the crews on his return said that in the area of Stalingrad, 'Greif' was subjected to fourteen attacks by Soviet fighters within forty minutes. The pilots reported that they managed to shoot down one of the attackers, and a powerful concentrated fire from the towers and tail gun repelled the other attackers.

Despite the difficulty of landing in Gumrak and the poor organization of the airfield, experienced crews successfully coped with this mission. For example, He 111 Hauptmann Karl Mayer from III./KG 27 took off from Novocherkassk at 12.30 and landed in Gumrak at 14.05. The bomber made a landing approach from the southern direction over the village of Beketovka.

---

30 The fate of Kurt Schede became clear only after seventy-four years! At the end of 2016, the wreckage of He 177 was found in a ravine near the village of Talovaya Balka (Svitlovodsky district of the Kirovograd region of Ukraine). Only small fragments of the bomber were preserved, but included the nameplates and badges of the pilots which established that this was the plane of Major Schede and his crew. Probably during the return to Zaporozhye due to bad weather, it was decided to land at the reserve airfield in Kirovograd. However, the 'Greif' did not reach it for some reason and crashed. Later it was established that the radio operator 'E8+FH' got in touch and reported that the plane was fired at by anti-aircraft fire from the ground while flying over Polyakovka. Apparently 'friendly fire' was the cause of his death.

After successfully landing, the crew unloaded the plane themselves, took on board ten wounded soldiers and at 14.55 left for the return flight. At 16.10, in the dark, the bomber returned to Novocherkassk. He 111 Oberleutnant Thofehern from III./KG 27 took off from Novocherkassk at 12.30 and landed at Gumrak at 14.00. The plane passed over the village of Beketovka at an altitude of 4,500 meters, then began a spiral descent to the airfield; 15 minutes after landing, the officers who organized the unloading arrived. Then came the Luftwaffe staff doctor, who was regulating the boarding of the wounded on the plane. During loading, shell explosions were seen at the Gumrak railway station and in the northern part of the airfield. At 14.45, a He 177 bomber appeared in the sky, which dropped cargo containers on parachutes. They fell near the train station. At 15.00, the He 111 Oberleutnant Thofehern took off and landed in Novocherkassk at 16.20. Hauptmann Mayer, commander 9./KG 27, participated in this mission and included the following in his report:

> Starting the engines and taxiing for take-off was significantly complicated by the completely insane wounded, who could no longer be taken with them. Some of them tried to prevent the launch by lying in front of the chassis. The Festung garrison, including senior officers, believed that the German deblocking forces were close, in front of Kalach-na-Donu. The aircrews did not give any information when they were asked questions about where the front line was located. It is to be feared that when the real state of affairs becomes known, the onslaught on landing planes will have to be repelled by force of arms.

Mayer's report confirmed the famous Russian saying 'hope dies last'. Despite the disastrous situation, the soldiers and officers of the 6th Army at that time still believed in the Führer's 'genius' and possible salvation. They thought that the Wehrmacht was doing everything possible to achieve this. In fact, in mid-January, the German command was finally convinced that the 6th Army was doomed. Generals were concerned only with the more important task of stabilizing the crumbling front, plugging huge gaps, and saving other armies from capture, including those withdrawing from the Caucasus. Generalfeldmarschall Manstein and Hitler cynically called on the 6th Army to fight so that it would bind as many Russian troops as possible and prevent them from being prematurely transferred to other sectors. Freezing and starving soldiers were sacrificed to save the Eastern front from collapse.

And with this mission they coped. As of 10 January, the Don front forces operating against the 6th Army numbered 280,000 men (210,000 soldiers), 23,600 guns and mortars, 9,300 vehicles, 41,000 horses, 254 tanks, and 222 anti-aircraft guns. At the same time, attacking the living 'dead' from the 6th Army, the Soviet troops suffered quite large losses. In the period from 10 to 15 January, the armies of the Don front lost 5,500 soldiers killed and 16,000 wounded.

On the night of 17–18 January, the Soviet air force conducted the most successful operation against the Luftwaffe air transport bases. A large group of bombers carried out a raid on the Zverevo airfield. As a result, thirteen Ju 52s were destroyed at once, including two from I./KGzbV 1 (W.Nr. 3144, W.Nr. 6578), three from I./KGzbV 172 (W.Nr. 6426, 7657, 10026) and three from KGr.zbV 500 (W.Nr. 2937, 5606, 6628), three from KGr.zbV 9 (W.Nr. 6682, 7534, 7661), and one plane from KGr. zbV 50 (W.Nr. 7495), one plane from II./KGzbV 172 (W.Nr. 5385) and one plane from KGr.zbV 900 (W.Nr. 6642). Another twenty Ju 52s were seriously damaged. And the next day, the situation was worsened by a heavy snowfall, which greatly hindered the work of the German airfields. As a result, only two Ju 52s landed in Stalingrad on 18 January. But the Russians recorded a flight of sixty-three transport planes over the blockade ring. As usual, He 111 bombers, flying in any weather, helped out. Landing in Gumrak new He 111 H-16 W.Nr. 8207 of 7./KG 27 was damaged (40 per cent) as a result of an air attack by Soviet aircraft. The bomber added to the vast dump of German aircraft, and the crew was taken out by another He 111.

In the evening, commander of 2./KG 55 Oberleutnant Horst Rudat landed in Gumrak. On the return flight, he managed to take out seventeen wounded soldiers in his He 111. At 20.40 that evening, three more bombers from KG 55 took off from Novocherkassk. But only one He 111 'G1+BR' Leutnant Georg Leopold from the 7th Staffel was able to land in Gumrak. However, it failed to take off and the crew had to be evacuated on another plane. Two other planes, after several unsuccessful landings, were forced to simply drop food containers on the airfield and return at the Novocherkassk.[31] According to German data, KG 55 lost two He 111 H-6 on this day (W.Nr. 7322, 7698). During the air attack of Russian bombers on Kantemirovka airfield, the last 'Aunt Ju' from Tr.St.Lw 'Don' were destroyed (W.Nr. 7667, 7673, 10019 and 10038).

---

31 Zefirov M.V. Aces of the Luftwaffe: Bomber aviation. – Moscow: AST, 2002. p. 332.

'Luftwaffe betrayed us and this is a crime against the 6th Army!'

Despite the fact that the Luftwaffe pilots made every effort to supply the dying 6th Army, its staff, led by Paulus, was dissatisfied with their actions. The commander of the doomed army feverishly searched for the culprits in the impending inevitable catastrophe. After a long and methodical analysis in a cold and dirty basement, Paulus finally found the 'traitors' among his Luftwaffe comrades. He considered the transport traffic insufficient and was outraged by the fact that many of the planes were dropping cargo from the air instead of landing.

Paulus contacted von Manstein and demanded that General Luftwaffe be sent to him for negotiations. Manstein called von Richthofen, who asked Milch about it. As a result of these bureaucratic procedures, the 6th Army headquarters decided to send the commander III./KG 27 Major Erich Thiel. On the morning of 19 January, he flew to Stalingrad Pocket at the head of the He 111 group. The flight took place in conditions of heavy clouds at an altitude of 1,500–2,000 meters. Guided by the radio beacon, the bombers came to the target. From an altitude of 1,500 meters, Gumrak was clearly visible from the cluster of crashed planes and many craters around the runway. Shortly after the planes landed at 11.00, ten Russian planes appeared in the sky. But in Gumrak, anti-aircraft artillery was still active, and they did not dare to attack lower than from a height of 800–1,000 meters.

To Thiel's surprise, the airfield was completely deserted. There were no unloading teams or soldiers in sight, and numerous cargo containers were scattered everywhere, half-buried in snow. Soon Major Thiel found himself in the Paulus headquarters dugout, which was still located in the Gumrak area. In addition to Paulus, the meeting was attended by the chief of staff of the 6th Army, Generalleutnant Schmidt, commander of the LI army corps General der Artillerie von Sydlitz, Oberst Elchlepp, Oberst Rosenfeld and Oberleutnant Kolbenschlag. In response to claims about the poor performance of the airfield, Paulus broke out with angry curses. He said that every plane that landed saved the lives of 1,000 people, while dumping cargo containers does not bring any benefit. Many of them were simply not found, and the army no longer had fuel for cars to collect them:

Paulus said:

> The last horses were eaten. Can you imagine that the soldiers
> pounce on the old carcass of horse, open the head and eat

113

the brains raw? What do I, as commander-in-chief of the army, say when a man comes to me and make a request, Mr. Generaloberst, give me a piece of bread! Why did the Luftwaffe promise that the supply will be carried out? Who is the responsible person who chose this opportunity? If I had been told that it was impossible, I would not have blamed the Luftwaffe, because then I could have broken through, then when the collapse occurred, I was strong enough to force the break, today it is too late.

Generalleutnant Schmidt was even more categorical, effectively blaming the Luftwaffe for the army's impending demise:

So you come here and want to justify the Luftwaffe, which committed the worst betrayal ever committed in German history? Someone suggested it to the Führer? Luftwaffe betrayed us and this is a crime against the 6th Army!

Pauius said:

Landing in Stalingrad must be completed, even if the plane crashes. So the Luftwaffe didn't do their duty. You can't leave it up to the crews to decide whether they can land or not, but you have to order them, and if someone doesn't follow that order, they will be court-martialed![32]

At the end of the conversation, he even told the pilot that he was talking to him from the next world, because he was actually already dead...

When Thiel returned to his plane, it was still not unloaded, but was already badly damaged by artillery fire, and the flight engineer had been killed. From 15.00, Russian U-2 light bombers in groups of three or four began to circle over the airfield. This continued until nightfall. The weather was cloudless, and the bright moonlight illuminated Gumrak well. Thiel saw immediately that the plane taxiing for the start had been damaged by falling bomb fragments. U-2s continued to circle the airfield until 22.00, replacing each other. Only at 22.00, when the snow began to fall, did the Russians leave. After unloading, twenty wounded were taken on board and Major Thiel came on board with them. The Ju 52 took off safely and

---

32 Boelcke Archiv.

delivered it to Zverevo air base. Thus this deadly mission, in which Major Thiel played the role of whipping boy, ended in nothing. Paulus, of course, could not think of calling into Stalingrad the true traitors of the Wehrmacht: Hitler and Göring.

The night of 19–20 January was the last time a large number of planes landed in Stalingrad. Hauptmann Mayer wrote in his report:

> The location of Gumrak could only be found by secondary landmarks. The direction finder itself was overloaded, but worked satisfactorily. At the airfield, a beacon signaled. The airfield itself was clearly visible on a moonlit night. The runway was marked with a green and white light. Landing was extremely difficult and only feasible for good crews. Two lamps were barely enough. The third, red light, was probably disabled by the enemy... After landing, the aircraft had to immediately turn off the runway to make way for landing aircraft. At the end of the runway, through the runways, the planes came into the parking lot of broken planes. Wreckage of aircraft is a great danger for landing, and especially for taking off aircraft, since the runway is very short. The landing plane veered slightly to the left on landing and went into a bomb crater. This fault is located next to the runway. Unloading of aircraft was again to be carried out by the crews themselves. Because of this, there were long delays. Unloading takes 30 to 40 minutes without refueling. Since taxiing after landing and taxiing for take-off are only possible on the runway, there are delays in unloading and, as a result, accumulation of aircraft at the end of the runway. This creates a big obstacle for taking off and landing aircraft. The onslaught of wounded that night was apparently less as a result of more planes landing. After receiving 10 wounded, we rolled out to the start. Then the planes that arrived for landing had to gain altitude and wait until the runway was clear. The take-off itself was very difficult due to the texture of the surface (snow about 20 cm deep significantly slowed the plane).[33]

This night in Gumrak was not a good one for all the crews. Near Sovkhoz 'Kotluban', Fw 200 C-3/U5 W.Nr. 0095 'F8+DH' made an emergency

---

33 Boelcke Archiv.

landing with a cargo of crackers and underwear. The plane was completely destroyed, and the crew of Oberfeldwebel Karl Gruner, consisting of six people, was captured.

The mission on 19 January was again a failure for aircraft from I./ FKG 50. Eight He 177s that took off for the delivery of goods in Stalingrad failed to find the agreed drop zone due to poor visibility and returned back. At the same time, due to bad weather conditions, some bombers landed at a reserve airfield in the city of Kirovohrad. At the same time, the landing was accompanied by a number of accidents. The wing of He 177 A-3 W.Nr. 15241 'VD+UP' demolished the roof of the hangar, and it lost its tail wheel. The damage was quickly repaired and the next day 'Greif' flew to the city of Zaporizhia. However, when landing, it suffered an accident, which resulted in the death of four crew members.

On 20 January the area of Stalingrad warmed up a little, and it began to snow. The Soviet air force was inactive, and the German air force became more active. During the day and night, the Russians observed heavy air traffic over the blockade ring (226 transport planes flew). In the Pitomnik area, one He 111 and one Ju 52 were shot down by anti-aircraft artillery. According to Soviet information, their crews were killed. This information completely coincides with the German data. He 111 H-6 W.Nr. 8205 of 2./ KG 100 and Ju 52 W.Nr. 7598 from KGr.zbV 700 went missing during supply flights for the 6th Army.

Despite all the difficulties and hardships, the 6th Army continued to fight heroically and fulfill its sacrificial mission. From 15 to 20 January, the Don front lost 6,000 soldiers killed and missing, and another 16,000 were wounded. Thus, in ten days of fighting, the Soviets lost 32,000 men in the Stalingrad area, or 15 per cent of their soldiers.

On 21 January, the Russians recorded the passage of 142 transport planes in the Pocket and 113 flying in the opposite direction. The 16th air force flew 178 sorties and reported one downed He 111.

Meanwhile, the situation continued to deteriorate. On 22 January, the Russians broke through the front in the northwestern part of Stalingrad Pocket. At 15.00, the 51st and 52nd Guards rifle divisions of the 21st Army reached the vicinity of Gumrak village. The last airfield suitable for the landing of transport planes was under threat. In the south, the Voroponovo railway station was captured. The length of the Pocket from west to east had been reduced to 20 km.

Among the 178 transport planes that flew over the blockade ring was the He 111 H-6 W.Nr. 7870 '1G+JM' Feldwebel Haug from 4./KG 27. It took

Above: Ju 52 'G6+EC' from 3./KGrzbV 105 flies in the Demyansk Pocket.

Right: Original drawing of the battle of Russian fighters with the Ju 52s group, 8 March 1942.

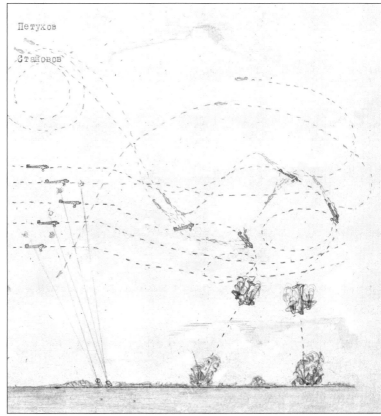

Петухов

Станонов

LaGG-3 fighter before takeoff.

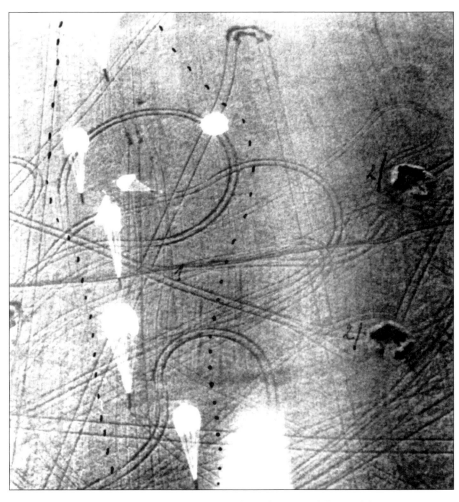
Cargo containers on parachutes in the air. (Photo from Boelcke Archiv)

The Russians studying the wreckage of He 111.

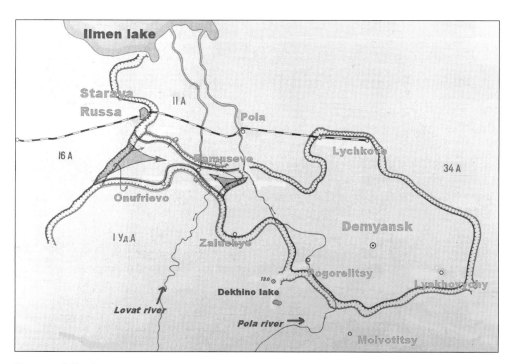

Demyansk Pocket.

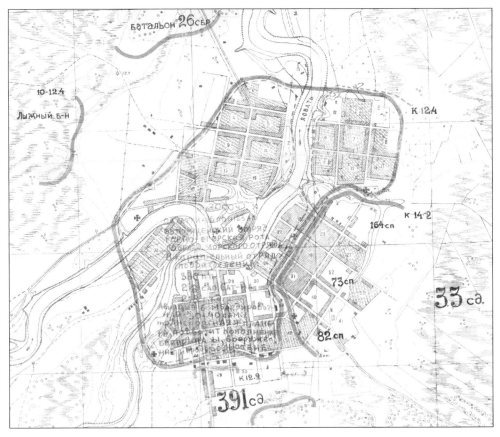

Original Russian scheme of the siege of small town Holm (14 February – 12 April 1942).

Ju 52 from 1./KGzbV 1 in low-level flight.

Right: Cargo containers in the bomb bay of the He 111 bomber.

Below: Cargo glider Go 242. (Photo from Boelcke Archiv)

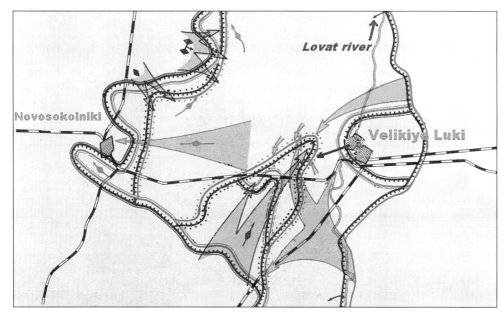

Battle plan for Velikiye Luki.

Russian soldiers during the battle in Velikiye Luki.

German tanks Pz.IV and Pz.III, abandoned near the rampart in Velikiye Luki.

Above: He 111 H-6 '1G+DH' from KG 27 before departure to Stalingrad. (Photo from Boelcke Archiv)

Right: Loading cargo containers into the He 111 bomber. (Photo from Boelcke Archiv)

He 111 H-6 '1G+HH' during a flight to Pitomnik airfield.

Above left: *Stalingrad Pocket*. Soviet caricature of 1943.

Above right: *Stalingrad Cauldron*. This cartoon was drawn by an unknown German soldier in Stalingrad Pocket. It was found by Russian soldiers after the death of the 6th Army.

Fw 200 C-3 W. Nr. 0046 'SG+KV' in the Pitomnik airfield. The KG 40 logo is clearly visible on the fuselage.

Above: He 111 bomber before another mission to supply the 6th Army. (Photo from Boelcke Archiv)

Right: The crew of the He 111 "1G+DK" from 3./KG 27. Far left navigator Hans Reif. (Photo from Boelcke Archiv)

He 111 H-6 W. Nr. 7870 '1G+JM' after the accident at the airfield 'Stalingradskij'. 22 January 1943. (Photo from Boelcke Archiv)

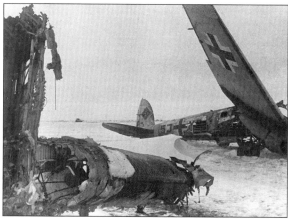

Above: Part of 'A ring of dead metal'. Abandoned German Ju 87, He 111 and Ju 52 aircraft at Pitomnik airfield.

Left: The wreckage He 111 '5J+M?' from III./KG 4 in the area of Pitomnik airfield.

Exhibition of German aircraft captured in the Stalingrad Pocket area. Moscow, summer 1943.

Joseph Stalin and his entourage inspect German planes. In the background is the Fw 200 C-3 W. Nr. 0046.

Transport planes Ju 52 over the Mediterranean sea.

The Ju 52 group is flying at a low level over the Mediterranean sea. The picture was taken from a Bf 110 fighter.

The huge transport airplane Me 323 looked like a real monster.

Allied fighters attack the Me 323 flying over the sea.

Glider tug He 111 Z Zwillinge.

Above: View from the left cabin of the Zwillinge.

Left: In the sky the He 111 Z Zwillinge looks very much like a dragon.

The Ju 52 from TG 3 drops cargo containers from a low level for III Army Corps troops. February 1944.

He 111 from KG 27 in Ukrainian airfield. (Photo from Boelcke Archiv)

Ju 52 in the area of the village of Shanderovka.

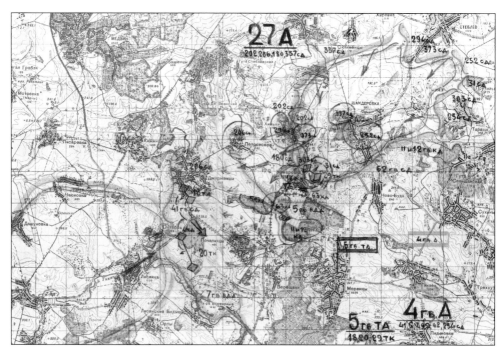

Original Russian map of the final stage of the breakout of the German group from the encirclement in the village of Shanderovka area.

Unable to escape from the 'Pocket' German soldiers are sent to captivity…

Above: He 111 H-20 from 6./KG 27 during the 1st Panzer Army supply operation (1. Panzerarmee). Me 323 from TG 5 is visible in the background. (Photo from Boelcke Archiv)

Right: He 111 H-20 in flight. (Photo from Boelcke Archiv)

German soldiers waiting to be evacuated.

Typical spectacle of another Wehrmacht collapse…

Drawing of Budapest made by a Russian army artist.

Above: Budapest street after the fighting.

Right: He 111 H-16 from 14.(Eis/N)/KG 27. (Photo from Boelcke Archiv)

Russian 85-mm anti-aircraft gun on the street in Budapest.

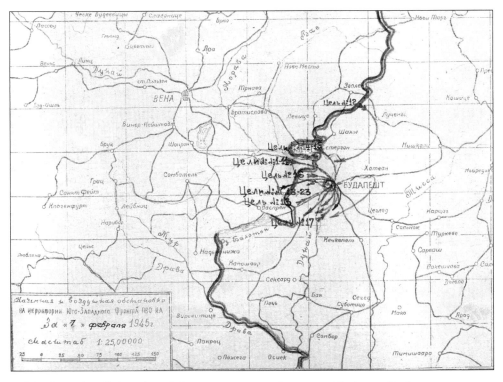

Original Russian flights plan of German transport planes over Budapest Pocket.

Destroyed by explosions Széchenyi Chain Bridge and Royal Palace.

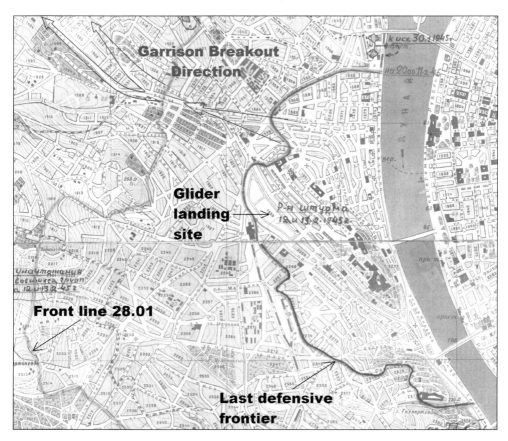

Diagram of the last phase assault of the Budapest Pocket.

Left: Remains of cargo glider that crashed into a house.

Below: Kaiserstrasse in Breslau.

Cargo container with food.

Residential building turned into a stronghold.

Concrete bunker for the civilian population.

Russian soldiers view the wreckage of the Ju 52 that fell on Breslau.

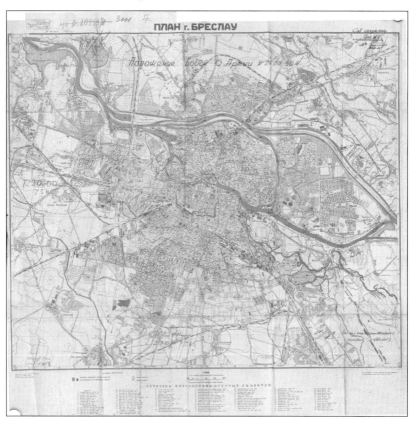

Original Russian map of Breslau.

off from Novocherkassk air base at 08.35 and landed safely in Gumrak at 09.50. After 40 minutes, the bomber began to take off, but one of the landing gear fell into a shell crater. Such situations were especially tragic for the wounded. They had survived, received their 'ticket from hell' and were finally on the plane taking off. It seemed that all the worst was over and suddenly the accident happened... The Haug crew was evacuated from Gumrak on He 111 '1G+CP' at 11.25. He 177 strategic bombers again participated in supply missions. And it was again unsuccessful... On the approach to the target, both aircraft were suddenly attacked by Soviet fighters (according to the pilots, they were 'Supermarine Spitfire' with English markings!?) As a result, He 177 W.Nr. 15240 'VD+UO' received eighteen hits in the wings, armored lower-gondola, tail tower, propellers and rudder, but managed to safely reach the airfield Kalinovka. The second 'Greif' was damaged in one of the engines, but it was able to return to base. Fw 200 C-4 W.Nr. 0071 'KF+DH' was also damaged, but was able to fly to German territory and made an emergency landing. His damage was estimated at 50 per cent. Later, the plane was partially dismantled and taken to Germany by rail.

On 23 January, the weather around Stalingrad was frosty and cloudy. Russian soldiers were already 700 meters from the village of Gumrak. Three containers of food intended for starving Germans landed on the positions of the 13th guards rifle division, which greatly pleased the starving Russian soldiers. In this regard, German planes trying to land had to choose other places. The report of one of the 2./KG 27 crew reads:

> After the Gumrak airfield was in Russian hands, we landed 23.01.1943 in a nearby village on a deeply snow-covered field on the edge of moving remnants of the troops. The site was marked only with a red cross landing. Soon after landing, the wheels sank into the snow almost to the axles, so that the plane almost turned over. How do we get out of here?! Several other vehicles were already in place with a broken undercarriage, caught in snow-covered craters from the explosions. Our plane was quickly unloaded, and I got a fuel tanker and leaked enough gas that it was enough for the return flight. Suddenly, a crowd of fleeing soldiers in a panic tried to storm our plane to get out of the Pocket. With pistols, we could still hold them back. Then we invited several seriously injured people with a medical orderly and the crew of the

broken plane. Then we rolled to the start. I let the air gunner go forward to identify possible shell craters. Suddenly we were attacked by Russian fighters. One burst of shells passed 50 meters in front of us, Ivan did not calculate. This was our salvation! At the start, I first gave full throttle for a while, slowing down the landing gear, then the plane barely started moving. I moved slowly down the slightly curved surface. I tried to lift the plane, but it barely broke away from the snow.[34]

The plane narrowly avoided a crash on take-off, and then miraculously missed the wires of a high-voltage power line. But its pilot still managed to take off safely, and then immediately disappeared into the low-hanging clouds that protected them from the Russian fighters waiting around. As a result, the bomber reached its air base. Another plane, He 111 H-6 W.Nr. 7360 '1G+HU' Oberleutnant Johann Herzog, crashed on take-off from Novocherkassk. Its entire crew of five was killed.

The transport planes' missions from I./FKG 50 also ended in another failure. During the flight to Stalingrad He 177 A-1 W.Nr. 15232 'E8+FK' (pilot Oberleutnant Schpohr) went missing immediately after dropping 'food bombs'. Two more 'Greif' failed to discharge their goods and turned back. In general, I./FKG 50 was not able to make a significant contribution to the supply of the fortress, but it suffered heavy losses. Following the attack by a Soviet fighter, Fw 200 C-4 W.Nr. 0179 'GC+SH' was able to fly to the German territory and made an emergency landing in the area of Voroshilovgrad. Its damage was estimated at 40 per cent, and the aircraft was later written off. In addition, another supposedly 'faulty' Ju 86 W.Nr. 4045 was destroyed by its crew in Salsk.

On 24 January, the Russians entered Gumrak. There they captured another 'cemetery' of 120 aircraft of various types, 3,200 vehicles, several ammunition depots and two hospitals packed with wounded soldiers of the 6th Army. The railway station had seven locomotives and two trains.

On this day, only forty transport planes were recorded as dropping cargo by parachute. Among them again were bombers from KG 27. In the area of Stalingrad, they came under heavy anti-aircraft fire. He 111 H-16 W.Nr. 8220 '1G+BS' from 8./KG 27 was badly damaged, which had a direct hit that tore off two-thirds of the rudder and damaged the right engine.

---

34 Boelcke Archiv.

Despite this, the pilot of Feldwebel Frank was able to keep the plane in the air for 2½ hours on one engine and safely land in Novocherkassk; damage to the aircraft was estimated at 40 per cent, but even in this condition, the He 111 could continue to fly! He 111 H-16 W.Nr. 8192 '1G+FT' of 9./KG 27 was also damaged by anti-aircraft fire. Pilot Oberleutnant Günther Schuldt was wounded in the elbow by a Soviet shell. Navigator and radio operator managed to take control of the plane, and blindly flew it to German territory and made a night emergency landing; 22-year-old Schuldt was sent to a hospital in Taganrog (Lazarett Lw 7/IV). However, the young man was disappointed and deeply depressed by his 'military fate'. He did not want to go home crippled and at 16.15 on 28 January shot himself… Although many soldiers of the 6th Army could only envy his 'military fate'.

After Gumrak's takeover, the last runway for transport planes was the 'Stalingradskij' airfield. It was a small area on the western edge of the city, on which the snow was somehow tamped down. The landing lights consisted of several dim lamps. Only the bravest and most experienced crews could land there. However, at least twelve aircraft from KG 27 managed to land at Stalingradskij before it was captured by the Soviets.

On 25 January, the Don front finally pushed the remnants of the 6th Army to the western outskirts of Stalingrad. The first units of the 6th Army began to surrender. In the evening, the remnants of the 297th infantry division and the 20th Romanian infantry division, led by generals Drebber and Dimitriu, as well as the 6th signal regiment, surrendered. In total, by this time the Soviets had already captured 17,500 soldiers, and along the way released 2,500 Red Army men from German captivity. But the Russians still suffered heavy losses from the 6th Army, which was fighting back with its last strength. From 20 to 25 January, the Don front lost another 16,000 soldiers killed and wounded, and another 519 died of frostbite.

On this day, a group of three German soldiers, escorted by Red Army men, appeared at the NKVD post near the Karpovskaya railway station. The group was heading west towards Kalach. One of the employees of the Soviet security service asked the Red Army men: 'Where are you taking the prisoners?' There was only a strange muttering in response. When checking, it turned out that the 'escort men' were Germans disguised in Red Army uniforms, and the 'prisoners' were officers of the staff of 9. Flak-Division Luftwaffe and its commander, Oberstleutnant Richard Haizmann! Former division commander General Wolfgang Pickert left Stalingrad in mid-January on his personal plane to meet Erhard Milch. He never returned, saying that he 'could not make a landing'. Haizmann assumed command, along the way devising a thorough escape plan from the Pocket. Under the guise of a 'group of prisoners', he managed to walk 35 km in the direction of Kalach, from where Haizmann was going to go further in the direction of Rostov-on-Don.[35]

Air traffic continued to decline rapidly. The Russians recorded a flight of sixty-six transport planes to Stalingrad. But not all of them were able to complete their missions. According to the report of a pilot of 2./KG 27:

> On January 25, the weather improved. I received orders to drop supplies along with four other aircraft in a completely clear sky over the captured city. So, in bright sunlight and without fighter cover, we flew south-east of Stalingrad, over a wide swampy area, riddled with many waters of the Volga, we were going to descend to the height of the drop. But there we were met by concentrated anti-aircraft fire, so that we had to turn away. Suddenly we were attacked by a chain of Russian fighters. We again went on the defensive in close formation, as we too were out of the anti-aircraft fire zone. As a result of our strong opposition, the Russians did not hesitate to allow us to fly home. It became clear that day operations here in the Stalingrad area were no longer possible.[36]

On this day, 5 He 177 A-1s from I./FKG 50 again appeared over Stalingrad, but this time in the role of bombers. Together with twelve Ju 88A from I./KG 51, they conducted the first air attack on Soviet positions in the Pitomnik area, dropping 128 SD50 fragmentation bombs on them.

The culmination of the brutal battle came on 26 January. At 10:00 (Moscow time), the 51st Guards rifle division, which had previously captured Pitomnik and then Gumrak, broke into Stalingrad and joined with units of the Russian 62nd army near the village of Krasnyi Oktyabr. The Pocket was split into two isolated parts. German soldiers spontaneously surrendered in droves, but many fanatics continued to offer fierce resistance.

Due to bad weather, the last battles in the area of Stalingrad took place almost without the participation of aircraft. German planes continued to

---

35 Records show that the only German soldier who managed to walk through the ring of the blockade and reach the positions of the German troops was an Unteroffizier from 9. Flak-Division

36 Boelcke Archiv.

drop cargo containers at night. In one of these sorties a Ju 86 W.Nr. 0252 piloted by Feldwebel A. Mueller was lost. This was the last combat loss of this type of aircraft in the area of Stalingrad. On 31 January another such plane (W.Nr. 0208) was inactivated at the Taganrog airfield, where it remained for seven months until 31 August. After the capture of the city by Soviet troops, it was included in the list of captured trophies. This old bomber had been produced in Germany since 1936, a total of 390 units were made. Of these, 128 were exported (Spain, Sweden, Portugal, Chile, Hungary). At Stalingrad, forty-six Ju 86s from KGr.zbV 21 and KGr.zbV 21 were lost, which became the 'swan song' of this aircraft.

On the afternoon of 29 January, the last combat loss of a Soviet aircraft in the battle of Stalingrad was recorded. An starshina Demidov's Il-2 was shot down by anti-aircraft fire over the northern part of the city. According to Soviet information, the pilot flew the burning plane to a German dugout and blew it up. On the same day, Fw 200 C-3 W.Nr. 0025 'F8+FW' at the airport of Zaporizhia was damaged in a Soviet air raid. Its damage was estimated at first at 15 per cent, then at 25 per cent, but later it was simply written off.

During 30 January, the Russians recorded seventy-six transport planes flying over Stalingrad, including sixty at night. The report of the pilot from 2./KG 27:

> In the city, the places of cargo dumping were marked by bonfires. Not far from the target, we reduced engine power and began to descend in a gliding flight. The acoustic-controlled Russian anti-aircraft searchlights swung wildly back and forth, never taking their eyes off us. At the destination, containers with food were dropped from a height of about 50 meters, as well as boxes with food from the entrance hatch. What may have fallen into Ivan's hands is unknown. In 'gratitude', he rewarded us with a hell of a firework display. However, we continued to return safely. In the last actions we saw no longer a military sense, but, at most, a friendly service for valiant fighters in a cruel city.[37]

Individual German soldiers continued to try to escape from the Pocket. So, from the central part of the city at 11.30, a Soviet truck with a closed body passed through the positions of the 57th Army. Its cabin was covered with

---

37 Boelcke Archiv.

metal sheets. The Russian soldiers did not shoot at it, thinking it was their own. Half an hour later, in the area of the Sklyarov farm, this truck was detained by Soviet patrols. It contained twelve Wehrmacht Unteroffiziere trying to drive in a westerly direction.

On this day, Generaloberst Paulus sent a congratulatory telegram to the Führer on the occasion of the coming to power of the Nazis (the main holiday of the Third Reich). In it, he loyally reported that 'the swastika flag is still flying over Stalingrad'. In response, a grateful Hitler sent a radio message awarding the title Generalfeldmarschall to Paulus. Unknown historical fact: on the same day (probably with the Führer's approval), Paulus officially surrendered command of the 6th Army to the commander of the 71st infantry division, Generalmajor Roske. Thus, Hitler legally removed Paulus from responsibility for the future fate of the remaining troops and the likely capitulation. According to the popular version, the assignment of the title Generalfeldmarschall was a direct hint of suicide. But given the new facts we have found, we can assume that Hitler did not want Paulus to commit suicide, but wanted to evacuate him from Stalingrad. According to German military traditions, Generalfeldmarschall could no longer lead a separate army. Therefore, he could leave the Pocket with a clear conscience for a new post.

But the evacuation of Paulus from Stalingrad at that time was difficult to implement. Only one German aircraft – the Ar 232 – could perform such a mission, and such aircraft were at the disposal of Luftflotte 4 and Sonderstab Gen.Feldm.Milch. Ar 232, together with a pair of Me 323 D, passed combat tests on the Eastern front. There is no information that these aircraft flew in Festung, probably they delivered goods to the advanced Luftwaffe airfields.

But there probably wasn't enough time to prepare for an extremely risky mission. By the evening of 30 January, the Russians had reached the vicinity of the Ispolkom (Stalingrad regional Executive Committee)[38] building, in the basement of which was the headquarters of the 6th Army.

On the night of 31 January, the Russians observed fifteen planes dropping cargo containers in the vicinity of Stalingrad Tractor Plant. The effectiveness of this operation was hardly high, but the Germans lost two of their aircraft. Fw 200 C-3 W.Nr. 0034 'F8+GW' was shot down by fire from the ground at a low altitude. All six crew members of the Oberfeldwebel Karl Wittman were reported missing. Ju 290 V2 W.Nr. 90-0008 was damaged and crashed during an emergency landing in Kharkov.

---

38 Administration of the Stalingrad region

In the morning, the Ispolkom building, which was the headquarters of the 6th Army, was surrounded by units of the 38th motorized rifle brigade Colonel Burmakov. After brief negotiations at 10.00 (Moscow time), a group of Soviet officers led by the chief of staff of the 64th Army, Major General I.A. Laskin, entered the basement where Generalfeldmarschall Paulus was located and arrested him.[39]

During 1 February, the Russians recorded a flight of twenty-four transport planes in the area of Stalingrad. They were mostly He 111 from KG 55. The pilots noted that the entire southern part of Stalingrad was plunged into darkness, while from the northern part of the destroyed city, surviving groups of German soldiers were still giving light signals to aircraft to drop supplies. Most of the containers were dropped on the southern edge of the Stalingrad Tractor Plant.

On this day, the northern group of the 6th Army still offered fierce resistance. The Soviets managed to occupy only a few ruins, with the 62nd and 65th armies losing about 800 men killed and wounded. The defense in the area of Stalingrad Tractor Plant was very powerful, based on a network of strongpoints, adapted to a long circular defense. And the Germans could stay there for another couple of weeks (if they continued to be supplied by air). But on 2 February, the remaining German units also capitulated. 'One of the most selected and equipped armies of invaders and enslavers ended its historical path with an inglorious defeat', – the journal of military operations of the Russian Don front reported triumphantly. During 1 and 2 February, 45,000 German soldiers (including twenty-four generals) surrendered.

On the afternoon of 3 February, one He 111 from 9./KG 27 flew near Stalingrad. Its pilot, E. Kamm, wrote:

> 100 meters below the cloud cover, we went off course and did not have time to orientate ourselves again until we found traces of a shipwreck in the frozen Volga. Now we were flying about 100 meters above the Volga in a south-westerly direction to Stalingrad. On the ice of the Volga (it was from 1 to 2 km wide),

---

39 According to the popular version, the last refuge of Paulus and his staff was the basement of the Central'nyi Univermag (department store). This information is given in the memoirs of his adjutant Wilhelm Adam, as well as in Soviet memoirs. There is even a sign on the preserved Univermag building stating that 'Paulus was captured here'. But according to the official act of the Don front about the capture of Paulus, it happened in the Ispolkom building, which was very similar to the Univermag. It was located in the next block, but has not been preserved to this day.

the replenishment of Russian armies with tanks and trucks 40 km long was moving! In parallel, the remnants of the 6th Army trudged in the other direction. They, too, were stretched out for many kilometers in this miserable campaign. The food we left behind will be appropriated by the Russians. We received the first return fire of anti-aircraft guns only in Stalingrad. The western bank of the Volga is very steep and about 200 meters high. So, the anti-aircraft gunners had to shoot from above down, which was our happiness.

This flight was a kind of 'farewell message' from the Luftwaffe to the soldiers of the 6th Army.

Stalingrad became one of the main crimes of the Nazis against the German armed forces. Hitler had previously sacrificed German soldiers to his madness, but it was the senseless death of the 6th Army that clearly showed the murderous nature of the Führer to many Germans who had been deceived by the Nazis.

From the point of view of strategy, this sacrifice was absolutely useless. Contrary to the popular myth that the 6th Army had shackled large Russian forces and the Soviets had suffered heavy losses (and this was indeed the case, only from 10 to 30 January the losses of the Don front amounted to 57,000 soldiers), the Stalingrad Pocket defense did not have any serious impact on the course of hostilities on the Eastern front. If the 6th Army had capitulated on 8 January, when the situation was already hopeless, many German soldiers would still have had a chance to survive. The fact is that due to snow drifts and interruptions in the operation of railway transport, the liberated Soviet troops could not be quickly transferred from the Stalingrad area. This assumption is confirmed by the fact that after the final surrender of the last German defenders of Stalingrad (2 February), Soviet units arrived at other parts of the front only by the end of February. But by then the Wehrmacht had already overcome the crisis, and the Army Group 'South' had launched a counter-offensive. As for the losses, according to a recent article by President Putin the Soviet army lost about half a million people in the battle of Rzhev alone. It is important to emphasize that for the bloody Stalinist regime, the human lives of Soviet people meant nothing, and the incompetent Soviet generals-butchers were ready to fight to the last Russian soldier.

But the fanatical defense and senseless postponement of the inevitable capitulation meant that those German soldiers who had miraculously survived were so exhausted that they could not survive the harsh Stalinist captivity. Most of them died of typhus fever and never returned home…

The following general statistics sum up the organization of the air bridge in Stalingrad Pocket. From 24 November 1942 to 2 February 1943, the Luftwaffe carried out 4,691 sorties to supply the fortress. A total of 8,250 tons of cargo were delivered to Stalingrad, including 4,000 tons of food rations, 1,562 tons of ammunition and 1,736 cubic meters of fuel. The average figure, therefore, was 138 tons per day; 24,760 wounded and 5,150 people who held various positions and technical specialists were evacuated from the Pocket by air. Only 30,000 people, that is almost 15 per cent of the number surrounded.

The total losses of the Luftwaffe during maintenance of the air bridge comprised 409 aircraft. Of these, 234 aircraft were irretrievable losses and 175 were damaged by more than 25 per cent on the German scale. The figure common in historical literature that says more than 1,100 transport planes crew members died, went missing and were captured is most likely greatly exaggerated. But in any case, many experienced pilots and flight school instructors were killed and captured. Thus, although the losses of the transport fleet were not as huge as many authors have claimed, we must admit that the German transport aircraft could not afford such a catastrophic defeat.

When assessing the defeat of the Luftwaffe, it is necessary to keep in mind the losses of the Kampfgeschwader, although they were significantly lower. For example, I./KG 100 lost eight aircraft and four crew during the supply operation. However, the involvement of bombers to perform transport operations, a successful measure in terms of tactics, led to serious strategic consequences. The fact is that hundreds of bombers and their experienced crews not only suffered losses, but, most importantly, could not perform their direct function for a long time. Which, of course, had a disastrous delayed effect for the Luftwaffe as a whole.

Chapter 5

The 'Giant'

'…and you will think that there are no Germans there.'

On 8 November 1942, the Allies launched operation 'Torch' to land British and American troops in Morocco and Algeria. The goal of the new military campaign was to destroy the Axis powers' positions in North Africa with simultaneous offensives from the west and east. The Allied command believed that the Germans would have great difficulties in supplying troops in the event of long operations and would not be able to transfer the necessary reinforcements to Africa in a short time. Their conclusions were also supported by the important fact that at this time the Wehrmacht was engaged in fierce fighting in the Volga, Caucasus and Moscow regions. However, they miscalculated and underestimate the internal reserves of the Third Reich. In addition, the Allies did not know that the Luftwaffe already had a flotilla of huge Me 323 transport planes.

Back in the fall of 1941, Professor Willy Messerschmitt proposed to equip the Me 321 cargo glider with its own engines to finally solve the problem of towing it. As the need for new transport aircraft at the front had become obvious by this point, the idea was quickly approved by RLM technical management (Techniques Amt). In early 1942, the designers began work. The first prototype of the Me 323 V1, converted from the Me 321 B glider, flew on 20 January. It was powered by four engines, had a conventional glider landing gear (jettisonable on take-off) and landed on four extendable skids. In March, testing of the Me 323 V2 with six Gnome-Rhone 14N/1140 engines began. A special 10-wheel bogie of complex design was already developed for it, consisting of two pairs of small and three pairs of large wheels, which formed two five-wheeled tandems located on both sides of the fuselage. Thanks to this, the aircraft could be used on unprepared airfields. The results of the first flights were so successful that, without waiting for their completion, RLM ordered a pilot series of ten aircraft under the designation Me 323 D-0. Six of them remained at the disposal of the Messerschmitt company for further testing and modifications, and four were transferred to unidentified transport squadrons for front-line testing. Their results were also recognized as satisfactory, and in the summer of 1942, mass production began of the Me 323 D-1 version, which corresponded to the Me 323 V3 prototype.

The armament of the first Me 323 D series consisted of two MG 15 machine guns located in the upper part of the fuselage above the loading hatch and two MG 15s in the upper part of the fuselage at the rear edges of the wings. In the Me 323 D-6 modification, two additional MG 131s were installed above the radio operator cabin, one facing forward and the other facing back. In the side windows of the fuselage, there were fasteners that provided the ability for transported troops to fire their own MG 4 if necessary. Loading and unloading was carried out according to a specially developed method, which was monitored by one of the crew members. By monitoring the ramp sensors in the hull, he controlled the uniformity of load distribution, preventing uneven pressure on the bottom. Piece loads, such as crates and barrels, were loaded through the side doors and evenly spread out behind the main load. It was important to distribute the load balance correctly so that it did not affect the plane's alignment during the flight. After placement, the cargo was secured with special devices to prevent it from sliding and shifting to the tail during take-off. The cargo compartment of the aircraft became slightly smaller than that of the airframe, and the load capacity was reduced to 10–12 tons. It was no longer able to transport tanks, but it could still take on board an 88 mm anti-aircraft gun with a tractor or a heavy truck with a trailer. The aircraft could carry fifty-two barrels of fuel, or 8,700 standard loaves of bread, or 120 soldiers – or sixty wounded on stretchers (instead of 200 and 100 on the Me 321, respectively).

In 1942, twenty-six 'Giants' were manufactured. In August, the first transport aviation group was formed, which received the Me 323 – I./KGzbV 323. Its first commander was Major Gunter Maus. Until 1 November, the unit underwent combat training at the Leipheim airfield. The group then moved to the Eleusis airfield in Greece, from which it made several test transport flights to the island of Crete.

Meanwhile, in October 1942, the entire special purpose Geschwader (KGzbV 323) was formed under the command of Oberstleutnant Gustaw Damm, which included II./KGzbV 323 under the command of Oberstleutnant Werner Stefan. Each Gruppe was to have three Staffel of six aircraft (eighteen Me 323 in total), and the total staff strength of the Geschwader was fifty-four aircraft. If the 'Giants' had been sent to Stalingrad, the 6th Army would have received much more cargo and the Festung would have been able to withstand Soviet attacks much longer. But the first serious operation in which six-engine monsters took part was the supply of German troops in Tunisia.

Hitler ordered the immediate occupation of southern France and simultaneously landed troops in the French colony of Tunis in order to establish a strong foothold there. Bombardment groups and other aviation units were urgently transferred to the Mediterranean Sea. However, the most impressive, and even surprising, achievement of the Luftwaffe was the increase in their transport fleet.

The creation and long-term retention of a beachhead in Tunisia was simply impossible without an air bridge, because sea communications were constantly attacked by the British fleet. As a result, the number of transport planes involved in this theater increased from 205 available in early November 1942 to 673 by March 1943. By the end of 9 November, 3,000 soldiers had been airlifted to Tunisia. By 10 November, these troops had established a beachhead and defensive perimeter. Within two weeks, the German units here already numbered 11,000 men. Heavy equipment, vehicles, armored personnel carriers and artillery, including new heavy 'Tiger' tanks arrived in Tunisia by sea.

KGzbV 323 played a major role in creating the bridgehead. Each 'Giant' was able to deliver 12 tons of cargo to Africa in one mission. Thus, the total load capacity of the aviation group of eighteen Me 323s was 216 tons of cargo. On 8 November, I./KGzbV 323 relocated to Lecce, Italy, where it began regular flights to Bizerta. Later, 'Giants' operated from air bases in Palermo and Naples. Initially, the Me 323 carried mainly military equipment: 8.8 cm flak, howitzers, tractors, trucks and armored personnel carriers. 'Competitors' Ju 52 at this time delivered fuel and ammunition to the beachhead. On 10 November 1942, KGzbV 323 suffered its first combat loss when Me 323 D-1 W.Nr. 1107 was destroyed at El Aouina airfield (Tunisia) during a raid by British Beaufighters from the 272nd Sqdn. RAF.

On 22 November, I./KGzbV 323 suffered its first operational loss. Me 323 D-1 W.Nr. 1103 was damaged while landing at the airport of Piacenza, sustaining 60 per cent damage and was later written off. On 23 November, Me 323 D-1 W.Nr. 1110 was heavily damaged at Bizerta airfield during an Allied air raid (80 per cent damage).

Let's describe how a typical flight to Africa of the crew of Oberleutnant E. Peter took place on the morning of 26 November. Me 323 D 'DT+IG' took off from Naples with the tank destroyer 'Marder' on board (the weight of this self-propelled gun was 11 tons). After two hours of flying over the sea, the 'Giant' landed in Bizerta. After unloading, 4 tons of empty gasoline barrels were placed in the cargo compartment, after which, at 13.05, Me 323 set off on its return journey. However, soon after take-off, the pitch of the propeller of number 5 engine failed, and then, because of overheating, it caught fire. Me 323 D turned back to Bizerta. There, the engine was extinguished, and the screw was removed from it. At 15.15, the transport took off on five engines and again headed for Italy. An hour later, the DT+IG landed safely in Sicily. On the same day, the crew of Oberleutnant E. Peter had taken the 'Giant' to the main base of I./KGzbV 323 in Lecce, where the aircraft was repaired and put back into service. By the way, experienced pilots sometimes managed to lift the Me 323 into the air with four engines, but this procedure was very risky.

On 2 December Me 323 D-1 W.Nr. 1203 made an emergency landing due to technical reasons in the area of Termoli in Italy. The huge plane made a capotage (overturn) and was completely destroyed. At the same time, three crew members; five were injured. From 1 November to 10 December, I./KGzbV 323 performed eighty-two transport flights and transported 865 tons of cargo. During this period, four aircraft were lost.

Soon an additional 167 Ju 52/3m arrived from the Eastern front to help the 'Giants'. They entered the newly formed temporary air groups KGr. zbV 'Wittschok', KGr.zbV 'Frankfurt', KGr.zbVS 7, KGr.zbVS 11 и KGr. zbVS 13. The 'S' in the designations meant school (Schule), these units were created from aircraft and personnel of training units. It was only after arriving at the Assembly area that the pilots first met the commanders of their Gruppe and Staffeln. Although these crews were very brave and their morale was very high, they naturally had no operational experience or appropriate qualifications. For this reason, each Gruppe included one Staffel consisting of experienced pilots.[1]

However, these improvised units did not have long to fly over the warm waters of the Mediterranean sea. According to the saying, 'It never rains but it pours', on 23 November, the 6th Army was surrounded in Stalingrad, and there, too, it was urgently necessary to create an air bridge. Therefore, on 26 November, 150 newly arrived Ju 52s were sent to Luftflotte 4. At the same time, another problem arose. The Rommel army in Libya was

1 Pegg M. Transporter Volume Two: Luftwaffe Transport Units 1943-1945. Luftwaffe Colours. – Classic Publications, 2008. p. 98.

retreating so rapidly to the west that it was beyond the range of the Ju 52s that supplied it from Crete. Soon after 20 November, all aviation groups were urgently relocated to southern Italy and Sicily, from where they began to fly to the Cabes and Castel Benito airfields, located on both sides of the border between Tunisia and Libya.

Meanwhile, an attempt by the Allies to capture Tunisia with one decisive blow and throw German troops into the sea failed. On 12 December, the Americans and British launched an offensive, but were stopped in the course of persistent fighting. Then the Germans launched a counteroffensive and drove the enemy back to their original positions. As a result, by 26 December the front line was stabilized, and the fighting took a positional character. And with this favorable result for the Germans, there was a lot of credit to transport aircraft and especially aircraft from KGzbV 323. The Allies were shocked when they registered that a line of defense had appeared from scratch in just a few days, and even with tanks, rocket-propelled mortars and anti-aircraft guns. Some even had a saying about it: 'You can land on a desert island and you will think that there are no Germans there. But before you can get around it, you will find German positions there.' The Allies at first did not even suspect the existence of the Luftwaffe's huge transport planes, capable of transporting even heavy guns and armored personnel carriers. In early January, four-engine Ju 90 and Ju 290 aircraft joined flights to Tunisia, from which was formed, on 3 January, a separate transport Staffel – LTSt. 290 (from April 22-Tr. Fl.St. 5).

The tactics of using transport planes in this theater of war had particular characteristics. During flights over the Mediterranean, Ju 52s usually went without fighter cover in groups of fifty to sixty aircraft, in order to conduct concentrated defensive fire in the event of an attack. Flights were often practised at low altitude directly above the water, so the group was less visible at a long distance and could not be detected by radar. Most often, such tactics helped to avoid losses, but the proximity of enemy air bases soon had an effect.

Transport planes were increasingly subjected to attacks, both during flight and on the ground. For example, on 9 December, a group of thirty to thirty-five Ju 52s took off from Castel Benito airfield. On board one of them, part of the transport squadron Fliegerkorps X, was flight engineer Hermann Rahm. The group 'Aunt Ju's took a course for the Trapani airfield in Sicily and flew at an altitude of about 30 meters, accompanied by two Bf 110s and two Ju 88s. Between the coast of Tunis and the island of Lampedusa, the group was suddenly attacked by British fighters. According to Rahm, two or three Ju 52/3m were shot down, including the one he was in. The plane caught fire and fell into the sea. Rahm and the pilot of the plane managed to escape. Two days later, the pilots, who were floating on an inflatable raft, were picked up by a British submarine. German crews who fought in the Mediterranean had a better chance of survival than their Luftflotte 4 colleagues who were flying over the snow-covered Russian expanses in the same days. Here, at least, they could not die from the cold, and if they were captured, they were guaranteed humane treatment and medical care.[2]

Since arriving in the Mediterranean, the Staffel in which Rahm served had been delivering spare parts, fuel and other supplies to El Agheila, in Libya. However, all efforts were useless and on 16 December, German troops left this Libyan city. On 23 January 1943, the British 8th Army captured Tripoli and reached the Tunisian border on 4 February. From then on, only one air bridge operated instead of two.

Every day about 100 aircraft, in small groups accompanied by Bf 109 or Bf 110 fighters, flew over the sea in both directions. Whereas in Stalingrad the main airfield that hosted the Ju 52 and their colleagues was Pitomnik, here the air bases at Bizerta and El Aouina became such for a few months. After unloading cargo, the wounded were loaded into the planes, but unlike their comrades from the 6th Army, who were suffering from the cold and icy wind on a snow-covered field, their stretchers lay on the much warmer, brown African sand.

German airfields were periodically subjected to air attacks, often resulting in large losses of aircraft. The most successful for the Allies was the American bombing of the El Aouina air base. On 18 January, thirteen B-17 from 97.BG and thirty-three P-38s from 1. FG. completely destroyed twenty-three Ju 52/3m at once. Also during the American attack, fifteen transport planes were severely damaged, and thirteen aircraft were lightly damaged. Almost at the same time, a similar raid on the Zverevo air base was made by the Russians. As described above, the Soviet bombers managed to destroy fourteen transport planes, and another twenty were seriously damaged. Thus, in one day, the Allies in different places on different continents deprived the Luftwaffe of seventy Ju 52 transport aircraft.

---

2 Pegg M. Transporter Volume One: Luftwaffe Transport Units 1937–1943. Luftwaffe Colours. – Classic Publications, 2007. p. 99.

But the loss of the 'Giants' for a long time remained at a low level. On 6 January, the Me 323 D-1 W.Nr. 1213 was damaged (50 per cent) in a hard landing at Pomigliano airfield. Obviously, this aircraft was repaired and put back into operation. On 11 January, Me 323 D-1 W.Nr. 1111 'RD+QK' was shot down over the Mediterranean sea by an American P-38J fighter from the 14th FG (pilot – Lieutenant V. Moor). Nine crew members and sixteen passengers – Wehrmacht soldiers – were killed; interestingly, an American pilot reported that he had shot down a 'six-engine Italian flying boat'. On 15 January, the Me 323 D-1 W.Nr. 1211 was shot down over the Mediterranean by a P-38J fighter from the same 14th FG. This time the Lightning pilot, Lieutenant Schipman, reported that he had shot down a 'six-engine transport plane of unknown type'. Nine crew members and three passengers were killed.

Meanwhile, on 2 February, the remnants of German troops on the Volga surrendered, which allowed the release of the transport aircraft forces involved there and would transfer some of the Ju 52s to the Mediterranean. Responsibility for the air bridge to Tunis lay with the Air transport command 'Mediterranean sea'(LufttransportFührer 'Mittelmeer'), which had its headquarters in Rome. In early 1943, it was led by Oberst Rudolf Stark, who was replaced in February by Generalmajor Ulrich Buhgoltz, who had previously commanded KGr.zbV 3 in southern Russia.[3]

In February, the fighting in this theater of operations was relatively successful for the Germans. On 30 January, the German 21st Panzer division and three Italian divisions from 5th Panzer Army Generaloberst von Arnim went on the offensive and on 18 February, recaptured Sbeitla, only recently occupied by the Allies. At the same time, in the south, the troops under Generalfeldmarschall Rommel dug in on the fortified 'Maret' line. On 6 March, Rommel launched an offensive against the 8th British Army, which ended in failure. After that, the 'Desert Fox' fell into pessimism and rightly considered further defense pointless. On the night of 9 March, Rommel flew to the Führerhauptquartier Werwolf in Vinnytsia (Ukraine), where he tried to convince Hitler of the need to immediately evacuate troops from Africa to Europe; the Führer refused to do so. Just as in the case of Stalingrad, he believed that the bridgehead in Africa should be defended to the last possible opportunity, 'shackling' significant enemy forces there and stalling for time. Rommel was ordered not to return to his troops, but to 'rest a little' and to go for treatment.

---

3 Pegg M. Transporter Volume One: Luftwaffe Transport Units 1937-1943. Luftwaffe Colours. – Classic Publications, 2007. p. 99.

During February, I./KGzbV 323 suffered only two losses. On 10 February the Me 323 D-1 W.Nr. 1214 was damaged in an accident. Three crew members were killed and four others were injured. On 14 February, Me 323 D-1 W.Nr. 1139 'RF+XM' was shot down over the sea by flight gunners of an American B-25 Mitchell bomber from the 310th BG. 'Giant' made an emergency landing on the water, and the crew moved to a lifeboat. The pilots were soon rescued by a Do 24 flying boat.[4]

Often the crews of Ju 52 and Me 323, despite their weak weapons, successfully repelled the attacks of enemy fighters. For example, on the night of 12–13 February, a Ju 52/3m from KGr.zbV 'Frankfurt' was attacked by a British night fighter, which made three attacks. However, the flight gunner managed to shoot it down, and the transport airplane reached the airfield safely. According to English data, a Mosquito from the 23rd Sqdn. RAF was shot down, which had taken off from the Malta airfield at 21.50 and went missing along with its crew (Flight Sergeant Clunes and Sergeant Marston). In another episode, when two Me 323 Ss were returning to Italy from Tunisia, they were attacked by an American P-38 Lightning long-range fighter. However, it was shot down by coordinated fire from two flight gunners of one of their planes.

In March, six 'Giants' were lost, with operational losses still equal to combat losses. On 1 March, Me 323 D-1 W.Nr. 1208 crashed at Trapani airfield; twelve passengers were killed and three pilots were injured. On 10 March, during an Allied air raid on an airfield in Tunisia, Me 323 D-1 W.Nr. 1205 and Me 323 D-2 W.Nr. 1231 were destroyed; on 20 March, Me 323 D-2 W.Nr. 1234 was shot down by fighters off the east coast of the island of Sardinia. Two days later, due to engine failure, the Me 323 D-1 W.Nr. 1222 crashed during take-off from the airfield at El Aouina in Tunisia; three crew members were killed. On 26 March, the Me 323 D-1 W.Nr. 1131 crashed during take-off from the same airfield; three pilots were killed and seven were injured. On 5 March, LTSt. 290 also suffered its first loss. During the night, a Ju 290 A-1 W.Nr. 0154 'J4+AH', which had just entered service, was damaged when landing at Sidi Ahmed airfield. But its crew, led by Hauptmann Kurt Fogel, was not injured.[5]

---

4 II./KGzbV 323 at this time was engaged in transport operations in the rear areas of the Third Reich, although it has not been possible to establish where exactly they flew. For example, on 15 February the Me 323 D-1 W.Nr. 1200 from this group was damaged on landing at the airfield of Lemberg (Lvov) in western Ukraine.

5 The plane was never repaired, and on 1 May, after the capture of Tunis, it fell as a trophy to the Allies.

From 23 February to 28 March, I./KGzbV 323 operated 160 transport flights from Italy to north Africa (320 departures in total). Thus, the 'Giants' during this period suffered an average of one loss for every fifty-three sorties (one combat loss for 106 sorties, including losses on the ground). These figures clearly refute the popular myth of the 'vulnerability' and 'helplessness' of these huge transport planes against Allied aviation. At the end of March 1943, II./KGzbV 323, comprising twenty-three Me 323 D, finally arrived in Italy. At that time, the I./KGzbV 323 consisted of fifteen Me 323, and the total number of aircraft of Geschwader thus reached thirty-eight planes.

During the week from 30 March to 5 April, three more 'Giants' were lost due to technical reasons. On 30 March, a Me 323 D-1 W.Nr. 1130 'RF+XD' crashed while landing at Castelvetrano airfield in Italy; eight crew members were injured. On 1 April the Me 323 D-1 W.Nr. 1104 crashed during take-off from the airport of Vicenza; this time, two pilots were injured. On 5 April, a Me 323 D-1 W.Nr. 1125 crashed while landing at the same air base; three people were killed and eight were injured. Note that most often 'Giants' crashed during take-offs and landings. There are two possible explanations for this fact.

First, the aircraft was rushed into service (there was only 7½ months between the first tests to the beginning of combat use). This progressive design might have needed more thorough testing and troubleshooting.

Second, landing such a huge object, especially with cargo, was not easy even for experienced pilots. The slightest violations of the flight mode (including a sudden change in weather conditions) caused the aircraft to lift its nose or, conversely, lift its tail, or stall (reduction in the lift coefficient), and it was extremely difficult to restore normal mode. The power of the transport airplane engines was also insufficient. At the slightest deviations from the necessary parameters (for example, a strong cross-wind gust or a small roll), the handling tended to deteriorate, and the aircraft began to sway and stall. The situation was complicated by the low power of the engines, which did not allow the pilots to quickly compensate for the problems in piloting this aircraft. In short, flying on the 'Giants' was a real 'attraction' for the pilots, comparable to a ride on a roller coaster!

But in the course of operation, all these shortcomings were carefully recorded, studied, and then based on numerous reports of pilots, new instructions and recommendations for operation were compiled. As a result, the accident rate of Me 323 gradually decreased and until the end of operation of these 'monsters' was kept at an acceptable level.

Operation 'Flaks'

Until early April, despite some aircraft losses, the air bridge across the Mediterranean continued to operate successfully. Meanwhile, the Allies were preparing for a decisive offensive against the German-Italian bridgehead. In parallel, they were thinking of additional ways to undermine the resistance of Axis powers. The Americans and British carefully studied the traffic of German air transport and belatedly realized what an important role this intercontinental air bridge played. It was decided to focus the aviation efforts on destroying the Luftwaffe transport planes in the air, and on the ground, during attacks on its airfields in Africa and Italy. This Allied operation was codenamed 'Flaks'. For its implementation, long-range fighters (P-38 and others) were transferred to air bases in Algeria and in the part of Tunisia that had been recaptured from the Germans.

The air operation started on 5 April simultaneously with the beginning of the offensive of British troops on the position of Wadi Akarit and American troops in the sectors of Gafsa and Fonduk. The efforts of the RAF and USAF immediately produced significant results. On the first day, Lightnings (twenty P-38s from 96.FS, 82.FG and twenty-six P-38s from 1.FG) managed to intercept a large group of thirty-one Ju 52/3m. After the attack, the Americans recorded seventeen downed transport planes on their combat account (the most distinguished were Captain Welsh, Lieutenants M.E. Larson, J.W. Jorda, Shaw, Bancroft and Mackay, who scored two aerial victories each). In a combat account, Mackay also recorded personally shooting down a twin-engine aircraft, the type of which he identified as 'Fw 187' (in fact, it was a Bf 110 G from II./ZG 26). As a result of air combat over the sea, fourteen transport planes and several escort fighters were shot down. Another ten 'Aunt Ju' were destroyed on the ground as a result of air attacks by B-24 Liberator bombers against airfields. The Italians lost five Fiat G.12 and 2 SM. 82. another sixty-five aircraft were damaged. Thus, on the first day of Operation Flaks, ninety-four aircraft were put out of action. Among them was one 'Giant'. Me 323 D-1 W.Nr .1215, which was heavily damaged (45 per cent) during a raid by American B-17 bombers from 97.BG and 307.BG to air bases in Tunisia. The aircraft was not recommissioned and was later written off.

On 7 April, the second loss was sustained by LTSt. 290. However, as in the previous episode, it was an operational loss. Ju 290 A-1 W.Nr. 0152 was seriously damaged (50 per cent) when landing at Megrine airfield. Its crew, led by Major Gugo Viskandt, was not injured. The valuable four-engine aircraft could not be restored and was written off.

Luftwaffe and Regia Aeronautica suffered heavy losses on 10 April. The pilots of Lightnings from 71. FS were credited with eighteen downed Ju 52 and four MS. 200 (the most distinguished was Lieutenant Meldrum Sears who shot down four transport planes). The 82. FS account recorded twelve downed Ju 52s, and another transport airplane shot down the B-25 crew from 310.BG. In fact, five German Ju 52s and eleven Italian transport planes were shot down over the Mediterranean on this day.

On 11 April, the crew of the P-38s from 95.FS in the area of Cape Bon attacked a large group of aircraft flying on the Tunis–Palermo route without a fighter escort. American pilots reported twenty-two Ju 52s were shot down; Lieutenant W.J. Schildt and Lieutenant J. R. Meyer each won three aerial victories. In fact, eighteen Ju 52s were shot down.

For KGzbV 323, the first 'black day' in a series of disasters was 13 April. Me 323 D-1 W.Nr. 1215 (previously damaged during an air attack on 5 April) and Me 323 D-2 W.Nr. 1232 were destroyed at an airfield in Tunisia during an Allied air raid. In the same place, Me 323 D-1 W.Nr. 1132 crashed due to engine failure; II./KGzbV 323 lost three more 'Giants' – Me 323 D-1 W.Nr. 1116, Me 323 D-1 W.Nr. 1221 and Me 323 D-2 W.Nr. 1233 were destroyed during the raid of the American Flying Fortress from 97.BG and 307.BG to Castelvetrano airfield.

As noted above, the losses were also borne by the Italian transport aircraft, which also took part in the supply of Tunisia. For example, on 16 April, three Spitfires from 92 Sqdn. RAF, piloted by Flight Lieutenant Neville Frederick Duke,[6] Flying Officer Tomas W. Savage and Pilot Officer Gordon A. Wilson in the Cape Bon area, intercepted a group of eighteen SM.82s. According to British data, five SM.82s were shot down, while two victories were on the battle account of Lieutenant Duke. According to Italian data, however, only two SM.82s were shot down in this battle.

On the evening of 17 April, a large group of sixty-eight Ju 52s took off from Bizerta. They were returning to Sicily with German and Italian service personnel. The Ju 52s flew low over the sea in three groups, accompanied by

---

6 Flight Lieutenant Duke was the most successful British Ace in the Mediterranean. He began his service here in November 1941 on a Tomahawk Mk.IIB fighter. Here he fought for a long time against the Afrika Korps Rommel aviation in the Tobruk area, then was sent as an instructor to one of the aviation schools in Egypt. And in November 1942, Duke was appointed commander of 92 Sqdn., after which he went to Tunisia. Thus the crews of Italian transport planes faced experienced pilots.

Bf 109s, Bf 110s and Italian Macchi C. 202 fighters (twenty-one fighters in total). Due to the air convoy taking too long to prepare (because of fog at the start airfield), the British learned of the flight and prepared for it. Transport planes were detected by radar and intercepted over the sea. About 18.00, north of Cape Bon, the closing group was suddenly attacked by eighteen P-40 Tomahawk fighters. As a result, the battle ended in a real crush for the Luftwaffe. Of the sixty-eight Ju 52s, thirty-three were shot down and nine were damaged. The escort fighters also suffered serious losses – ten fighters (nine Bf 109s and one Bf 110). The rest of the transport planes turned back to Tunis. Damaged and burning planes landed directly on the beaches of the coast. And only six Ju 52s were able to eventually fly to Sicily.

However, the worst disaster occurred five days later. On 22 April, sixteen Me 323 from I. and II./KGzbV 323 went on another flight to Tunisia with a cargo of gasoline. The huge planes were flying in free formation at some distance from each other and low over the water. Traditionally, in the first half of the route, 'Giants' were accompanied by Italian Macchi C.202 Folgore fighters, then Bf 109s from II./JG 27, based in Tunisia, took over the watch for protection from Allied fighters. The flight went according to plan and nothing indicated impending trouble.

However, on the approach to the African coast near the island of Zembra, the course of transport planes unexpectedly crossed with a large group of friendly Ju 52s flying in the opposite direction. To avoid a collision, the pilots of the Me 323 began to maneuver and had to break the battle formation (given the size of the aircraft, it was quite large!). The pilots of the Bf 109 did not immediately understand the situation and slightly moved away from the 'Giants'. And it was at this most unfortunate moment that a large group of British, South African and American fighters suddenly appeared in the sky. These were P-40K from the 1st, 4th and 5th Sqdn. SAAF[7] and Spitfire from the 250th, 260th Sqdn. RAF and 31st FS.

In the ensuing air battle, fourteen giant transport planes were shot down:

- six from I./KGzbV 323: Me 323 D-1 W.Nr. 1126, W.Nr. 1134 and W.Nr. 1135; Me 323 D-2 W.Nr. 1242, W.Nr. 1248 and W.Nr. 1253;
- eight from II./KGzbV 323: Me 323 D-1 W.Nr. 1114, W.Nr. 1115 and W.Nr. 1124; Me 323 D-2 W.Nr. 1225, W.Nr. 1226, W.Nr. 1239, W.Nr. 1245 and W.Nr. 1254.

---

7 South African Air Force – the air force of South Africa.

According to the pilots of the escort fighters, because of the cargo of gasoline, huge planes simply exploded and flared up like torches. One 'Giant' immediately landed on the water; 119 crew members out of 138 were killed (only nineteen managed to escape). Among the dead was commander II./KGzbV 323 Oberstleutnant Werner Stefan, who was flying in one of the planes as a passenger, as well as two of the three Staffels commanders – Hauptmann Kube and Hauptmann Ruge. As a result, only two 'Giants' reached their destination. However, one of them for some reason (perhaps because of the damage) stayed in Africa for some time. Only one Me 323 managed to return to the Trapani airfield on the same day. At the same time, the planes took an incredible number of soldiers out of Tunisia – 340. Of these, 120 were placed lying between the engines inside the wings.

The day after the battle at Zembra island, General Eisenhower's headquarters published a special message, which read:

> Allied tactical aircraft patrolling part of the sea between Sicily and Africa, found a German compound of 20 large six - engine transport planes Me 323, accompanied by 40-50 fighters. Allied planes, without hesitation, attacked the enemy and within ten minutes destroyed all transport planes, and of the accompanying fighters shot down 8 German Me 109 and 2 Italian aircraft. Large transport planes transported troops and fuel from Sicily to Tunisia.

Aerial victories were recorded on the combat account of Allied pilots as follows: Major Peterson of the 5th Sqdn. SAAF and Lieutenant Green of the 4th Sqdn. SAAF were recorded to the combat account of 2.5 downed Me 323; Lieutenant Marshall of the 4th Sqdn. SAAF was recorded on the combat account with two Me 323 shot down and Lieutenant Weingartz of the 5th Sqdn. SAAF also with two Me 323s shot down. All of the above pilots flew the P-40K. In addition, two downed Me 323s were recorded on the combat accounts of Lieutenant Gilson and Lieutenant van der Veen of the 1st Sqdn. SAAF who flew the Spitfire. Pilots from the 250th Sqdn. and the 260th Sqdn. RAF recorded one downed Me 323 as a group victory, and the pilots of the American Spitfire from the 31st FS downed two Me 323s in the group. Note that by this point, the Allies were already aware of the existence of 'Giants'.

II./JG 27 lost only three Bf 109s during this battle. Two pilots were missing, and the third was picked up by the rescue service. While protecting transport planes, German fighters managed to shoot down one Spitfire and four P-40 Kittyhawks.

In total, between 18 and 24 April, while servicing the air bridge to Africa transport aircraft, the Luftwaffe lost sixty-four aircraft (fourteen Me 323 and fifty Ju 52) and 320 pilots. Along with it, 240 tons of supplies were lost. As for the massacre of the 'Giants', it is often cited as an example of the absolute defenselessness of these transport planes. However, it should be recalled that these aircraft flew between Europe and Africa from November 1942, that is five months, while incurring minimal losses. 'Giants' delivered 15,000 tons of cargo to the bridgehead, including ninety-six self-propelled artillery guns and armored personnel carriers, 616 guns, 360 trucks and tractors, and forty-two radio stations. It was largely thanks to KGzbV 323, which made 1,200 sorties (600 flights), that the Wehrmacht was able to quickly establish a line of defense there and hold it for a long time. The 22 April was a 'black day' for Luftwaffe transport aircraft due to a difficult set of circumstances, but each such disaster approximated the imminent collapse of the Third Reich.

The first months of operation showed that the combat survivability of the Me 323 was significantly higher than that of the Ju 52. The plane was very difficult to set on fire. Even after receiving numerous hits, it continued to fly. Suffice it to say that during one of the battles, the B-26 Marauder bomber fired all the ammunition (4,250 rounds!) from their own nine 12.7 mm machine guns (and the Americans fired incendiary and explosive bullets). Even after such a crushing attack, the Me 323 D still escaped heavy damage. 'Giant' was also generally more maintainable than 'Aunt Ju', although reviously it had seemed that the Ju 52 had no equal in the speed of recovery from severe damage. Due to all these features, the Me 323, already in Africa, was nicknamed 'Leukoplast-Bomber' by the Germans.

The total losses of transport aircraft by the Luftwaffe and Regia Aeronautica as a result of Operation Flaks from 5 to 24 April were 141 aircraft, including 123 Ju 52, fourteen Me 323 and four SM.82. Another sixteen aircraft were retired during the same period due to accidents and catastrophes. As a result, on 25 April, Reichsmarschall Göring ordered all transport flights to Tunisia to be conducted only at night. This led to a reduction in losses, but at the same time reduced the amount of cargo delivered to the bridgehead.

After the massacre in the area of the Zembra island, the remaining 'Giants', along with the surviving pilots from II./KGzbV 323, were transferred to the I./KGzbV 323 Geschwader, and II./KGzbV 323 went to be re-formed in Leipheim. Aircraft from I./KGzbV 323 continued to fly to North Africa, but in very limited numbers. Nevertheless, there were some losses. On 25 April, a Me 323 D-2 W.Nr. 1223 burned down at Castelvetrano airfield while refueling.

Meanwhile, on 22 April, the Allied ground forces launched a decisive offensive along the entire front. The Germans and Italians defended fiercely, but were gradually driven back to the sea. On the morning of 5 May, the sky over North Africa was clear. This did not bode well for the defenders of the bridgehead. At dawn, columns of American and British bombers appeared in the sky, dropping thousands of tons of bombs on the positions of Axis troops. Then there were clouds of ground-attack aircraft and fighters that made massive air attacks against trenches, artillery positions, tanks, roads and airfields. At 03.30 hours, two British divisions went on the offensive in the center of the front. By the middle of the day, they had broken through the main line of defense of the German troops, and in the evening they reached the city of Tunis. The bridgehead was split into two parts, formed the northern Pocket in the Bizerta area, and the southern Pocket on the Bon Peninsula.

During the first week of May, the remaining transport planes delivered only ammunition to Tunisia, while evacuating the wounded, as well as various Luftwaffe support units from Bizerte and from Cape Bon. To ensure the maximum number of flights, the crews flew almost daily with small breaks between departures. Moreover, the planes took on board a lot of cargo, often exceeding the maximum allowable take-off weight. Several remaining 'Giants' from I./KGzbV 323 also participated in the flights. On the way back, they took out hundreds of wounded and even prisoners.

While providing these transport operation, two very mysterious 'Giants' disasters occurred. On 6 May, Me 323 D-1 W.Nr. 1118 exploded in the air for an unknown reason and fell into the water near the Italian city of Ancona. The next day, Me 323 D-2 W.Nr. 1250 'C8+FN' also exploded in the air over one of the airfields in Tunisia. Most likely, these disasters occurred as a result of sabotage. On 10 May, Me 323 D-2 W.Nr. 1247 was destroyed at the Trapani airfield as a result of an Allied air attack.

The last flight of the Ju 52 from Tunis took place on the night of 12 May, when only a small piece of land on Cape Bon remained in the hands of the defenders. On the same day, in defiance of Hitler's crazy orders demanding defence of the beachhead until the last possible moment, Axis troops laid down their weapons. On 13 May, the Allies crushed the last pockets of resistance; 250,000 soldiers, half of them Germans, were captured. It was a disaster similar to the collapse in Stalingrad. But unlike the starved and hard-pressed soldiers of the 6th Army, most of whom later died of typhus and other diseases, the captive Tunisian soldiers were in relatively comfortable conditions. Most of them survived and then returned to their homeland.

The total losses of transport aircraft for six months (from 8 November, 1942, when operation Torch began, until the surrender on 12 May 1943) amounted to more than 350 transport planes. Among them were twenty-three Me 323s, of which eighteen were shot down by fighters, two were destroyed at airfields and three were severely damaged as a result of accidents. These losses were roughly proportional to the losses of the air bridge in Stalingrad Pocket, but the share of combat losses of transport planes in Africa was incomparably higher.

Chapter 6

From Sardinia to Kuban

Transport reform

After the disasters in Stalingrad and Tunisia, no major Pockets appeared at the front for some time. Given Hitler's maniacal desire to destroy the Wehrmacht, this was a real miracle. Thanks to this respite, the thinned transport aircraft of the Luftwaffe could spend a long time (nine months) rebuilding its divisions and even afford the luxury of correcting organizational shortcomings made during the rapid growth of the late 1930s. Unlike the fighters, reconnaissance aircraft, bombers, and ground-attack aircraft, the transport Geschwader, Gruppe and Staffel did not have any clear organizational structure until April 1943. Despite the large number of operations and units involved in them, there was no clear chain of command, and there was no single authority to oversee aircraft maintenance and crew training. With the exception of KGzbV 1, which was formed at the beginning of the war, no unit operated on a permanent basis. The creation of aviation groups for special operations continued to be improvised. In fact, transport aircraft worked on a situational principle, and its concentration on different sections of the front was achieved by constantly moving aircraft and crews from place to place.

All these organizational problems became apparent during the deployment of the long-lasting air bridges to Stalingrad and Tunisia during the winter of 1942/1943. Meanwhile, the war continued to drag on, and the need for air supply of certain units was constantly growing. Therefore, in May 1943, the Luftwaffe command finally decided to carry out a large-scale reorganization of transport aircraft. The Geschwader and special purpose Gruppe were now to be formed and operated on a permanent basis and were converted into transport squadrons (Transportgeschwader – TG) and transport air groups (Transportgruppe TGr). A total of five transport Geschwader and four separate Gruppe were formed.[1]

---

[1] Pegg M. Transporter Volume One: Luftwaffe Transport Units 1937-1943. Luftwaffe Colours. – Classic Publications, 2007. p. 113.

The strength of the transport Geschwader was 217 aircraft, including five aircraft in the staff link and forty-eight aircraft in each Gruppe. Gruppe was divided into four Staffel of twelve aircraft. Along with the reorganization, plans for the production of the Ju 52, which was still the main aircraft of transport aircraft, were increased. As a result, production of this type of aircraft peaked in 1943, when a total of 887 Ju 52s were produced. At the same time, in addition to the standard Ju 52/3m, transport units began to receive a large number of modifications of the Ju 52/3mg8e, which was distinguished by an increased wingspan, the presence of a loading hatch in the roof, and side doors on both sides of the fuselage. At the same time, the post of inspector (commander) of transport aviation was introduced, which was taken by Generalmajor Friedrich-Wilhelm Morzik, who is already known to readers.

Table. Reorganisation of Luftwaffe transport units in May 1943

Name of the unit before it was reformed	Name of the new unit
Stab./KGzbV 1	Stab./TG 1
I./KGzbV 1	I./TG 1
II./KGzbV 1	II./TG 1
III./KGzbV 1	III./TG 1
IV./KGzbV 1	IV./TG 1
Stab./KGr.zbV 3	Stab./TG 2
KGr.zbV 600	I./TG 2
KGr.zbV 800	II./TG 2
KGr.zbV 106	III./TG 2
Stab./KGzbV 2	Stab./TG 3
KGr.zbV 9	I./TG 3
KGr.zbV 50	II./TG 3
KGr.zbV 102	III./TG 3
I./KGzbV 172	IV./TG 3
KGr.zbV 'Surf'	Stab./TG 4
KGr.zbV 105	I./TG 4
KGr.zbV 500	II./TG 4
KGr.zbV 400	III./TG 4

Name of the unit before it was reformed	Name of the new unit
KGr.zbV 700	IV./TG 4
KGr.zbV 'Word'	Stab./TG 5
I./KGzbV 323	I./TG 5
II./KGzbV 323	II./TG 5
III./KGzbV 323	III./TG 5
KGr.zbV 5	TGr.10
KGr.zbV 108	TGr. 20
KGr.zbV 23	TGr. 30
KGr.zbV 300	*Erganzungstransportfliegergruppe*

The reorganization also affected KGzbV 323, which suffered heavy losses in the battles. On 1 May, on the basis of KGr.zbV 'Word' was formed to Stab./TG 5, I./KGzbV 323 was renamed to I./TG 5, and II./KGzbV 323 was renamed to II./TG 5. Previously formed III./KGzbV 323 (on the basis of the training KGr.zbV 900), respectively became III./TG 5. Note that from this point in the history of the Geschwader 'Giants', there is some confusion. This is due to the incompleteness of the surviving documents and contradictions in different sources. So, according to one source, on 21 May, the I./TG 5 was sent for reformation to Leipheim, where it received new Me 323 E aircraft. According to other sources, II./TG 5, previously withdrawn to Germany, was already disbanded on 22 June 1943 due to heavy losses in equipment and personnel. III./TG 5 was allegedly used for some time on the Eastern front and was also disbanded in June 1943. It turns out that in May–June, 'Giants' should not have been on the Mediterranean at all. However, this did not prevent them from continuing to fly there and regularly incur losses. Moreover, up to the summer of 1944, German documents mention the 1st and 6th, 7th and 8th Staffel, as well as II./TG 5 and even IV./TG 5. Recall that initially air groups equipped with Me 323 had a composition of two Staffel. Probably, none of the Gruppe (II./TG 5, III./TG 5) were disbanded in 1943. The serial numbers of newly formed Staffels were chosen at random, regardless of the presence of formed units. For example, as noted above, there was a 1st and 6th Staffel, but the 2nd, 3rd, 4th, and 5th did not exist.

The production of the new Me 323s made it possible to quickly make up for the losses. After the production of 104 aircraft of the 'D' production series, the production of a new modification of the aircraft under the 'E' index began. Trying to take into account the feedback of pilots who noted the shortcomings of the defensive weapons of the aircraft, the designers gradually turned the huge transport airplane into a real flying fortress. On the upper surfaces of the wing between the middle and outer engines were installed two rotating towers HDL 151 with hydraulic drive, equipped with 20 mm guns MG 151. Then they were replaced with EDL towers (which had a smaller profile) with an electric drive and the same gun. As a result of strengthening the defensive armament of the aircraft, the power structure of the wing was slightly changed, and emergency hatches were made under the defensive installations. These improvements led to an increase in the weight of the aircraft from 27,330 kg to 29,000 kg and a simultaneous reduction in the load capacity to 10 tons. The crew was increased to seventeen persons (two pilots, two flight engineers, radio operator and twelve flight gunners). This modification was designated Me 323 E-2 and thanks to its improved characteristics, it became the most produced transport aircraft of this type. From April 1943 to April 1944, ninety-eight planes entered service (Me 323 E-1 W.Nr. 1253–1299, Me 323 E-2 W.Nr. 130015–130055 and finally Me 323 E-3 with W.Nr. 330001–330010). At least two Me 323 Ss were converted from the cargo version to the 'escort' gunship version (Waffenträger). Of all the 217 'Giants' built, 181 aircraft were delivered directly to the Luftwaffe. In 1942 – twenty-six, in 1943 – 121, in 1944 – thirty-four planes. The highest rate of aircraft production was achieved in February 1943, when twenty-seven Me 323s were assembled.

After the Wehrmacht disaster in Tunisia, transport planes of the Luftwaffe on the Mediterranean had very little time to rest and replenish. Soon the Ju 52s had a new task: the evacuation of the German garrison from the small Italian island of Pantelleria, located between Africa and Sicily. The operation was started on time and was successful. Almost all the Germans were removed from the island before it was captured by the Allies on 11 June.

The strategic situation in the Mediterranean had changed dramatically. After the fall of Tunis, the entire German-occupied coast of southern Europe, from France to Greece, was exposed to the threat of an attack by the Allied armies. However, the Führer was less pessimistic about the results of the Tunisian military campaign and the situation that followed. In June 1943 Hitler, talking about the strategy of the Anglo-Americans, admonished General der Panzertruppen von Senger, sent as a liaison officer with the Italian command in Sicily, said: 'The Allies, having failed in their attempt to jump over to Sicily immediately after landing in north Africa, have already lost their war in the Mediterranean.' Subsequent events clearly showed the degree of stupidity and incompetence of this pompous rascal, who became the head of the German people.

In the spring of 1943, the German command led by Hitler, fell victim to a very insidious strategic misinformation prepared by British intelligence. According to it, the next goal of the Allies was to be the island of Sardinia and the coast of the Balkan Peninsula. On 9 May, the documents planted by the British fell into the hands of OKW officers, and three days later it indicated in its Directive that 'Allied operations should begin as soon as possible,' and 'activities related to Sardinia and the Peloponnese are of paramount importance in comparison with all others'. On 14 May, the Führer informed Großadmiral Dönitz that 'the discovered Anglo-Saxon directives confirm our guesses that their planned attacks will be directed mainly against Sardinia and the Peloponnese'.

As a result, Greece and the islands of Rhodes, Crete, Corsica, Sardinia were urgently sent troop reinforcements, as well as additional guns and ammunition. And this at a time when reserves were sorely lacking on the Eastern front. Me 323 aircraft were also actively involved in transport operations. They mainly operated transport flights between the mainland, Sardinia and Corsica. Meanwhile, the RAF and USAF continued to literally massacre Luftwaffe transport aircraft in areas adjacent to Italy after the victory in Tunisia. Therefore, transport planes suffered regular losses. On 20 May, near Villacidro airfield (Sardinia), American P-40K fighters from the 325th FG shot down Me 323 D-1 W.Nr. 1128 'C8+CB' and Me 323 D-2 W.Nr. 1240 'C8+KB' from St.I./TG 5. Of their crews, four people were killed and six others were injured. Another Me 323 D-2 W.Nr. 1234 'C8+GR' was shot down by a P-40K fighter from 319.FS, piloted by Flight Officer John W. Smallsred. On the same day, two Ju 90 B-1s (W.Nr. 90-0003 'JH+CH' and W.Nr. 90-0006 'J4+HH') were destroyed at the Italian Grosseto airfield during bombing by American B-17s.

Two days later, TG 5 lost 3 'Giants' at once:

- Me 323 E-1 W.Nr. 1259 was shot down by American fighters over the sea east of the island of Sardinia. 5 pilots were killed and 4 were injured;
- Me 323 D-2 W.Nr. 1237 was destroyed at the airfield of Trapani as a result of the Allied air raid;
- Me 323 D-2 W.Nr. 1235 ' C8+GP '(tail number' X1-H') from 6./TG 5 damaged at Castelvetrano airfield in an Allied air attack. Despite the fact that the damage was not critical (40 per cent), this aircraft was later written off and disassembled for spare parts.

On 30 May, during a massive raid by American B-17 bombers on Pomigliano airfield, three 'Giants' were destroyed at once: Me 323 D-1 W.Nr. 1137, Me 323 D-2 W.Nr. 1238 and Me 323 E-1 W.Nr. 1260. This was the first loss of the aircraft Me 323 production series 'E'.

In June, TG 5 suffered only one loss. On 18 June, Me 323 D-2 W.Nr. 1227 in the central part of the Mediterranean sea was shot down by ship's air defense fire. The crew was saved. Probably, this 'Giant' was flying to Greece or back.

On 10 July, the huge Allied fleet, contrary to the Führer's forecasts, began landing on the island of Sicily. The small German-Italian garrison could not offer serious resistance and soon began to retreat to the north-east coast. Although the Italians fled Sicily in a panic, between 3 and 16 August German troops, including parachutists delivered by transport planes, managed to organize effective rearguard actions, which allowed the main part of the troops to be evacuated across the Strait of Messina to Italy by 17 August.

TG 5 again suffered heavy losses during this period. On 17 July, as a result a massive Allied air raid on Pomigliano airfield again three 'Giants' were destroyed: Me 323 D-2 W.Nr. 1249, Me 323 E-1 W.Nr. 1256 and Me 323 E-1 W.Nr. 1275. On 18 July, the Me 323 D was attacked and damaged by fighters, but nevertheless managed to land safely at Pistoia airfield. When trying to take off with only four engines running, the plane failed to gain altitude and crashed (60 per cent damage). On 21 July another pair of 'Gigants': Me 323 E-1 W.Nr. 1271 and the Me 323 E-1 W.Nr. 1278 was destroyed at Grosseto airfield during an air attack by Allied aircraft.

On 23 July Ju 90 B-1 W.Nr. 90-0007 'J4+JH' from 1./Tr.Fl.St 5 was shot down in combat with an American B-26 bomber over the sea near Bastia (Corsica). However, the crew of the Oberfeldwebel Boldt was rescued by a German ferry of the 'Zibel' type.

On 26 July, Me 323 E-1 W.Nr. 1267 'C8+DG' and Me 323 E-1 W.Nr. 1270 'C8+EG' were attacked by Beaufighters over the sea in the area of Cape Rera off the island of Maddalena after taking off from Venofiorino airfield on the island of Sardinia at 12.10. One plane made an emergency landing on the island and crashed; the other did not reach land, but sat on the water and sank.[2] Crew losses were – Me 323 E-1 W.Nr. 1267 'C8+DG' – three killed (including pilot Oberfeldwebel W.J. Klar) and

---

2 In May 2012, it was found and examined by divers, at the moment it is the only known surviving remains of Me 323.

six wounded; on Me 323 E-1 W.Nr. 1270 'C8+EG' – five killed (including pilot Oberfeldwebel H. Boge) and six wounded.

On 30 July, Me 323 E-1 W.Nr. 1274 made an emergency landing on the island of Corsica after being fired on by an American B-26 bomber (pilot – Captain Wynne S.G. Maydwell) from the 14th Sqdn. RAF. The plane was severely destroyed (80 per cent damage), and four pilots from the crew of Oberfeldwebel Walter Honig were injured.

At the end of July, two 'Giants' (Me 323 E-1 W.Nr. 1279 and Me 323 E-1 W.Nr. 1291) were abandoned in a faulty condition on the airfields of Sicily during the retreat. On 1 August Me 323 E-1 W.Nr. 1266 was destroyed during an air attack against the Cappadocia airfield.

On 5 August, Me 323 E-1 W.Nr. 1262 was severely damaged during an emergency landing at the Venofiorino airfield in Sardinia. Although the damage was estimated at 45 per cent, the aircraft was not repaired. 'Giant' was decommissioned and disassembled for spare parts. On 17 August, Me 323 D-1 W.Nr. 1140 and Me-323 D-1 W.Nr. 1143 were destroyed in an Allied air attack on the Istris airfield (Greece).

The next day, Me 323 D-1 W.Nr. 1213 suffered heavy damage (65 per cent) due to the bombing of the Pisa airfield. This plane was 'long-lived'. Back in early January, it was severely damaged during a hard landing at the Pomigliano air base. The aircraft was then repaired and survived the entire Tunisian campaign and most of the summer of 1943.

During the battle of Sicily, the TG 5 lost sixteen Me 323 for various reasons. This period was particularly unfortunate for Geschwader. And the total number of lost aircraft reached sixty-nine units.

On 19 August, Ju 290 V-2 W.Nr. 0151 'J4+BH' crashed during an emergency landing at the Rome–Ciampino airport.

On 3 September 1943, the divisions of General Montgomery's 8th British army were the first to land on Italian soil. In fact, a second front (the Western Front) of confrontation with the Nazis appeared in Europe. To the Führer, finally, it became clear that this was the main goal of the Allied offensive. Therefore, he ordered the urgent occupation of Italy and Rome, as well as the evacuation of troops from the islands of Sardinia and Corsica (where they had been transported with great difficulty six weeks earlier, due to Hitler's stupidity).

The transfer of troops took place by sea and by air. On 19 September, the evacuation of German soldiers from Sardinia was completed without any difficulties. The removal of troops from Corsica was carried out by eighty Ju 52/3m, several SM.82 from III./TG 1 and twenty Me 323 from

II./TG 5. Ju 52 from II. and III./TG 1, II. and III./TG 2, III./TG 4 were based at the airfields of Florence, Lucca, Pistoia, Pontedera and Pisa. The Me 323 and Savoia-Marchetti SM.82 aircraft were based at Grosseto air base. In addition to the 'Aunt Ju', III./TG 2 used several Italian aircraft captured by the Germans from their former allies. In total, 27,000 people were airlifted out of Corsica during the evacuation operation, including an Italian parachute regiment that voluntarily remained loyal to Germany. Most of the heavy equipment, vehicles and guns were transported by sea. On 14 September, French troops landed on the island of Corsica, but they acted very hesitantly, which allowed the Germans to complete the evacuation by 5 October. The Allies claimed that they managed to shoot down thirty transport planes, including twenty-six Ju 52/3m and four SM.82, but such impressive numbers of German losses were a strong exaggeration.

TG 5 lost seven aircraft during this operation. On 5 September Me 323 E-1 W.Nr. 1268 was heavily damaged (65 per cent) at Grosseto airfield. On 12 September, the Me 323 D-1 W.Nr. 1106 crashed during a forced landing on the island of Sardinia. One pilot from his crew was killed, and two others were injured. On 23 September, Me 323 D-1 W.Nr. 1122 and Me 323 E-1 W.Nr. 1282 were destroyed at Pisa airfield during another massive Allied air raid. On 30 September, a Me 323 E-1 W.Nr. 1285 and Me 323 D-1 W.Nr. 1216 were shot down by a Spitfire Mk. VII from a GC.III/3 squadron of the Free French air force near Bastia during the evacuation of German troops from Sardinia. On the same day, the faulty Me 323 E-1 W.Nr. 1112 was blown up by German sappers on one of the airfields of the island of Corsica.

These were the last TG 5 losses in the Mediterranean. During ten months of combat work in this region, Geschwader lost seventy-five 'Giants' for various reasons. Against the background of the volume of production of these aircraft (147 Me 323 in 1942–43), such losses can be called catastrophic. In order to transport such a volume of cargo in the conditions of overwhelming air supremacy of Anglo-American aviation, Luftwaffe transport aircraft had to sacrifice itself again to the stupidity of Hitler. It is clear that with all the self-sacrifice and full concentration of forces, the German transport planes units could not sustain such huge losses indefinitely.

In the autumn, the military situation in the Mediterranean stabilized, and the fighting in Italy became protracted. This allowed the Luftwaffe to withdraw battered units for rest and replenishment, and then transfer to the Eastern front, where the need for transport aircraft increased dramatically.

149

Missions on 'Kuban-Brückenkopf'

In the supply of Stalingrad Pocket, cargo gliders were barely used. According to some reports, the use of such was planned 'as a last resort', and such an extreme case, apparently, had not yet happened by January 1943. It was not until 20 January that the 1st airborne squadron (LLG 1), with sixty-four glider tugs and 170 cargo gliders DFS 230 and Go 242, was sent to ensure the air bridge in Stalingrad.

However, by the time this unit was relocated at the disposal to the Luftwaffe 4th air fleet, it was too late. Shortly before the disaster in Stalingrad, it was decided to use Me 321 cargo gliders to supply the 6th Army. Both Staffels equipped with them were in France at the time. Due to the urgency, the crews did not have time to prepare. Literally within a day, eleven 'Giants' were attached to the He 111 Z glider tugs and sent from the city of Reims directly to the banks of the Don river, in fact, the flight route passed through all of Europe. If we stand back from the real situation and think objectively, if all eleven cargo gliders reached Stalingrad, they could simultaneously deliver up to 350 tons of food to the starving 6th Army. However, it was obvious that their arrival could not affect the situation in Stalingrad, and all eleven cargo gliders would inevitably 'decorate' the next cemetery of German transport planes with their giant debris.

The flight of eleven air monsters from the GS Kdo aviation group took place in terrible weather conditions. They flew over the cities of Zhytomyr and Poltava to the air bases of Stalino (now Donetsk) and Makeyevka. During relocation, the Me 321 were forced to stand for long periods on snow-covered intermediate airfields, where it is very difficult to maneuver heavy cargo gliders. The first two He 111 Z arrived at Makeyevka airfield only on 28 January, when it was too late to fly to Stalingrad...

But work for the huge cargo gliders was still found. While the 6th Army was dying in Stalingrad, the Wehrmacht was urgently withdrawing troops from the Caucasus and creating a new line of defense. The 1st Panzer army of General der Kavallerie Eberhard von Makensen was retreating towards Rostov-on-don on a mission to save the crumbling front of Army Group 'Don'. At the same time, the commander of the 17th Army, Generaloberst Richard Ruoff, was ordered to withdraw to the city of Krasnodar with the mission of creating a strong defense and holding a bridgehead there. In an optimistic scenario, the Führer wanted to use it to resume the offensive to the oil fields, and in a pessimistic scenario, this bridgehead was planned to be used to protect the approaches to the Crimea.

On 12 February, the Germans evacuated Krasnodar, and two weeks later they withdrew over the river Protoka to the so-called 'Poseidon line', while to the south, mountain riflemen and mountain rangers took up a defense on the well-fortified hills around the village of Krymskaya. It was turned into a powerful strong point, prepared for a long defense. By early spring, the 17th Army had retreated to a convenient 120-kilometer line, protected in the north by numerous marshes, in the center by marshes rivers and canals, and in the south by numerous heights. This line was defended by twelve German and four Romanian divisions. Thus arose the Kuban bridgehead, which the Germans called 'Kuban-Brückenkopf'.

To supply the 17th Army, a huge fleet of many different types of vessel (tugs, fast barges and ferries) was formed. But sea transport could not fully meet the needs of the beachhead, especially in the spring during storms on the Black Sea, so the Luftwaffe had to organize an air bridge in Kuban. The GS Kdo, equipped with Me 321 cargo gliders and He 111 Z glider tugs, played an important role in its work. Based at Bagerovo air base in Crimea, they delivered food and ammunition to the 17th Army for two months from February to March. On return flights, the Giants evacuated thousands of wounded soldiers. At the same time, thirty people were placed in the glider tug itself, and 100 wounded soldiers were in the towed cargo glider. In addition to the 'Giants', the He 111 Z was towed by Go 242 cargo gliders, two pieces per flight. The operation also involved the Hs 126 glider tugs towing Go 242 cargo gliders.

However, the most effective actions were KGr.zbV 200, which was armed with four-engine Fw 200 Condors. After unsuccessful missions in the area of Stalingrad, during which the air group lost nine aircraft, from 4 to 13 February Condors performed seventy-six flights from air bases at Zaporizhia and Bagerovo to the Kuban airfields (Krasnodar, Timoshevskaya and Slavyanskaya). In total, 116 tons of ammunition, 12 tons of heavy weapons, 76.6 tons of food and 4 tons of fuel were transported. On return flights, 1,887 German soldiers and officers were taken out, including 830 wounded. At the same time, all the missions passed without losses due to the lack of any counteraction by Soviet aviation and air defense.

Specialized aviation group III./KG 4 Major Werner Klosinski, previously involved in the supply of the Velikiye Luki Pocket and Stalingrad Pocket, was also based in the Crimea from 30 January. One of the tasks of the He 111 crews was to tow Go 242 cargo gliders with ammunition and food through the Kerch Strait. On the beachhead, bombers and cargo gliders landed at specially prepared airfields at Timoshevskaya and Slavyanskaya.

On the way back, as a rule, the wounded were taken out. Periodically the III./KG 4 carried out bombing sorties. The main targets of air attacks were Soviet ports on the Black Sea, as well as railway stations and airfields. For example, on 20 February air strikes were carried out on the port of Tuapse and the airfield at Gelendzhik; and on 25 February on railway stations in Armavir, Krasnodar and Kropotkin. Between 3 and 10 March a series of night raids were made on the airfields of Krasnodar and Adler. It was the base for Soviet bombers and attack aircraft, striking blows at the German troops.

After completing several missions it turned out that the Bagerovo airfield, at which was based III./KG 4, was too narrow and cramped to land bombers at night. After five He 111 crashed, the group was moved to Saki airfield.

In April, He 111 bombers were equipped with a new high-altitude sight 'Lotfe 7D', which significantly improved the accuracy of bombing, including from high altitudes. In late April to May 1943, III./KG 4 mainly bombed Soviet troops trying to break through to Novorossiysk and Krymskaya, and also conducted a night hunt for trains on the railway lines from Krasnodar to Kropotkin and from Armavir to Maykop.[3] The function of towing gliders gradually passed to the Ju 52 units transferred to the Crimea. In April, GS Kdo returned to Germany, and then was transferred to France at Dijon and Negre airfields in view of the expected Allied amphibious operation there.

Despite a series of fierce attacks, the Russians never managed to break through the front of the 17th Army. The only serious success of the Soviets was the capture of the village of Krymskaya on 5 May. After this, the bridgehead was the scene of continuous battles for several months, which cost the Russians huge losses, but did not bring them any success.

The Wehrmacht confidently held the 'Kuban-Brückenkopf' until the autumn of 1943. But after the failure of Operation Zitadelle and the subsequent Russian counteroffensive, the southern wing of the Eastern front collapsed again. On 22 August, the Red Army occupied the city of Kharkov, and by the end of the month, the Russian southern front had broken through German positions on the Mius river, after which it launched a large-scale offensive on the city of Melitopol. On 8 September, the city of Stalino (now Donetsk) was liberated. On 12 September, north-west of Stalino, Soviet tanks pushed back the German 4th Panzer army to the city of Konotop, and two days later reached the approaches to the city of Nizhyn. In these

---

3 Gundelach K. Kampfgeschwader 'General Wever' 4. – Motorbuch Verlag Stuttgart, 1978. pp. 231 – 233.

circumstances, the defense of Kuban bridgehead lost its meaning, and on 3 September, the 17th Army headquarters received preliminary permission from Hitler to evacuate German troops to the Crimea.

The evacuation (Operation Brunhild) was carried out systematically between 9 September and 9 October. During this time, 177,355 German soldiers and officers, 50,139 Allied soldiers and officers (Romanians and Slovaks), 28,436 Hiwi[4] (Russian volunteers), 16,311 wounded, 27,456 civilians, 115,477 tons of military cargo (including 27,670 tons of ammunition, 29,500 tons of food, 13,940 tons of forage), 21,230 vehicles, seventy-four tanks and assault guns, 1,815 artillery pieces and 74,657 horses were transported by sea from the bridgehead. In addition, transport planes of the Luftwaffe removed another 15,661 people and 1,153 tons of military equipment from the Gostagaevskaya airfield.

In total, from 1 February to 30 September 1943, Fligerkorps I carried out 13,536 transport flights for the transportation of people and cargo (during this period, 135,230 people were transported). Another 2,901 flights were made by cargo gliders. The operation for maintenance of an air bridge in Kuban bridgehead took place almost without opposition from the Red Army air force. The losses of transport planes and cargo gliders were minimal.

---

4 German abbreviation of the word Hilfswilliger, auxiliary volunteer, Russian prisoners of war who voluntarily joined the Wehrmacht.

Chapter 7

Korsun 'meat grinder'

'We are fighting a very strong, persistent and stable army…'

At the beginning of 1944, the main events on the Eastern front took place in its southern sector – in Ukraine. During the winter the Army Group 'South' Generalfeldmarschall Erich von Manstein repelled the endless attacks of the Red Army. However, it was not the Soviets with their talentless generals who were the main threat to the German Eastern front. The inevitable death of the Wehrmacht was embedded in the pathological psyche of Hitler. Even the talented commander von Manstein could not resist the destructive passions of his commander-in-chief. The Führer, obsessed with stupid fanaticism, demanded to hold the line along the Dnieper river, even after the Russians from the numerous bridgeheads they had captured were deeply wedged into the German defenses. The same typical scenario of the sacrifice of German troops was repeated again. As a result, on 28 January 1944, units of the XI and XXXXII German army corps were surrounded on the southern bank of the Dnieper river in the of Korsun.[1] The Korsun Pocket was created in which there turned out to be 56,000 soldiers: nine infantry divisions, one security division, five assault guns divisions, three sapper battalions, four construction battalions, 5th SS Infantry Brigade Wallonien (SS-Sturmbrigade Wallonien), 5th SS Panzer Division 'Wiking' (5.SS-Panzerdivision 'Wiking'), Estonian SS infantry battalion Narwa, 810th Armenian infantry battalion, Russian Kuban cavalry regiment and other units. General der Artillerie Wilhelm Stemmermann was in overall command of the group. At first, the Pocket perimeter was quite large, but then the blockaded area quickly shrank to 35 km in diameter.

---

1 In many studies and memoirs, including German ones, Korsun Pocket is mistakenly called the Cherkasy Pocket (Kessel von Tsherkassy). In reality, the city of Cherkasy was located outside the ring of the blockade.

Then events began to develop according to the standard scheme for the mad command of Hitler: preparing and conducting a deblocking strike from the outside and organizing the air bridge. But, in the case of the Korsun Pocket, the Führer immediately 'allowed' the encircled troops to break through in a southwesterly direction.

Responsibility for supply by air to the blockaded group was assigned to Fliegerkorps VIII (VIII. Fl. Korp.). Initially, the operation was assigned to I., II. and III./TG 3, commanded respectively by Major Hans Ellerbrok, Major Otto Baumann and Major Paul Risch. Ju 52 aviation groups operated from Uman, Golta and Proskuriv airfields. Inside the Pocket, the transport planes' reception was organized at Korsun airfield.[2] The Hungarian 5/2. V. Szd fighter squadron was assigned to escort and protect the Ju 52.

Flights on the new air bridge began on the morning of 29 January, when the first fourteen Ju 52s took off from Uman airfield with 30 tons of ammunition on board. The wounded were sent on the first return flight, which by this time amounted to more than 2,000 people. Then light anti-aircraft batteries were delivered to the Pocket for the defense of Korsun air base. He 111 bombers were also re-engaged on the organization of the air bridge. The already familiar mission was assigned to KG 27 'Boelcke'. At the beginning of February, this Geschwader was based at Golta and Proskuriv air bases and had forty-four serviceable aircraft.

Table 1. Availability of aircraft in KG 27 on 30 January 1944.

Gruppe	Staff number	Total He 111	Combat-ready planes
Stab/KG 27	4	1	0
I./KG 27	37	34	24
II./KG 27	37	22	12
III./KG 27	37	15	8
In total	115	72	44

The opposing Soviet side also became active in the air and on the ground, trying to disrupt Korsun Pocket's supply plans. The Soviets, thanks to the pernicious passion of Hitler, already had a wealth of experience in operations

---

2 Pegg M. Transporter Volume One: Luftwaffe Transport Units 1937-1943. Luftwaffe Colours. – Classic Publications, 2007. p. 132.

to encircle German troops, and it was no secret to them that the Germans would immediately organize an air bridge. Therefore, in the first days anti-aircraft batteries were placed along the ring of the blockade. In addition, in the sky over the Pocket Russian fighters began a barrage. However, the Germans could not have held the crumbling Eastern front for so long if the Russians did not have their psychopathic 'commander' Stalin and his favorite, talentless, Soviet generals. Even after so many typical operations to blockade German Pockets, the Russians could not effectively hinder the air bridge organized by the Germans. 'Stalin's falcons' throughout the war were haunted by two main vices, the consequences of which were often used by the Luftwaffe pilots. The Russians were unable to master low-altitude combat skills and were unable to fly in bad weather. Therefore, the Ju 52 crews, knowing these features of Russian fighters preferred to fly in a closed formation at an altitude of about 500 meters. However, this tactic was fraught with danger. Despite the constant change of routes and approaches to the target from different directions, the Ju 52s were subjected to fire from the ground, including from small arms. And not all the crews of the German transport planes had enough endurance and skills to keep the formation and height.

Soon Soviet intelligence established the fact of participation in the operation to supply the encircled German troops TG 3. The Russian report said, 'The 3rd transport group of the 4th air fleet consisting of 38 Ju 52 aircraft arrived at Uman airfield to help the encircled group.'

On 1 February, the weather conditions changed dramatically. In the Korsun Pocket area, the weather was relatively clear. In the morning, a group of planes from III./TG 3 arrived at the Pocket. On the way to the goal, transport planes had to constantly maneuver, dodging shells and machine-gun bursts. Some crews flew directly over the trees to make it difficult to detect from the ground. It was a very nervous and risky flight. As a result, the commander of the group, Major Risch, contrary to strict instructions, decided to fly at a high altitude on the way back. As it turned out, this was a fatal mistake. As soon as all the Ju 52s took off and gathered in battle formation, they were suddenly attacked by a large group of Russian fighters. As a result, twelve aircraft were shot down at once, including the Ju 52 of Major Risch himself. Another three Ju 52s were damaged, two of them then made emergency landings on German territory, and one crashed while landing at the airfield.

According to Soviet information, on this day, six La-5 fighters from the squadron of Senior Lieutenant Pyotr Bazanov (3rd Guards IAP) accompanied six ground-attack aircraft Il-2 (mission – bombing the Korsun railway station). When approaching the target area, the pilots suddenly saw a large group of transport planes. Bazanov left a pair of La-5s to accompany the ground-attack aircraft, and four fighters attacked the transport planes. Russian planes approached the Ju 52s from behind and fired cannons and machine guns from a short distance.

After returning to his airfield, Bazanov reported that he and his wingman Ivan Ivanov had each shot down four Ju 52s, and pilot Ivan Bogachev had shot down two Ju 52s. At this time, the commander of the 10th IAK Major General M.M. Golovnya was at the airfield, who did not believe the report of the squadron commander, calling it a 'fantasy'. But Bazanov insisted on his version. Then Major General Smut on his personal Yak-9, accompanied by La-5 under the control of Bazanov, flew to the battle area. On the ground, they saw ten large fires from burning Ju 52s that were transporting fuel. Then they noticed another pair of Ju 52s that were standing on the ground after the crash landing. Golovnya and Bazanov fired at them, but at that moment they were attacked by Hungarian Bf 109 fighters. Each of the Russian pilots lead the battle alone, but everything ended well. Major General Golovnya flew to Kiev (his Yak-9 took off with outboard fuel tanks), and Senior Lieutenant Bazanov landed at his airfield. Subsequently, the pilot was credited with four aerial victories over the Ju 52 on this day. For Senior Lieutenant Bazanov, German transport planes were a familiar target during the 6th Army's blockade of Stalingrad, he had personally shot down four Ju 52s and two more transport planes in a group with other Russian fighters.[3]

On this day, the Hungarian 5/2. V. Szd suffered its first losses. In the Korsun area La-5 fighters from the 3rd Guards IAP shot down a Bf 109 G-4 hadnagy (Leutnant) Gyorgy Debrody, which carried out a mission to accompany the Ju 52. The pilot made an emergency landing on Russian territory. Soon Debrody witnessed an air battle, during which his friend hadnagy (Leutnant) Miklos Kenyeres from the same squadron shot down a La-5. Debrody began to wave his arms and managed to attract the attention a comrade of Kenyeres. Without hesitation, he landed his Bf 109 next to Debrody! At the same time, on the other side of the field, Soviet infantrymen could already be seen running and shouting. Kenyeres threw out his parachute and flight jacket to make room in the cramped cockpit.

---

3 In total, Peter Bazanov won twenty personal and three group victories during the war, including shooting down eleven Ju 52s.

Debrody sat on the lap of a comrade, after which they immediately began to take off. At the same time, one pilot pressed the pedals with his feet, and the second operated the control handle. Two Hungarians managed to make a fantastic take-off, sitting on top of each other and moving on the chassis in the mud and snow. At low altitude, the Bf 109 flew over hills teeming with Russian infantry and safely reached the Uman air base. Debrody and Kenyeres were among the best aces of the Hungarian air force. Debrody was 2nd in the number of wins, Kenyeres 5th. But they didn't have long to fight together after their lucky escape.

In total, the Russian 5th Air Army carried out 417 sorties on this day, and the pilots reported twenty-five downed aircraft.

After heavy losses on 1 February, the Korsun Pocket supply operation was entrusted to commander II./TG 3 Major Otto Baumann. He decided to find a compromise between low-level flights and high-altitude flights. From now on, Ju 52s flew in large groups at an altitude of 1,500–2,000 meters, accompanied by Bf 109s from JG 52. However, fighter escorts were constantly lacking, so formations of thirty-six Ju 52/3m followed with limited protection of two or three Bf 109s. However, in bad weather conditions, this modest escort was quite enough for reliable protection.

On 2 February, a large group of prisoners from Korsun Pocket fell into the hands of the Soviets. The Germans, hoping for good treatment in captivity, passed all the information they had to Russian intelligence. They said that the officers demanded that the soldiers show fierce resistance and did not lose heart. They were promised that in three to four days, three Panzer divisions would begin their offensive from the south, which would break through the blockade ring and deblock the 8th Army. However, the command of the Russian 2nd Ukrainian front did not believe the stories of the captured Germans and looked at the situation with optimism. At that time, ten rifle divisions and three tank corps were located on the outer ring of the blockade, and eight rifle divisions, three cavalry divisions, four tank regiments and one tank brigade were located on the inner ring. The Russians had 243 tanks in this area. 'Thus, the superiority of forces on our side, which makes it possible, combining the offensive with the defense, to repel any enemy tank attacks from the south and southwest and defeat the encircled enemy divisions,' said the journal of combat operations of the 2nd Ukrainian front.

On this day, the Korsun Pocket area was heavily overcast and raining. The Russian 5th Air Army carried out 202 sorties and reported seven downed aircraft. During the mission to supply the Pocket in the area of

Horodyshche, He 111 H-16 W.Nr. 162112 '1G+KS' from 8./KG 27 was shot down; its entire crew of five (Leutnant Helmut Schoen, Unteroffizier Erich Gunther and Unteroffizier Rudolf Michel, Feldwebel Hans Bottcher and Feldwebel Paul Kosubek) was missing. It was later revealed that the 23-year-old navigator, Gunther, was captured. However, he never returned to his homeland. The crew of the other He 111 H-16 '1G+BR' from the same Staffel was more lucky. In the area of Horodyshche, it was also damaged by anti-aircraft fire, while the flight engineer and flight gunner were injured. But the plane was able to safely return to the Golta airfield.

Commanders of Staffel transport used different tactics to reduce losses. One option suggested that transport planes reached the target area at an altitude of 3,000 meters, then spiraled down to a height of 200 meters, dropped cargo containers, then spiraled back up to an altitude of 3,000 meters, then headed for the base. These maneuvers were very dangerous and often resulted in losses. Therefore, the commander of 8./KG 27 Karl Anselm began to use a different tactic for his He 111s, similar to that often used by Ju 52 crews. The bombers flew to Korsun Pocket at a low level, directly above the trees and hills. Russian anti-aircraft gunners, seeing the He 111 rushing over the ground, simply did not have time to aim and deploy the barrels, and the attacks of Russian fighters at this height were not dangerous. At the drop point, the group rose to a height of 200 meters, dropped the cargo, and then again at a low level went to German territory.

On 3 February, the weather became even more overcast, the air temperature was plus 3°C. The activity of the Russian air force decreased to 166 sorties, the pilots reported two downed aircraft. From 29 January to 3 February, an average of 120–140 tons of cargo were delivered to Korsun Pocket, and 2,800 injured people were evacuated from there during this period.

On 4 February, the clouds cleared a little. The Russians recorded a flight of fifty transport planes over the blockade ring. The 5th Air Army carried out 306 sorties, including 113 to attack ground targets in the Pocket and on the outer ring. Air attacks were also conducted against Luftwaffe air bases outside Korsun Pocket. Twenty-two Il-2 ground-attack aircraft from the 5th ground-attack aviation corps (5th SHAK) and thirty La-5 fighters from the 10th IAK struck the Uman airfield. Soviet pilots reported thirty-four Ju 88 and Ju 52 aircraft destroyed on the ground. However, such excellent results, as always, were a strong exaggeration.

On 5 February there was heavy fog and rain in the Korsun Pocket area. Because of this, Russian aircraft did not take to the skies at all. German transport planes continued to fly despite the bad weather. Russian soldiers constantly reported Ju 52 low-altitude flights in the north and south directions. Seventy transport planes flew over the positions of the 5th Guards tank army; the order of the headquarters of the 2nd Ukrainian front was 'to combat the enemy's transport planes flying through our territory towards the encircled troops, the troops are ordered to use all means and capabilities: firing volleys of duty units, shooting from anti-tank guns, field artillery, all anti-aircraft artillery and machine guns'.

Meanwhile, the operation to unblock the encircled German group developed slowly. On 1 February, from the south (from the area of Antonovka and Kaligorka), German troops went on the offensive. From the north, Russian positions were attacked by encircled troops. Tanks and infantry were moving to meet each other to link up in the settlement Shpola area. By 5 February, the Germans had made marked progress in both directions, significantly narrowing the blockade ring. But at the same time, the Russians attacked the defense perimeter from different directions and began to quickly compress it. On 4 February, the 52nd Russian army advanced only 14 km to the west. The next day, cavalrymen of the 4th Guards army surrounded and captured the important German stronghold of Olshana, located south of Korsun. In addition, the Soviets moved significant reserves to the Shpola area and were able to repel further attacks. On 7 February, the headquarters of the 2nd Ukrainian front stated:

> Despite the fact that the German group has been completely surrounded for several days, and the offensive of our troops is steadily compressing the encirclement ring, despite the complete failure of unblocking the encircled troops from the south and the inability to get out of this ring of fire, despite the fact that the encircled bear huge losses in manpower and equipment, there are no indications of demoralization and disorganization in the encircled divisions. German surrender is a rare occurrence, the resistance of persistant counter-attacks do not stop. This phenomenon shows once again that we are fighting a very strong, persistent and stable army.

The Russian 5th Air Army carried out only sixteen sorties during the day, fourteen of them for reconnaissance.

On 6 February, a Bf 109 G-4 hadnagy (Leutnant) Miklos Kenyeres from 5/2. V. Szd was shot down by anti-aircraft fire while performing a mission to escort a Ju 52 to Korsun Pocket. The pilot parachuted over Soviet territory and landed in the forest. These events were witnessed by a friend of Kenyeres – hadnagy (Leutnant) Gyorgy Debrody, whom Kenyeres saved five days previously in a similar situation. But this time the 'military fate' was not so favorable for the Hungarian pilot. There was no question of landing in a 'friendly' area to save Kenyeres. Debrody made several circles over his friend and had to return to the base. Miklos Kenyeres tried to reach the German positions, but two days later he was captured by the Russians. 'A Hungarian pilot Kenyeres was captured,' the journal of combat operations of the 2nd Ukrainian front reported. During the interrogation, he said that he fought in the '5/2 Hungarian Royal fighter squadron, part of the 102nd aviation brigade. The division is engaged in support of German transport planes'.[4] The reason for using Hungarian fighters to escort the Ju 52 was extremely trivial. In this section of the Eastern front, there were simply no German fighters. JG 51 in its entirety was based north – in Belarus, and JG 52 in the Crimea and southern Ukraine. If such circumstances had taken place on the Western front, all German transport planes supplying this Pocket would have been destroyed within a few days. And, here on the Eastern front, defenseless German transport planes could act almost with impunity.

'Transport aircraft of the enemy, despite very bad weather, continued to operate'

In early February, it became clear that the efforts of one transport Geschwader (TG 3) and of one bomber Geschwader (KG 27) to supply the groups of XI and XXXXII German army corps were not enough. Soon, additional Luftwaffe units were brought in to supply Korsun Pocket.

---

4 On 16 November 1944, Gyorgy Debrody was shot down in a frontal attack against a Soviet Yak-9 fighter 46 km east of Budapest, over his homeland. He was severely wounded and did not participate in aerial combat again until the end of the war. In May 1945, he surrendered to the Americans. Miklos Kenyeres survived Soviet captivity and returned to his homeland. The comrades who parted during the supply of German troops in the Korsun Pocket area eventually met again, and then emigrated to Spain together.

On 6 February, I./KG 4[5] Major Hans Bätcher moved from Sarabuz airfield (Crimea) to Novo-Nikolayevka airfield, located in the Ukrainian city of Vinnitsa. In the afternoon, the bombers made their first sorties in Korsun Pocket. Bätcher's own plane, according to the records in his Fleigerbuch, took off at 12.30. This was the 645th combat flight of this ace of bomber aviation, who a year before had taken an active part in the supply of Stalingrad Pocket. This time Bätcher dropped five cargo containers Mun C250, then returned safely to base at 14.35.[6] Commander I./KG 4 completed the next mission on 7 February at 06.55. The flight duration was exactly two hours.

On 8 February, Bätcher took to the air twice. The first mission started at 07.20, and at 09.00 the bomber returned to its airfield. After a little more than two hours of rest, at 11.20 Bätcher took off again.

On this day, the He 111 H-16 '1G+MN' of 5./KG 27, piloted by Oberleutnant Schmolka, was on a special mission. A press photographer on board filmed the cargo containers dumping process for *Adler* magazine. When the footage was delivered to the editorial office, the German magazine's management did not like it for some reason. Since there were no computers, let alone graphic editors at that time, and the possibilities of the physical retouching of photographic materials were very limited, there was an unpleasant hitch. The way out of this situation was found very quickly. The publication just replaced some of the photos from Korsun Pocket with photos taken in completely different missions, except more spectacular. We must admit that in the future, there was no shortage of color photos of the

---

5 Former I./KG 100. In October 1943, the 'old' I./KG 4 completed a protracted rearmament with He 177 'Greif' bombers. According to the original plans, 'Griffons' was supposed to equip the entire Kampfgeschwader 'General Wever', but for a number of reasons, this was abandoned. As a result, the Luftwaffe command decided to conduct a small reorganization. I./KG 4 was renamed I./KG 100 and remained in the west as part of this Geschwader. In return, KG4 received a 'new' first group, the former I./KG 100 under the command of Bätcher, who was promoted to the rank of Major on 1 November.

   The Gruppe was listed as part of KG 4 only formally and still remained an elite aviation group. In October 1943, I./KG 4 operated from the Nikolayev-OST air base, then was based in Kirovograd, and from November settled for a long time at the Sarabuz airfield (Crimea). During the winter, He 111s carried out a kind of 'circular defense' there: in the north, they regularly bombed the crossings over the Siwash being built by Soviet sappers, and in the east the Red Army's captured bridgehead in the Kerch region. Occasionally, the crews conducted reconnaissance over the sea and carried out raids on the ports of Tuapse and Novorossiysk, and a railway line running along the coast of the sea of Azov.

6 Fleigerbuch Hans Georg Bätcher. pp. 190–191.

surrounded German troops in the photo archives of German magazines. At this time, the forces of Wehrmacht units, isolated and abandoned in the many Pockets and the strength of the Luftwaffe's transport aircraft, which continued to supply them by air, continued to diminish.

The Russian 5th Air Army carried out 232 sorties during 8 February, mainly to attack ground targets in the area of the Horodyshche. At the same time, the planes dropped 22,000 propaganda leaflets, but shot down (according to Soviet data) only two German planes. On this day, the Soviets issued an ultimatum to the encircled troops on behalf of Marshal of the Soviet Union Zhukov, General of the Army Konev and General of the Army Vatutin. Its text was typical and actually copied a similar ultimatum put forward thirteen months previously by the 6th Army in Stalingrad. The Russians suggested that the encircled Germans surrender in full force and hand over all their military equipment intact to the Russians. In exchange, they were promised they could keep their military uniforms, insignia, orders and officers' cold weapons, to provide food, medical care, and after the war depart to any country in the world.

However, the Germans did not even respond to this 'gentleman's' offer by the Russians. The offensive of the deblocking group developed successfully. Unable to break through to Korsun Pocket from the south in the area of Shpola, the German III Panzer corps launched an offensive from the south-west along the axis of villages of Tihonovka, Lysyanka and Shanderovka. The four Panzer divisions that were part of it were able to quickly break through the Russian front. On 7 February, the Germans captured the village of Vinograd, and the next day occupied the villages of Tat'yanovka, Kosyakovka and Repki. At the headquarters of the 2nd Ukrainian front, the optimistic mood changed to panic. It became clear to the Russians that the Germans were breaking through to the Lysyanka–Shanderovka settlement line in order to join the encircled 8th Army troops in this area.

However, the beginning of the thaw made the roads almost impassable. There were 126 tanks and assault guns in the German strike group. Due to the thaw and Rasputitsa, heavy armored vehicles consumed three times more fuel than usual, but the fuel trucks were hopelessly stuck. The crews had no choice but to resort to delivering fuel on foot in buckets. The 'carriers' didn't cope well with the task; boots constantly stuck in the mud, then in the soft snow. Shells were also sorely lacking. It seems that the Germans would not be able to break through to their surrounded comrades in such conditions.

But soon, out of the fog at a low level, appeared the outwardly clumsy Ju 52 transport planes – splattered with mud and covered with soot! To get away from anti-aircraft fire, desperate pilots descended almost to the ground, literally hiding behind trees or low hills. Containers of ammunition, gasoline, and food rations fell to the sides of muddy roads. Mud and snow softened the impact of the containers on the ground to such an extent that even the heavy boxes of shells for tank guns did not receive any damage. With the delivery of gasoline things were more difficult. Every fifth barrel of fuel exploded on impact, but the rest reached their 'addressees'! When night fell and frost fettered the mud, the most experienced pilots landed in the open area along the roads by the light of their headlights.

On 9 February, in the area of Korsun, there was a heavy fog, sleet, and the air temperature was about 0°C. The Russians recorded a flight of 200 transport planes over the blockade ring. Among them were bombers from I./KG 4. Major Bätcher on this day set another record in his busy flying career. It carried out four Korsun Pocket supply missions at once (at 12.30, 15.45, 19.45 and 22.35). This intensity was the result of desperate requests for supplies from the deblocking group and the encircled troops. In total, He 111 Major Bätcher dropped 5 tons of cargo during the day. At the same time, only during the first 'lunch' flight did the plane's crew see two Soviet fighters in the sky. The rest of the flights took place without any opposition from the enemy.

The group of bombers from 1./KG 27, which took off from the Golta air base, was much less lucky. In the area of Korsun, they were attacked by Soviet fighters who shot down a He 111 H-16/R1 '1G+AH'. The bomber fell on the territory of Korsun Pocket, and all its crew (Feldwebel Theodor Klein and Feldwebel Konrad Schmidt, Obergefreiter Rudolf Bonisch, Obergefreiter Werner Kuhlen and Obergefreiter Ernst Schuwolka) were killed. Another He 111 H-16/R1 '1G+CH' received damage to the cockpit from enemy fire (navigator and radio operator were injured), but was able to return to base.

The Russian 5th Air Army flew eighty-eight sorties. The pilots reported ten downed Ju 52s. Planes of the 2nd air army twice attacked the Vinnitsa air base. The first raid involved twelve Il-2 ground-attack aircraft and sixteen La-5 fighters; the second – thirteen Il-2 ground-attack aircraft under the cover of eighteen fighters. Soviet pilots claimed twenty heavily damaged enemy transport planes. Ground-attack Il-2 aircraft from the 8th Guards SHAD shelled and bombed German troops inside the Pocket, including the landing site for transport planes near the village of Cherepen. The pilots reported that they destroyed six Ju 52s on the ground during the attack.

Meanwhile, the Russian 4th Guards army captured the German stronghold of Horodyshche, located southeast of Korsun Pocket. All the streets of the ruined city were filled with abandoned and burned cars, boxes, various goods and weapons were scattered everywhere. This was evidence that the Germans could no longer hold the entire defense perimeter; retreating, they concentrated all the defense in major strongpoints.

On 10 February, the Russians recorded a flight of 159 transport planes in the Korsun Pocket. Among them again was He 111 Major Bätcher. On this day, he made only one flight in the Pocket. The Russian 5th Air Army carried out eighty sorties, including forty-three to attack ground targets and landing sites of German aircraft in the Korsun area. The pilots reported eleven planes destroyed on the ground.

On this day, an experienced crew from the 587th Night Bomber Regiment (NBAP) (pilot Captain K.V. Ryzhakov, navigator Junior Lieutenant V.M. Firsov) received a 'combat task' directly from Stalin. Their mission was to use a Po-2 biplane in the afternoon to drop twelve pennants on Korsun Pocket with personal letters from Generalfeldmarschall Paulus and other German generals who were captured in Stalingrad. These 'gifts' were intended for the command of the encircled German group, and were intended to undermine their morale. The log of combat operations of the aviation regiment recorded:

> 16.15 departure from the Fursy airfield. 17.15 landing at Dashukovka airfield for refueling. Departure at 17.30. Heavy anti-aircraft fire over the target. At 18.15, pennants were dropped from a height of 50 meters. 19.15 landing on the Fursy airfield. Po-2 received 8 direct hits of small-caliber shells.

Whether the letters reached the recipients is unknown, but after successfully completing the mission to drop the pennants, the Po-2 crew was awarded the Order of the Red Banner. This example clearly shows the level of mental abilities of Stalin's generals and how much time and effort they spent on the implementation of such naïve, and frankly stupid, ideas.

On 11 February, the Korsun Pocket area still had warm and rainy weather, the air temperature was plus 4°C. The 5th Air Army carried out thirty-nine sorties, including twenty-four sorties to attack ground targets. The Russians bombed and strafed German aircraft landing-sites in the Korsun area several times and reported seventeen Ju 52s destroyed on the ground.

On this day, Major Hans Bätcher carried out three missions to supply the encircled troops. And each time the load of his bomber consisted of five 250-kilogram cargo containers with food and ammunition.[7] The flight at 14.45 on 11 February was the pilot's 655th and, as it turned out, last mission on the Eastern front. Despite the fact that a pair of Soviet fighters was trying to attack the bomber, at 16.10 it landed safely at the Novo-Nikolayevka airfield. Three days later, Bätcher was seconded to the headquarters of Luftflotte 4, and Hauptmann Ernst Gopel became commander of I./KG 4 instead.

On 12 February, the battle (the outcome of which would determine the fate of the blocked German group in the Korsun Pocket) reached its culmination. German tanks reached the Hnylyi Tikych river and reached the outskirts of the village of Lysianka. At the same time, the encircled troops began to break through in a south-westerly direction from the settlements of Steblev and Tarascha. 'The enemy's transport aircraft, despite very bad weather, continued to operate, dropping cargo to the encircled troops,' says the journal of combat operations of the 2nd Ukrainian front. 'A total of 150 flights of combat aircraft and sixty flights of transport aircraft were recorded.' At noon, an unusual incident occurred. At the fork in the road north of the village of Skalevatka, there was a former German Panther tank in ambush (buried and camouflaged) captured by the Russians from the 20th tank corps. Suddenly, a Ju 52 appeared out of the trees at a low altitude. The plane made a couple of circles over the tank, then dropped a container with 120 75-mm shells and a barrel of gasoline next to it. The pilots knew the silhouettes of German tanks well and took this one in the Russian service for a German one. The Russian crew of the German tank was very happy to receive such a valuable gift from the enemy.

The Soviet command took desperate measures not to let the Germans out of the Pocket, but the movement of Russian troops, as well as German ones, was hindered by the terrible Rasputitsa caused by rains and snow melting. T-34 tanks got stuck and sank in impassable mud, fuel trucks could not deliver them fuel. The artillery also could not pass to the areas of concentration. The horses that towed the guns could not get through the marshes that had formed. 'The troops are operating in extremely difficult conditions with complete impassability of roads, with a shortage of fuel for

---

7 Fleigerbuch Hans Georg Bätcher. pp. 192–3.

tanks and cars,' stated the headquarters of the 2nd Ukrainian front. 'The food supply of the soldiers is at the expense of local resources.'

The Russian air force was also experiencing serious problems. Because of the Rasputitsa, airfields were unsuitable for intensive take-offs and landings, most of the aircraft were idle. Many pilots after completing the mission could not find their air base, and landed on any flat ground, directly on the snow. The army command demanded that the air force obtain accurate information about the enemy and its movements. However, the air force could not comply with this order due to bad weather and a shortage of reconnaissance aircraft. Extraordinary measures were needed. On 12 February, the commander of the 1st ground-attack aviation corps (1st SHAK) General Alexey Ryazanov even had to form a special squadron consisting of six Il-2 ground-attack aircraft, which were supposed to perform a reconnaissance mission. Experienced crews of 'Zementbombers',[8] well-oriented on the ground, had to fly at a low level over German territory and control the movement of German tanks.

Although the Soviet troops were not surrounded, the air bridge on the opposite side was also operating intensively. The Russian air force had to spend a lot of effort to supply its troops in the Korsun Pocket area. For example, from 8–16 February, the 326th Night Bomber Division (NBAD), equipped with Po-2 aircraft, made 822 transport flights. At the same time, some of the cargo was dropped from the air, and some was unloaded during landings. In total, during this period, 49 tons of fuel, 65 tons of ammunition, and 620 rockets for Katyusha multiple rocket launchers (the Germans called them 'Stalin's Organs') were delivered to the Soviet troops.

On 13 February, He 111 bombers attacked the positions of the Russian 5th Guards tank army, which, with its endless slaughts, prevented the German group from breaking out of Korsun Pocket. Meanwhile, the German air bridge continued to work intensively. Ju 52s regularly flew over the heads of Russian tankers who had suffered significant losses from German bombs following in the area of Shanderovka and back. The Russian 5th Air Army flew 128 sorties, including sixty-four to attack ground targets and Korsun airfield. The pilots reported the destruction of twelve transport planes on the ground.

On 14 February, it was snowing heavily in the Korsun Pocket area. The Russian air force was inactive, which meant that there was no intelligence

---

8 'Zementbomber' is a common nickname of the Russian attack aircraft Il-2, which is apparently associated with the unreliability and clumsiness of this poorly designed and poorly built aircraft, which Stalin liked very much.

information about the German forces. The Russian command had no idea what was going on inside the blockade ring. When the Russian 52nd army reached Korsun in the evening in a fog, they found only empty streets and fifteen faulty Ju 52 aircraft. The Germans had already left to the southwest, moving all remaining units to the area of Shanderovka. But single Russian fighters still continued to fly in the Korsun Pocket area. He 111 H-16 W.Nr. 162104 was attacked by a fighter over Korsun; flight gunner Feldwebel Erwin Schrott and radio operator Unteroffizier Friedrich Brunner were injured. The bomber returned safely to the Proskuriv airfield (45 per cent damage), but the 20-year-old Brunner died in hospital eight days later. The 'military fate' of the other crew from 6./KG 27 was more cruel. The He 111 H-16 '1G+MP' W.Nr. 160967 which took off at 06.30 from Proskuriv airfield fell in the area of Stoblov for an unknown reason. The entire flight crew (Unteroffizier Johannes Vollmer, Gefreiter Gunther Bubik and Gefreiter Rudolf Menzel, Obergefreiter Heino Borchmann and Obergefreiter Johann Hanjes) joined the long list of missing persons.

On the night of 14–15 February, bombers from I./KG 27 continued their supply missions to blockaded German forces. When performing this flight at 00.31 He 111 H-16 '1G+DN' W.Nr. 161915 made an emergency landing inside Korsun Pocket for an unknown reason. Subsequently, the crew members were able to reach the German positions, with the exception of navigator Unteroffizier Erich Kuhne, who went missing.

On 15 February, Soviet intelligence belatedly found out that the Germans were burning and blowing up equipment that could not be taken with them and were preparing for a decisive break from the encirclement. However, the Soviet troops were completely unprepared for this development due to Rasputitsa and incompetent command. Russian tanks by this time were left without fuel and shells. For example, the 27th tank brigade had fifty T-34 tanks, but there was only enough diesel fuel to refuel a third of the tanks, and ammunition for only half of the available tanks. To prevent a German breakthrough, two Guards airborne divisions were urgently deployed. Incompetent Soviet generals ordered the soldiers of these divisions to dig in the open and repel the attacks of German tanks with anti-tank guns and grenades!

The Russians recorded a flight of twenty German transport planes over the blockade ring on 15 February. They dropped cargo containers from a low altitude near the village of Shanderovka.

On the night of 16 February, seventy transport planes flew over the positions of the 5th Guards tank army, which was desperately trying to contain the deblocking attack of German troops in the area of Lysyanka.

In the headquarters of Fleigerkorps VIII (VIII. Fl. Korp.) from the encircled German troops came a desperate radio message that the ammunition was running out. In order to save their comrades some TG 3 crews performed five missions a day at the limit of human capabilities.

During this period, transport planes flew mostly at night. There were two reasons for this: at night, dirty airfields froze, and landing on them became safer; in addition, the night sky allowed the transport planes to avoid contact with Soviet fighters.

German bomber crews also continued to sacrifice themselves. A He 111 H-16/R1 W.Nr. 161 929 '1G+BH' from 1./KG 27 crashed during a night sortie to supply the encircled troops near the village of Hristinovka. While flying at low altitude, the plane touched the ground, then fell and caught fire. Crew of five (Feldwebel Kurt Sperling, Feldwebel Heinz Blust, Unteroffizier Willibald Markus, Unteroffizier Max Raab and Obergefreiter Reinhard Beck) was killed.

On 16 February, the advancing German forces completely captured the village of Lysyanka and expanded the bridgehead on the north bank of the Hnylyi Tikych river. By 19.00 on the same day, they captured the village of Oktyabr'. As a result of fierce fighting, the strike group managed to break through a 20-kilometer-long corridor towards Korsun Pocket. Now parts of the III Panzer corps and the group General der Artillerie Stemmermann were separated by about 7 km.

On the night of 17 February, a breakout of the encircled German group from Korsun Pocket began on a 4.5-kilometer-wide front. At 03.00, a huge column headed by tanks and assault guns reached the positions of the 180th rifle division and the 5th Guards airborne division, which were defending in the area of the villages of Komarovka and Hil'ki. The Russian soldiers, who had almost no artillery or shells, were quickly crushed. After that, the Germans rushed in a continuous stream in a south-westerly direction. When dawn broke, the Russians saw several columns of German infantry, tanks, and convoys of wounded moving from the village of Shanderovka in the direction of Hil'ki. The headquarters of the 2nd Ukrainian front ordered the commanders of aviation units to collect all serviceable aircraft and strike at the breakout Germans. But the order was not carried out. Because of a heavy snowstorm that reduced visibility to 1 kilometer, no Russian aircraft took to the sky.

The effectiveness of the operation to unblock Korsun Pocket was largely due to the dedicated work of German transport planes. Over the course of seventeen days, TG 3 crews completed a total of 1,500 missions. During this time, more than 2,000 tons of cargo were delivered and more than 2,000 wounded were taken out.

However, the organization of the air bridge in Korsun Pocket cost the Germans significant losses. The Soviets claimed to have shot down and destroyed 329 aircraft on the ground, including 179 Ju 52s. Of course, these data were very different from reality and were inflated by the Russians several times.

The Luftwaffe did suffer heavy losses in this operation, but they were not as heavy as in Stalingrad. For example, the TG 3 lost 32 Ju 52/3m when supplying the Korsun Pocket. Another 113 aircraft were damaged in various ways, mainly by anti-aircraft fire from the ground and due to accidents. KG 27 lost five He 111 shot down and missing, and three more bombers were damaged. Twenty-two crew members sacrificed themselves to save the encircled troops.

Although the breakthrough was successful and a second 'Stalingrad' did not take place, the damage to the Wehrmacht in terms of privation, suffering and death of German soldiers was enormous. It was in every sense a Pyrrhic victory. Of the 56,000 soldiers who were surrounded, 37,000 eventually managed to make their way to the German forces. But at the same time they had to abandon all the artillery and heavy equipment; 11,000 German and Belgian soldiers, and Russian volunteers (Hiwi) were captured. All the drama and desperation of the surrounded German soldiers is well demonstrated by one egregious fact. Among those who did not escape from Korsun Pocket was 55-year-old General der Artillerie Stemmermann, who at dawn personally led his troops in the attack. The chaos and confusion of the Germans fleeing for their lives was so great that they did not notice the loss of their commander!

On 18 February, near the village of Petrovskii (halfway between the settlements of Shanderovka and Lysyanka), the Russians found a corpse in a general's uniform on the snow. He was carrying a soldier's book, a driver's license issued on 28 August, 1930, a hunting ticket issued on 1 April 1941, and other documents with photographs. They included the name Wilhelm Stemmermann. In addition, the body was identified by German prisoners who were personally familiar with the General. By order of General of the Army, Konev General der Artillerie Stemmermann (Hitler awarded him posthumously the Knight's Cross of the Iron Cross with Oak Leaves) was buried with military honors in a separate grave in the cemetery of the village of Jurjincy. This was a rare case when a Russian commander showed respect for a German commander.[9]

---

9 Subsequently, the Soviet totalitarian historians have completely misrepresented the facts about this battle and its finale. They lied that the German generals were the first to escape from Korsun Pocket in heavy tanks, escaping from there 'over the mountains of corpses of their soldiers'.

The main reason for this respect was the horror experienced by the Russians in a terrible and bloody war. Potentially, the Germans were not only able to take Moscow, but could also reach Novosibirsk. Soviet military leaders knew first-hand the consequences of the crushing blows of the German war hammer. Fortunately for the Russians, Hitler's vices to a greater extent contributed to the extermination of the Wehrmacht and the Luftwaffe, as well as to the destruction of his Communist enemies, and ultimately led to the collapse of the Third Reich itself.

Responsible for the collapse of the operation to destroy the German group, Ivan Konev, General of the Army and commander of the 2nd Ukrainian front, made a false report to Stalin, in which he tried to pass off his failure as a major victory. 'Our troops – infantry, tanks, cavalry and artillery – fell on the enemy, fire, bayonet, tracks and sabers during the day led to a merciless destruction of the enemy,' he wrote. Sovinformburo – the main information and propaganda body of the Soviet Union during the war – also announced the complete defeat and degradation of Wehrmacht. 'Captured Germans told that for the last 3–4 days soldiers and officers of the surrounded troops committed mass suicides,' the message said. 'Wounded German soldiers and officers were killed and burned by order of the Main command … The encircled German troops left 52,000 corpses on the battlefield, 11,000 soldiers surrendered.' Stalin believed in the deception and on 20 February awarded Ivan Konev the title of Marshal of the Soviet Union.

In fact, the Soviets suffered more damage in the operation to block Korsun Pocket than the encircled Germans. In total, 80,000 people were lost (killed and wounded), including 24,286 killed, dead and missing, as well as 850 tanks and self-propelled guns. For example, in the 5th Guards tank army of General Rotmistrov (staff strength of about 800 tanks), by the end of the battle, only forty tanks had survived.

Chapter 8

Hundred 'Pockets' on Hitler's uniform

Kamenets-Podolsky Pocket

Despite all the sacrifices made, the situation for the Wehrmacht was constantly getting worse. Thoroughly battered Army Group 'South' had not yet had time to take a breath after the Korsun 'meat grinder', as in early March, the Red Army launched an even more large-scale offensive on a huge area from Pripet Marshes to the mouth of the Dnieper river. The bloodless divisions could not hold off this pressure for long. The Russians pushed the Germans back in all directions and began to move rapidly towards the Carpathians.

In the southern sector of the Eastern front, the Germans were in complete chaos. Hitler's 'strategy' led to more and more new crises and catastrophes. The German divisions that were struggling to break out of the encirclement were usually rendered non-combatant and almost without weapons (all heavy weapons were destroyed or abandoned) and could no longer fight fully. The resulting gaps in the front line were plugged by poorly prepared 'new' divisions. Further, the Soviets struck again; the Führer forbade retreat, and another sacrifice to the bloody god of war began.

Instead of a single front line, there were various battle groups formed from units that happened to be in the same area. German infantry and Panzer divisions were mixed up with each other, losing a clear structure and control system. An even bigger problem was the numerous volunteer formations and rear units that had lost their functions and turned into a disorganized crowd. The German command practically lost control of the situation. Communication between isolated battle groups was carried out mainly by radio. All this was supplemented by cloudy and rainy weather, which led to the premature onset of Rasputitsa. All ground supply lines were cut or operated inefficiently. Air bases were disorganized and worked with the overexertion of forces.

On 25 March 1944, a huge German group with a total strength of about 200,000 people was completely surrounded in the area of the city of Kamenets-Podolsky. There were Gruppe 'Beukelmann' Gruppe 'Maus', Gruppe 'Gollnik', Kampfgruppe 'Hotin', Gruppe 'Chevallier', 75th Infantry Division, 82nd Infantry Division and 168th Infantry Division, 18th Artillery Division, 1st Panzer-Division, 6th Panzer Division, 7th Panzer Division, 16th Panzer Division and 17th Panzer Division. General command over these motley units was exercised by the 1st Panzer Army headquarters (1. Panzerarmee) led by Generaloberst Hans-Valentin Hube. Simultaneously with the emergence of the Kamenets-Podolsky Pocket, some units of the 4th Panzer Army (4. Panzerarmee) were encircled in the area of the city of Tarnopol. Thus, 120 km north-west of the city of Kamenets-Podolsky, Tarnopol Pocket arose.

Luftflotte 4 again received the routine order to organize an air bridge to supply the encircled German troops. However, each subsequent mission to supply the encircled troops created new insurmountable difficulties for German transport aviation, exhausted by endless sacrifices.

After the Stalingrad disaster, the Luftwaffe did not, and could not, draw the right conclusions about the development strategy and tactics of using transport aircraft. Due to the pathological traits of Göring and his 'carefully'chosen inner circle, the Luftwaffe turned from a separate branch of the armed forces into a rusty 'crutch' to support the terminally ill invalid that the once brilliant Wehrmacht had become by 1944. As in 1942, the new air bridge was built by improvisation and plugging holes. As early as January 1944, due to a shortage of aircraft, the staff strength of transport Geschwader was reduced from 217 to 192 aircraft. Transport Gruppen were reduced to three Staffel, which included sixteen aircraft each. This decision was primarily due to the decline in production of transport planes. While 1,028 transport planes were produced in 1943, including 887 Ju 52/3m, the following year this figure fell to 443, of which 379 were 'Aunt Ju'. Moreover, there was no real replacement for the long-obsolete Ju 52. German transport aircraft on the Eastern front could operate minimally effectively only thanks to the incurable defects fighters and anti-aircraft artillery of Red Army.

The vicious practice of using bombers to deliver supplies to the encircled German forces was further developed in 1944. As a result of this and a number of other reasons, the bomber Geschwader of the Luftwaffe degraded and the level of professional training of pilots steadily fell. The attempt to introduce new models of bombers ended in shameful failure. The Luftwaffe leadership could no longer think of strategic bombing of the deep Russian rear. The harsh reality was that there was a shortage of bombers to tactically contain the advancing Russian forces, which also added to the already monstrous Wehrmacht crisis.

The operation to supply 'fresh' Pockets formed in 1944 was assigned to the 2nd Air transport command (Tg.Fl.F.2) led by Generalmajor Friedrich-Wilhelm Morzik. To supply the encircled German groups in a short time he managed to collect a very significant force of transport aircraft:

- III. and IV./TG 1, I./TG 4 at Kalarashi airfield. They were equipped with SM.82 and Ju 52 transport planes;
- III./TG 2 at Galati airfield (Ju 52);
- I./TG 1 and II./TG 2 at Karli Chiki airfield (Ju 52);
- one Staffel from I./TG 3 at Constanța airfield (Ju 52);
- I./TG 2 (Ju 52), TGr. 30 (He 111 H-20) and Schleppgruppe two (Ju 87 B glider tugs with Go 242 and DFS 230 cargo gliders) at Bacau airfield;
- II./TG 5 (Me 323) and separate Transportstaffel 5 (Ju 290, Piaggio P.108T)[1] at Zilistea and Focșani airfields;
- III./TG 3 (Ju 52) at the Dana Chiki airfield. In addition, several Gruppen bomber aircraft were additionally allocated to supply the Kamenets-Podolsky Pocket:
- I./KG 4 'General Wever' (He 111) at Milec airfield;
- and II./KG 27 (He 111) at Lemberg airfield (city of Lviv).

In total, these units had about 300 aircraft (150 Ju 52, 100 He 111 and about fifty other aircraft of various types).

By 25 March, most of the assigned units had arrived at dirty and overcrowded air bases. The organization of work at the airfields was very different from German standards and more in line with the disorder accepted by the Russians. Technical staff refueling aircraft used hand pumps directly from barrels of gasoline. Despite the bad weather, the operation to organize the air bridge began the next day. Landing inside the Kamenets-Podolsky Pocket was carried out at the Proskuriv air base, which was the only place that was suitable for this purpose. However, the Kamenets-Podolsky Pocket differed in that it was, so to speak, a 'Wandering Pocket' ('Wandernde Kessel'). The units defending its western front were gradually advancing,

---

1 Piaggio P.108T (P.108T) transport modification of the Italian heavy four-engine bomber, produced in small quantities. The aircraft had a length of 23 m, a wingspan of 32 m, and a range of 3,500 km. It could carry up to sixty people.

and those in the east were also gradually withdrawing, while preventing the encirclement front from contracting. Therefore, in the future, along the route of retreat, a special team conducted reconnaissance of the area and organized temporary landing sites. The temporary landing site was indicated by radio beacons and light signals. Special code signals in the form of crosses, circles and triangles were also developed. For example, KG 27 between 22 March and 11 April used thirty different landing sites and designated places to dump cargo containers: Kurylowce-Murowane, Sauca, Wierzbowiez, Nefedowcze, Dunajewce, Sinkoff, Bolschaja Lewada, Berezanka, Bricani Targ, Wonkowzy, Lipcani, Gruzka, Rozca, Nowa Sulita, Kamenez Podolsk, Hotin, Surzence, Marianowka, Borszczow, Ulaskowce, Jezierzany, Nowosiolka, Kostiakowa, Mielnica, an der Straße Jagielnica-Czortkow, Fluste Miaste, Glebozcek, Worwolince, Berestek, Gleboka, Jagielnica (given in the German designation).

At the end of March, the airfield in the city of Kamenets-Podolsky was mainly used for cargo delivery. Ju 52, He 111 and Me 323 kept landing there until the Soviet tanks arrived on the outskirts of the city.

The authors do not have complete data on Luftwaffe losses for this period, but the example of KG 27 shows that they were significant. On the first day of the operation – 26 March – this Kampfgeschwader lost two aircraft. At 12.18, a group of bombers from the 4th Staffel took off from Lemberg airfield (city of Lviv). Some of them had to dump the cargo at the Bolschaja Lewada landing site, others at the Berezanka landing site. During the flight over Kamenets-Podolsky Pocket, two He 111 H-20s (W.Nr. 700260 '1G+AM and W.Nr. 700271 '1G+HP') experienced were problems with their engines. One of the bombers was able to fly to German territory and make an emergency landing 2 km north of the city of Lviv. The second German plane went missing with a crew of five people. Another bomber (He 111 '1G+LM') was damaged by ground fire. The flight gunner was injured, but the plane returned safely to the air base.

Although the fact that the surrounded Germans were being supplied by air in this sector was recorded by Russian intelligence, the Soviet air force did not interfere with the operation of the air bridge. This strange fact has a logical explanation. The fact is that the data received by Russian intelligence was incomplete. Intelligence information obtained directly as a result of aerial surveillance was practically absent. This was due to the fact that the Luftwaffe airfields were located 150–250 km or more from Kamenets-Podolsky Pocket and were scattered over a large area. At such a long distance, Soviet reconnaissance planes (of which there were only fifteen in this sector of the front) simply could not fly. As at the beginning of the war, in 1944 the function of tactical reconnaissance for the Soviets was most often performed by conventional fighters, whose range did not exceed 100–120 km in winter.

The analysis of indirect data obtained during the interrogation of prisoners, the analysis of transport planes' flight routes and other information, produced few results. This was largely due to the extremely low competence of Russian intelligence officers and the outright stupidity of the country's leaders. Despite the huge amount of speculation and gossip collected, the Russians had no idea how Luftwaffe transport aircraft was organized, where it was based, and what types of aircraft were involved in organizing the air bridge.

Thus, the concentration of Luftwaffe transport aircraft was not recorded by Russian intelligence, and no other types of aircraft, other than the usual Ju 52, were noticed.

The efficiency of the Soviet air force was not the best either. Formally, the mission of fighting Luftwaffe transport planes in the area of Kamenets-Podolsky Pocket was to be carried out by the Russian 2nd Air Army (2 VA). By the end of March 1944, it consisted of four air corps and five separate air divisions, totaling 709 aircraft (279 fighters, 159 ground-attack aircraft, fifty-seven bombers, 199 night bombers, and fifteen reconnaissance aircraft). At the same time, the Russian Air Army command estimated the number of Luftwaffe forces at 642 aircraft (based on intelligence data).

Based on the situation, on 27 March the command of the 2nd Air Army (2 VA) assigned its units a priority mission of direct support to the advancing Soviet troops. And only the 10th fighter aviation corps (10th IAC) in cooperation with the 224th attack aircraft aviation division (224th SHAD) was assigned a mission to 'fight against enemy transport aircraft in the area of the village of Dunaivtsi'. At 14.56, the crews of Pe-2 bombers from the 202nd bomber aviation division (202nd BAD) bombed the village of Dunaivtsi and reported that a group of Ju 52s was standing in a nearby field. At 19.40, six Il-2 ground-attack aircraft, accompanied by four fighters, attacked this site and reported the destruction of two transport planes, ten trucks that were under loading, and damage to several more German aircraft.

The next day, 2nd Air Army (2 VA) fighters were mostly engaged in attacks on ground targets, according to Russian reports. Russian bombers and ground-attack aircraft attacked concentrations of German troops in the area of the Tarnopol Pocket and the crossing of the Dniester river. Although the fight against German transport aircraft was also an important mission of the 2nd Air Army (2 VA), no success in this direction was reported by the Russians. This situation was highly typical for boastful Russian official reports, where success was usually exaggerated.

On 29 March, the command of the Soviet air force for the second time ordered units of the 2nd Air Army (2 VA) to 'prevent the operation of enemy transport aircraft in the area of the village of Dunaivtsi'. But unlike air attacks on crossings and clusters of vehicles and tanks (the crews of Soviet bombers reported dozens of destroyed German trucks), no information was received about the success of the fight against transport planes.

As happened before, the Soviet troops blocking the Germans in the Kamenets-Podolsky Pocket were also often supplied by air. For example, the 208th Night Bomber Division (NBAD) (208th NBAD) delivered ammunition for Russian tank units directly to the front line. Luftwaffe activity increased significantly compared to the previous days. 'In large groups of 30-40 bombers accompanied by 3-4 fighters, and sometimes without cover, German planes bombarded the battle lines of the troops of the 13th and 60th armies', the Soviet journal of combat operations reported. At the same time, the intensive work of the German transport aircraft, as well as the places of its base and landing (in addition to the mentioned village of Dunaivtsi) were again not recorded by Soviet intelligence.

'The enemy's aircraft continued to be active,' the Russian combat report for 30 March reported. 'In the area southwest and west of Tarnopol, enemy bomber aircraft bombed the battle formations of the 13th and 60th armies… A total of 65 flights of aircraft were recorded, including 40 transport planes.' Twenty-four fighters from the 331st Fighter Aviation Division (331st IAD) were specially assigned to intercept transport planes, but their actions were unsuccessful due to bad weather. However, all transport planes of the Luftwaffe suffered losses. During a flight to supply German infantry, a He 111 H-20 W.Nr. 700274 '1G+GK' from 2./KG 27 went missing with a crew of five.

And only on the last day of March, the 2nd Air Army (2 VA), according to Soviet documents, achieved the first serious success in the fight against transport planes of the Luftwaffe. On that day, at an altitude of 600–800 meters, there was cloud cover, light snow, and visibility was from 4 to 10 km. In the morning, the crews of Russian reconnaissance planes reported that German transport planes were landing and taking off en masse right on the northern edge of the city of Kamenets-Podolsky. In this regard, the fighters of the 5th fighter aviation corps (5th IAC) and the 10th fighter aviation corps (10th IAC) were ordered to attack them. The pilots made several raids in the specified area and reported ten Ju 52s shot down in the air and four more German transport planes destroyed on the ground.

The authors do not have information about the losses of Ju 52, but serious losses from the actions of Russian aviation were suffered by He 111s from KG 27. During take-off from the Kamenets-Podolsky airfield with the mission of transferring a radio beacon to another landing site He 111 H-20 W.Nr. 700414 '1G+AK' from the 2nd Staffel was suddenly attacked by low-flying Russian planes. As a result, the German bomber suffered much damage and was unable to take off. Two crew members (radio operator and flight gunner) and three radio operators who were on board as passengers were injured.

On the morning of 1 April, He 111 H-20 W.Nr. 700212 '1G+DP' from 6./KG 27 first dropped cargo containers near the settlement of Rusha, then landed in Kamenets-Podolsky Pocket to pick up wounded soldiers. At 10.55, the bomber took off, but was soon attacked and shot down by Russian fighters. The entire crew of five people was missing. A similar mission was dertaken by He 111 H-20 W.Nr. 700155 '1G+BM' of 4./KG 27. After dropping cargo containers near the village of Rusha, the plane landed in Kamenets-Podolsky Pocket. After loading the wounded soldiers on board, it took off and headed northwest. Soon, in the area of Koszowa, it was suddenly attacked by Russian fighters. As a result, flight engine Unteroffizier Paul Retschlag was killed on board and two crew members were injured (radio operator Gefreiter Dieter Kreh and flight gunner Obergefreiter Karl Scholz). However, the He 111 managed to evade the chase and landed safely at Lemberg air base (city of Lviv).

On 2 April, 2nd Air Army (2 VA) aviation regiments received the same missions as before. In particular, it was again ordered to 'fight the enemy's transport aircraft'. In fact, the Soviet air force was inactive on this day. 'The air force of the 2nd VA did not fulfill the task they were facing because of bad weather conditions and unsuitability of airfields,' the Russian combat summary reported.

However, the Germans also faced problems, and starting from 2 April, deliveries to Kamenets-Podolsky Pocket by air were somewhat reduced due to weather conditions. During the day, there were constant snowstorms and low clouds in the Pocket area. Transport planes began to fly mostly at night, when weather conditions were more favorable. The German pilots again worked with incredible dedication. Planes began taking off right after dark. The Ju 52, He 111, Ju 290 and Me 323 took off at intervals of three to five minutes. Each crew tried to perform the maximum number of sorties to supply their comrades, many made up to four or five missions a day.

Meanwhile, on 3 April, the Russian air force almost did not go up in the sky. Only the 5th ground-attack aviation corps (5th SHAK) and 331st IAD were active. At the same time, a pair of Il-2 ground-attack aircraft (master-Captain Vatkov) attacked German vehicles in the locality of Mushkatovka. During the first approach to attack, the pilots suddenly saw seven Ju 52s standing on the south-western edge of the settlement. After that, ground-attack aircraft made another approach to attack and fired at transport planes. According to Captain Vatkov's report, one enemy aircraft was damaged. In general, the success in the fight against the German transport aircraft was again very modest.

On 4 April, weather conditions improved. The Luftwaffe not only activated flights to Kamenets-Podolsky Pocket, but also launched a series of airstrikes against Soviet troops and airfields. So, at 11.00, a pair of Fw 190 ground-attack aircraft suddenly attacked the Zubuv airfield, damaging two Yak-9 fighters and injuring seven people from the ground staff. At 13.05–15.35, a group of German ground-attack aircraft made a second raid on the same target, dropping five high-explosive bombs and several containers with small fragmentation bombs. As a result, sixteen Yak-9 fighters were damaged and one person was killed.

During this period, the 2nd Air Army (2 VA) was again virtually inactive. And this time it was not the weather that prevented it, but a shortage of aviation oil. It was completely absent from seven of the sixteen airfields where the 2nd Air Army (2 VA) was based. Three more airfields were out of petrol, and six Russian airfields had close to zero fuel supplies. The airfields themselves were still unsuitable for take-offs and landings due to the effects of rain. In this difficult situation, the Russian commander was forced to send light night bombers Po-2 (also U-2) to launch a daytime bombing strike on the surrounded German group. The 208th Night Bomber Aviation Division (208th NBAD) and the 326th Night Bomber Aviation Division (326th NBAD) flew sixty-five sorties and lost one aircraft. The strange decision to use low-speed biplanes during the day was explained simply – it was easier to take off from dirty airfields. 'Active struggle' with Luftwaffe transport aircraft was conducted only by fighters of the 10th fighter aviation corps (10th IAK). According to the pilots' report, seven Ju 52s were damaged at a site 1 km southwest of the village of Ivankovo (not confirmed by German data).

On 5 April, the 2nd Air Army (2 VA) combat summary reported: 'The enemy's transport aircraft, despite strong opposition from our aircraft and heavy losses, continued to transport cargo for the encircled groups'. Over exactly which Soviet units provided this 'strong opposition', and what 'losses' the enemy's transport aircraft suffered however, the Russians were modestly silent.

The Germans again twice attacked Zubuv airfield, where the 5th IAK was based, and destroyed two Yak-9 and one Li-2, and damaged four Yak-9 fighters. Russian losses were four people. Soviet fighters did not take off to intercept, as 'the airfield was not suitable for operation'. In total, about 300 flights of Luftwaffe aircraft were recorded in the Kamenets-Podolsky Pocket area.

On 7 April, the 331st IAD received orders: 'Destroy enemy transport aircraft on the Brody-Podgaytsy line.' But the Soviet battle report did not report any success in this direction on this day. Po-2 biplanes, accompanied by Yak-1 and Yak-9 fighters, were again widely used for bombing German troops during the day.

On 8 April, the 19th IAP received a special mission to conduct a free hunt against transport planes in the area of the settlements of Yahilnytsya and Tluste. Again, no information about downed German planes was received by the 2nd Air Army (2 VA) headquarters. Apparently, the Russian pilots simply did not find any targets. Despite the increased number of flights due to improved weather conditions (cloud cover at an altitude of 800–2,000 m, visibility was up to 8 km), the Soviet air force still operated chaotically, in small groups or even as separate aircraft. Planes had to be towed from parking lots to the runway by tractors, and there was a chronic shortage of fuel and engine oil (fuel trucks got stuck in the mud, and supplies were carried out mainly by air).

On the night of 10 April, pilots of the 208th NBAD accidentally discovered a 'night airfield' 10 km southwest of the village of Yahilnytsya, where German transport planes were supposedly landing. Soviet aircraft crews reported five transport planes landing and taking off and four more standing on the ground unloading. Light bomber Po-2 dropped bombs on the airfield, reporting one destroyed transport airplane of unknown type. The next day, Russian fighter pilots from the 10th IAC found another temporary airfield 8 km west of city Buchach, where four Bf 109s, one Bf 110 and two Ju 52s were located. Soon this target was attacked by five Il-2 ground-attack aircraft from the 224th SHAP. The pilots reported one Ju 52 destroyed on the ground.

In this way, the German reports of a fairly weak response from the Soviet air defense and aviation during the supply of surrounded units of the 1st Panzer Army (1. Panzerarmee) were true. At the same time, German pilots complained more about anti-aircraft fire than about attacks by Soviet fighters. Transport planes' flight routes were constantly changing, and areas free of anti-aircraft guns were selected. Dumping cargo containers on parachutes was widely practised. The He 111 H-20 typically carried nine 250-kg containers, or eight 250-kg containers and one 500-kg container. The Ju 52 also took on board containers that were dropped manually through a cargo hatch or open doors. At the last stage of the operation, 1st Panzer Army (1. Panzerarmee) was ordered to eat at the expense of requisitioned food from the local population. Therefore, transport planes focused on delivery mainly of ammunition, gasoline and spare parts for tanks to the blocked German troops.

On 8 April, after hard fighting and a 300-kilometer dash to the west, the advanced German units joined the II SS Panzer Corps (II. SS-Panzerkorps) in the area of Buchach. The last sorties of transport planes to supply the already unblocked German group were carried out on 10 April. Although soldiers of the 1st Panzer Army (1. Panzerarmee) ate almost all their horses, and most of the heavy weapons got stuck in the mud and were abandoned, almost all 200,000 people escaped capture and death.

Luftwaffe transport aircraft performed about 8,000 flights to supply Kamenets-Podolsky Pocket, delivering 4,000 tons of cargo to the encircled troops. This was an average of 200–250 tons per day. This was close to the minimum supply requirement, which back in 1942 was requested by the fallen 6th Army in Stalingrad.

Kovel Pocket

In addition to the 'Wandering Pocket' in the area of the city of Kamenets-Podolsky in the same period, the Luftwaffe supplied by air two more surrounded German garrisons. In mid-March, the 2nd Belorussian Front troops advancing through the forests along the Pripet Marshes reached the town of Kovel (150 km northeast of Lviv). Since this was the last strong point on the way to the city of Brest-Litovsk, located in the deep rear of the Army Group 'Mitte', still defending on the banks of the Dnieper river, the German command issued orders to defend the city 'at all costs'. Hitler declared Kovel the next Festung. As a result of the active resistance of German troops, the Soviets surrounded the city of Kovel, but could not advance further. As a result of all these events, Kovel Pocket was formed.

On 25 March, a small strike group using Panther heavy tanks managed to break through to Kovel Pocket and deliver supplies and reinforcements there. Two days later, German troops began an operation to unblock the encircled garrison. Since during the same period the Luftwaffe were busy supplying Kamenets-Podolsky Pocket and the garrison of another Festung – Tarnopol Pocket (more on this later), the supply by air of Kovel Pocket was carried out irregularly. In addition, DFS 230 cargo gliders from Schlepp. Gr.1 were used for the transport mission.

On 2 April, during a mission to drop cargo containers to the garrison Kovel Pocket He 111 H-20 W.Nr. 700490 '1G+CL' of 3./KG 27 was damaged by anti-aircraft fire; flight gunner Obergefreiter Franz Tripold was injured on board. The plane suffered 20 per cent damage, but was able to return safely to the Krosno air base.

On 3 April, St./JG 51 suffered heavy losses during sorties to escort the Ju 52 in the Kovel area. In the morning, two fighters were shot down: Fw 190 A-5 W.Nr. 157230 Unteroffizier Franz Kindler and Fw 190 A-6 W.Nr. 550885 Oberfeldwebel Kurt Walz. Unteroffizier Kindler parachuted out and was later captured, while Oberfeldwebel Walz was killed. According to Soviet data, on 3 April the commander of the 163rd Fighter Aviation Regiment (163rd IAP), Lieutenant Colonel P.A. Pologov, east of Kovel Pocket (near the village of Kolodyajnoe) shot down a Ju 52 and two Fw 190, and he RAM the Fw 190 with his own plane. The Russian pilot escaped by jumping out with a parachute.

On 5 April, with the continuous support of Ju 87 and Hs 129 ground-attack aircraft, two German Panzer divisions managed to crush the Russian defense and break through the blockade ring. Later, the corridor was expanded and the city of Kovel remained in the hands of the Wehrmacht. Thus, although for objective reasons the air bridge in Kovel Pocket existed for a short time, it played a significant role in supplying the blocked group of German troops.

Tarnopol Pocket

Much more dramatic was the 'military fate' of a small German garrison in the city of Tarnopol (120 km south-east of the city of Lviv). On 26 March, the Germans took up a circular defense in the hope of a quick release.

The supply of the Tarnopol Pocket was mainly carried out by He 111 bombers from KG 27 and TGr. 30, as well as by DFS 230 cargo gliders from Schlepp.Gr.1. The operation took place in the face of strong opposition from Soviet air defense, especially anti-aircraft artillery. Therefore, all missions took place only in the early morning and evening with limited visibility. Adverse weather conditions (snowstorms with strong winds) also made it very difficult to pilot cargo gliders. Glider pilots had to show great skill and endurance to save their own lives and deliver supplies to their surrounded comrades. The dangerous landing technique required them to accurately perform a number of very risky maneuvers. After detaching from the He 111 glider tugs, the cargo gliders pilots had to overcome the barrage of Russian anti-aircraft guns, find a small runway on the outskirts of the city, and land on it from the first approach. To increase the chances of success in the face of Russian anti-aircraft artillery, the Germans were forced to improvise and make some risky additions to the dangerous tactics of landing gliders. After detaching from the glider tugs, cargo gliders circled in the air for a while, while the bombers descended and began to bomb the positions of Russian anti-aircraft batteries, dropping one or two fragmentation bombs. Thus, the desperate crews of the He 111, making several passes, forced the Russian anti-aircraft gunners to press to the ground and diverted their fire. At this time, DFS 230 cargo gliders were rapidly gliding towards the city and landing.

However, pilots of successfully landed cargo gliders were not taken back for use in following missions. After that, qualified pilots, whose training took a lot of time, became simple infantrymen. Since the days of Holm Pocket much had worsened for the Luftwaffe and the Wehrmacht. There were simply no Fi 156 aircraft to save the brave and valuable pilots of cargo gliders. Thus, after delivering supplies to the encircled troops, the pilots got their hands on weapons and joined the garrison at Tarnopol Pocket. The shortage of aircraft forced the Luftwaffe, as in the case of towing cargo gliders, to charge the He 111 crews to perform two missions in a single flight. The bombers that dropped cargo containers into the fortress also carried fragmentation bombs on an external sling, which were previously dropped on Soviet positions around the city.[2] This excessive overexertion of the bomber pilots created additional difficulties for them and led to losses.

The degree of risk to the bombers used to supply the blocked German group can be demonstrated by a number of combat episodes. On 29 March

2 Pegg M. Transporter Volume Twu: Luftwaffe Transport Units 1943-1945. Luftwaffe Colours. – Classic Publications, 2008. p. 136.

in the district of Tarnopol Pocket He 111 H-20 W.Nr. 700195 '1G+AN' from 5./KG 27 was damaged by Russian anti-aircraft fire. Radio operator, flight engineer and flight gunner were injured as a result of shrapnel hits. However, the bomber returned safely to base, and its damage was estimated at 5 per cent.

On 30 March, a He 111 H-20 W.Nr. 700226 '1G+AC' from 6./KG 27 was shot down during a flight to supply the Tarnopol Pocket. The burning bomber fell on the city 300 meters from the Catholic church. The entire crew of the Hauptmann Ralf Selter was killed. In addition, Russian anti-aircraft gunners damaged another bomber, He 111 H-20 W.Nr. 700267 '1G+EP' from the same Staffel. A flight gunner was injured, but the plane managed to drop cargo containers and then return to base.

The Russian air force was not very active due to bad weather. It was not until 31 March, when the sky became clear, that the Soviets gathered their strength. Twenty-six Pe-2 dive bombers, eighty-three Il-2 ground-attack aircraft accompanied by forty-one fighters made a massive raid on the Tarnopol Pocket. Then, in the evening of the same day, a second raid was made on the city with the participation of twenty-seven Il-2 ground-attack aircraft accompanied by thirty-four fighters. A total of 45 tons of bombs were dropped on the target, causing numerous fires.

Meanwhile, the situation of the German garrison was getting worse. As long as the landing site remained in the hands of the defending Germans, the volume of deliveries was kept at the level of 12–15 tons per day. After it was captured, transport planes could only dump cargo containers by parachute. As a result, the volume of deliveries immediately decreased to 8 tons per day. However, even these loads most often didn't get to the surrounded Germans. On 1 April, the garrison commander Generalmajor von Neidorf reported by radio that only five of the ninety cargo containers dropped the previous night had ended up in the hands of German soldiers. The rest landed in enemy territory, drowned in lakes and swamps, or were simply lost among the ruins of the city.

Meanwhile, the Soviet forces continued to tighten the encirclement. By 4 April, the Russians had captured most of the city of Tarnopol. And from the south-west to Pocket the deblocking German group tried to break through. Aware of the desperate situation of the defenders of the Tarnopol Pocket, on the night of 14 April, the German units made a last-ditch attempt to unblock the garrison. However, the desperate attack did not achieve its goal. At the same time, He 111 aircraft continued to drop cargo containers on parachutes to supply the Tarnopol Pocket. On 6 April, KG 27 suffered another loss during this mission; He 111 H-20 W.Nr. 700540 '1G+IK' from the 2nd Staffel went missing in the area of Tarnopol Pocket along with a crew of five people. This was another sacrifice of young pilots for the sake of continuing the senseless struggle.

At noon on 15 April, the last radio message came from Pocket that Generalmajor von Neidorf had fallen in battle... Fighting on the outskirts of the city of Tarnopol subsided after two days;[3] 2,400 German soldiers and officers joined the list of prisoners.

The greatest contribution to the supply of encircled German groups in the southern sector of the Eastern front was made by TGr. 30 Major Walter Hornung. From 25 March to 8 April, this aviation group, flying He 111 aircraft, made 1,285 transport flights, delivering 11,020 cargo containers with a total weight of 1,670 tons. On 9 June, Hornung was awarded the Knight's Cross for successful completion of the tasks.

The number of Luftwaffe transport aircraft were steadily dwindling, and there was almost nothing to replace them with. Ahead of the German armed forces there were still many hard trials. They were waiting for the collapse that was already inevitable. Almost all of the Luftwaffe's further efforts were reduced to endless attempts to postpone this bitter finale.

---

3 Pegg M. Transporter Volume Twu: Luftwaffe Transport Units 1943-1945. Luftwaffe Colours. – Classic Publications, 2008. p. 136.

Chapter 9

Shadow of Stalingrad on the Danube

Another collision between two psychopaths

The second half of 1944 was a period of new defeats and catastrophes for the Third Reich. In the West, the Allies landed troops in France and eventually drove the German armies back to the western borders of the Reich. In the East, the Wehrmacht lost vast territories from the city of Leningrad to the Crimean Peninsula. In the south, German troops were forced to abandon most of Italy and almost the entire Balkan Peninsula. In addition, Hitler lost his 'allies' – Bulgaria and Romania. Air attacks by British and American bombers on German territory reached a climax, and all major cities and factories were methodically reduced to ruins. Therefore, in the autumn of 1944, many people rightly thought that the collapse of Hitler's empire was closer than ever.

But at the end of the year the situation suddenly changed. After a stunning summer of success, the Red Army bogged down into the German defenses in Courland, East Prussia, Poland and Slovakia. From September to December 1944, only fierce positional battles were fought on most of the Eastern front. The reasons for this sudden stop must be found in the psychological and physical state of both sides of the military conflict. Duped by Nazi propaganda, the German people and the Wehrmacht were ready to make the last bloody sacrifices – not only for the sake of the infuriated Führer, but also under the threat of an invasion of the Third Reich by Soviet troops full of vengeance. They had already experienced how terrible this revenge could be, and this horror gave them new strength to resist. A significant reduction in the length of the front line allowed the Wehrmacht to bring its battered divisions into relative order and free up 'reserves', which together with the newly formed divisions significantly strengthened the defense. The concentration of all German industry in the hands of the state on the Soviet model led to a temporary increase in the production of military products.

From the Soviet side, there were also serious reasons for slowing the offensive. Contrary to the prevailing myth of the limitless human resources of the USSR, by 1944 the Russians began to experience a serious shortage in completing their army units. Many experienced Red Army soldiers in 1944 were not in the best physical condition after numerous injuries. The weapons produced in giant military factories using simplified technologies were of terrible quality. The complexity of equipment supplied by lend-lease caused the Soviet soldiers endless surprises. Soviet mechanics and drivers had a culture of not servicing American and British tanks and vehicles, which often led to them failing, unable to withstand the harsh conditions barbaric operation.

The temporary suspension of the Red Army promotion caused Hitler unreasonable optimism. He issued an appeal to the nation, in which he stated that in the current difficult conditions, Germany must stand, thanks to fanatical resistance and the use of 'wonder weapons' (Wunderwaffe). He convinced his small-minded colleagues that the Third Reich had a chance to 'rise from the ashes like a Phoenix'.

But at this turning point the Führer had a new headache, which interrupted his euphoria about the current 'generally optimistic situation'. Hungary, another 'loyal' ally of Germany, hastened to withdraw from the lost war. To prevent another crisis, the Führer used a secret plan aimed at solving the unpleasant Hungarian problem. On 16 October, when the Red Army was already fighting in the eastern part of that country, a military coup planned by Hitler took place in the capital, Budapest. As a result, the 'duplicitous' regent of the Kingdom of Hungary Miklós Horthy was arrested, and the Hungarian nationalist leader Ferenc Szalasi became head of Hungary instead. This event was the beginning of the Hungarian disaster. The fanatic Szalasi decided to fight alongside the Nazis, regardless of the victims and destruction. A brutal military regime was imposed in the country, repression of Jews and pacifists began, and the Hungarian army was ordered to 'fight to the end' against the threat of communism.

At the end of October, the 2nd Ukrainian Front troops were able to capture the entire eastern part of Hungary after heavy fighting, accompanied by large tank battles. After breaking through German positions near Kecskemét, Russian T-34 tanks reached the south-eastern suburbs of Budapest for the first time on 29 October. There they were stopped only by pre-dug anti-tank ditches. There was panic in the city, and many residents fled to the western parts of the country. But the German Army Group 'South' (Heeresgruppe Süd), under the command of Generaloberst

Johannes Friessner, managed to cope with the crisis. The German Panzer divisions, which were urgently deployed to the area of the breakout, were able to defeat the Russians and push them back to the city of Kecskemét. The situation in this sector was temporarily stabilized, allowing Hitler to temporarily ignore the Eastern front and prepare for a stupid adventure in the Ardennes. But soon Stalin became concerned, dissatisfied with the slow progress of Soviet troops in Hungary. He ordered the 3rd Ukrainian Front troops stranded near the Yugoslav capital of Belgrade to retarget their attacks on southern Hungary. As a result, the Red Army in this sector doubled its forces and in mid-November resumed attacks along the entire front east and north of the Danube. German and Hungarian divisions could not withstand the pressure of the superior Russian forces, gradually retreating to the west.

On 19 December, the Soviets, who had previously crossed the Danube south of Budapest, launched another offensive and broke through the Army Group 'South' (Heeresgruppe Süd) front southwest of the Hungarian capital. Generaloberst Friessner proposed to withdraw some of the troops from the eastern bank of the Danube and evacuate Pest – the eastern part of the city. However, the Acting Chief of the General Staff of the Army High Command, Generaloberst Heinz Wilhelm Guderian, citing the Führer, forbade any retreat. 'The Führer believes that the loss of Budapest at the time of a successful German offensive in the west will reduce the effect of the latter by 50 per cent,' he said.

On 24 December, the ring of Soviet encirclement around the city of Budapest finally closed and formed Budapest Pocket. At the same time, at first there was little evidence of danger in the huge city – trams were running along the streets, shops were open, and residents were preparing for Christmas. The population was not going to turn their ancient city into a battlefield, hoping that the German troops would again push back the Russians. But Hitler and Stalin had a different opinion.

The commander of the IX.SS-Gebirgskorps (IX SS Mountain Corps), 56-year-old SS-Obergruppenführer und General der Waffen-SS und Polizei Karl Pfeffer-Wildenbruch, was appointed head of the defense of the next Festung. He was ordered by the Führer to organize a circular defense and fight for every house. The commander of Army Group 'South' (Heeresgruppe Süd), Generaloberst Friessner, who insisted on the evacuation of Budapest, was dismissed with the phrase, 'Führer thanks you', and replaced by General of the Infantry Otto Wöhler, who did not put forward such 'defeatist' proposals from then on. At the same time, infantry reinforcements and Panzer divisions were being urgently transferred from East Prussia to Hungary. The retention of Budapest and the western part of Hungary became the focus for Hitler, for which he was willing to sacrifice even the territory of Germany. As had happened many times in such situations, the Führer ordered the organization of an air bridge to supply the garrison of Budapest Pocket and prepare a deblocking strike from the west. By the end of December 1944, the diameter of the blockade ring of the German group was an impressive 40 km.

The battle of Budapest was somewhat similar to the battle of the Russian city of Holm on the Lovat river in February–April 1942, only on a larger scale. Holm was also located on two banks of the river, had a round shape, and in the middle was a bridge. The city was surrounded on all sides by the Red Army, and the front line was to the west. But Holm was a small town dominated by two-story houses, while Budapest (located 1,300 km southwest of Holm) was the largest and most beautiful city in Eastern Europe. Several giant bridges connected the western and eastern parts of the city. From a military point of view, Budapest was ideally suited for long-term defense. The city was about 20 km in diameter. The eastern part of the city – Pest – is located on a plain, and its plan was based on three rings of streets intersected by radial avenues. It was mostly built up with large brick houses of gallery type, most of which were built in the late nineteenth and early twentieth centuries. Near the Danube embankment there were several blocks of huge buildings in neo-Gothic and neoclassical style. The largest were the Hungarian Opera House, the Hungarian Parliament Building, the Hungarian National Museum, and the university, among others. The western part of the city is Buda – in which are preserved the features of a medieval city with narrow streets and massive multi-storey stone buildings. On the right bank of the Danube, opposite the huge bridges (Széchenyi Chain Bridge – and Elisabeth Bridge), there are large hills – Gellert Hill (220 meters high) and the huge Castle Hill. There was also the ancient Buda Castle, which became a natural citadel for the defense of the city.

The Budapest Pocket garrison numbered 70,000 soldiers, including 33,000 Germans and 37,000 Hungarians. These were SS Cavalry Division 'Florian Geyer' (SS-Kavallerie-Divisionen 'Florian Geyer'), SS Cavalry Division 'Maria Theresia' (SS-Kavallerie-Divisionen 'Maria Theresia'), 271st Volksgrenadier Division (271. Volksgrenadierdivision), 13th Panzer Division (13. Panzerdivision), Panzer-Division 'feldherrnhalle' and parts of other divisions that accidentally happened to be in Budapest at the time of the Russian Encirclement.[1] Hungarian troops were represented by the Hungarian Third Army under the command of tabornagy (Colonel General) Ivan Hindy, which included the Hungarian 1st Panzer Division, the Hungarian 10th Infantry Division and the Hungarian 12th Reserve Division. In addition to German and Hungarian soldiers, at the beginning of the siege, there were approximately 800,000 civilians in Budapest who were forced to become hostages of this brutal battle.

A special operational headquarters was set up to supply the Budapest garrison, headed by Generalleutnant Gerhard Konrad (former commander TGr. 30 Walter Hornung was appointed as his assistant). III./TG 2 and III./TG 3, which had sixty-four Ju 52 transport planes, were placed under his command. Also involved in supply missions were the airborne I./LLG 2 (Do 17 and Ju 87 glider tugs, DFS 230 cargo gliders) and the Hungarian transport squadron (Ju 52). But these units were not enough to supply the 70,000-strong garrison of Budapest Pocket.

He 111 aircraft were also traditionally involved in supplying the encircled group. These were bombers from Stab./KG 4 and I./KG 4 'General Wever', which at the end of December 1944 were based at Novy Dvor airfield in Slovakia. Also involved were He 111 from II./KG 4, which were located at the large Wiener Neustadt air base in Austria. Before the encirclement of Budapest, these aviation Gruppen were idle for some time due to lack of fuel. However, at the height of the crisis in Hungary, they were allocated the necessary fuel reserves from a special 'Führer reserve'. Thus, the He 111 had the opportunity to show itself in the traditional role of bomber. On 23 December, He 111s appeared again in the sky after a long pause; they bombed positions of the Red Army. On the night of 24-25 December, bombers from KG 4 launched an air attack against a Russian crossing of the Danube near the town of Dunaföldvár.

After this 'warm-up', both bomber Gruppen were ordered to supply Budapest Pocket together with transport Gruppen. In early January, the III./KG 4 Major Herbert von Kruska arrived in Wiener Neustadt. Thus, the Kampfgeschwader 'General Wever' met in full for the first time since June 1942. 14.(Eis/N)/KG 27, based at Malacky airfield, 34 km north of Bratislava,

---

1 During the battle, the SS men tore off the stripes indicating that they belonged to the Waffen-SS. They knew that the Russians hated this branch of the army and executed all the SS men they found. Once captured by the Russians, the soldiers always hid the true name of their divisions, giving pre-invented legends. Thanks to this precaution, the Soviets did not know until the end of the battle that the city was being defended by the Waffen-SS, and there is complete confusion in Russian documents with the names of German divisions.

were also involved in supply missions to the city. On 29 December, these 'railway hunters' made their first sorties to supply Budapest.

Since the distance from the air bases to Budapest Pocket was small, and the supply needs of the encircled troops clearly exceeded the capabilities of the weakened Luftwaffe, the crews again had to work with dangerous overstrain, sometimes making two or three departures per night.[2] Inside the fortress, transport planes landed on several avenues in the eastern part of the city, since the only Ferihegy airfield was captured by the Soviets on 27 December.

In addition to organizing an air bridge, in full compliance with the Führer's order, the operation to unblock Budapest Pocket began. Already on the night of 2 January 1945, the IV SS Panzer Corps (IV. SS-Panzerkorps), under the command of SS-Obergruppenführer Herbert Gille, unexpectedly launched an offensive parallel to the Danube (Operation Konrad I). The Germans managed to quickly break through the front and put the Russians to flight. The operation took place with strong (by the standards of 1945) support of aircraft and river vessels, which landed to the rear of the Soviet troops and shelled the banks of the Danube.

On 4 January, the Luftwaffe and Royal Hungarian Air Force flew 900 flights. Bombers and ground-attack aircraft launched continuous attacks on Soviet positions. On 6 January, the Germans captured the towns of Esztergom and Mány. However, on 7 January, the Wehrmacht unexpectedly broke off its offensive west of Budapest Pocket, but launched a new attack west of Lake Velence. The next day, the deblocking group captured the localities of Pilisszentlélek, Moča and Gyula. On 8 January, the Soviet command seriously feared that German tanks were about to break through the blockade ring and reach Budapest Pocket from the west or southwest. But the beginning of Rasputitsa and increased Russian resistance forced the IV SS Panzer Corps to stop the offensive at the moment when the western outskirts of Budapest were 17 km away. The latest success was the capture of several localities north-east of Esztergom. After that, the 'cunning' SS-Obergruppenführer Gille, who had orders from the Führer not only to unblock Budapest, but also to push the Red Army back across the Danube, began regrouping and transferring his divisions to the north bank of Lake Balaton.

Meanwhile, in early January the Russians began to storm the eastern part of Budapest Pocket; 18th Guards Rifle Corps advanced from the south, and

---

2 Gundelach K. Kampfgeschwader 'General Wever' 4. – Motorbuch Verlag Stutgart, 1978. pp. 320–21.

the 30th Rifle Corps attacked from the north. In addition to the Russians, their new 'allies' – the Romanians – took part in the assault. Since the time of Stalingrad, amazing events had taken place. Now the most complete (in terms of participation in the war against the Soviet Union) allies of the Germans fought against them with the same enthusiasm. Thus, the eastern sector of Pest was allocated for the offensive of the Romanian 7th Army Corps.

On 3 January, the Soviets seized 155 blocks of houses in the northern part of the city and forty-nine city blocks in the southern part (in the Soroksár district). The Russian 5th Air Army (5 VA) and Royal Romanian Air Force flew 1,000 sorties, most of which were designed to attack ground targets in Budapest Pocket. Russian and Romanian pilots reported twenty-two German planes shot down and two Ju 52 transport planes destroyed on the territory of the city.

A He 111 H-16/R1 W.Nr. 162353 '1G+LY' (crew commander Oberleutnant Josef Herrmann) went missing during a flight to Budapest during the night. This was a heavy loss for the Luftwaffe, because the lost experienced crews were replaced by inexperienced newcomers, whose probability of death from enemy fire or from a banal accident was incomparably higher. One of the pilots of 14. (Eis/N)/KG 27 recalled:

> At this point, most of the crews had just arrived from air school and had no combat experience. Sorties for the mission of supplying surrounded units made great demands on the pilots, especially towards the end, when the drop areas became smaller.
>
> Therefore, we came up with a special tactic that increased the probability of successful completion of the mission. At first we flew past Budapest to the south, flying past without hindrance numerous anti-aircraft guns along the Danube river, which at that point flows to the south. Then, at an altitude of about 2000 meters, we turned back (upstream of the Danube), and smoothly descending with muted engines, flew in the direction of the city. Our goal was Nep-Stadion. The drop height of cargo containers should be between 80 and 120 meters. Keeping the optimal drop height was important for two reasons. If the height is less than optimal, the cargo container parachute will not have time to open, and if the height is more than optimal, it is likely that cargo containers will be carried by the wind to the Russians' positions.

The Russians placed a huge number of light and medium anti-aircraft guns in the immediate vicinity of the cargo containers dump sites. However, their observation posts were deceived by our tactics, and in most cases we reached the drop point without firing. After dumping cargo containers, we continued to play to the outskirts of the city, where we could turn the engines back on at full power. At the same time the flight height of 10 meters was normal.[3]

On 4 January, the Red Army captured 194 city blocks in Pest, and seven more city blocks were captured by Romanians. The Romanian 9th Cavalry Division had reached the outskirts of Hippodrome Kincsem Park. Aviation activity on this day sharply decreased due to heavy clouds and fog. Hungary experienced severe frosts up to minus 11°C.

On 5 January, the Russians captured 293 city blocks, including the entire Soroksár district, as well as an aircraft engine plant and a radio factory.

On 6 January, Red Army occupied 118 city blocks. At the same time, the commanders of the Russian divisions storming the eastern part of the city were accused by the Soviet commanders of 'slowness'. The Germans defended every block stubbornly, and when the Russians got too close and dragged in heavy weapons, the Germans quickly retreated to the next strong point, and everything began again. At the same time, Russian soldiers spent a lot of time sweeping up captured buildings, going around basements and attics in search of the Germans. Along the way, they searched apartments and robbed them, stealing the abandoned property of residents. The command of the 7th Guards Army was forced to issue a special order prohibiting the seizure of civilian property by Russian soldiers. On this day, the Soviets registered the passage of 100 German aircraft, half of which delivered supplies to Budapest Pocket.

On 7 January, the Budapest area warmed up sharply, with the air temperature rising to 0°C. The city was covered with heavy clouds, accompanied by snow and rain. As a result, the fighting took place without air support. The Russians captured sixty city blocks in the northern part of Pest and seventy-seven blocks in its southern part. In the area of Kispest there were fierce tank battles.

On 8 January, the Russians captured another 160 city blocks.

On 9 January, the battle for the vast eastern part of the city reached a turning point. The German garrison, beginning to run out of ammunition,

---

3 Boelcke Archiv.

and was no longer able to hold the extended line of defense. As a result, on the orders of SS-Obergruppenführer Pfeffer-Wildenbruch, German and Hungarian soldiers left their far-advanced strongholds in the southern part of Pest during the night and retreated closer to the city center; 728 city blocks were immediately evacuated in the urban areas of Pesterzsébet, Kispest, Kossuthfalva and most of Wekerle. The encircled garrison had to leave the last landing area of the transport planes. On this day, Soviet observers recorded a flight of fifteen transport planes over the blockade ring. Russian and Romanian planes did not fly due to bad weather.

From 10 January, the Russians began regular shelling of bridges across the Danube with 152-mm and 203-mm howitzers. Later, the destruction of the bridges involved bombers from the 5th Air Army (5 VA), which also constantly bombed these targets. But the bridges of Budapest were so strong and massive that, despite the constant direct hits of bombs and shells, none of them could be destroyed. On this day, the Germans further reduced the held bridgehead, giving the Red Army another 831 city blocks in the northern part of Pest without a fight. The Russian air force was again inactive due to bad weather. At least ten German transport planes flew over the blockade ring to supply Budapest Pocket.

On 11 January, the Soviets took over another urban area – Angyalföld, located in the northern part of Pest. Soldiers of the 18th Guards Rifle Corps captured most of the Népliget Park and reached the old Kerepesi Cemetery. On this day, the Soviets created a separate Budapest group of troops consisting of the 18th Guards Rifle Corps, the 30th Rifle Corps and the Romanian 7th Army Corps. It was headed by Major General Ivan Afonin.[4] He was ordered to launch a decisive attack, the purpose of which was to cut the German defenses into pieces. By the evening of 14 January, the Russians planned to capture the rest of Pest. In this regard, the 5th Air Army (5 VA) was ordered at 12.00 on 12 January to make a massive bombing attack against the central part of Budapest.

---

4 Major General Ivan Afonin – one of the most odious characters of the Red Army. A narrow-minded and incompetent General, a protégé of Marshal Zhukov. He never spared the soldiers under his command, following the most insane orders of his superiors. On 12 April,1944, General Afonin personally shot the chief of intelligence of the 237st Rifle Division, Major Andreev, because of a personal hostility. Thanks to Marshal Zhukov's intercession with Stalin, General Ivan Afonin escaped a military trial for this crime. During the Soviet-Japanese War, he performed an adventurous operation in the spirit of Otto Skorzeny. On 19 August 1945, General Afonin, with a battalion of machine gunners on planes, unexpectedly landed at Mukden airfield (now Shenyang), where he personally captured the final Emperor of the Qing dynasty Puyi along with his entourage.

In the morning, however, the city was again heavily cloudy and raining. Therefore, the planned bombing did not take place. Russian and Romanian infantry had to storm the next city blocks without air support. After fierce fighting, they managed to capture 126 city blocks, of which eleven blocks fell to the 'allied' Romanian troops.

The next day, despite bad weather and fog, Russian planes still took to the air and carried out 242 sorties to attack ground targets in Budapest Pocket. However, the weather prevented accurate bombing. The efforts of the Russians were in vain, the bombing did not cause serious damage to the defenders.

On 14 January, the Soviets seized another 242 city blocks in Pest, as well as a railway goods station.

On 15 January, another 216 blocks passed into the hands of Red Army. On this day, the participation of Romanians in the storming of the Hungarian capital ended. The Romanian 7th Army Corps was withdrawn from the city.

On 16 January, despite the continuing snowfall, the weather in the area of Budapest improved significantly, visibility increased to 4–15 km. 5th Air Army (5 VA) flew 520 sorties and reported twenty-two downed German aircraft. Il-2 ground-attack aircraft and bombers repeatedly bombed and shelled city buildings on the eastern bank of the Danube.

At 13.00 (Moscow time), a pair of Yak-3 fighters from the 659rd Fighter Aviation Regiment (659rd IAP), flying out to investigate in the area of the small town Mor, accidentally met with two Ju 52s. Lieutenant Nikitin, piloting one of the Yak-3 fighters, attacked one of the German planes and shot it down. According to the pilot's report, the transport airplane crashed in the area of Tata.

At 17.30, a group of twelve Yak-3 fighters flew to the Budapest Pocket area. At an altitude of 3,500 meters, the pilots saw a group of three Ju 52s, which were accompanied by ten Bf 109 fighters. The Russian fighters split into two groups. Five Yak-3 fighters attacked the transport planes, while another Yak-3 group engaged the Bf 109s. Further events developed very dramatically. Yak-3 Captain Pavlovsky, from a distance of 50 meters, attacked the tail of the Ju 52, after which it caught fire and fell 10 km west of the city of Sárbogárd. The pilot saw one of the crew members of the Ju 52 jump out on a parachute. Junior Lieutenant Buikevich shot down another Ju 52, which fell west of the settlement of Ivancha. Next, Junior Lieutenant Buikevich attacked another Ju 52. According to the combat report of Buikevich downed transport airplane fell south-east of the town of Kiskunfélegyháza. Junior Lieutenant Vasilyak, who was behind his group, soon found two more Ju 52s in the area of the village of Vértesacsa at an altitude of 2,800 meters. Transport planes were accompanied by two Bf 109 fighters. Yak-3 Junior Lieutenant Vasilyak fired at transport planes, after which they separated and began to descend. German (or Hungarian) fighters tried to attack Yak-3, but he evaded them. The Junior Lieutenant Vasilyak caught up with one of the Ju 52s flying at a low level and once again attacked it. The plane caught fire in one of the engines, after which it dropped five cargo containers and tried to make an emergency landing near the city of Csákvár.

At 17.35, a Yak-1 Senior Lieutenant Korolev from the 611rd Fighter Aviation Regiment (611rd IAP) flew to intercept a group of Ju 52s dropping cargo containers in Budapest Pocket. In the area of the settlement Sharashd Yak-1 he found and caught up with a group of three Ju 52. During the attack, Senior Lieutenant Korolev shot down one of the German transport planes.

On 16 January, the Red Army captured 113 blocks in Pest, coming close to the Hungarian Parliament Building and bridges over the Danube.

On 17 January, the resistance of the German garrison suddenly increased. During the fierce fighting, the Russians managed to capture only thirty-six city blocks. But this was only due to the fact that on this day the SS-Obergruppenführer Pfeffer-Wildenbruch received permission from Hitler to completely evacuate the bridgehead on the eastern bank and transfer the remaining troops to Buda. At night, the German soldiers secretly left the front line according to a pre-made plan and crossed the bridges to the western part of the city. But the evacuation could not be carried out in full. The Soviets learned about the upcoming operation from the prisoners they had captured the day before, and in some areas they forestalled the Germans with unexpected attacks. As a result, the organized evacuation eventually turned into a stampede. When Russian soldiers and tanks appeared on the Danube embankment chasing the Germans, all the bridges across the river were blown up one by one.[5] But many Germans and Hungarians had not yet managed to cross to the other side. Abandoned by their comrades and trapped face to face with

---

5 According to Soviet data, Elisabeth Bridge was blown up by the Russians on the night of 17/18 January (at 02.30 Moscow time) by the 11th Assault Engineering company sabotage group. The group secretly crossed the front line on 15 January, penetrated to the bridge from the west bank. Yefreytor Arkady Nikolsky managed to get across the bridge to the explosive charge, put a fuse in it, and then managed to move away from the bridge by 300 meters. After the explosion, the entire group of four people returned safely to their own, and Nikolsky was awarded the title Hero of the Soviet Union for this dangerous mission.

the advancing Russians, they were forced to either continue fighting or surrender. The majority reasonably preferred captivity. As a result, on the morning of 18 January, the Russians immediately captured 18,000 people abandoned by their comrades on the eastern bank of the river; 318 artillery pieces, forty-seven tanks, seventeen self-propelled guns, nine armoured personnel carriers and 255 motorcycles were also captured.

In mid-January, in Austria, there were heavy snowfalls. For two days, the Wiener Neustadt airfield was covered with a layer of snow almost a meter thick. Not only the technical staff, but also all the pilots participated in clearing the 900-meter-long and 30-meter-wide runway. Even the staff officers and commander II./KG 4 Major Hesse picked up shovels. After two days of continuous operation, the bomber flights to Budapest Pocket resumed.[6]

On 18 January, between 21.10 and 23.56, fifteen He 111 of 14.(Eis/N)/ KG 27 and six Ju 52 of TG 2 flew in groups of two to six aircraft over Budapest Pocket, dropping cargo containers over Buda. In total, on this day, the Russians recorded a flight of forty-two transport planes over the ring of the blockade.

To reduce losses, German pilots used the old technique of avoiding Russian anti-aircraft artillery fire. Transport planes flew over the front line at an altitude of 3,000 meters, and on the approach to the target area dropped to an altitude of 1,000 meters. Only when directly above the city did they descend to the required height for dropping cargo containers. According to Soviet radar stations, the approach course to Budapest always passed over the Danube, usually from the south.

That night, several transport missions were performed by Unteroffizier Edgar Spraiter, from 14.(Eis/N)/KG 27. By that time, he had already flown 379 combat missions and was a very experienced pilot. Flights to Budapest were associated with risks not only because of Russian anti-aircraft guns, but also because of the dangerous terrain in the form of high hills. Unteroffizier Spraiter recalled:

> Unteroffizier Werner was flying a height of 3000 meters, then the plane descended and dumping cargo containers from 400 meters. He should have started to gain altitude immediately after the dropping the cargo containers, because there was a mountain ahead. But he didn't! After closing the

---

6 Gundelach K. Kampfgeschwader 'General Wever' 4. – Motorbuch Verlag Stuttgart, 1978. pp. 322–23

doors of the bomb bay, I noticed this, and at the last moment I managed to grab and pull the wheel, otherwise we would have crashed.[7]

On 19 January, between 00.04 and 06.00, another thirty He 111 and ten Ju 52s flew over Budapest Pocket, dropping another batch of cargo containers. According to Russian data, not only cargo, but also 'reinforcements' were delivered to the city. Soviet observers repeatedly recorded parachutists landing on the Margaret Island, located on the Danube opposite the Hungarian parliament building. However, most likely these 'mirages' were caused by alcohol, which the Russians could find in large quantities in the destroyed city. This night He 111 H-20 W.Nr. 700014 of 1./KG 4 went missing with the crew.

As noted earlier, cargo gliders participated in the supply of Budapest Pocket. Their tactics were as follows: glider tugs reached the area south of the city, uncoupled cargo gliders at an altitude of 2,000–3,000 meters, after which the glider pilots had to gradually descend – with one approach to reach the landing site. After the Red Army took over the Vermezzo park area, a new landing site was urgently set up in Pest. This location was located between Attila Street and Naphegy Street west of Castle Hill. However, due to the high-rise buildings located nearby, landing there was fraught with danger. For example, the DFS 230 cargo glider 'H4+2-6' of 18-year-old Unteroffizier Georg Filius lost altitude prematurely during a southbound approach and crashed into the window of the fifth floor of a seven-story building at 35 Attila Street. After the disaster, the cargo glider stuck out of the breach in this house for a long time, becoming the subject of many photos.

After the destruction of bridges over the Danube in the battle for Budapest, there was a natural pause. The Germans fortified themselves in the western part of the city. From high the Castle Hill, they kept the entire river embankment in the area of the blown-up bridges under fire. The headquarters of the garrison and all the German and Hungarian divisions were located in a huge and deep tunnel under the Royal Palace. There was an ammunition depot, a gasoline barrel depot, and supply of food. Having sustained heavy losses during the assault, the Russians ceased attacking the German garrison and began regrouping their forces, adding significant reinforcements.

---

7 Boelcke Archiv.

Meanwhile, in Hungary, the temperature dropped to minus 18°C. This weather, which covered the burned ruins of city blocks with frost, gave Budapest the appearance of Stalingrad as it was remembered by the doomed Germans two years previously. It seemed as though the ghost of the 6th Army that had died on the banks of the Volga had been resurrected on the banks of the Danube. The similarity to the Stalingrad disaster was also highlighted by the fact that the Budapest Pocket garrison was formally part of the 'new' 6th Army. However, if the situation in Stalingrad Pocket was being followed by the whole of Germany, then in 1945 Budapest was just one of many places on the geographical map of Europe where a bunch of doomed German soldiers senselessly sacrificed their lives to Hitler's ideas.

On 20 January, the Russians crossed to Margaret Island. There they unexpectedly encountered strong resistance from the Germans, who had armored personnel carriers and artillery.

On the night of 20-21 January, the Russian air defense again recorded a transport flight into Budapest Pocket. Radar stations detected five He 111 and two Ju 52, which dropped cargo in the period from 18.00 to 23.40. That night the commander of the Budapest group of troops Major General Ivan Afonin drove his car from the headquarters in the city of Ercsi to Budafok (the old city district of Budapest, located in the southern part of Buda). Suddenly, his car was fired at by a German plane (most likely it was a Ju 87 D-5 from NSGr. 5), as a result Major General Afonin was seriously injured and the Major General of Managarov was appointed the commander of the Budapest group of armies instead. On the same night, He 111 H-20 W.Nr. 701132 '5J+GS' from 8./KG 4 was shot down by anti-aircraft fire over Buda, and its crew added to the lists of missing persons.

On 21 January, between 21.20 and 23.50, thirteen He 111 and three Ju 52 dropped cargo at Budapest Pocket. At the same time, Russian observers again recorded the landing of the ghost parachutists. At 23.01, the Russian radar searchlight-seeker station (RAP-150) from the 583th Anti-aircraft Regiment performed a vertical search for targets. Suddenly, a He 111 was illuminated coming at a low level to the western edge of Budapest. The pilot immediately banked the plane to the right, descended, and disappeared into the darkness. But soon the German plane, trying to gain altitude, was caught by the beam of another Russian searchlight. Abruptly changing course, the bomber went into a horizontal flight, but again was illuminated by several searchlights. Probably as a result of performing sharp maneuvers, the crew was blinded, lost orientation and He 111 crashed into a four-story house located in the vicinity of the old city cemetery. As a result of the accident, the entire crew was killed.

At 00.45-07.00 twenty-four He 111 and six Ju 52 singly and in groups (from two to five aircraft) dropped cargo containers over Budapest. Edgar Spraiter, flying a He 111 H-16 '1G+EY' from 14.(Eis/N)/KG 27, recalled:

> The fifth flight of the crew of Unteroffizier Werner. Takeoff at 01.25 am in a blizzard and severe frost… Budapest was obscured by clouds, and I decided that east of the city, where there were no hills or mountains, we could drop as low as possible to fly to the fortress. That night, we were the only plane that made it to Buda Castle. It was very nice to receive a radio message of gratitude from our fellow infantrymen who were defending the Castle.

In total, the crew then dropped eight cargo containers with food. On the way to Budapest Pocket this He 111 H-16 W.Nr. 160915 '1G+EY' had problems with switching the pumps that fed fuel from the additional tanks to the main fuel tank. Despite technical problems and bad weather, after completing the mission, the He 111 landed safely at Wiener Neustadt airfield.[8]

'From the plane flying at a low level, a terrible picture observed…'

The frosty morning of 22 January turned a new page in the bloody drama of Budapest Pocket. First, dozens of Russian bombers appeared over the ruins, and attacked the southern and northern Buda neighborhoods from a low level. Then, after a heavy artillery barrage at 13.00, the Russian troops went on the offensive. However, the Germans put up a fierce resistance and at the cost of heavy losses, the Russians were able to capture only twenty blocks of the city.

During the attack, the Soviets got their hands on a very informed and talkative prisoner – ornagy (major) of the general staff of the Hungarian Army and an employee of the military technical institute, Imre Rodvani. He spoke in detail about the composition and number of Hungarian troops in the city. Rodvani also told the Russians that the garrison was commanded

---

8 Boelcke Archiv.

by SS-Obergruppenführer Pfeffer-Wildenbruch, whose headquarters were located in the tunnel under the Royal Palace. The high-ranking Hungarian prisoner told the Soviets that there were constant rumors among the encircled soldiers that they were about to break through to the west, either towards Esztergom or towards Székesfehérvár.

On this day, the Russians did not record transport planes flying over Budapest Pocket. All forces of the German transport aviation were thrown in support of the IV SS Panzer Corps (IV. SS-Panzerkorps), seeking to unblock Budapest Pocket. Thus, on the 3rd Ukrainian Front, where the German offensive was developing, 168 flights of Ju 52s and He 111s were recorded, delivering supplies for German tank divisions directly to the front line.

On 23 January, the Russians managed to capture only one city block in Budapest. Frosty weather (24 January in the area of Pocket was minus 19°C) contributed to the actions of aviation. But the Soviets in this sector were no longer strong enough. For example, planes of the 5th Air Army (5 VA) were forced to simultaneously support Red Army attacks on the northern bank of the Danube (in Slovakia), strike at a deblocking German group, and bomb Budapest Pocket. As a result of this dispersal of forces, the numerical superiority of the Russian air force did not give any tangible benefit.

On 25 January, 5th Air Army (5 VA) flew a total of 526 sorties, but only half of them were on a mission aimed at bombing Buda. The main problem for the garrison was not aviation, but Soviet artillery; 278 howitzers (including seventy-two 203-mm guns) fired at Buda around the clock from the eastern bank of the Danube, the north-western and south-western outskirts of the city.

On 26 January, weather conditions changed again. In Hungary, it warmed up sharply and heavy snow began to fall again. The Russians were able to capture thirty-five city blocks in the western part of Budapest. In the evening and at night, the Russian air defense recorded a flight of four He 111 to Budapest Pocket.

On 27 January, the Russians captured another twenty-seven city blocks. Meanwhile, the situation of civilians who had unwittingly found themselves in a war zone was becoming increasingly dire. The city's economy was completely destroyed, the water supply did not work, electricity and gas were not supplied. Water was extracted from artesian wells and pre-prepared reservoirs. The headquarters of the Hungarian troops blocked in Budapest Pocket sent a desperate radio message to their command. It reported that there are 43,000 civilians in Buda territory controlled by the garrison who urgently needed food, medicine and milk powder for children. 'The possibility of landing transport planes is excluded,' stated the message.

Due to poor visibility, the Russian air defense recorded only three aerial targets that day. At 20.40, a Ju 52 was spotted in the Budapest area at an altitude of 1,500 meters; at 21.50, a He 111 flew over the city. All aircraft entered the city from the north-west (from the city of Esztergom), and left the south-west course (towards the city of Székesfehérvár). At 23.30 hours, Russian searchlights illuminated a He 111, after which 1575th Anti-aircraft Regiment anti-aircraft guns opened fire on it. After the attack, one of the engines of the German plane caught fire. The damaged He 111 made an emergency drop of two cargo containers and then began to descend sharply. According to Soviet data, a German bomber fell into the Danube.

At 00.20 on 28 January, another He 111 appeared over Budapest, dropping cargo containers. Then the German transport planes began to fly over the city one by one. After ten minutes, Russian searchlights illuminated a bomber flying over the city at a low level. The 11th battery of the 1575th Anti-aircraft Regiment opened fire on it. After four volleys from automatic anti-aircraft guns, the plane caught fire and fell in the area of Castle Hill. At 01.50, Russian anti-aircraft gunners shone searchlights on a single He 111 that came under fire from the 12-battery 1575th Anti-aircraft Regiment. According to Soviet data, the burning plane fell on the Royal Palace. At 04.20, the Russian radar station detected another target moving towards Budapest. After ten minutes, a Ju 52 appeared from the clouds, which lowered the flight altitude to drop cargo containers. After firing from automatic anti-aircraft guns, the plane caught fire and crashed on the western bank of the Danube. In the evening of the same day, transport planes' flights to Budapest Pocket continued. At 23.30, the 13th battery of the 1575th Anti-aircraft Regiment shot down one He 111 flying at a low level over the western part of the city. On this day, the Russians captured eighteen city blocks of Buda.

On 29 January, from 00.29 to 06.00, the Russians recorded a flight of forty-six Ju 52 and six He 111 to Budapest Pocket. Russian air defense system reported about five German transport planes shot down. At 00.55, the 11th battery of the 1575th Anti-aircraft Regiment opened fire on a He 111, which was flying at an altitude of 700 meters and was illuminated by searchlights. After the attack, the plane caught fire and fell on Pest. At 01.35, the same battery of automatic anti-aircraft guns fired at another He 111 flying at an altitude of 800 meters. According to a Russian report, it caught fire and fell on the western bank of the Danube. At 02.00 and 03.00, Russian anti-aircraft artillery shot down two more He 111, which fell in the area of the Royal Palace. At 04.56, the searchlights illuminated another target, which was immediately fired at by Russian anti-aircraft guns. It was a Ju 52 flying at an altitude of 900 meters. The plane managed to make an emergency drop of cargo containers, then caught fire and crashed vertically near the positions of the 2nd battery of the 1575th Anti-aircraft Regiment. Between 20.33 and 21.18, the Russians recorded a flight of three more Ju 52s that dropped cargo containers in the Royal Palace area.

Although it had been a long time since the Stalingrad disaster, many of the aspects of supplying the encircled German garrison were repeated in Budapest. The contents of the dumped cargo containers sometimes caused indignation and bewilderment among the defenders of Budapest Pocket. For example, in some of the cargo containers were yellow flags to indicate where unexploded ordnance fell. Sometimes among the contents of the containers were carefully packed Iron Crosses, which should have been awarded to the defenders of Budapest. All this garbage, according to the German command, was supposed to replenish the defending garrison with food and ammunition.

Also surprising is that German transport planes dropped cargo containers on four separate occasions that included the Knight's Cross of the Iron Cross with Oak Leaves for SS-Obergruppenführer Pfeffer-Wildenbruch. It was only on the fourth attempt that the reward reached the recipient. On 29 January, on the eve of the next anniversary of the Nazis' rise to power, special 'holiday' cargo containers were dropped on the city with donations from Hitler's chief bloody executioner, the ReichsFührer SS Heinrich Himmler. When they were opened by the defenders of the garrison, they found sweets, cigarettes and cans of canned horse meat(!). Such 'gifts' were perceived by German soldiers as a sophisticated mockery, because horse meat was the basis of their diet in the Pocket. The next day, an official protest against the contents of Himmler's cargo containers was sent over the radio from Budapest Pocket.[9] These egregious facts were another proof of the psychological state of the Third Reich management, who had long lost touch with reality and lived in a world of their own pathological dreams.

At the end of January in the area of Budapest, it got cold again – to minus 14°C. On 30 January, the Russians captured 123 more city blocks

---

9 Pegg M. Transporter Volume Twu: Luftwaffe Transport Units 1943–1945. Luftwaffe Colours. – Classic Publications, 2008. p. 166.

and completely occupied Margaret Island. Over the city constantly flew Il-2 ground-attack aircraft which with low-level flight bombed and shelled buildings on the streets of the city. The 2nd Ukrainian Front combat magazine reports that 6,000 German and Hungarian soldiers were captured on this day in Buda.

During the day, the 1575th Anti-aircraft Regiment reported three downed transport planes. At 02.00, a Ju 88 was shot down and crashed on the western bank of the Danube. At 03.10, the 13th battery of the 1575th Anti-aircraft Regiment opened concentrated fire on a Ju 52. A damaged German plane managed to emergency drop cargo containers with 75 mm shells that fell on Soviet territory. According to Russian information, after some time, this heavily damaged German transport airplane fell on Buda. At 22.52, the 10th battery of the 1575th Anti-aircraft Regiment fired on another Ju 52 flying over the Danube at an altitude of 500 meters. Damaged by anti-aircraft fire, the plane caught fire and fell on Pest. In total, on this day, Russian observers recorded a flight of seventeen transport planes over the ring of the blockade.

On 31 January, Russian air defense recorded a flight of thirty-two transport planes over Budapest Pocket (from 00.11 to 04.25). Of these, twelve were identified as He 111, four as Ju 88, and sixteen as Ju 52. All transport planes entered the target area from the southwest (from the city of Székesfehérvár), and went to the northwest (towards the city of Esztergom).

The 1575th Anti-aircraft Regiment reported six German planes shot down. At 01.00, the 14th battery of the 1575th Anti-aircraft Regiment shot down a He 111 (fell into the Danube), at 01.15, the 13th battery of the same Regiment shot down a Ju 52 (fell on German territory). At 01.35, the 3rd battery of the 1575th Anti-aircraft Regiment shot down a Ju 52 (crashed on German territory). At 01.43, the 4th battery of the same Regiment shot down a Ju 52 (fell on the south-western edge of the city). At 02.20, the 15th battery shot down a He 111 H-20. The plane crashed in German territory, the crew jumped out with parachutes, it was probably W.Nr. 700026 '5J+EC' from St.II./KG 4 (the pilot and navigator were killed, and the other three crew members were injured, but escaped). At 03.45, the 2nd battery of the 1575th Anti-aircraft Regiment shot down a Ju 52 that crashed on German territory. The high efficiency of Russian anti-aircraft artillery fire indicated in Soviet documents is seriously questionable. Most likely, the Russian anti-aircraft gunners greatly overestimated their success. The claimed crash sites of downed aircraft (German territory, the Danube) did not allow us to verify the validity of applications for victory by anti-aircrafters over German transport planes.

On the night of 1 February (from 01.00 to 04.45), thirty-four He 111 and eighteen Ju 52 flew over Budapest. The city was heavily overcast and foggy, so Russian searchlights could not illuminate any targets. The Russian anti-aircraft guns were silent.

On the night of 1–2 February (from 05.54 to 07.34), thirty-four He 111 and seven Ju 52 flew over Budapest. This time all the planes flying over the Danube, turned around over the river and headed to the target from the north. The KG 4 pilots recalled that on the way to the target they were met by the beams of dozens of searchlights and a strong barrage of Russian anti-aircraft fire. Cloudy weather reliably protected transport planes from Russian anti-aircraft guns. However, the cloud cover that saved the pilots also reduced the accuracy of the cargo containers drop. It is worth remembering that the inefficiency of delivering supplies using cargo containers had already been proven in Stalingrad. A similar story was repeated in Budapest Pocket. A significant number of cargo containers fell on Soviet positions, in deserted ruins or in the Danube. Dumping was done in the dark, and the search for cargo containers usually started in the morning. Even the discovered cargo containers did not give the garrison any hope of getting precious food. It was often found that some of the contents had already been stolen by starving civilians. The troops took a variety of measures to facilitate the search for dumped cargo containers, up to marking the areas of discharge with light signals. However, there was simply not enough fuel to carry out these labor-intensive tactics on a permanent basis in the dilapidated city.

At the beginning of February 1944, despite the lack of supplies and the loss of many strongholds, the situation in Budapest Pocket was still stable. And there was gasoline. Russians recorded at least nine German tanks and four self-propelled guns on 1 February, which were constantly maneuvering through the streets of the German part of Budapest, shooting at Russian infantry. In total, Russian intelligence had established the presence of sixty tanks and forty-six self-propelled guns in Buda. At the same time, the Russians themselves had only nine tanks in the city. Due to the need to repel German de-blocking attacks from the west and southwest of Budapest, the Soviet group was severely weakened and, by 1 February, it had only 44,000 soldiers. Thus, thanks to the dedication of the German tankers who were rushing to Budapest, the agony of the garrison itself was significantly prolonged. However, the situation of the encircled group was getting worse all the time. There were already 10,000 wounded people in the Budapest Pocket infirmaries, most of whom received no assistance.

In early February, the area of Budapest was heavily overcast, with constant rain and heavy snowfall. The Soviet air force was again inactive. The Russians attacked the encircled garrison several times, but despite heavy losses they were unable to approach Buda Castle. Many Russian commanders did not want to send troops to suicide attacks, spreading rumors that 'the Germans will soon capitulate themselves'. At the same time, Soviet soldiers who were in the city constantly cursed the Russian pilots and anti-aircraft gunners. The infantrymen who were constantly risking their lives could not understand why their comrades, who were in relative safety, let the German transport planes pass to the city, allowing them to supply the doomed garrison of Budapest Pocket.

The situation on the outer ring of the blockade also looked depressing. At dawn on 18 January, the IV SS Panzer Corps (IV. SS-Panzerkorps) launched Operation Konrad II, which came as a complete surprise to the Soviet command. However, this rapid (for 1945) operation was only a pitiful shadow of the Blitzkrieg of 1940. After cutting through the Soviet defenses between Lake Balaton and Lake Velence, the Germans covered a distance of 50 km in eight days and reached the banks of the Danube near the cities of Dunapentele and Adony (south of Budapest). On 23 January, the SS captured the village of Kápolnásnyék (2 km south of the city of Ercsi), where the headquarters of the Russian Budapest group of troops was located. On 24 January, separate German Tiger tanks broke through to the southern edge of the village of Baracska. On this day, the Soviet command was afraid that the Germans would cross the Danube and break through to Budapest Pocket from the south-east. In this regard, it ordered the urgent removal of the Russian 27th Army from the front north of the Danube and transfered it to the south-eastern vicinity of Pest, as well taking up the defense on Csepel Island. The last Russian tank reserve, the 23rd Tank Corps, was thrown into the southern vicinity of Buda.

If SS-Obergruppenführer Herbert Gille had a clear order to unblock Budapest, it would most likely have been executed. But Hitler set Gille a great task – 'to defeat the Russians southwest of the city'. As a result, instead of attacking directly at Budapest Pocket, German Panzer divisions struck in a north-westerly direction, trying to encircle four Russian corps. Consequently, SS-Obergruppenführer Herbert Gille achieved some success, but dispersed his few forces over a wide area and eventually got stuck 15 km from the southwestern outskirts of Buda. The pause allowed the Russians to concentrate new forces in the area of the breakthrough. On 27 January, the Soviets launched a successful counter-attack on the IV SS Panzer Corps

(IV. SS-Panzerkorps). By early February, SS-Obergruppenführer Herbert Gille was forced to abandon almost all of the captured territory. As a result, the ambitious Operation Konrad II in Hungary ended in complete collapse for the Germans. In fact, it was the equivalent of the Ardennes counteroffensive operation, carried out on a much smaller scale, but with the same shameful consequences.

After the failure of the deblocking operation, the commander of the garrison at Budapest Pocket, SS-Obergruppenführer Pfeffer-Wildenbruch naively requested a directive from Hitler regarding the future prospects. In response, the Führer ordered him to stay on the occupied lines, and, in extreme cases, go to the Royal Palace and return fire to the last cartridge. Hitler also stated that the Budapest garrison was performing an 'important historical mission', shackling many Russian troops and preventing them from invading Austria. So, having already struggled to survive at Stalingrad, the units and individual soldiers of the 6th Army were again ordered by their Führer to accept 'death for the sake of victory'. The surviving soldiers in the destroyed Budapest had to once again sacrifice themselves to show the world the 'genius' of the outstanding 'strategist', Adolf Hitler.

Meanwhile, the air bridge in Budapest Pocket continued to operate. On 3 February, the Russians recorded a flight of twenty-five transport planes over the blockade ring.

At 04.55 on 4 February, the 5th battery of the 1575th Anti-aircraft Regiment opened fire on a Ju 52 flying over the Danube. The first shots of automatic anti-aircraft guns missed the target, but then the gunners more precisely took aim and were able to get into the cabin of the slow-moving 'Aunt Ju'. Russian observers reported that the downed plane fell on Pest. At 07.20, the 13th battery of the 1575th Anti-aircraft Regiment fired on a He 111 flying at an altitude of 1,000 meters. The bomber's engine caught fire, but it continued to fly north, losing altitude. Russian anti-aircraft gunners opened a frenzied fire, after which the plane fell on the western bank of the Danube. Between 01.00 and 03.00 on 5 February, Russian anti-air defense recorded a flight of five transport planes over Budapest. From 04.37 to 16.00, eleven more planes flew over the city. Among them were Do 17 glider tugs towing DFS 230 cargo gliders. Russian observers mistakenly identified the Do 17 as 'Ju 88'.

The view of Unteroffizier Edgar Spraiter from 14. (Eis/N)/KG 27, a direct participant in the events, is interesting; from 4 February he continued to fly with his old crew, whose members returned to the front after recovery or vacation. Unteroffizier Spraiter recalled:

> On that day, we made five flights to Budapest. The first departure is at 3 am, and the other four after 17.00. At the first departure, it was still the blackest night and a snowstorm. So we tried to reach Buda Castle on a low-level flight over a bend in the Danube river. Since the Danube flows through the mountain range here, we were fired upon by the Russians from the high banks. After the Russian searchlights also illuminated us, we had to go into the clouds. In this situation, it was pointless to look for Buda Castle, so we turned back. On the way back, we saw other returning German transport planes. Their crews also realized the futility of mission in such difficult conditions. Despite heavy cargo containers, strong crosswinds and snow, we were able to land safely in the 'ice gorge' of the landing strip.

On the night of 4–5 February, German air traffic increased. Russian observers recorded a flight of sixty He 111 and Do 17 and nineteen Ju 52. Several low-flying German transport planes became easy prey for Russian anti-aircraft gunners. At 20.20, the 4th battery of the 1575th Anti-aircraft Regiment shot down a Ju 52 (crashed on German territory). At 21.23, the 2nd battery of the 1575th Anti-aircraft Regiment shot down a plane identified as a 'Ju 88' (crashed in the northwestern part of the city, one pilot jumped out on a parachute into German territory). At 22.10, the 9th battery of the 1575th Anti-aircraft Regiment shot down the He 111 (fell on German territory). At 22.29, Russian searchlights illuminated a Ju 52 approaching the cargo containers drop point at an altitude of 800 meters. After a direct hit by anti-aircraft shells, the aircraft's right wing caught fire. After that, the Ju 52 managed to emergency drop four cargo containers with food (fell on Soviet territory), and one of the pilots jumped out on a parachute. Then the downed Ju 52 crashed into the roof of a building on Dobrofonoi street. A Russian capture team was sent to search for the pilot who parachuted out, but he managed to hide under the cover of darkness among the ruins. Unteroffizier Spraiter continues:

> The weather improved in the evening, but it was very cold. Because of the Russian anti-aircraft guns, we flew about 3,000 meters above the burning city, turned back northeast of Budapest, and flew to the city blocks at a low level. I knew

Budapest very well from my day trips with Unteroffizier Werner, and now I was well-versed. From the plane flying at a low level, a terrible picture [was] observed. A solid layer of smoke clouds hung over the burning city at an altitude of about 60 meters. We flew over the burning streets, past the bell towers, in the direction of Buda Castle. Over the Danube, the plane was climbing sharply to Buda Castle, we were dropping our cargo containers and trying to get out of the searchlights and anti-aircraft guns as quickly as possible.

The Russian anti-aircraft defense already knew about our flights and was on the alert. Up to twelve searchlights were constantly searching the sky for incoming and outgoing German transport planes. In good weather, we headed for Buda Castle and flew at an altitude of about 3,000 meters. Then we flew with muted engines, dropped cargo containers at a low level and immediately gained altitude. But that day, because of the weather and dense clouds of smoke, we flew only over the Danube river.[10]

At 23.20, the Russian radar searchlight-seeker station (RAP-150), located on the southern edge of Buda, was searching for targets. Suddenly, a cargo glider was illuminated, which was being towed by an unidentified aircraft (the searchlight did not hit the glider tug). After that, the cargo glider detached, went down and began to maneuver, trying to get out of the beams of the Russian searchlights. The pilot lost his bearings and landed near the Ferashvarosh railway station. On landing, the cargo glider's left wing fell off. The pilot tried to escape, but was shot by a Russian sentry. When examining the fuselage of the cargo glider, it turned out that it had transported mines to the besieged garrison. At 23.30, the 11th battery of the 1575th Anti-aircraft Regiment fired on a Ju 52 approaching Castle Hill at an altitude of 500 meters. After concentrated fire from automatic anti-aircraft guns, the plane caught fire and fell on Pest. In total, Russian anti-aircraft gunners reported the destruction of seven transport planes on this day. 'The enemy air force, despite the bad weather, continues to drop cargo by parachute to the encircled troops,' the 2nd Ukrainian Front combat magazine reports for 4 February.

---

10 Boelcke Archiv.

'Dense mass of thousands of drunk, ragged, unshaven, dirty and lousy, nobody operated crowd of Germans, like sheep, rushed ahead through the battle formations ...'

On 4 February, the Soviet Budapest group of troops launched another decisive assault. However, the Russians again failed. At the cost of heavy losses, they managed to capture only fourteen city blocks. In such a crisis situation, intellectually 'gifted' Soviet commanders began to act 'creatively'. In order to undermine the morale of the enemy, they used the so-called 'round-the-clock schedule of battles'. The essence of this 'progressive' approach consisted of incessant attacks on the German garrison, literally giving the enemy no rest day or night. The Russians even drew up an official schedule of disturbing attacks on the garrison at Budapest Pocket. For example, the 108th Guards Rifle Division conducted a 'general assault' from 10.30 to 21.00. From 21.00 to 03.00 there were reconnaissance assault groups. From 03.00 to 07.00, a 'night assault' was held. From 07.00 to 10.30 – intelligence groups were active again.

On the night of 5 February, Luftwaffe transport aviation continued its intensive flights to Budapest Pocket. Russians recorded a flight of fifteen He 111, Ju 52 and Do 17 glider tugs (identified by Russian observers as 'Ju 88') between 03.00 and 06.00. The 1575th Anti-aircraft Regiment again fired at planes flying over the city and reported two downed Ju 52s. On this day, after a long break, the Luftwaffe launched air attacks against Soviet positions in Budapest. Between 19.50 and 21.09, another five He 111 from KG 4 dropped cargo containers for the garrison. Meanwhile, the Soviets got their hands on another talkative prisoner – a soldier from the 13th Panzer Division. He said the garrison was preparing for a breakthrough, and that forty armoured personnel carriers had already been prepared and disguised by the Germans in the area of Sashedy hill for this purpose.

On the night of 7 February, the Russians recorded just one flight of a German transport airplane in Budapest Pocket. 'At 03.45, the 13th battery of the 1575th Anti-aircraft Regiment opened fire on He 111 and a cargo glider towed by it, flying at an altitude of 1000 meters, which illuminated was a searchlight,' the anti-aircraft Regiment combat log records. 'Cargo glider loaded with food fell 2 km from the battery. The crew consisted of one Unteroffizier of the German army who was taken prisoner.' In the afternoon, the Russians were able to capture Sashedy hill and thirteen city blocks with a surprise attack; 2,700 German and Hungarian soldiers (including 800 wounded in hospitals) did not have time to retreat to the central part of Buda and were captured. It was only on this day that Soviet intelligence learned that a landing area for cargo gliders was being set up in the park to the west of Elisabeth bridge.

By this time, the situation of the Budapest Pocket garrison had already become critical. Food rations for soldiers were reduced to 100–150 grams of bread and 50 grams of fat or canned food per day. Sometimes starving soldiers were given hot soup made from horse meat, which was traditionally the basis of the 'food menu' in German Pockets. However, despite the lack of food, air delivery of ammunition remained a priority. The cargo containers dropped by German aircraft contained mostly mines, 75 mm shells, grenades and ammunition. The daily rate of ammunition consumption for the Germans was set at sixty rounds for the rifle and 700 rounds for the machine gun. The medium-caliber guns had a daily supply of twenty rounds. Shooting from 105-mm and 152-mm howitzers was conducted only in emergencies. The situation of the Hungarian troops in Budapest Pocket was even worse. The Germans did not want to share their meager supply of ammunition with their allies, so the Hungarian soldiers were given only five rounds per day. The typical daily diet of a Hungarian soldier consisted of sweet coffee (for breakfast), lean bean or potato soup (for lunch), and horsemeat soup (for dinner).

On the morning of 7 February, there was heavy cloud cover in the Budapest Pocket area, with bouts of fog and snow; the air temperature was 0°C. Russian air defense recorded a flight of forty-five transport planes over the ring of the blockade. The first group of German transport planes passed over Budapest in the period 07.20–08.10, the second in the period 19.54–21.55. Due to poor visibility, the Russian anti-aircraft gunners could not shoot accurately, they could only hear the hum of aircraft engines flying in the darkness at a low altitude. According to German data, He 111 from 14.(Eis/N)/KG 27 flew over the city again. However, not all missions were completed successfully. He 111 H-16 W.Nr. 933309 '1G+FY' was severely damaged by anti-aircraft fire on the way to Budapest, 30 km from the city. The plane turned around and managed to emergency drop cargo containers, and then the crew made an emergency belly-landing at Pandorf air base.

On the afternoon of 7 February, Bf 109 reconnaissance planes flew over the city. The Russian air force was inactive due to bad weather. On this day, the Red Army captured fourteen more city blocks at the cost of heavy losses and approached the last line of defense around Castle Hill. The Germans thoroughly prepared for the last fight near their 'Alamo'. Massive stone barricades and extensive minefields were built along the streets adjacent to Castle Hill.

On the night of 8 February, due to continuous clouds and fog, only individual crews of the German transport aviation flew to Budapest. At 00.00-00.06, a pair of He 111s from KG 4 flew over the city, followed by three more bombers at 00.46–02.33. The next night (at 00.48–00.58), the Russians recorded only two Ju 52s flying over the city.

On 9 February, the Russians captured fourteen city blocks, and on 10 February, sixteen city blocks. Some Red Army units reached the railway leading to the south station, and thus reached the main line of defense of the German garrison. The city was still foggy and snowing, which made it difficult for the Soviet artillery to work. Russian aviation did not operate. In the period from 15.30 to 23.57, the Soviet air defense recorded a flight towards Budapest Pocket of eight He 111, eight Ju 88, eight Ju 52 and one cargo glider. Because of poor visibility, the Russian searchlights could not illuminate any targets, and the anti-aircraft artillery was silent.

On the night of 10 February (between 00.01–02.50), Russian observers recorded a flight of thirty-three transport planes to Budapest, half of which were identified as Ju 52. For the first time in a long time, He 111s from KG 4 not only dropped 'Food bombs' for the encircled garrison, but also dropped high-explosive bombs on Soviet positions in Buda. In order to minimize losses from friendly fire, the simplest communication was organized between the garrison at Budapest Pocket and the attacking bombers. When approaching the target, the German infantry gave light signals about their location, so the bombs fell in the designated places.

On 10 February, taking advantage of heavy cloud cover, a single He 111 from 14. (Eis/N)/KG 27 and KG 4 made a day flight to supply the Budapest Pocket.

On 11 February the flights of the German transport aviation continued. At 01.05–04.36, ten single He 111s flew over Budapest at short intervals, dropping cargo containers for the garrison. From 07.20 to 08.10, seven more He 111 flew over the Pocket. The Russian air defense was again inactive due to poor visibility. On this day, the battle for Buda reached its climax. The Soviets were able to break through the defenses in the south and captured Gellert Hill, located opposite Buda Castle. The Germans and Hungarians were forced to evacuate 114 city blocks at once, and retreated to Buda Castle. The Russians captured sixteen abandoned tanks and self-propelled guns, 191 artillery pieces, and twenty-six artillery tractors. By the end of the day, the Pocket area was reduced to 3 sq. km; 16,000 German and

5,000 Hungarian soldiers remained in the encircled garrison. In addition, the Germans had six more tanks and self-propelled guns and a small supply of fuel for them. Assessing the current disastrous situation, the commander of the SS-Obergruppenführer garrison, Karl Pfeffer-Wildenbruch, embarked on a suicidal breakout from the encirclement.

Subsequent events have similarities to the ending of the battle for Velikiye Luki Pocket. At 19.00, in the front line occupied by the Russian 42nd Rifle Regiment 180th Rifle Division (the big intersection of Margaret Avenue and Krisztina street near the modern Széll Kálmán tér metro station), the sound of roaring engines and clanking tracks was suddenly heard in the fog and darkness. Then the silhouettes of heavy Panzer tanks appeared from the ruins, with German soldiers on board. After crushing and shooting Russian guns at point-blank range, they rushed through the streets of Budapest in a north-westerly direction. Behind the tanks and self-propelled guns (this was the vanguard of the 13th Panzer Division and the Panzer-Division 'Feldherrnhalle'), a huge crowd of shrieking Germans rushed out of the fog and snow. The war diary of the 180th Rifle Division described this breakthrough:

> Dense mass of thousands of drunk, ragged, unshaven, dirty and lousy, nobody operated crowd of Germans [sic], like sheep, rushed ahead through the battle formations, broke through them, using the darkness and Hungarian conductors, has spread in a westerly direction, trying to reach the area adjacent to Budapest forest.

This vivid description was no exaggeration. It was Hitler's fatal mistakes that turned German soldiers into something similar to 'a flock of sheep'. According to the memories of the surviving soldiers of the garrison, civilians also tried to break out of the city – even women with baby strollers; however, confirmation of these facts could not be found in Soviet documents.

The right flank of the 180th Rifle Division was almost destroyed and the escaping Germans and Hungarians streamed out of the city. The Russians tried to close the gap, but poor visibility and confusion in reports prevented them from assessing the situation in the area of the German break until dawn.

After learning that the garrison was able to break out of the mousetrap, the men of the 2nd Ukrainian Front went into a wild rage. The Russians knew that if Stalin found out about this failure, they would all be immediately killed or, at best, sent to the Gulag for twenty-five years. Soviet commanders tried to correct the situation at any cost. All Russian reserves were urgently dispatched to the vast area that separated Budapest and the nearest German troops on the outer ring of the blockade. The 5th Air Army (5 VA) received an order to fly off all serviceable aircraft and destroy the fleeing enemy group with air strikes. But snow and fog continued to protect the Germans and Hungarians in the forests west of Budapest. Visibility was only 1-2 km, so even to establish the exact location of the group from the Pocket was difficult. According to a pre-prepared plan, the group, having reached the forest area north of Budakeszi, divided into combat groups, which then moved in different directions. Although the Russians repeatedly claimed to have destroyed and captured all the Germans who escaped from Budapest Pocket (such information was recorded in the report of the Soviet command to Stalin), this was not entirely true. In fact, at least 621 people were able to reach Wehrmacht positions in the Gran area by 16 February. Although the rescue of about 1 per cent of the original number of Budapest Pocket was a miracle, it was a terrible indication that, on the whole, the Russians had not greatly distorted reality.

The commander of the lost SS-Obergruppenführer Pfeffer-Wildenbruch garrison was one of the last to leave Buda Castle. However, he was not among the German soldiers who fought their way out of the city. SS-Obergruppenführer Pfeffer-Wildenbruch chose a more 'original' way of escape from the Russians. Together with tabornagy (Colonel General) Ivan Hindy (commander of the Hungarian troops in Budapest), the chief of police of Budapest, the commandant of the Royal Palace and other officers, he tried to escape from Buda Castle through the sewers. This group of 'like-minded people' made their way through the darkness and stench of shit, experiencing terrible hardships. But despite such a 'clever' escape plan, on the afternoon of 12 February they were all captured by the Russians on the western outskirts of Buda. However, this is not the end of the Budapest Pocket story.

The fact is that a significant group of Germans and Hungarians did not dare to break through, and continued to defend themselves in Buda Castle. They needed emergency supplies, so the air bridge continued to operate. On the night of 12 February (19.08–24.00), twenty-two He 111 from KG 4 'General Wever' carried out the last mission to supply the remnants of the garrison. Crews watched as gunfire flashed and fires burned on Castle Hill. These 'fireworks' were a good reference point. Many cargo containers on parachutes descended smoothly, disappearing into the darkness of the ruined city. The crews of the German transport planes could only speculate about what was happening below…

It was only on the morning of 13 February that the Soviets took full control of Budapest. After that, the entire city was at the mercy of the soldiers. Mass rapes and the murder of captured and wounded German soldiers began (the authors managed to find documentary evidence of this massacre in Soviet documents), robberies and other atrocities. This bloody and inhuman massacre, accompanied by primitive cruelty, is still called by many Russian 'patriots' the 'liberation of Budapest'.

Summing up the work of the air bridge in Budapest Pocket, we can give the following figures. In a month and a half, approximately 1,500 tons of cargo were delivered to the encircled city (an average of 34 tons per day). And quite a significant part of the cargo was delivered by dropping cargo containers because of the inability to land inside the Pocket. Only from 1 January to 6 February, German planes delivered about 3,000 cargo containers to Budapest Pocket, including about 400 cargo containers with shells. According to German data, I./LLG 2 towed forty-eight cargo gliders to Budapest. Such insignificant volumes of cargo delivered in comparison with the supply of Stalingrad Pocket clearly indicate the deplorable situation of Luftwaffe transport aircraft.

Despite favorable conditions, new aircraft, radar stations and combat experience, the Russians were not able to interrupt the air supply of the Budapest Pocket garrison. German transport aviation lost forty-four aircraft during this air bridge operation, including thirty-six Ju 52/3m, seven He 111 and one Ju 87. Thus, the effectiveness of Soviet aviation and anti-aircraft artillery in comparison with 1942 still remained low.

The Battle for Budapest Pocket clearly showed the sad results of the incompetent leadership of Hitler and Goring. The agony of the bloody Nazi regime became a fact for the whole world, and the collapse of the Third Reich was only a few months away.

Chapter 10

The 'miracle' Breslau

Exemplary Festung of the Third Reich

The series of disasters on the Eastern front forced Hitler to prepare for the Soviet invasion of German territory. Vaterlandes was to be the last victim in his plan to destroy all life. However, from the brilliant victories of Blitzkrieg (which Hitler had nothing to do with) to the Berlin Pocket, the Wehrmacht and Luftwaffe had to go quite a long way. Starting in the winter of 1942, Hitler began to use a favorite means of implementing his 'victory strategy' – a fanatical defense. This immediately leads to a series of endless crises and catastrophes at the front. Things were getting worse on the battlefields every year. After the Stalingrad disaster, it finally became clear that the main reason for the approaching collapse of Germany was not the steadfastness of the Soviet people or the 'skill' of incompetent Soviet commanders, but the military incompetence of Hitler. However, no serious attempts to physically eliminate the Führer were made, and the cultured, educated and intelligent Germans, like a 'flock of sheep' obediently went to the slaughter. Moreover, by February 1943, Hitler's paranoia had been transformed by Nazi propaganda into the idea of 'total war'. As the catastrophe unfolded on the Eastern front, one of the key elements of the idea of 'total war' became German fortress cities. They were supposed to serve as a kind of barrier in the path of the 'Asian avalanche' by which the Red Army was meant. The main goal of the garrison and the population of such Festung (town-fortress) was self-sacrifice for the sake of a change in the situation at the front. According to Hitler, such a sacrifice should have been the greatest reward for any German citizen or soldier devoted to Nazism.

Obtaining the status of fortress for the city meant to organize the advance construction of fortifications around it and the placement of a permanent garrison in it. Hitler trusted only the most loyal members of the Nazi party and the Waffen-SS to lead and conduct combat operations in such Festung. The supply was to be carried out mainly by air. The possibility of de-blocking was not provided for, and the surrounded garrisons were ordered to defend themselves until all possibilities were exhausted and die with 'honor' for the sake of the Führer.

It should be noted that all major cities in East Germany were most favorable for the implementation of the 'strategy' of these kind of fortresses. The idea of fanatical defense was not an invention of the Nazi leader. Hitler's predecessors in the seventeenth and eighteenth centuries were also fans of fortresses and initially built cities in East Germany as town-fortresses. Therefore, each had numerous castles, bastions, forts, ditches, ramparts and escarpments from their foundation. All these structures were improved during the Kaiser's era. The cities of East Germany therefore, (unlike Budapest) were perfectly suited for a long siege. Their defense could be conducted not only by army units, but also by units of the people's militia (Volkssturm).

On 25 July 1944, Hitler issued an order proclaiming the large city of Breslau Festung. As stated above, the city of Breslau itself was convenient for defense. Strong fortifications built in 1914 during the First World War were preserved around it. The city had many ancient stone buildings and a citadel located on a high hill in the central part. In addition, the area was protected by a canal between 20 and 35 meters wide.

On 1 September, Generalmajor Johannes Krause was appointed commandant of Festung. A detailed plan for the construction of defensive structures was drawn up. One of the German officers who took part in the defense of Breslau noted that it 'provided for the presence of an outer and inner ring. The outer ring of defense was to be 120 km long. Five divisions were to take up positions on this line.' Then the same officer made a significant note: 'The construction of this frontier was a purely party project.' Thus, according to Hitler's plan, the defender of the eastern borders of the Reich was not to be the Wehrmacht, but the Nazi Party.

On 12 January, the Soviets launched a general offensive aimed at Berlin. The Russians quickly broke through the front, which Hitler significantly weakened by sending several Panzer divisions into Hungary. On 17 January, the Germans fled Warsaw without a fight, and a week later the first Festung, the city of Posen, was surrounded. Then, during February, the fortresses of Arnswalde, Kolberg, Glogau and Breslau were sequentially blocked. However, the Russian offensive did not achieve its ultimate goal. The point of the wedge rested on the Oder river near the city of Kustrin, while its huge flanks stretched along Pomerania and Silesia, the old provinces of the Kingdom of Prussia. The Russian armies fanned out across this vast area, then were stopped by Rasputitsa and the fanatical resistance of the German garrisons.

However, until the beginning of 1945, the city of Breslau still did not look like a fortress. The hasty creation of defensive structures of the 'inner ring' began only in January, when it became clear that the Red Army was already 'on the threshold'. As the crisis worsened, it became clear that the front-line city was run by high-ranking Nazis, not Wehrmacht generals. On 19 January, Gauleiter Lower Silesia Obergruppenführer SS Karl Hanke ordered the civilian population of Breslau, first of all women and children, to leave the city urgently. Columns of refugees stretched to the west, in the direction of Dresden; 250,000 people went on a difficult journey, accompanied by snowstorms at a temperature of minus 20°C. Due to poor organization of the transition, about 18,000 people died from hypothermia. Nevertheless, the energetic actions of Gauleiter Hanke were highly appreciated by Hitler. Reich Ministry of Public Enlightenment and Propaganda Joseph Goebbels wrote about it in his diary: 'If all our Gauleiter in the east were like this and worked like Hanke, then our situation would be better than in reality. Hanke is a prominent figure among our Gauleiters operating in the east.'

Meanwhile, all available forces were thrown into the hasty preparation of Breslau for a long defense: Wehrmacht and Volkssturm units, and able-bodied men from the urban population. As a result, the Germans managed to create a strong defense fortress. City streets were blocked with barricades, ditches and rubble were laid on the roads, and approaches to the defended objects were heavily mined. Numerous stone structures, gardens, and parks were used to conceal firepower. The outer ring of defense was located about 30 km from the outskirts of Breslau. From the western and south-western direction, the city was protected by an anti-tank ditch 3 meters deep and 4 meters wide. Meanwhile, on 1 February, instead of the ailing Generalmajor Krause, Oberst (Generalmajor from 6 February 1945) Hans von Alfen was appointed commandant of the Breslau garrison.

On 14 February, OKW reported that the town-fortress of Breslau was blocked by Soviet troops, although on that day it was still possible to evacuate the wounded from the city in a southern direction. The next day, Generalmajor von Alfen announced that the enemy had completely surrounded the city and thus from that day we can talk about the emergence of the Breslau Pocket. The total length of the front around the city was then 72 km, and the front line was 9-10 km from its center. The garrison consisted of approximately 50,000 men, mostly scattered Wehrmacht units (remnants of the 609th Infantry Division, remnants of the 20th Panzer Division), several Waffen-SS units, integrated units of the Luftwaffe and Kriegsmarine, and several battalions of Volkssturm. They had only seven tanks, eight self-propelled guns, and a small number of field guns. Soviet intelligence estimated the fortress garrison at about 31,000 men, 124 guns, about fifty tanks, and assault guns. In addition, there were about 80,000 civilians left in the city, which also turned out to be a considerable force. The inhabitants of Breslau – overwhelmingly German – considered the arrival of the Red Army a disaster, so they actively helped the military.

The city was surrounded by troops of the 1st Ukrainian Front – Marshal of the Soviet Union Ivan Konev. 'We had surrounded Breslau securely, and the only question now was when and at what cost we would be able to take it,' he wrote in his memoirs. For the blockade of the city, Marshal Konev allocated the 6th Army, which included six rifle divisions, an artillery corps, 31st Anti-Aircraft Artillery Division, and many other artillery and mortar units. At first, Marshal Konev hoped that Breslau would be taken quickly. However, the city proved to be a tough nut to crack for the Russians. Thus, the Russian 6th Army blocking Breslau was diverted from participating in the offensive to the Oder river, and then to Berlin.

At the time of the encirclement, the city had several warehouses with ammunition and food. However, it was clear from the very beginning that the supplies available there were not enough to sustain the garrison and the civilian population of Breslau Pocket for a long time. It became necessary to organize the supply of the surrounded German garrison by air. Starting from 10 February, responsibility for the organization and operation of an air bridge in the fortress was fully assigned to Lufttransportchef der Wehrmacht OKL Generalmajor Fridrich-Wilhelm Morzik. He had a lot of experience in this kind of work, which was gained from the supply of Demyansk Pocket. For supply the Breslau Pocket, it was decided to use Ju 52/3m from I./TG 1, II./TG 1, III./TG 2, III./TG 4, IV./TG 4 and TG 3, He 111 from TGr. 30, KG 4 and 14.(Eis)/KG 55. The final destination of the air bridge was Gandauer airfield, located on the north-western edge of the city (5 km from its center).

On the night of 15 February (before the encirclement), the first four Ju 52s landed at Gandauer airfield. They delivered 4 tons of ammunition and equipment, and on the way back they transported forty-three wounded soldiers. In the evening, the first He 111 H-20s from I./KG 4 took off from

Klotzsche air base (11 km north of Dresden) to Breslau. When approaching the target area, their crews were guided by the signals of a radio beacon available at Gandauer airfield. Then at night, eighteen Ju 52/3m from II./TG 3 landed there, taking off from the Juterbog-Damm airfield (62 km southwest of Berlin). A total of fifty-seven Ju 52s flew to Breslau Pocket on the night of 15–16 February, of which fifty-three transport planes completed the mission. They brought 36 tons of ammunition and equipment to the fortress, and on the way back evacuated 212 wounded and seven civilians. In addition, cargo containers on parachutes with a total weight of 21.9 tons were dropped from transport planes that night.

On the evening of 16 February, bombers from III./KG 4 and 14.(Eis)/KG 55 Hauptmann Franz Schmidt joined the air bridge. On the night of 17 February, twenty-two He 111 H from TGr.30 and 14.(Eis)/KG 55, as well as forty-seven Ju 52/3m, flew to the Gandauer airfield. This time, however, their crews are faced with serious difficulties. It turned out that the Russians had applied radio interference to the low-power radio beacon at Gandauer airfield. Not hearing its signals, and not being able to accurately reach the airfield in the dark, the pilots of four He 111 and 22 Ju 52 were forced to turn back.

Those planes that did manage to land at Gandauer airfield delivered 48 tons of various cargo. Then they took 508 wounded, ninety-one civilians and eight military specialists on return flights. At the same time, the Ju 52s took off with a serious overload, with an average of twenty-four passengers in each plane. The pilots had to demonstrate all their flying skills.

By order of the commandant the fortress began an urgent search for more powerful radio equipment. Generalmajor von Alfen recalled:

> It was good that this kind of misstep occurred early enough, so we still had time to fix it. And where to look, it soon became clear – at the Shengarten airfield (now Starachowice), 10 km west of Breslau Pocket, which was previously used by Luftwaffe flight schools. But it was already practically on the front line. As a result, the Shengarten combat tour happened under constant Soviet fire. Nevertheless, the search party managed to find and safely remove the radio station, which the Red Army radio operators could no longer drown out.

On 18 February, forty-one He 111 H and forty-five Ju 52/3m dropped cargo containers on parachutes to the Breslau Pocket garrison, totaling 83 tons.

Twenty-five Ju 52s were able to land at Gandauer airfield based on visual landmarks. On the way back, they evacuated 227 wounded.

On the night of 19 February, thirty-one He 111 and forty-five Ju 52 took off for Breslau Pocket. This time, seventy-six aircraft landed at Gandauer airfield, including all bombers. They delivered cargo totaling 97.7 tons, and then removed 626 wounded, ninety civilian refugees, and 1.3 tons of communications equipment.

After the new radio beacon was put into operation, cargo was delivered into the fortress by air in two ways. It was either unloaded from planes landing at Gandauer airfield, or dropped in Breslau Pocket on cargo containers on parachutes, guided by radio signals. The delivery method had to be selected by the Gruppen commanders who participated in the air bridge operation, taking into account numerous factors, primarily weather conditions, the activity of Soviet aviation and the availability of aircraft.

On the night of 20 February, twelve Ju 52/3m delivered 36 tons of cargo to Gandauer airfield. They evacuated 226 wounded and thirty-five civilians, and took away twenty parachutes for cargo containers that could be reused. The following night, twenty-seven Ju 52s landed there with 53.5 tons of ammunition, equipment, and food. On the way back, they took on board 346 wounded, thirty-two refugees and ninety-four parachutes for cargo containers.

However, on the night of 22 February, only one of the eight Ju 52/3m that were supposed to deliver ammunition and equipment for the Breslau Pocket anti-aircraft batteries landed at the fortress. This plane took out twenty-four wounded people on the return flight.

On the night of 23 February, bad weather conditions prevented landing at Gandauer airfield. Therefore, the crews of thirty Ju 52 were ordered to drop cargo containers on parachutes. This was done by twenty-five aircraft that dropped cargo containers with a total weight of 38.1 tons. Losses amounted to at least two aircraft. One of them, Ju 52 W.Nr. 641016 '4V+MK' from 2./TG 3 was shot down by anti-aircraft fire, the crew of Leutnant Ernst Stolbe was killed. A second Ju 52, W.Nr. 7759 from 7./TG 3, which took off from Breslau Pocket with wounded soldiers was caught in a snowstorm, got lost and crashed in the Czech Republic near the Snezka mountain.

On the night of 25 February, twenty-five Ju 52/3m took off, of which fifteen landed at Gandauer airfield. On one of them was Oberstleutnant Wilhelm von Frideburg, who was supposed to control the operation of the air bridge inside the blockade ring.[1] Transport planes brought 29.4 tons of various cargo, and then took out 140 wounded and forty-two parachutes for cargo containers. The following night, all fifteen Ju 52s landed at Gandauer airfield. They delivered 29.5 tons of cargo, and on the way back took 140 wounded and sixty-two parachutes for cargo containers.

On the night of 27 February, twenty-seven of the thirty-two Ju 52s that took off arrived at Gandauer airfield. They delivered 41.7 tons of ammunition, equipment and food, as well as seven soldiers. The return flights carried 142 wounded, eight military personnel and sixty-five parachutes for cargo containers. SS-man Hendrik Ferten recalled:

> At night, both soldiers and civilians watched the flight of 'Junkers' through the night sky cut by searchlights. The men listened with bated breath, hopeful and terrified, to the roar of the aircraft engines, drowned out by the cannonade of Russian anti-aircraft guns. Often we witnessed Junkers in flames falling to the ground with helpless people on board.

'A clearing' of death

Despite the working air bridge, the situation of the garrison at Breslau Pocket during the fighting gradually deteriorated. German units, slowly retreated to the center of the city. Hitler closely monitored the situation in the fortress, and often personally gave orders regarding what he considered to be necessary defensive measures. One of his major decisions was to order the construction of a second airfield inside the blockade ring. Hitler took into account the experience of Budapest Pocket, which did not have a suitable airfield inside the blockade ring. In his opinion, this fact greatly accelerated the collapse of Budapest Pocket. On 23 February, Generalmajor von Alfen received an order from the Führer: 'In order to guarantee the supply of Breslau by air, even in the event of the loss of the Gandauer airfield, preparations for the construction of an airfield inside the city must begin immediately.' Next, he was asked to report on the proposed location of the airfield and the approximate time of its construction.

---

1 From 4 July to 30 November 1942, he commanded KG 51, then in 1943 he commanded KG 76. From 11 August 1944 to 26 January 1945, Oberstleutnant von Frideburg directed BFS 6 (pilot training school for instrument flight), which among others actively used Gandauer airfield.

The commandant of the fortress himself was thinking about this at the beginning of February. Then, to create an 'internal' airfield, he found two places in the north-eastern part of the city, adjacent to the eastern edge of Scheitniger Park (now Szczytnicki Park). The first was the city's Hermann Göring Stadium (now Olympic Stadium Wrocław), and the second was Frizenvize (now Wrocław sports Park), which housed a sports complex of about 14 hectares, including a football field, a sports hall and a 20-meter parachute tower. However, at the beginning of the blockade, when all forces were thrown on the defense, Generalmajor von Alfen was forced to postpone the construction of a new airfield.

Oberstleutnant von Frideburg was appointed head of construction preparation for additional airfield. He found that the Hermann Göring Stadium and Frizenvize are located in an area where the ground is heavily flooded with meltwater in the spring. Its condition during this period made it much more difficult or heavy transport planes to land and take off, and made it unsuitable for use as an airfield. As a result, both sites were rejected as alternative airfields. It was necessary to find another place inside the fortress where it would be possible to equip a runway with a length of at least 1,300 meters. The only suitable option was the straight Kaiserstrasse (now Grunwald Square), which was about 1,500 meters long and wide enough.

The choice of location for another airfield served as the basis for the conflict between the commandant of the fortress Generalmajor von Alfen and Gauleiter Hanke, whom Hitler began to refer to as the 'head of the defense of Breslau'. Gauleiter Hanke was favor of the Kaiserstrasse option, while Generalmajor von Alfen insisted on Frizenvize. Oberstleutnant Frideburg believed that the approach of aircraft to the alternate airfield at Kaiserstrasse would only be possible if the wind direction coincided with the direction of the strip; that is, only with a south-westerly or north-easterly wind. The dispute was eventually resolved by Hitler himself. He sent the following order to Breslau: 'The construction of the internal airfield is entrusted to Gauleiter Hanke. The commandant of the fortress is obliged to provide him with the necessary specialists and explosives.'

A large amount of work had to be done on Kaiserstrasse to get the necessary lane width for transport planes to land. First, the lampposts along the street were removed, along with tram rails and wires, and overhead telephone line cables, as well as felling all the trees. Some of the buildings were then demolished, including the Evangelical and Catholic churches, which the clergy strongly objected to. After that, it was necessary to remove the debris from the demolished houses, which could be used to create barricades in other parts of the city. And all this had to be done mostly manually.

By order of Gauleiter Hanke, thousands of women and teenagers from the civilian population of Breslau were mobilized to work on the airfield at Kaiserstrasse. They had to work hard day and night to ensure that the construction schedule was met. One of the participants later recalled:

> Sappers blew up an entire city block with residential buildings, streets, squares, alleys and monuments. Our job was to level the area so as to get a flat airfield... We loaded the carts with broken stones. Full carts were taken to the edge of the field and overturned there. Then the construction debris was used for leveling.

The authors do not have an exact answer to the reasonable question of how the women and teenagers ended up there. They had to leave the city on the orders of the Gauleiter before the Russian encirclement of Breslau. We can only assume that either a part of the female population ignored the orders of Hanke (which seems to be a very dubious version), or these women and teenagers came to the city from settlements located near Breslau during the rapid Russian offensive.

Meanwhile, the events of the night of 28 February showed that Generalmajor von Alfen and Gauleiter Hanke were not arguing about the suitability of alternate airfields, and who had the power in the city– the Nazis or the Wehrmacht. From Alt-Lenewitz airfield (15 km east of Torgau), He 111 H and Do 17 from TGr 'Herzog' took off. He 111 towed six Go 242 cargo gliders, and Do 17 towed thirteen DFS 230 cargo gliders, which carried soldiers and officers of the 2nd battalion 25th Parachute Regiment. Interestingly, their commander – Hauptmann Herbert Trotz – had flown to the fortress on the night of 25 February. Over Breslau Pocket, the planes and cargo gliders were illuminated by Russian searchlights, and heavy anti-aircraft fire was directed at them. At an altitude of 1,970–2,160 meters above the city, German crews uncoupled. Some cargo gliders landed on the airfield at Kaiserstrasse, while other cargo gliders landed at Frizenvize. Thus, both alternate airfields turned out to be quite suitable for cargo glider landings.

The following night (1 March), eighteen Ju 52/3m landed at Gandauer airfield and delivered 228 soldiers and officers from the 2nd and 3rd battalions of the 25th Parachute Regiment, as well as 4 tons of weapons and ammunition to the fortress. This delivery was undertaken at the request of Gauleiter Hanke, who insisted on strengthening the Breslau garrison. After them, another thirty Ju 52s landed there, carrying 46 tons of cargo and another thirty soldiers. On return flights, all these transport planes took out 330 wounded, six civilians and twelve military specialists, as well as ten empty cargo containers for weapons and 107 parachutes for cargo containers. Russian anti-aircraft gunners reported six German transport planes shot down.

On the night of 3 March, only six of the fifteen Ju 52s that took off for Gandauer airfield landed there. They delivered another fifty-two people from the 25th Parachute Regiment, 6 tons of weapons and ammunition, including ten grenade launchers. They then removed eighty-eight wounded, thirty military and six civilians, as well as thirty parachutes for cargo containers from Breslau Pocket.

Since work on the construction of the Kaiserstrasse airfield was also carried out during daylight hours, it was difficult for Soviet pilots flying over the city not to notice them. As a result, the area was subjected to shelling and Russian air raids on a daily basis. One of the women residents of Breslau remembered:

> We were often shelled by Soviet artillery. But we had already gained some experience and were able to assess the proximity of shells, so we only rarely went into hiding. Soviet fighter-bombers were much more dangerous. As soon as one of the guards noticed such a plane, he turned on the alarm, after which all the workers began to look for shelter. Often the alarm was announced too late. I once saw six young girls come under fire from the plane's onboard weapons at once... At least once a day, Soviet bombers arrived, and the carefully leveled surfaces were again covered with craters.

Soon the situation with the Kaiserstrasse equipment began to resemble a vicious circle. Residents cleared and leveled the landing site, and Soviet aircraft and artillery regularly 'plowed' it. This street had become a truly cursed place for the residents of the city. A German priest said about it: 'Hundreds of girls and women who, like slaves, are chased to work by party functionaries. They are killed or crippled by low-flying Russian planes, but Hanke orders them to build further. He intends to follow the Führer's orders.' It is estimated that the civilian losses of Breslau during the work on Kaiserstrasse amounted to at least 10,000 people by the end of the siege. But most likely these figures are repeatedly exaggerated, since the air attacks of the Red Army air force were neither regular nor accurate.

The Germans called the airfield at Kaiserstrasse 'a clearing', and the name had a double meaning. From the sky, it looked like a clearing in a dense forest among dense urban development. And in the minds of the locals, it was a place that divided them into the living and the dead...

The conflict between Generalmajor von Alfen and Hanke was naturally resolved in favor of the Gauleiter, who had support in the Nazi leadership. On 2 March, commander of Army Group 'Mitte' Generalfeldmarschall Ferdinand Schörner appointed Generalleutnant Hermann Nichoff (who had previously commanded the 371st Infantry Division) as the new commandant of the fortress. He had a wealth of combat experience, including fighting in Kamenets-Podolsk Pocket in March–April 1944. Generalleutnant Nichoff was able to fly to Breslau Pocket only on the third attempt on the night of March 4 to 5.[2] The Ju 52 he was flying was the only plane to land at Gandauer airfield that night. In addition to the Generalleutnant, the aircraft brought seventeen more soldiers from the 25th Parachute Regiment to the fortress, and then evacuated twenty wounded, and the crew of another transport airplane that had been hit on one of the previous nights.

By the time Generalleutnant Nichoff arrived, Gandauer airfield was already under constant artillery fire, and the city was regularly subjected to day and night air attacks by Russian ground-attack aircraft and bombers. Major Chereshnev, Navigator of the Li-2 bomber from the 340th Bomber Aviation Regiment (340th BAP) recalled:

> The weather was flying, visibility was excellent. Not a cloud in the sky. Major Bobryshev and I arrived first, dropping photoflash bombs. We saw a large city as in the daytime. Bridges, blocks of high-rise buildings, and streets were clearly visible. Bobryshev turned the plane around, and we began to enter the target. We were supposed to bomb the racetrack where Hitler's transport aviation was delivering supplies for the encircled troops [meaning alternate airfield Frizenvize]. Ju 52 planes were circling in the sky, and the frightened anti-aircraft gunners, not knowing whether they were their own

---

2 The former commandant Generalmajor von Alfen remained in the encircled city until 25 March, when he was assigned to Army Group 'B' on the Rhine. After that, he safely left the fortress with another transport plane.

or others, were firing automatic guns. However, this did not prevent us from dropping the bombs exactly on target. As we turned to go back, we saw a flaming torch moving eastward. The white domes of parachutes flashed below.

The Soviets, imitating the Germans, tried to exhaust the garrison strictly on schedule. Early in the morning, Breslau Pocket was bombed, in the first half of the day, artillery fire began, which was replaced by Il-2 aircraft. At noon there was a pause, and in the evening and at night heavy bombers again appeared over the city, dropping incendiary bombs. However, due to bad weather (snowfall, haze and fog) in the area of Breslau in March, air attacks were carried out only sporadically. For example, on 2 March Silesia was cloudy and windy, the air temperature was plus 1°C. Russian aviation did not fly. The next day, some of the aircraft operated, but due to heavy clouds and snow, most of the missions were not completed. On 4 March, snow fell again in Lower Silesia, making visibility very difficult. In the following days, snowfall and rain continued.

The assault on Breslau Pocket was very sluggish and slow. On 1 March, the 6th Army of the Russians managed to capture only three small blocks in the southern part of the city. On 3 March, six city blocks were occupied. On 4 March, Red Army men managed to capture only two destroyed houses. On 5 March, the Russians captured six city blocks. The next day there was fighting in four blocks in the southern part of the city. The Russian infantry complained about the mass use of Panzerfaust grenade launchers by the Germans, which caused heavy losses to the soldiers. The assault from the northern direction was generally considered unpromising due to the fact that the area was completely shot through from the hills and the old fortress located on the banks of the Oder river. On 7 March, the 6th Army captured three city blocks and a church building.

On the morning of 9 March, a massive air attack was planned against the southern part of the Breslau Pocket, which was to involve 600 bombers and 300 ground-attack aircraft Il-2. But due to heavy cloud cover over the city, the 2nd Air Army (2 VA) again carried out only scattered bombing raids in small groups of aircraft. As a result, the Russian infantry, which rose to the attack, was again able to capture only three city blocks. The next day, the Russian air force was again inactive. Only on 11 March, was the 2nd Air Army (2 VA) able to carry out a strong air attack against the Breslau Pocket, which involved 830 aircraft. But most of the crews of Russian bombers, due to poor visibility, were again unable to hit their designated targets in the southern part of the city.

Minor Russian hooliganism

When it was not possible to take Breslau on the move, Marshal Konev's headquarters had a problem – how to prevent the surrounded garrison from being supplied by air. Initially, this task was expected to be solved by the 71st Anti-aircraft Division under the command of Colonel Grigory Svet. Already on 22 February, batteries of anti-aircraft guns of this division taken up positions near the city. They were supposed to shoot down German planes flying to Gandauer airfield. At the same time, the scheme of their location shows that the anti-aircraft gunners blocked the approaches to the fortress only from the northern direction. At that time, this was the right decision, since transport planes Ju 52 were actually then heading to Breslau Pocket on the 'northern' route.

However, the Luftwaffe has always been distinguished by its ability to respond quickly to the current situation. Therefore, very soon other routes were developed to provide air bridges, which made it possible to avoid flying over the positions of Soviet anti-aircraft guns. After that, the headquarters of the 71st Anti-aircraft Division was not in the best position. Not having the strength to cover all directions at once, they could not quickly change the positions of the batteries of anti-aircraft guns, especially large-caliber ones. Therefore, in order to prevent the work of the German air bridge as much as possible, the Soviets had to improvise and use unusual methods to counter the Germans.

On 26 February, the Red Army men captured the village of Neukirch (now part of the city), at the western edge of Breslau. They were unable to advance further, and the front line stabilized between Neukirch and the Gandauer airfield located just 3.5 km to the east of it. Neukirch had an airfield, and Soviet pilots flying in the area of Breslau Pocket noticed that the location of the main landmarks near it and near Gandauer airfield is almost the same. After studying their messages, the head of the camouflage service of the 2nd Air Army (2 VA) Major V.I. Lukyanov reported to the command: 'The enemy's transport aviation crews fly at night to Breslau and deliver various cargoes to the besieged. If you set Neukirch to the same mode of operation of the airfield as in Breslau, the Germans will probably be mistaken.'

The commander of the 2nd Air Army (2 VA) Colonel General S.A. Krasovsky found the subordinate's offer tempting. After discussing the details of the upcoming operation of the false airfield, he ordered Major Lukyanov to allocate an aircraft for reconnaissance of the existing German airfield in Breslau. Then a special group of fourteen people headed by Senior Lieutenant Golyshev went to Neukirch, which tried to turn it into an exact copy of the Gandauer airfield. Further, the work of the twin airfield was organized as follows. Every day after dark, a Po-2 (also U-2) biplane took to the air, the crew of which determined which light sign the Germans used to mark the Gandauer airfield at night. As soon as the reconnaissance plane returned, the same sign was displayed in Neukirch, which was supposed to mislead the Ju 52 crews.

To a certain extent, this trick was successful. Although German planes continued to drop cargo containers on parachutes over Gandauer airfield, some of them were unloaded in the dark over Neukirch. In total, in March–April, 149 tons of various cargo were dropped at the twin airfield, according to Soviet data. Five transport planes and four cargo gliders landed there by mistake. Of the cargo captured by the Soviets, the Russian soldiers were most impressed by the carefully sealed leather bag with awards intended for the defenders of Breslau. In the Red Army, it was unacceptable to deliver awards by air for soldiers and officers still involved in the struggle.

The Russians came up with other ways to interfere with German transport planes. They placed their anti-aircraft searchlights close to the front line and tried to blind the pilots coming in to land at Gandauer airfield. But soon the German gunners were able to localize the searchlight positions and fire at them. As a result, the Russians had to move their searchlight installations at least 6 km away from the city. In addition, the positions of Soviet anti-aircraft batteries were periodically subjected to air attacks. For example, on 5 March, fourteen Fw 190 F-8s from I./SG 4 completed such a mission. This Gruppe, under the command of Major Fritz Schroter, was based at the Proßnitz airfield (as the Germans called Prostějov, Czech Republic), 175 km south of Breslau.

On the night of 6 March, fifty-three Ju 52/3m took off for Breslau Pocket, and forty-six of them were able to land on the new runway at Kaiserstrasse. They delivered ninety-four soldiers with weapons, including thirty machine guns, and 61.5 tons of various cargo. They then removed 471 wounded and 149 parachutes for cargo containers from the fortress, which were re-usable.

The following night, six out of fifteen Ju 52s arrived at Breslau Pocket. They delivered 3.7 tons of cargo, and took out sixty-one wounded, three Feldjäger with documents and twenty parachutes for cargo containers. On the night of 8 March, three Ju 52/3m landed at Kaiserstrasse with 3.7 tons of cargo on board. On the way back, twenty wounded people and the same number of parachutes for cargo containers were loaded into them.

That night, a Ju 52 W.Nr. 10140 '4V+CL' from 3./TG 3 went missing along with five crew members (pilot Leutnant Andreas Dennewill).

It quickly became clear to the Soviets that the available anti-aircraft guns and searchlights from the 71st Anti-aircraft Division, as well as the 'twin airfield', were not enough to interfere with transport planes of the Luftwaffe. They decided to involve night fighters, which in the Red Army air force were a rarity. The 18th Air Army (18 VA) had an unusual unit, the 56th Aviation Division Long – Range Fighters (AD IDD) under the command of Colonel B.V. Bickii. It consisted of the 45th Aviation Regiment Long-Range Fighters and the 173rd Aviation Regiment Long-Range Fighters. They were armed with twin-engine American Douglas A-20 G-1 Havoc aircraft.

Initially, they were ground-attack aircraft, armed with four forward 20mm guns and two Browning.50 caliber machine guns. In July 1943, the Russians converted them into long-range night fighters. An additional 1,036-liter fuel tank was installed in the bomb bay, which increased the flight time to eight hours. The aircraft was equipped with the airborne radar system Gneiss-2. Three of its knife-like antennae were slanted up in the upper fuselage, directly in front of the pilot's cabin, which is why the plane was nicknamed 'Ruffe'.

In March 1945, Colonel Bickii, after learning of 'problems' in the Breslau Pocket area, suggested that the commander of the 18th Air Army (18 VA) use his division to block the surrounded fortress from the air. Already on 13 March, 173rd Aviation Regiment Long-Range Fighters were transferred to Rudniki airfield, located 111 km east of Breslau. Later, the 45th Aviation Regiment Long-Range Fighters also flew there.

Each regiment had thirty-two Douglas A-20 G-1 Havocs and thirty-nine crews, as well as a radar company with a ground-based long-range radar system. A ground-based radar system was installed at four points around Breslau. They could detect a plane flying at an altitude of 1,000 meters at a range of up to 35 km. However, the accuracy of determining the coordinates of the target was not high.

The tactics of the Russian night fighters were as follows: 'Ruffes' Douglas A-20 G-1 Havoc, taking off from Rudniki airfield, were displayed on the target according to the ground radar system. Then, when approaching the target, the airborne radar system Gneiss-2 was activated. It could detect a 'bomber' type target at a distance of 300 to 3500 meters with an accuracy of up to five degrees in angular coordinates. When an enemy was detected, the operator of the airborne radar system had to give instructions to the pilot to enter the attack position. However, this was only a theory.

For a month and a half (from mid-March to May), the crews of the 45th Aviation Regiment Long-Range Fighters and 173rd Aviation Regiment Long-Range Fighters carried out 246 night flights to the Breslau Pocket area. But the operators of the airborne radar system and pilots were able to detect the target in only in sixty-eight cases – of which fifteen were visual, in the beams of searchlights; eleven times, by commands from the ground according to the ground radar system; and eight times, when searching freely using the airborne radar system. The other thirty-four times the target was detected visually in moonlight. At the same time, Russian night fighters were only able to attack the enemy in thirteen cases, but only two crews were successful! Captain Kaznov had two downed He 111s on his combat account, and Lieutenant Shesterikov had one cargo glider on his account.

To justify their complete failure, the Russians claimed that 'in many cases, they forced the crews of transport planes of the Luftwaffe to refuse to perform the task'. Allegedly, the Germans, seeing a night fighter behind them, dropped the cargo 'anywhere' and in a panic unhooked the towed cargo gliders away from Breslau. As a result, according to the Russians, about a hundred German soldiers landed on Soviet territory.

'The witch's ring'

By mid-March, the 10th Air Defense Corps, under the command of Major General P.G. Slepchenko, was transferred to the vicinity of Breslau instead of the 71st Anti-aircraft Division. It was armed with 640 anti-aircraft guns, 380 anti-aircraft machine guns and 150 anti-aircraft searchlights. The 310th Fighter Aviation Division Air Defense Colonel A.T. Kostenko, which had 115 aircraft, also carried out orders from the 10th Air Defense Corps. Later, between 1 and 16 April, five additional Anti-aircraft Regiments, six separate Anti-aircraft Divisions, and other units were transferred to the corps.

In the area of Breslau Pocket the Anti-aircraft batteries of the 10th Air Defense Corps were placed in such a way as to ensure the creation of a dense ring of anti-aircraft fire around the fortress to prevent its supply by air, as well as firing at ground targets. For this reason, Russian Anti-aircraft batteries were located 2.5–3 km from the front line, and sometimes closer.

Soon the crews of transport planes of the Luftwaffe felt a significant strengthening of the Soviet anti-aircraft ring around the Breslau Pocket. One Ju 52 radio operator recalled:

The Russian air defense was surprisingly strong. Our reconnaissance aircraft counted about ninety medium and heavy anti-aircraft artillery batteries and at least 100 searchlights, which were concentrated near Breslau. The number of Russian fighters operating at night is difficult to determine. At first, our losses were not great.

But that all changed in mid-March. Our Staffel, which had ten crews and planes, lost four crews and five planes in the second half of March alone. One crew managed to escape. Our comrades were able to jump out of the burning plane, and then landed on parachutes on the territory that was controlled by our troops. Colleagues who participated in the supply of Stalingrad by air, said that the Russian air defense at Breslau was much more powerful. Landing at the Gandauer airfield was also difficult because the advanced Russian units were located just half a kilometer from the runway. As soon as we approached, we were blinded by searchlights and machine-gun fire. In addition, the Russians, only hearing the noise of engines, began to fire mortars at the airfield territory…

During the landing and departure from Gandauer airfield, we saw the glow of raging fires in the city. On the way back, we dropped leaflets written in Russian. Radio communication between German troops and the encircled Breslau, which was necessary in the conditions of night flights, was significantly hampered by enemy radio stations. As a result, we often missed the city, immediately falling under enemy anti-aircraft fire.

In such conditions, not all crews could safely reach the target area. For example, on the night of 10 March, thirty-five He 111 H and twenty-two Ju 52/3m flew there, but only twelve He 111 and ten Ju 52 were able to land. They delivered ammunition and equipment for the fortress anti-aircraft batteries, and then removed sixty-one wounded, one Feldjäger with documents, and six parachutes for cargo containers. The next day, only one He 111 dropped cargo containers over the Breslau Pocket with a total weight of 1.4 tons.

The situation sometimes resembled a kind of 'swing'. For example, on the night of 12 March, out of forty-two He 111s from KG 4, TGr. 30 and 14.(Eis)/KG 55 heading for Gandauer airfield, thirty-eight planes landed there, delivering 26.3 tons of various cargo. And of the forty Ju 52s, only twenty-seven aircraft completed this mission, carrying 44.3 tons of ammunition, 1.5 tons of various equipment, seventeen soldiers and one anti-tank gun. They evacuated 190 wounded people from Festung. The Russians recorded a flight of eighty-seven transport planes over the blockade ring.

The following night, due to heavy Soviet anti-aircraft barrage, only five of the sixteen He 111s from TGr. 30 were able to land at Gandauer airfield. But at the same time, twenty-six of the thirty-two Ju 52s that took off were safely landed there. Russians recorded a flight of fifty-five transport planes over the blockade ring, with Russian anti-aircraft artillery reporting seven German planes shot down.

On the night of 14 March, fifty-nine Ju 52/3m took off for Breslau, of which forty-four landed at Gandauer airfield and alternate airfield Kaiserstrasse. They delivered 27.5 tons of equipment and eight soldiers with weapons, and on the way back they took on board 228 wounded and six parachutes for cargo containers. Russian anti-aircraft artillery reported six Ju 52s shot down. That night, the Ju 52 of the TG 4 commander Major Erich Reymann was shot down. It was a painful loss of an experienced pilot and an excellent organizer who had hundreds of transport flights under his belt.

On 15 March, twelve of the fifteen He 111 H from TGr. 30 that took off landed at Gandauer airfield, as well as twenty-five of the forty-one Ju 52s that took off. They delivered 12.3 and 27.5 tons of cargo, respectively. Transport planes took out another 180 injured and fifty parachutes for cargo containers. Russian anti-aircraft gunners claimed six downed Ju 52s.

Any decrease in the number of planes landing at the fortress affected not only the volume of cargo delivered, but also had a strong impact on the morale of the garrison. By order of Generalleutnant Nichoff, out of the twelve hospitals deployed in the city, only those whose recovery was not expected for the next two months wounded were evacuated along the air bridge. In other words, only the seriously wounded and crippled were taken out, while the rest could return to service. Oberfeldwebel Wal of the ambulance service, who was responsible for the removal of the wounded, recalled.

> For the night transport of the wounded from the Gandauer airfield, the maximum number of them was located in the adjacent buildings and barrack. We delivered the wounded to the airfield in the shortest possible time. The number of 'sitting' and 'lying down' wounded in crowded hospitals was constantly updated by phone... Transportation of the wounded was carried

out not only by ambulances, but also by buses. Everything was done to get them on their way as soon as possible.

Usually, the Ju 52 could fit no more than twenty-eight people, but some pilots managed to load thirty-two at once!

On the night of 16 March, all thirteen He 111 from TGr. 30 that flew to Breslau Pocket completed the mission. They dropped cargo containers on parachutes with a total weight of 12.4 tons, including medicines and medical equipment for fortress hospitals. Of the thirty-six Ju 52/m3 that took off, twenty-four planes landed at Gandauer airfield, delivering another 37.7 tons of cargo, and then evacuating thirty-nine injured people. Russian anti-aircraft artillery reported two downed Ju 52s.

On the night of 17 March, fifty-seven He 111 and twenty-nine Ju 52 took off at Gandauer airfield, of which three and six aircraft respectively did not reach the target. The garrison in Breslau Pocket received 92.8 tons of ammunition, equipment, and food at once. One of the Ju 52/m3 radio operators recalled:

> At 04.30, we turned into the city. There is no connection to Gandauer airfield completely, so we turned to Frizenvize. Despite the fact that we were flying at an altitude of 250–300 meters, it is impossible to make out anything. We went to the place where cargo containers were supposed to be dumped. Suddenly we came under fire from two 37-mm guns at once. Something cracked in the tail of the plane. We repeatedly found ourselves in the beams of enemy searchlights. Our pilot tried to maneuver between them, then tried to gain altitude. At the same time, the 'bombs' (cargo containers) with mail and provisions were severely damaged by anti-aircraft shell fragments. You didn't have to think about dropping them anymore. We tried to make our way north from this 'the witch's ring' as unobtrusively as possible. Suddenly there was a bluish gleam on the propellers and edges of the wings. Russian searchlights were looking for us, but they couldn't find us in the dense clouds.

This Ju 52 with numerous holes from Russian anti-aircraft fire at 06.10 safely returned to the air base in Klotzsche. The other four transport planes went missing that night in the area of Breslau Pocket.

On the night of 18 March, eighteen Ju 52s took off for the mission at Gandauer airfield, of which only six landed at the fortress. At the same time, all twelve He 111 from TGr. 30 landed safely there. In total, Luftwaffe aircraft delivered 33.6 tons of various cargo, and then took out seventy-three wounded and twenty parachutes for cargo containers.

The following night, twenty-one He 111 out of twenty-three departures arrived at Gandauer airfield, along with all twelve Ju 52/m3. They delivered 43.3 tons of cargo.

On the night of 20 March, all eighteen He 111 landed at Gandauer airfield. Another ten Ju 52/m3 of the forty that took off dropped cargo containers on Breslau. In total, the fortress garrison received 31.2 tons of ammunition and equipment.

Despite all the difficulties, the air bridge continued to work properly. On 21 March, twelve of the fifteen He 111s and six of the twelve Ju 52s that flew there, landed at Gandauer airfield. They delivered 18 tons of weapons and ammunition, and then removed eighty-one wounded, two high-ranking officers and twenty parachutes for cargo containers.

At night on 22 March, twenty-three He 111 from TGr. 30 flew to Breslau Pocket, of which only one was forced to turn back due to technical problems. Also, twenty-six Ju 52/m3 flew to the fortress, of which only twelve reached their targets. In total, they delivered almost 45 tons of cargo to the encircled garrison. On the way back, transport planes took on board ninety-five wounded and twenty-four parachutes for cargo containers. Following them, a second 'wave' of ten transport planes Ju 52/m3 took off at Gandauer airfield. This time, only four aircraft carrying 7.9 tons of cargo landed safely at the airport.

Hitler spoils everything

At the end of the war, Hitler began to interfere in the planning and conduct of even the smallest and most insignificant military operations; the air bridge in Breslau was no exception. At the end of March, Gauleiter Hanke sent a radio message to Berlin asking them to send heavy 150 mm infantry guns to the fortress. At the same time, its commandant Generalleutnant Nichoff repeatedly stressed that it did not need guns at all, but ammunition. Despite this, the Führer reacted favorably to the request, and ordered the delivery of the weapons to the Breslau Pocket.

The Luftwaffe reported to Hitler that the guns did not fit in the Ju 52, and therefore it was not possible to deliver them by air to the surrounded city. The Führer regarded this as 'unwillingness to support the air bridge'. He pointed out that the guns and their calculations could be transported on six cargo gliders.

On the night of 23 March, nineteen He 111 dropped cargo containers with a total weight of 16.2 tons to the garrison at Breslau Pocket. That night, three He 111 H-20s from KG 4 towed Go 242 cargo gliders and three Do 17 towed DFS 230 cargo gliders. Cargo gliders carried three 150 mm guns, gun service, and a supply of shells. On approach to the fortress, two of the Go 242 cargo gliders and one DFS 230 cargo glider were shot down by Russian anti-aircraft fire. As a result, only one 150-mm cannon was delivered to the city. The adventure, begun at the insistence of Hitler, ended in another collapse.

The next day, twelve He 111s landed at Gandauer airfield and delivered 10.4 tons of various cargo to the garrison Festung. Another aircraft from KG 4 towed a Go 242 cargo glider, which successfully landed at Kaiserstrasse. On 24 March, the OKW combat magazine noted that the supply of Breslau is hampered by enemy searchlights. To date, 65 Junkers have gone missing, which is an irreplaceable loss, since their production has been stopped. On the same day, the commandant of fortress Generalleutnant Nichoff wrote in his diary: 'Delivery to Breslau has become extremely difficult due to increased anti-aircraft fire and increased searchlights.'

Bf 109 becomes a transport airplane

Heavy losses of transport planes forced the Luftflotte 6 command to look for alternative ways to supply the Breslau Pocket. In mid-March, it was decided to use single-engine Bf 109 day fighters for air bridge. The nearest airfield from which fighters could operate was Schweidnitz (now Świdnica, Poland). From it to the fortress was about 50 km to the northeast. I./JG 52 was based there, commanded by Hauptmann Erich Hartmann, the Luftwaffe's most successful Ace and holder of the Knight's Cross of the Iron Cross with Oak Leaves, Swords and Diamonds.

The mission to supply the Breslau Pocket was given to 2nd Staffel, Oberleutnant Rudolf Trenkel. The planes of this Staffel were to carry one small cargo container each containing ammunition and medical supplies. They had parachutes made of red silk so that they could be located faster on the ground.

In general terms, the tactics of the Bf 109 during sorties to supply the Breslau Pocket looked like this: Pilots from 2./JG 52 on the way to the city were covered by fighters Bf 109 from other Staffel. After dropping the 'food bombs', all the fighters launched assault attacks on the positions of the Soviet troops, or conducted a 'free hunt' in the area.

In practice, however, the German pilots had to face a serious opponent in the face of Soviet anti-aircraft artillery. On 15 March, a Bf 109 G-14 W.Nr. 465260 of Oberleutnant Trenkel was heavily damaged directly over the Breslau Pocket. The pilot was seriously injured, but was able to reach the location of his troops, and near the town of Strehlen (now Strzelin, Poland), 35 km south of Breslau, jumped out by parachute. He was sent to the hospital and no longer participated in the battles. The next day, the Bf 109 G-14 W.Nr. 465354 did not return from a flight to supply Breslau Pocket. The fate of its pilot, Feldwebel Heinz Schindler, was unknown and he has been listed as missing ever since. Then, on 20 March, a similar fate befell another pilot 2./JG 52 – Fähnrich Reiner Gawel, his Bf 109 G-14 W.Nr. 465472 also did not return from the mission to supply the fortress.

At least one of these pilots was captured by the Soviets, because the very next day, Russian intelligence became aware that JG 52 were participating in flights over Breslau and dropping ammunition to the garrison.

On 21 March, to Schweidnitz airfield flew III./JG 52 under the command of Major Adolf Borchers holder of the Knight's Cross. He also joined the air bridge in Breslau Pocket. The next day, led by the commander the pilots dropped six cargo containers on the city, and then during the 'free hunt' shot down five Russian planes, two of which were on the account of Major Borchers. At the same time, the Bf 109 G-14 W.Nr. 786145 was damaged by anti-aircraft fire. Its pilot made an emergency landing on belly at Shengarten airfield.

On 23 March, fighters from I./JG 52 flew to Breslau Pocket, dropping eight cargo containers. The next day, this mission was accomplished by twelve Bf 109s from the same Gruppe.

The accuracy of dumping cargo containers left much to be desired. The heavy fire of Soviet anti-aircraft guns did not allow German pilots to stay over the city for a long time, choosing the right moment for dropping at low altitude. The familiar story was repeated. A significant number of cargo containers never got to the defenders of Breslau Pocket. Some of them fell on Soviet positions, some on swampy and flooded territories from where they could not be recovered.

The assault on Breslau Pocket was still slow. Unlike the assault on Budapest Pocket, the Soviet 6th Army did not show fanaticism. With the tacit consent of Marshal Ivan Konev, they conducted the siege formally. The Russians did not launch attacks from different directions, but carried out attacks in separate sectors. The 6th Army headquarters regularly reported on the captured city blocks, but still did not put much pressure on the German garrison. On 18 March, the Russians launched a 'decisive offensive', but again only pushed the Germans deeper into the city. The attacking Russian troops reached the Hindenburg square and the FAMO factory (Fahrzeug-und Motoren-Werke GmbH).[3] However, it was not until 27 March that the facility and several surrounding city blocks were completely captured. The Russians were unable to advance further, and the assault was temporarily suspended.

At the end of March, Silesia finally got warm weather. The air temperature rose to between +15 and +17°C. However, it was still overcast and raining. Rasputitsa and low clouds hindered the movement of Soviet troops and aviation operations. And only at the very end of the month, the saving cloud cover that reliably protected the ancient city from massive raids dissipated...

'...However, the fight is not over yet'

Since the area southwest of the city was flooded by early April, Generalleutnant Nichoff correctly concluded that the assault on Breslau would continue from the west. In addition, it was very convenient to attack Gandauer airfield from there. To defend this area, the commandant of the fortress utilized his best forces: two parachute battalions, 21st Bataillon Volkssturm, the main part of the artillery, heavy anti-aircraft guns installed for direct fire, about twenty 2-cm-Flak-Vierling 38, as well as available tanks and assault guns.

On the morning of 31 March – Easter Saturday – an ominous silence hung over the Breslau Pocket. It was broken only at 18.00, when the Soviet artillery began a heavy fire on the city. At the same time, bombers appeared in the sky. Hendrik Felten, who served in the SS-Festungs-Regiment 1, recalled:

> Soviet artillery smashed buildings one by one with their
> 280-mm shells, while squadrons of planes rained bombs

---

3 This plant was part of the Junkers concern and produced a variety of military equipment (heavy semi-tracked tractors Sd.Kfz. 9, Panzer II tanks, 'Marder' tank destroyers, 'Wespe' self-propelled guns, 5cm PaK 38 (Sf), etc.

on the city, which was already on fire. A mushroom-shaped smoke screen hung over Breslau. Anyone who saw this smoke and the city burning like a torch might have thought Breslau has come to an end... However, the fight is not over yet.

Then at night, Po-2 light night bombers (also U-2) from the 208th Night Bomber Aviation Division Colonel L.N. Yuzeyev flew over the city at low level, dropping 50-kilogram bombs and firing tracer bullets into the streets. On the same night, a Ju 52 from IV./TGr.1, which was piloted by the very experienced pilot Feldwebel Eduard Jikal (403 sorties), went missing.

At dawn on 1 April, when the sun's rays had not yet broken through the wall of smoke that covered the ground, the Soviet artillery thundered again. The shelling of Breslau Pocket continued for six hours. Around 12.00, the planes also began dropping leaflets calling on the German garrison to surrender. Interestingly, until this day, trams had continued to run in the city, their movement stopped only after the network of contact wires was disabled during the shelling and air attacks on 1 April. After that, trams were used to create barricades on city streets.

In between air raids artillery and Katyusha multiple rocket launchers (the Germans called them 'Stalin's Organs') fired on the same areas. After this massive preparation, the Soviet tanks moved towards the Gandauer airfield. During the ensuing battle, the Germans suffered heavy losses, including the loss of their 88 mm anti-aircraft guns. The Soviets, however, having broken through the German defenses in the first half of the day, were not able to develop their success before dark. During the night, Generalleutnant Nichoff moved reinforcements from other defense sectors and closed the gap in the city's defenses.

2 April was a 'black day' in the history of Breslau Pocket. The air attacks began at 08.00 and continued almost without interruption throughout the day. Pe-2 bombers from the 6th Guards Bomber Aviation Corps dropped 250-kg and 500-kg bombs on Festung. German anti-aircraft artillery was practically inactive, and shells were saved for firing at tanks. This allowed the pilots of diving bombers to descend to an altitude of 1,500–900 meters and attack their targets with impunity. The fires in the fortress did not stop. Fire spread from building to building and architectural monuments, sparing nothing in its way. Only the city hall remained intact. One resident of Breslau wrote: 'Heated by the heat, the bell begins to ring... The fire element is raging in our yard. The wood melts almost instantly in the hot swirls. Pillars of fire sparks rise to the sky to fall on neighboring roofs and give life to new fires.'

By the evening of 2 April, many city blocks of Breslau were in ruins, and the entire city center was almost burned out. Because of the raging fires, it was almost as bright as day. There was an unbearable smell in the streets. It came from damaged sewer pipes and mixed with the stench of decomposing corpses that had not had time to be buried.

The events of the two Easter days convinced the Germans that the Soviet command would achieve its goal by carpet bombing. However, on 3 April there was a lull again. The rains that started gradually stopped the spread of fires, and again closed the Breslau Pocket from Russian aircraft. Even in 1945 'Stalin's falcons' did not learn how to fly and find targets in difficult weather conditions!

Meanwhile, the air bridge in Breslau Pocket continued to function. On the night of 2 to 3 April, transport planes, approaching the city one by one from different directions, delivered the necessary supplies to the garrison. However, they landed in the fortress only in isolated cases. Most of the equipment, ammunition, and food was dropped in cargo containers on parachutes. At the same time, German pilots had to overcome the dense, echeloned fire of the Russian 10th Air Defense Corps units.

According to Soviet data, on the night of 2 to 3 April in the area of Breslau Pocket, anti-aircraft gunners shot down five Ju 52 and one Ju 88.

On 4 April, Russian ground attacks resumed. By evening, their tanks had reached the Gandauer airfield and occupied all the key positions around it. Only the airfield at Kaiserstrasse remained at the disposal of the fortress garrison; transport planes and cargo gliders could still land on it. However, in the conditions of the tightening ring of the blockade and constant artillery attacks, it was increasingly difficult to do this. It was clear to the defenders that within the next few days, aircraft landings would cease. The last three Ju 52s that delivered the next batch of cargo landed at alternate airfield Kaiserstrasse on the night of 6–7 April. On return flights, they took out fifty-two wounded soldiers and the crews of two planes that had been downed earlier. One of these aircraft – a Ju 52 from II./TG 2, which was piloted by Oberfeldwebel Alfred Kummer – went missing. After that, only cargo gliders and Fi 156 landed on Kaiserstrasse. These small planes delivered cargo to the Breslau Pocket, but their main mission was to transport important documents and evacuate cargo glider pilots.

After the loss of Gandauer airfield and the cessation of full use Kaiserstrasse, the problem of supplying the Breslau Pocket became acute. For example, on 7 April, four Bf 109 Ks from III./JG 52 flew to the fortress from Schweidnitz airfield with cargo containers. However, only one of them was able to drop the load on the target, and the garrison received only 640 kg of necessary equipment and ammunition. At the same time, the evacuation of the wounded almost stopped, since occasionally Fi 156 could only transport two or three people. As a result, the hospitals of Breslau Pocket were overcrowded, and the number of injured increased every day.

Now most of the cargo could be dumped only in cargo containers on parachutes. On the night of 8 April, nineteen He 111s appeared over Breslau, some of which were towing Go 242 cargo gliders. They dropped cargo containers with 18.2 tons of ammunition and equipment over the city. After them, a second 'wave' of four He 111 delivered cargo containers with food. That same night, Ju 52/m3 appeared for the last time in the sky over Breslau Pocket. Five planes dropped cargo containers on parachutes. By that time, the Luftwaffe had a shortage of these aircraft, and the remaining 'Aunt Ju' did not have enough spare parts and engines. From now on the main transport airplane was He 111.

Meanwhile, Soviet command planned another 'decisive' assault on Breslau Pocket for 10 April. It was to be preceded by a series of massive bombing raids on Festung. According to the plan, on the night of 9– 10 April, dozens of Po-2 (also U-2) biplanes from the 208th Night Bomber Aviation Division were to attack German strongholds and sites where cargo was dropped from transport planes. They were designated by special navigation lights that these Russian light bombers had to 'extinguish'. Then in the afternoon – between 12.10 and 13.00 – large groups of Il-2 ground-attack aircraft and Pe-2 dive bombers were to strike the city.

However, the implementation of Russian plans was again prevented by the weather. On the night before the assault, the area of Breslau Pocket was shrouded in cloud and fog. As a result, only twenty-six Po-2 biplanes (also U-2) took to the air and dropped shrapnel bombs on the city.

On the morning of 10 April, after a long artillery barrage, the units of the Russian 6th Army launched another offensive. Tanks accompanied by infantry moved in the direction of the city center. The first groups of Il-2 ground-attack aircraft and Pe-2 dive bombers appeared over the fortress at 16.40, when the cloud had cleared a little. However, the success of the Red Army was once again modest. From 1 to 14 April, only nineteen city blocks, six factories, four parks and two city squares were captured. Most of the city remained in the hands of the Wehrmacht.

The air bridge continued to function. For example, on the night of 14 April, fourteen He 111 aircraft from KG 4 dropped cargo containers on parachutes with ammunition, equipment and food totaling 15.8 tons.

However, unlike other Pockets, the Breslau garrison did not lack for food. The available supplies, even without the air bridge, could be enough for another month and a half of the siege.

Following the assault in the first half of April, accompanied by massive shelling and raids, the Soviets expected the garrison of Breslau Pocket to capitulate. However, this did not happen. The attack on Berlin had already begun, and 'Silesia Fortress' continued to hold on to the rear of the 1st Ukrainian Front.

Therefore, on 18 April, parts of the Russian 6th Army launched a new offensive on Breslau Pocket. The Russians managed to capture the Beckmann machine-building plant, an abattoir, and thirteen blocks in the western part of the city. However, the Soviets again suffered heavy losses. For example, in the battles in the western part of the city, the 349th Guards Self-propelled Guns Regiment lost thirteen out of sixteen of its self-propelled guns ISU-152.[4] The next day, the Linke and Hofmann plant, the gas plant, and eight city blocks were captured. However, the 'decisive assault' again failed. The fighting was for individual city blocks, but the Russian 6th Army failed to penetrate deeply into the German defenses. On 24 April, the Russians captured twelve blocks and the Dauber factory with heavy fighting. The last major success of the Red Army was the capture of the Arsenal building after the assault, which took place on 26–28 April.

On the night of 26–27 April, I. and III./KG 4 'General Wever' performed the last supply sorties in Breslau Pocket. Thirty He 111s dropped 24.1 tons of ammunition and various equipment to the garrison. On the night of 30 April to 1 May, Ju 52s appeared over the encircled fortress for the last time. Seven planes dropped cargo containers on parachutes. That same night, two Fi 156s landed at Kaiserstrasse. After delivering the cargo, they took off safely, taking on board several cargo glider pilots who had landed there the day before.

By the end of April, the commandant Festung Generalleutnant Nichoff realized that the garrison had exhausted all forces in heavy fighting. Later, after Hitler had committed suicide, he was given permission by Generalfeldmarschall Ferdinand Schörner to break out of the city. But such an action could only lead to more victims, and there was practically nowhere to break through at that moment! On the morning of 4 May, Generalleutnant

---

4 In total, the Russians lost eighty tanks and self-propelled guns during the siege of Breslau, including forty-seven ISU-152, seventeen IS-2, 11 T-34, five SU-122 and one ISU-122; 122 crew were killed.

Nichoff decided to start negotiations with the Soviet command. At 13.00 on 6 May, the garrison at Breslau Pocket surrendered.

The only one who managed to escape from the doomed Festung at the last moment was Gauleiter Karl Hanke. On 29 April, Hitler had appointed him the new Reichsführer-SS in place of the traitor Heinrich Himmler. This promotion, against the background of the dying Third Reich, allowed Gauleiter Hanke to leave the city 'with a clear conscience', the inhabitants of which he urged 'to die or win'. On the night of 6 May, the new Reichsführer-SS took off from Kaiserstrasse in a Fi 156 and, with some adventures, reached the area of Prague. But soon before taking up the duties of the new Reichsführer-SS, Hanke was killed in a shootout with Czech partisans.

On 6 May 1945 not only ended the history of Breslau Pocket, but also the German city of Breslau. The former capital of Lower Silesia, as well as other cities in the region, went to Poland. The surviving German population was forced to leave the city.

Summing up, we can say that the stubborn defense of Breslau Pocket played not only the role of a breakwater in the path of the 'Asian avalanche', but in general did not affect the course of military operations on the Eastern front. Objectively, it was a senseless slaughter of Russians and Germans in order to fulfill the orders of two psychopaths: Hitler and Stalin.

Now a few words about the results of the Luftwaffe's activities in supplying the Breslau Pocket. German data on the operation of the air bridge in Breslau Pocket is contradictory. According to one report, the Luftwaffe flew about 3,200 sorties to supply the German garrison (1,000 Ju 52 and 2,000 He 111); 5,600 tons of cargo were delivered to the fortress. According to other sources, from 15 February to 1 May, German aviation made about 2,000 sorties to supply the Breslau Pocket, delivering 1,496 tons of various cargo (67 tons were delivered by Fi 156). Perhaps in the first case we are talking about all departures and cargo, including dropped cargo containers on parachutes, and in the second only by landing method. In total, transport aviation evacuated about 6,600 wounded from Breslau Pocket (this figure almost coincides with the information of Soviet intelligence).

Data on the participation of specific Luftwaffe units in the implementation of the air bridge in Breslau Pocket is fragmentary and incomplete. For example, II./TG 3 performed 566 flights to the fortress, delivering 3,770 soldiers and 657 tons of cargo, and on the way back evacuated 3,282 wounded.

The Luftwaffe's total losses, including non-returnable and operational losses, were 165 aircraft (only II./TG 3 lost 52 Ju 52s). Twenty-one crew members were killed, eighty-four people were missing and twenty-three others were injured.

As far as the effectiveness of the Russian response to the implementation of the air bridge in Breslau Pocket is concerned, Russian attempts to abort the air bridge failed. The reasons for the failure are similar to those given in previous chapters of this book.

Chapter 11

Erhard Milch – chief planner of the collapse of the Luftwaffe

The figure is not for the facade!

The Luftwaffe is strongly associated with the rotund figure of the ever-smiling and 'bright' Hermann Göring. Relatively few people know the man behind this magnificent external 'facade', who played the role of a hard-working 'shadow' or 'gray cardinal'. While the Kriegsmarine, and especially the Wehrmacht, had a succession of leaders, the Luftwaffe was always led by the same person almost until the collapse of the Third Reich (von Greim took this position only for a few days). Why did a whole cohort of top Luftwaffe executives remain in the shadow of Göring? Were there any attempts to take his place and change the reputation of the 'madhouse' acquired by the German air force after 1942?

Perhaps the only person who had a real opportunity to unseat Göring was Generalfeldmarschall Erhard Milch. It was he who was the master of the fanatical and consistent displacement of his competitors and occupation of vacant positions. So, why did the second person in the Luftwaffe, who solved all personnel issues like a battering ram, never become the first? There are many answers to this intriguing question, but the authors want to draw readers' attention only to the psychological reasons for the failure of Milch.

We will begin our psychological analysis with the simplest of things, and what catches the eye of an external observer, with a description of the appearance of the second in command of the Luftwaffe.

Anyone who looked closely at the photos of this German Generalfeldmarschall would notice that Erhard Milch's appearance hardly met the standards of beauty. A large, almost rectangular head, deep-set eyes under overhanging brows, and a large, fleshy nose. An unusually high, oddly shaped forehead, did not make his face smart, but on the contrary, created a resemblance to the movie image of Frankenstein's monster. In some photos the full figure in combination with his average height made Milch look almost as wide as Göring. Of course, the military uniform hid the shortcomings of the appearance of this Luftwaffe leader, but against the background of his patron Göring, who glittered like a copper basin, Erhard Milch did not give the impression of a leader.

However, the unprepossessing appearance of this extremely ambitious man is not enough to explain the failure of hopes for absolute power in the Luftwaffe. Following the example of the psychiatrist Freud, it is necessary to understand the motives that played a major role in the rise of Erhard Milch's character and determined the limit of his career growth and subsequent collapse. It is advisable to start this difficult path by analyzing the childhood of the Luftwaffe functionary that interests us.

The secret of birth?

The first thing those are interested in Erhard Milch's biography will learn is the mysterious history of his father's nationality, or rather the myth of the future Luftwaffe Field Marshal's non-Aryan origin. As a rule, any popular biography of Milch is limited to a detailed discussion of this fact and a brief list of information from his track record.

In our opinion, the question of whether Milch had Jewish or German blood in his veins, or whether he belonged to a different nationality, did not play any significant role in his life and, most importantly, in his professional career. Moreover, after a brief trial and the usual Third Reich shenanigans, Milch was officially declared an Aryan.

However, biographers do not mention that in fact the young Erhard had no father at all, and was raised only by his mother and grandmother. In general, the relationship in the family between Milch's parents was so strange and intriguing that it could be a good example for describing sexual attraction in a book by Sigmund Freud. However, the Milch family was quite well-off in terms of financial support, and their children were never in need of anything. Eventually, the strange family broke up and Frau Milch moved with the children to Berlin.

Continuing the themes of Freud, it is logical to ask the question of who became the model of masculinity necessary for the normal development of the psyche of the young Erhard. Of course, there were men in his inner circle, including his possible real father, his mother's rich uncle Karl Brauer. However, we must admit that the real symbolic father figure for Milch was Kaiser Wilhelm, and then, in adulthood, this place was taken by Adolf Hitler. The fact is that the boy was brought up in an atmosphere of extreme nationalism and militarism, traditional for Germany at that time. There were other children in the family, but it is clear that the eldest son received the most attention from his mother and the greatest influence of pathological German nationalism.

Unfortunately, the authors do not have detailed information about Milch's childhood and youth. Therefore, we are forced to reconstruct some of his character traits based on the actions committed in adulthood. It can be assumed that, as a student at the prestigious private Königsallee school, Erhard demonstrated the traits that became the basis of the character of the future Field Marshal of the Luftwaffe, namely aggressiveness, an exorbitant ambitions, hypertrophied selfishness and monstrous stubbornness.

It must be admitted that the unrestrained propaganda of nationalism, patriotism and militarism, and other harmful influences within the family environment of the young Erhard, were laid down in the fertile ground of his nervous system.

The authors have reason to assume that Milch had a congenial defect in the psyche which defined his character. In the conditions of a specific social environment, this natural feature was transformed into a leading character trait that determined his future fate. Milch became utterly single-minded. During his speech at the Nuremberg Tribunals, he stated: 'Loyalty to the Kaiser and loyalty to my country were the only political teachings that I accepted both as an officer and in my parents' home.' Milch was completely devoid of doubt throughout his life, and the scope of his interests was extremely narrow. It was in the service of this ingrained idea of pathological patriotism that gave an incredible strength, and at the same time an incredible weakness to his character.

Happy 'military fate'. From Fähnrich to Generalfeldmarschall

Like many Germans from well-to-do families of that time, young Erhard saw no other fate for himself than the military profession. The eldest son, according to the old German tradition, simply had to become an officer.

Milch's specialty was artillery, and his military career began in 1910. Studying at the military school in the city of Anklam was extremely successful for the young gunner. At the final exams, he was the best of 120 candidates for officer rank. This energetic, military-minded cadet, who was even younger than his comrades, made an indelible impression on them. We can assume that this success was achieved not due to high abilities, but solely due to diligence, accuracy and exemplary discipline.

Milch entered the First World War with the rank of Leutnant. He fought on both the Eastern and Western fronts. The young soldier's efforts were noticed by his superiors, and in July 1915 Milch was transferred to the Luftstreitkräfte (Imperial Air Force) where he was trained as an air observer. That's how he began with aviation, which later became the main business of his life. The career of the future Generalfeldmarschall developed successfully, he felt very at home in the army. However, Milch was not at all a favorite of capricious military fate. His service was radically different from the life of the 'aristocrat' Göring, who spent the entire war jousting in the sky. Milch, as a company commander on the Western Front, experienced all the horrors of the land front. When commanding troops, the future State Secretary of the Reich Ministry of Aviation could be rude and stubborn, which sometimes saved the lives of his soldiers. The grind of the trenches did not shake Milch's faith in the Kaiser and the rightness of the 'unfortunate' Germany, which allegedly became a victim of British intrigues. Not only did he not become a pacifist, but on the contrary, he longed with all his being for revenge in the future war.

Milch met the end of the war in aviation as an air intelligence officer. In October 1918, Milch, who did not know how to fly an airplane, was appointed commander of Jagdgruppe 6. So for the first, but not the last, time in his life, he began to manage a unit that he did not know and did not understand.

Due to his character, Milch took the defeat in the First World War and the collapse of the German Empire stoically. Rather than crying over it or falling into a stupor, after the peace of Versailles, he tried to fight the German revolutionaries, whom he considered traitors. It was not until late 1921 that Milch retired with the rank of Hauptmann.

Considering that by developing civil aviation, he benefited a Germany offended by the terms of the Treaty of Versailles, Milch took up civil aviation. In this business, thanks to his boundless ambition, he achieved great success. However, Milch felt that only military service under Nazi-patriots could fully realize his ambitions.

In 1933, 'military fate' again turned out to favor Erhard Milch. After a long break, he resumed his military career. The rapid creation of the Luftwaffe became a kind of springboard for the take-off of the State Secretary of the Reich Ministry of Aviation. One promotion followed another. Like any born military man with unlimited ambitions, he was waiting for only one thing, a new war, and therefore new military ranks. Thanks to Hitler's obsession, these expectations didn't have to wait long.

In the Polish and Norwegian conflicts, Milch did not show any generalship talents, but was able to attract the attention of Hitler. In fact, all his activities were reduced to solving small economic issues at the tactical level and frenzied activity in the form of flying a private plane over the front line. However, the efforts and fanaticism of a man for whom the word 'impossible' did not exist were highly appreciated by the Nazi leadership. On 19 July 1940, Hitler personally awarded Erhard Milch the highest military rank of Generalfeldmarschall. After a brief experience in command of Luftflotte 5, Milch never again managed troops, but was exclusively engaged in administrative work and inspection of Luftwaffe military units. It was in this organizational work that his talent as a sadistic manager manifested itself. His inspections of Luftwaffe units at the beginning of the Second World War reached the point of complete fanaticism.

Despite the fact that many contemporaries and biographers call Milch a civilian in uniform, in reality, he was a born martinet. Throughout his career, he showed complete readiness to follow orders from his superiors and extreme rudeness, up to obscene language and physical abuse to subordinates.

Ice and flame. Milch and Göring

Milch was the complete opposite of his boss Göring (a detailed psychological description of Hermann Göring can be found in the book *Hitler's Strategic Bombing Offensive on the eastern Front. Blitz over the Volga, 1943*). The psychological qualities of the State Secretary of the Reich Ministry of Aviation complemented or compensated for the features of the Reich Minister for Aviation. This complement of physical characteristics and internal mental strength during the formation of the Luftwaffe played, of course, a positive role. Without the adventurism of Göring and the methodical planning and control of Milch, it would have been impossible to create a somewhat visually exaggerated, but still quite combat-ready air force in such a short time. However, as Hitler's military appetites grew and the Nazis dragged Germany into all-out war, relations between the State Secretary of the Reich Ministry of Aviation and the Reich Minister for Aviation became increasingly strained. Unlike Göring, Milch did not seek to be visible. He never shone like a copper basin or was hung with decorations like a Christmas tree. Despite the fact that Milch, like his boss, was obsessed with huge ambitions, he almost always remained in the shadows. However, soon this 'shadow' – to the surprise of the narrow-minded Göring – gradually became the most important person in the Luftwaffe.

And we must admit that after the Stalingrad disaster, Milch had a real chance to take the post of head of the Luftwaffe. Defeats and disasters made the pathological shortcomings of Reichsmarschall and the 'advantages' of the State Secretary of the Reich Ministry of Aviation very contrasting in the eyes of others. Against the background of Göring's disorderly lifestyle and complete disregard for his official duties, the zealous bureaucrat and sadistic Milch looked like a model of discipline and exemplary order. And these pairs of qualities can be continued for a long time. Moreover, against the background of Göring's mental illness, the psychopathic Milch looked like an example of good mental health. However, there were two Luftwaffe fathers with similar features, namely: stupidity, excessive conceit and a complete lack of moral standards.

At the beginning of 1943, Milch was at the peak of his influence in Hitler's environment and was close to the peak of his powers. He was State Secretary of the Reich Ministry of Aviation, Deputy commander-in-chief of the Luftwaffe, inspector General of Luftwaffe (Generalinspekteur der Luftwaffe), Director of air armament (Generalluftzeugmeister) and Chairman of the Board of Directors of Lufthansa. He jealously guarded every position. Göring fruitlessly spent several years trying to dismiss his deputy, but each time he did not have enough strength to achieve the result. Only at the very end of the war, when the 'impudent' Milch encroached on the most 'sacred' in the Third Reich – the unlimited powers of Hitler and angered the Nazi overlord – Göring finally managed to fulfill his long-held dream. However, even the complete failure of Milch did not mean the immediate elimination of the inconvenient Generalfeldmarschall from his immediate environment. Göring had to work hard to convincingly remove Milch from all the many positions he held in the Luftwaffe.

Primitive sadist

The main myth associated with Milch's activities continues the theme of his confrontation with Göring and the discussion about the reasons for the collapse of the Luftwaffe. Many biographers usually note with bitterness that the strategic planning of the State Secretary of the Reich Ministry of Aviation and his methodical work on the development of the German air force was completely spoiled by the impulsive Hermann.

However, an objective analysis of the facts shows that Milch is at least as much to blame for the collapse of the Luftwaffe as his boss. Moreover, many of the decisions made by Deputy Göring personally caused the German aviation industry, and indirectly the Luftwaffe, almost more irreparable strategic damage than all his 'hooliganisms' as Reichsmarschall. Here are just a few of the total mistakes that most clearly refute the myth of Erhard Milch's strategic talents and his exceptional managerial effectiveness.

Management practice involves a conscious choice of the main methods (management technologies) to achieve the goals set for the manager, taking into account changing external and internal conditions. Milch had never chosen or changed his management style. His manner of managing people was derived from the main characteristic of his character. The authors have already mentioned the pathological limitations of Milch's abilities. His outlook corresponded to that of a barrack Feldwebel, who trains his subordinate soldiers brilliantly, but is not capable of more than that.

Milch was a fanatic of command-and-control methods, and no amount of reality could change his firm belief in their effectiveness. A striking example of Milch's fanaticism is the collapse of the organization of the air bridge to Stalingrad. Even after the death of the 6th Army, he seriously argued that if he had been sent in time to lead the Luftwaffe transport aviation, the disaster could have been avoided. These primitive principles were the foundation of Milch's management of the aviation industry and were consistently implemented throughout his tenure as second-in-command at the Luftwaffe.

Trying to please Hitler, for the sake of short-term tactical reasons to accelerate the growth of aircraft production, Milch consistently carried out a total nationalization of the German aviation industry. By the early 1940s, private initiative and technical creativity, the source of progress in aviation, had been replaced by strict planning, centralized resource allocation, and control. This decision of Milch, which was fully approved by the Nazis, had disastrous long-term consequences. By the beginning of the war with the Soviet Union, talented German designers, bound hand and foot by strict requirements, were not able to create new aircraft designs. The freedom of creativity was replaced by the pointless activity of fulfilling the whims of Hitler, who considered himself a natural expert in all technical matters.

Thanks to the actions of Milch, until the end of the war German pilots were forced to fly hopelessly outdated aircraft models of the early '30s. Every new plane created in the state planning system turned out to be worse than the previous one, and the He 177 bomber, like many other practical results of Milch management, turned out to be just a flying disaster.

The popular version that puts all the blame for the Luftwaffe technical disaster on the alcoholic and drug addict Generaloberst Ernst Udet, who became the scapegoat for all the sins of Göring and Milch, can also be justly questioned. Milch, who took his place, not only did not change the situation with the production of new models of aircraft, but on the contrary, using the same adventurous methods of work as the Udet, brought the situation to a final collapse.

A natural consequence of the administrative management methods fanatically imposed by Milch was the growing tension in relations with German designers. After the suicide of Udet, the search for those responsible for the endless technical failures was focused on the leaders of aviation firms and leading design groups. It should be noted that Milch initially treated all German designers as planners of technical errors. All the leaders of aviation companies he perceived as his subordinates, and demanded from them unquestioning obedience. He did not understand the essence of technical creativity and denied the objective impossibility of performing crazy and contradictory technical projects. Any objections expressed to his plans were perceived as treason and betrayal. That is why he sought to dismiss and even court-martial almost all German aircraft designers of the pre-war period. In their place, he attracted all sorts of outcasts and crooks who promised him the creation of various samples of 'miracle' weapons.

Milch's complete inability to change the situation in the Luftwaffe and the aviation industry led him to total suspicion and search for enemies and spies, even in his own department. In later years, the 'talented manager' has managed his subordinates exclusively with threats of military courts and shootings.

Devoid of doubt; a Nazi patriot

We have already written that the innate aggressiveness and rigid character formed during life made it impossible for the Generalfeldmarschall to communicate constructively with others. Confident in the absolute correctness of his opinion, Milch was in permanent conflict and treated all high-ranking employees of the Luftwaffe, Wehrmacht and even Kriegsmarine with contempt. The only person who was never subjected to his scathing criticism was Adolf Hitler.

The fanatical loyalty to the Führer of the most insidious and unscrupulous man in the Luftwaffe has a simple explanation: Milch's single-minded determination to serve Hitler and Germany was the entire focus of his life.

The criminal who proclaimed himself the Führer of the Third Reich did not create something fundamentally new. He only revived the idea of German nationalism, the period of the second German Empire and clothed it in a new 'bright' package of primitive national socialism. People like Erhard Milch did not need agitation and never suffered from the pangs of conscience, choosing connections with the immoral environment of the Führer. They were, in fact, already Nazis, even before the creation of Hitler's party. They were not interested in swastikas and Nazi salutes and other idiotic attributes, they dreamed of world domination by Germany. We have to admit that in Germany at that time there were a sufficient number of such 'patriots' who were ready to commit any crimes and monstrous atrocities for the sake of pathological love for Germany.

Thus, the fact that Erhard Milch has been associated with the Nazi movement since the 1920s and provided financial and transport services to the leaders of the national socialist party during its formation is not surprising.

In turn, without such loyal German 'patriots' as Milch, the Nazis had no chance to come to power and hold it for a long thirteen years. Various kinds of fanatics for whom the word 'impossible' did not exist, always attracted Hitler, who was obsessed with primitive natural needs. It was these people that the Führer considered the most effective tool in his hands, evaluating loyalty and sacrifice much higher than abilities and competence. They were so masterfully manipulated, and they were so calmly sacrificed when necessary. In a conversation with a colleague, Milch described his loyalty to Hitler as follows: 'Even if he orders me to come to him on the waves, I will go without hesitation.' And these words were confirmed by the terrible actions of Milch. It was he who forced German pilots to sacrifice their lives. He court-martialed transport aviation pilots who allegedly failed to fulfil their duty to the soldiers of the doomed Stalingrad who were dying of hunger and disease.

'Aufschlagbrand!' (Burned down!)

It so happened that at the time of the death of Milch's brainchild – Luftwaffe, he had been out of business for almost a year'. What he did so expertly with his rival enemies happened to him. He was betrayed by former friends and partners and forced to resign. Even such a disastrous turn of his life as the collapse of the Third Reich and prison for crimes committed, Milch took stoically.

After serving a prison sentence, this war criminal never repented. Until the last day of his life, Milch did not change his opinion about his own rightness, he did not understand the monstrous nature of Nazism and portrayed himself as a victim of injustice. The former Generalfeldmarschall continued to claim that everything he did in high positions in the Third Reich was for the good of Germany.

References and Sources

16th Air Army. Military-historical essay on the combat path of the 16th Air Army (1942–1945). Moscow: Voenizdat, 1973.

17th Air Army in the battle from Stalingrad to Vienna. Moscow: Voenizdat, 1977.

Irving D. The rise and fall of the Luftwaffe. Life Of Generalfeldmarschall Erhard Milch. Moscow: Yauza, 2006

Alyabyev A. Chronicle of the air war. Strategy and tactics. 1939 – 1945 – Moscow: tsentrpoligraf, 2006.

Becker K. Luftwaffe: working height 4000 meters. – Smolensk: Rusich, 2004.

Welz G. Soldiers who were betrayed: notes of a former Wehrmacht officer. – Smolensk: Rusich, 1999.

Gubin B.A. Kiselev V. D. 8th Air Army. Military-historical sketch of the 8th Air Army's combat path in the Great Patriotic War. Moscow: Voenizdat, 1980.

Zefirov, M.V. Aces of world war II: the British Empire. Volume # 2. – Moscow: AST, 2004.

Zefirov, M.V. Aces of the Luftwaffe: Bomber aviation. Moscow: AST, 2002.

Nenakhov Y.Y. 'Wonder weapons' of the Third Reich. – Minsk.: Kharvest, 1999.

Archambault, C & Roba, Jean-Louis. *TGr. 30, les fantomes des poches de l'Atlantigue (2)*. Avions 132, France, 2004.

Gundelach K. Kampfgeschwader 'General Wever' 4. – Motorbuch Verlag Stutgart, 1978.

Giganten der Luft – Messerschmitt Me 321-323. Waffen-Arsenal Special 06. – Podzun-Pallas Verlag GmbH, 2003.

Kempski B. Szybowiec/samolot transportowy Me-321/323 Gigant. Typy Broni i Uzbrojenia 160. – Wydawnictwo Bellona, 1994.

Lagoda M. Ein blick in die Vergangenheit. Kriegsernerungen eines Feraufklarers aus Russland und dem Orient. Helios, 2011.

Möller, Christian. *Das letzte Aufgebot der deutschen Luftwaffe.* Helios Verlags- und Buchvertriebsgesellschaft, Germany, 2010.

Forsyth, Robert & Creek, J.Eddie. *Heinkel He 111. An Illustrated History.* Classic Publication, Great Britain 2014.

Forsyth, Robert & Creek, J.Eddie. *Junkers Ju 52. A History: 1930-1945.* Classic Publication, Great Britain 2014.

Pegg M. Transporter Volume One: Luftwaffe Transport Units 1937-1943. Luftwaffe Colours. – Classic Publications, 2007.

Pegg M. Transporter Volume Twu: Luftwaffe Transport Units 1943-1945. Luftwaffe Colours. – Classic Publications, 2008.

Waiss, W. Chronic Kampfgeschwader Nr. 27 Boelcke. Teil 3. 01.01.1942 – 31.12.1942. Helios Verlag, Aachen, 2005.

Waiss, W. Chronic Kampfgeschwader Nr. 27 Boelcke. Teil 4. 01.01.1943 – 31.12.1943. Helios Verlag, Aachen, 2007.

Waiss, W. Chronic Kampfgeschwader Nr. 27 Boelcke. Teil 5. 01.01.1944 – 31.12.1944. Helios Verlag, Aachen, 2008.

Archives

Archiv KG 27 'Boelcke'.

Central archive of the Ministry of Defence of the Russian Federation (TSAMO RF)

TSAMO RF. Foundation 221 Shap. Inventory 1351. Case 1024
TSAMO RF. Foundation 221 Shap. Inventory 1351. Case 1029
TSAMO RF. Foundation 235 Shap. Inventory 2092. Case 826
TSAMO RF. Foundation 20026 Shap. Inventory 1. Case 7
TSAMO RF. Foundation 336 Shap. Inventory 0005220. Case 0006
TSAMO RF. Foundation 221 Shap. Inventory 1351. Case 1022
TSAMO RF. Foundation 221 Shap. Inventory 1351. Case 1027
TSAMO RF. Foundation 20157 Shap. Inventory 1. Case 3
TSAMO RF. Foundation 22339 Shap. Inventory 0698517. Case 0001
TSAMO RF. Foundation 357 Shap. Inventory 5971. Case 104
TSAMO RF. Foundation 20018 Shap. Inventory 1. Case 11
TSAMO RF. Foundation 213 Shap. Inventory 2002. Case 376
TSAMO RF. Foundation 20207 Shap. Inventory 1. Case 19
TSAMO RF. Foundation 20048 Shap. Inventory 1. Case 10
TSAMO RF. Foundation 20025 Shap. Inventory 1. Case 5
TSAMO RF. Foundation 20026 Shap. Inventory 1. Case 7
TSAMO RF. Foundation 206 Shap. Inventory 262. Case 89
TSAMO RF. Foundation 48 Shap. Inventory 451. Case 98
TSAMO RF. Foundation 48 Shap. Inventory 451. Case 141
TSAMO RF. Foundation 206 Shap. Inventory 262. Case 189
TSAMO RF. Foundation 240 Shap. Inventory 2779. Case 861
TSAMO RF. Foundation 240 Shap. Inventory 2779. Case 1132
TSAMO RF. Foundation 20502 Shap. Inventory 1. Case 61
TSAMO RF. Foundation 240 Shap. Inventory 2779. Case 869

TSAMO RF. Foundation 332 Shap. Inventory 4948. Case 165
TSAMO RF. Foundation 302 Shap. Inventory 0004196
TSAMO RF. Foundation 236 Shap. Inventory 2673. Case 1008
TSAMO RF. Foundation 236 Shap. Inventory 2673. Case 1138
TSAMO RF. Foundation 236 Shap. Inventory 2673. Case 993
TSAMO RF. Foundation 20524 Shap. Inventory 1. Case 32
TSAMO RF. Foundation 302 Shap. Inventory 0004196. Case 0085a
TSAMO RF. Foundation 346 Shap. Inventory 0005755. Case 0171
TSAMO RF. Foundation 346 Shap. Inventory 0005755. Case 0169
TSAMO RF. Foundation 22738 Shap. Inventory 0151367s. Case 0005
TSAMO RF. Foundation 302 Shap. Inventory 0004196. Case 0091
TSAMO RF. Foundation 236 Shap. Inventory 2673. Case 1033
TSAMO RF. Foundation 236 Shap. Inventory 2673. Case 1061
TSAMO RF. Foundation 244 Shap. Inventory 3000. Case 827
TSAMO RF. Foundation 241 Shap. Inventory 2593. Case 332
TSAMO RF. Foundation 290 Shap. Inventory 0003284. Case 0701
TSAMO RF. Foundation 240 Shap. Inventory 2779. Case 1941
TSAMO RF. Foundation 370 Shap. Inventory 0006518. Case 0437
TSAMO RF. Foundation 240 Shap. Inventory 2779. Case 1905
TSAMO RF. Foundation 13607 Shap. Inventory 20368. Case 566
TSAMO RF. Foundation 13607 Shap. Inventory 20368. Case 763
TSAMO RF. Foundation 13607 Shap. Inventory 20380. Case 94
TSAMO RF. Foundation 240 Shap. Inventory 2779. Case 1911
TSAMO RF. Foundation 327 Shap. Inventory 0004999. Case 0295
TSAMO RF. Foundation 370 Shap. Inventory 0006518. Case 0445
TSAMO RF. Foundation 236 Shap. Inventory 2673. Case 2570
TSAMO RF. Foundation 236 Shap. Inventory 2673. Case 2555
TSAMO RF. Foundation 236 Shap. Inventory 2673. Case 2538
TSAMO RF. Foundation 236 Shap. Inventory 2673. Case 2583
TSAMO RF. Foundation 370 Shap. Inventory 0006518. Case 0304
TSAMO RF. Foundation 370 Shap. Inventory 0006518. Case 0306

Applications

Table 1. Statistics of air bridge to Stalingrad on December 1942

Дата	The total number of departures to supply the Pocket	Number of successful flights	Cargo delivered (tons)	Number of planes lost
1.12	42	40	85	3
2.12	78	70	120	1
3.12	?	?	?	3
4.12	88	74	143.8	1
5.12	37	29	?	2
6.12	96	44	72.9	6
7.12	145	135	362.6	13
8.12	126	107	?	13
9.12	?	?	?	2
10.12	?	?	?	11
11.12	141	117	?	12
12.12	?	?	?	13
13.12	95	73	133.7	3
14.12	98	85	135	1
15.12	57	50	91.5	1
16.12	129	97	?	11
17.12	71	47	129.9	2
18.12	46	31	85	2
19.12	179	146	273.3	5
20.12	128	113	215	1
21.12	180	144	362.3	2

Дата	The total number of departures to supply the Pocket	Number of successful flights	Cargo delivered (tons)	Number of planes lost
22.12	?	?	142	3
23.12	37	?	83.8	3
24.12	?	?	?	0
25.12	9	?	?	0
26.12	49	37	78	4
27.12	95	79	127	0
28.12	13	10	35.4	0
29.12	106	96	124.2	5
30.12	91	85	224.9	3
31.12	177	158	?	5
In total	?	?	?	131

Table 2. Statistics of air bridge to Stalingrad for January 1–13, 1943

Дата	The total number of departures to supply the Pocket	Number of successful flights	Cargo delivered (tons)	Number of planes lost
1.01	130	78	205	3
2.01	?	?	?	0
3.01	123	97	168.4	5
4.01	170	145	270.9	4
5.01	95	53	161.3	7
6.01	56	29	49.5	3
7.01	102	63	125.5	4
8.01	101	76	117.6	7
9.01	124	106	385.7	4
10.01	138	102	162.2	5
11.01	134	96	189.6	11
12.01	64	51	61.7	0
13.01	92	69	224.5	4
In total	1329	965	2121.9	47

Index

6th Army, ix, 56–5, 67, 71–3, 77, 81–7, 89, 91–2, 94–5, 98, 100, 102, 105–108, 110–14, 116, 118–19, 122–4, 128–9, 131, 141, 150, 157, 163, 181, 199, 207, 219, 227, 237–8, 241–2, 251

Anti-aircraft artillery, 15–18, 21, 23, 27, 32, 42, 65, 67, 71, 73, 77, 102–103, 113, 116, 160, 173, 183, 197, 203–204, 212, 215, 219, 232–4, 237, 239

Army Group 'B', 58–9

Army Group 'Don', 67, 108, 150

Army Group 'Mitte', ix, 1–2, 49, 55, 181, 226

Army Group 'Nord', 1–3, 44, 49–50

Army Group 'South' (Heeresgruppe Süd), 124, 154, 172, 187–8

Barbarossa, Operation, 1, 46

Bätcher, Hans-Georg, 63, 66–7, 72–3, 77, 81, 83, 86–7, 92, 162, 164–6

Breslau Pocket, 218–22, 224–32, 234–44

Budapest Pocket, 188–212, 214–15, 222, 237

Caucasus, 46, 83, 111, 126, 150

Dornier,
Do 17, 190, 207–208, 210, 224, 236
Do 215, 76, 80

Demyansk, ix, 1–33, 38, 44–6, 50, 62, 89, 219

DFS 230, ix, 35, 54, 150, 174, 182–3, 190, 198, 207, 224, 236

Focke-Wulf,
Fw 189, 54
Fw 190, 179, 182, 229
Fw 200, 27, 101, 103–104, 108, 115, 117–18, 121–2, 151

Fieseler,
Fi 156, 36–7, 50, 98, 183, 240–3

'Flaks', Operation, 135

Festung, xii, 58, 67–8, 77–9, 82, 85, 91, 95, 98–9, 101, 103–104, 106, 108, 111, 122, 128, 182, 188, 216–17, 233, 236, 238–9, 241–3

Fligerkorps I, 153

Friessner, Generaloberst Johannes, 188

Gandauer airfield, 219–22, 224–6, 228–9, 232–6, 238–40

261